P

LORDS & LIARS

The Secret Story of the Christie's-Sotheby's Conspiracy

By

Christopher Mason

London

GIBSON SQUARE

This edition first published in the UK in 2005 by

Gibson Square
15 Gibson Square
London N1 0RD

Tel: +44 (0)20 7689 4790
Fax: +44 (0)20 7689 7395

info@gibsonsquare.com
www.gibsonsquare.com

ISBN 1-903933-668

UK sales by Signature
20 Castlegate
York YO1 9RP

Tel 01904 633 633
Fax 01904 675 445

sales@signaturebooks.co.uk

Contents

List of People

SOTHEBY'S
Alfred Taubman, *Chairman, 1983-2000*
Judy Taubman, *His wife*
Diana 'Dede' Brooks, *CEO, 1994-1999*
Michael Ainslie, *CEO prior to Dede Brooks*
Lord Camoys, *Deputy chairman*
Henry Wyndham, *Chairman of Sotheby's, London*
Bill Ruprecht, *Successor to Dede Brooks as CEO*
Lord Westmorland, *Sotheby's director and master of the horse, close friend of the Queen*

CHRISTIE'S
Sir Anthony Tennant, *Chairman, 1993-1996*
Christopher Davidge, *Chief executive officer, 1993-1999*
Olga Davidge, *His second wife*
Lord Hindlip, *Chairman, 1996-2002*
Christopher Burge, *Star auctioneer in New York*
Jo Floyd, *Chairman, 1974-1988*
Lord Carrington, *Chairman after Floyd, 1988-1993*
Patty Hambrecht, *General counsel, later president of Christie's, Inc.*
Stephen Lash, *Head of Trusts and Estates, New York*

Ed Dolman, *Successor to Christopher Davidge*
Lord Bathurst, *Disgraced chairman*

OTHERS
Christopher Wood, *Christie's expert turned dealer, based in London*
John Siffert, *Counsel for Dede Brooks*
Steve Kaufman, *Counsel for Dede Brooks*
William J. 'Joe' Linklater, *Counsel for Christopher Davidge*
Jeff Miro, *Taubman's longtime lawyer and confidant*
David Boies, *Counsel for plaintiffs in the civil suit against Sotheby's and Christie's*
John Greene, *United States federal prosecutor*

22 December 1999

CLUTCHING A BLACK leather briefcase crammed with neatly filed documents, Christopher Davidge ventured out into the streets of London on an overcast morning three days before Christmas. Dressed sharply in a dark blue suit tailored to his diminutive physique, his graying beard and leonine hair clipped and coiffed to immaculate perfection, the fifty-four-year-old CEO of Christie's was embarking on an errand that he knew could destroy the reputations of both Christie's and its archrival, Sotheby's, and send one of the richest men in America to gaol.

The London art world was grinding to a halt for the Christmas holidays, and the normally bustling streets of St. James' were quiet. The only sign of life was at Fortnum & Mason, the royal grocer in Piccadilly, where American tourists were still clamouring for last-minute gifts wrapped in turquoise shopping bags emblazoned with royal coats of arms.

Hailing a cab in Piccadilly, he headed east to the City for his rendezvous with William Joseph Linklater, a senior partner in the international law firm of Baker & McKenzie. Reputed to be tough, suave and extremely effective, Joe Linklater headed the firm's criminal practice division in the United States.

With the precision of a general planning a surprise attack, Davidge had spent the past few days reviewing his stockpile of documentary ammunition. Ensconced in the candlelit drawing room of his flat, he had focused on the task that Linklater assigned him: to carefully index the dozens of pages of notes he had kept of his illegal meetings and agreements with his archcompetitor, Diana "Dede" Brooks, the CEO of Sotheby's. Also among the cache of documents Davidge carried were his confidential communications with Sir Anthony Tennant, Christie's former worldwide chairman, who had stepped down from Christie's board in 1998. Together, the contents of the plump file constituted a devastating chronicle of an illicit, undiscovered price-fixing conspiracy between the world's two leading auction houses.

Davidge's black London taxi pulled up at Baker & McKenzie's offices on New Bridge Street at ten A.M. With his cache of papers still firmly in his grasp he took the elevator to the third floor, where he was greeted by Joe Linklater, who had flown in from Chicago the night before. Finding Davidge to be apprehensive at first but engagingly frank about his role in the conspiracy, Linklater began examining the pile of papers that lay before him. His eyes lit up when the Englishman pointed to three pages of handwritten notes from Sir Anthony Tennant, one of which was headed "Paper given April 30."

Tennant's notes appeared to memorialize a series of agreements hatched between Christie's former chairman and a senior, but unnamed, official at Sotheby's. Davidge explained to Linklater that the mystery figure—referred to as "he"—was Alfred Taubman, the American multi-millionaire who was Sotheby's chairman and controlling shareholder. Taubman and Tennant, he noted, had breakfasted together in London on April 30, 1993.

After that breakfast, Davidge recalled, Tennant had told him to expect a call from Dede Brooks to follow up with the topics he had discussed with Taubman. This allegation appeared to be supported by a notation Tennant had made on the first page, indicating that he had given his breakfast companion Davidge's home telephone number.

With considerable glee, Linklater noticed that Tennant had concluded one page of his notes with a haunting twenty-six-word sentence which could he strategically highlighted to suggest that it was Taubman and Tennant—not Davidge—who had instigated and masterminded the conspiracy: "He and I should now withdraw,"

Tennant had written, "but stay in touch with a view to seeing how things go and intervening from on high if need be."[1]

Linklater realized that such a document, if handled adroitly, could get his client off the hook altogether.

SOTHEBY'S WAS in the midst of joyful celebrations in New York on the evening of January 11, 2000, as one thousand guests arrived at the company's newly expanded global headquarters to celebrate the launch of the art world's most eagerly awaited Internet auction site, Sothebys.com. Dominating the intersection of York Avenue and East Seventy-second Street with ten stories of glass brilliantly lit against the night sky, the new edifice stood out among a neighbouring cluster of red-brick nursing homes like a beacon of commerce, culture and corporate pride. Idling limousines were double-parked around the block as Wall Street titans, socialites in mink coats, corpulent art dealers and waif-thin models braved the cold night air to come and inspect the latest venture of the world's oldest international auction house.

The triumphant host of the evening's festivities was Dede Brooks, the company's six-foot-tall, hard-charging CEO, who was reputed to be the most powerful woman in the art world. Charismatic, visionary and endowed with prodigious energy, she had set out to become the public face of Sotheby's and had succeeded spectacularly.

Also on hand that evening was the firm's ebullient chairman, Alfred Taubman, an imposing figure in a three-piece charcoal-grey suit who exuded the confident air of a self-made man. Privately, Taubman was unenthusiastic about Sotheby's prospects on the Internet, but he had flown in from Palm Beach on his private jet to show his support as chairman. As guests poured out of the elevators onto the firm's new tenth-floor penthouse, they were greeted by muscle-bound waiters in black-and-white Sothebys.com T-shirts, proffering trays of wine, beer and champagne. In keeping with the populist Internet theme, revellers were served mini hot dogs instead of the usual foie gras and smoked-salmon canapés. The crowd was ushered into the north gallery, where they encountered long rows of candy-coloured Macintosh computers showing off Sotheby's elegant Web site with its handsome blue-and-white graphics.

"We believe that Sotheby's is uniquely positioned for the twenty-first century," Brooks declared in a booming voice as guests explored the bustling penthouse, which was adorned with an intriguing array of the objects Sotheby's intended to sell online.[2] The item receiving the most attention was a rare copy from the first printing of the Declaration of Independence, which was prominently displayed in a glass case. The fragile document was one of only four copies known to be in private hands and was expected to fetch between $4 million and $6 million.*

For many who laboured at Sotheby's, the evening seemed to signal an epiphany for the 256-year-old firm, which had strived to reinvent itself to meet the dawn of the new millennium. Dede Brooks had been the driving force behind Sotheby's initiative to capitalize on the Internet revolution, believing that vast profits could be made by expanding the firm's franchise to sell objects on the Web. Not everyone, certainly, had the ready cash to bid on a Cézanne masterpiece like *Rideau, cruchon et compotier,* a sublime 1893 still-life composition that Sotheby's had sold to a private collector for $60.5 million at its Impressionist and Modern sale in May 1999. But Brooks was convinced that hundreds of thousands of art-world novices worldwide might be willing to pay $600 for a pair of candlesticks—or perhaps $1,200 for a simple diamond engagement ring—by bidding on Sothebys.com.

It was a bold gamble. Start-up expenses for the new venture had already cost the firm $41 million and were expected to soar to $80 million by the end of 2000.

In making preparations for Sotheby's Web transactions, Brooks had masterminded a dramatic reinvention and overhaul of the company's worldwide business. It was a process that had strained the firm's senior staff to the uttermost for the past year. Fine-art and dec-

---

* The winning bidder for the Declaration of Independence was Norman Lear, the television producer, who purchased it on Sothebys.com in June 2000 for $8.1 million.

orative-arts experts, who normally had their hands full attracting everything from pocket watches to Brancusi sculptures to diamond tiaras for their department's live auctions, were under fire to sign up handpicked dealers to sell objects on Sothebys.com. It had been harrowing, but their efforts seemed propitious: Sotheby's stock had soared to a record high of $47 during the spring of 1999 in anticipation of the firm's Internet debut.

The new Sotheby's building was Alfred Taubman's pride and joy. Drawing upon a genius for retail design and marketing that he had honed during fifty years as a developer of luxury shopping malls, the tycoon had envisioned a handsome tower with a restaurant, art bookshop, spacious expert department offices and central escalators to encourage customers to explore seven stories of exhibition space and auction rooms. At his instigation, enormous freight elevators had been installed to make it possible for Sotheby's trucks to enter from a side entrance and be brought up directly to expert departments so that objects as precious and fragile as a medieval illuminated manuscript or a Calder mobile would suffer a minimum amount of handling.

Only twenty minutes into the party, Taubman was aghast when dozens of Macintosh screens displaying Sotheby's new Web site began flashing intermittently, then fizzled to black. Because of a highly embarrassing technical glitch, the server had crashed and could not be restored. Ripples of shock, dismay and amusement permeated the room as some guests realized that the fête designed to trumpet the Web site's arrival was turning into a fiasco.

Grabbing his raincoat and clutching a blue cashmere scarf around his neck, Sotheby's portly chairman stalked out of the reception early, looking like an exasperated godfather fleeing a raucous Sweet Sixteen party. Worse indignities were to follow shortly. Taubman had not yet heard the disquieting news, but earlier that day the Antitrust Division of the United States Justice Department had issued subpoenas to three of the Michigan-based companies under his control. Each subpoena demanded the production of Taubman's diaries, calendars, telephone bills and business and travel records since 1992 relating to his responsibilities as an owner and director of

Sotheby's Holdings. Without mentioning Sir Anthony Tennant or Christie's by name, the legal papers required Taubman to submit all documents relating to his contacts with "directors, officers, employees, agents or representatives" of "any other auction house. It was the beginning of the nightmare that would engulf Taubman and give rise to the most devastating scandal ever to befall the art world.

1

'Big Al'

WHEN ALFRED TAUBMAN strolled into the London premises of Sotheby Parke Bernet in October 1983 as the proud new owner of the fabled British auction house, he was greeted like a conquering hero. Grinning from ear to ear, the fifty-nine-year-old tycoon made his way through the lobby and ascended a well-worn staircase to the main salesroom. Sotheby's staff bombarded him from every direction with handshakes, cheery smiles and deferential nods, though many of them had never previously deigned to give the time of day to the shopping-mall mogul.

His sudden popularity came with his newfound status as the white knight who had emerged in the nick of time to rescue the financially ailing firm from a pair of highly leveraged New York corporate raiders, whose aggressive bid to seize control of Sotheby's had been branded "wholly unacceptable" by Sotheby's aristocratic directors.

Taubman could hardly believe his good fortune. He had acquired the crown jewel of the art world with the help of excellent timing and a consortium of powerful friends who had assisted him in rustling up a winning bid of $ 139 million. Wall Street cynics joked that "Big Al" from Michigan had foolishly overpaid for Sotheby's as a gift for his glamorous new wife, Judy, a former Miss Israel, who had once worked on the front counter at Christie's.

But Al Taubman was no starry-eyed spendthrift.

Guided by formidable commercial instincts, he was confident he could transform the company into a profitable enterprise. No one in the art world—least of all the conventional souls over at Christie's—

knew of his plans to expand Sotheby's global audience. But he intended to crush the competition by applying some of the marketing techniques he had mastered as a developer of luxury shopping centres to the sale of rarefied objects such as ancient Greek statues, Chinese porcelain, Old Master drawings and Impressionist paintings.

To prove he meant business, Taubman wanted to deliver a rallying speech to his new employees on both sides of the Atlantic, starting in London and then flying on the Concorde to New York to accomplish the task in a single day.

By nine A.M. every member of the London staff, from porters to senior directors, had assembled in the main salesroom to greet their new boss. Standing before them in a dark-grey suit he announced in a resounding voice that he was thrilled with his purchase of Sotheby's. He declared that he had the greatest respect for everything the company stood for, including its hardworking staff, and promised that everyone would receive a pay increase.

Having captured his audience's attention, Taubman moved on to the awkward crux of his oration: Never in his life, he told them, had he been treated so haughtily as he had during his experiences as a client of Sotheby's—though he acknowledged that Christie's came pretty darn close in terms of superciliousness and general rudeness. Alienating the customer was no way to run a business, he warned, and such conduct would no longer be acceptable.

"I want you to pledge that your manners will improve and that you will show that you care deeply about what customers think," Taubman said, sternly. "Your expertise and scholarship are beyond question, but you are in a service business and if you can't behave properly, you don't belong."[1]

Dozens of Brits accustomed to the snobbish, insular world of Bond Street were startled to receive a lecture on etiquette from a nouveau-riche American. But when he concluded his speech on a note of optimism for Sotheby's future, the new chairman received an enthusiastic round of applause, which was echoed that afternoon when he delivered a similar exhortation to all of the New York staff gathered in the large second-floor salesroom on York Avenue.

Behind the rapturous ovation, some were deeply sceptical. "When

Taubman came in, we all said, 'Oh, God! Shopping centres! What does *he* know?'" recalled John Stair, who ran Sotheby's restoration department.[2]

Others who had feared that their civilized universe was about to be disrupted by an ignorant businessman were pleasantly surprised. "Alfred was immediately perceived as *tactful*," noted Thierry Millerand, a European Furniture specialist. "He told us he was not going to get involved in telling us how to do our jobs, because the experts knew what they were doing. And that created very good vibes."[3]

Many senior directors who knew how close Sotheby's had come to the brink of extinction felt reassured. "Alfred was viewed as a saviour," recalled John Marion, Sotheby's gravel-toned New York chairman and star auctioneer. "We felt he wasn't going to break things up, and he would save Sotheby's reputation."[4]

TAUBMAN HAD APPEARED at a perilous moment for the legendary auction house. In 1982, it had stumbled into debt, caught short by a faltering economy and a profligate period of international expansion led by the firm's charismatic former chairman and chief auctioneer, Peter Wilson.

Wilson was an elegant buccaneer who roved the world's palaces, châteaux and villas, charming their owners with his encyclopaedic knowledge of every kind of work of art while convincing them to entrust something marvellous from their collections for sale at auction. Only Sotheby's, he argued, could be relied upon to deliver top prices for their treasures. Duchesses, earls, aging moguls and their progeny were assiduously cultivated in order to ensure that they would turn to Sotheby's, not Christie's, in times of death, divorce or debt—the "three Ds" that kept the auction houses in business.

Under his leadership, Sotheby's had become more dynamic than stuffy, blue-chip Christie's, more risk-minded and voracious in seeking the lion's share of goods for sale each auction season. But the Englishman's madcap pursuit of prestigious consignments to drive up sales had always been carried out with scant regard for the costs of doing business or the necessity of turning a profit.

In scrambling to cut its losses the company had laid off more than 25 percent of its two thousand worldwide staff by June 1982, and morale was at an all-time low. The firm was also obliged to close its auction operations in Los Angeles and London's Belgravia and to vacate its elegant leased quarters on Madison Avenue.

Sotheby's bleak prospects sent its stock price tumbling during the summer of 1982, making the company vulnerable to a takeover. "It looked to us like a giant mess," recalled an executive from one of the companies that looked into buying Sotheby's before abruptly withdrawing. "Our instincts were that this thing was a zoo. They have no internal controls. It's all this upperclass-Englishmen stuff. They don't know how to run a business."5

London's investment community was abuzz with speculation that a major U.S. company was on the verge of making a bid for Sotheby's. So the stock market and the art world reacted with astonishment when General Felt Industries, Inc., a manufacturer of carpet underlay in Saddle Brook, New Jersey, announced in December 1982 that it had acquired 1,623,500 of Sotheby's shares for $12.8 million, making it the largest single stockholder with a 14.2 percent stake in the company.

General Felt's stealthy assault was greeted with dismay by Sotheby's directors in London. They were indignant to learn that the American firm's co-chairmen Stephen Swid and Marshall C. Cogan— two men they had never *heard* of—wanted to sit down with the board to discuss Sotheby's future.

By the spring of 1983 the investors had assembled a war chest of nearly $100 million, most of it borrowed from American banks, and were ready to make a hostile bid.

Sotheby's directors were apoplectic at the prospect of being taken over by Cogan and Swid. Graham Llewellyn, the firm's chief executive, declared that if the raiders seized control of the firm he would "blow my brains out." Passions ran equally high in New York. "Instinctively, we did not like them," a senior Sotheby's expert recalled, "and we did not want them."6

THE SHIMMERING POOL beyond the porthole windows of Al

Taubman's all-white contemporary house in Palm Beach reflected a perfect azure sky one Sunday morning in late April 1983. He was sitting across the breakfast table from his English houseguest, David Metcalfe, when the jovial aristocrat surprised him with an investment tip that would change his life.

Taubman was eager for a new investment opportunity. He had been canvassing friends for worthy suggestions for months, but nothing had captured his imagination until Metcalfe looked up from his newspaper with a quizzical gaze and popped the question:

"How about Sotheby's?"[7]

Taubman chuckled at the outlandish suggestion at first. But he listened attentively as Metcalfe pointed out that the *Financial Times,* the *New York Times* and the *Wall Street Journal* were full of stories that week describing the British auction house's distress over the advances of Messrs. Cogan and Swid. Furthermore, Metcalfe explained, he knew firsthand from talking to his chum David Westmorland that Sotheby's was desperately searching for a white knight.

The timing appeared to be perfect.

"Well if they would be happy to talk to me, I would be happy to talk to them," Taubman said.[8]

Metcalfe was delighted to arrange an introduction. He knew that Westmorland was in the Bahamas staying with friends in Lyford Cay—a private community that was a favourite winter and springtime playground for transatlantic multimillionaires and aristocrats like Stavros Niarchos and Prince Rainier III of Monaco. With considerable relish he picked up the telephone to call his old friend.

David Fane, more formally known as the fifteenth Earl of Westmorland, was a tall, affable white-haired director and former chairman of Sotheby's. He also happened to be a devoted courtier and a close personal friend of Queen Elizabeth II since childhood. As master of the horse he rode before Her Majesty in royal processions wearing a splendid scarlet-and-gold ceremonial uniform. When Metcalfe reached him in the Bahamas, however, the earl was in his bathing suit, trying to catch a few rays of sun before heading back to London.

"Listen, David," Metcalfe said, excitedly. "Al Taubman, who's a great friend of mine, is interested in buying Sotheby's."[9]

THERE WAS LITTLE about the early life of Alfred Taubman to suggest that an English earl who traced his aristocratic lineage back to 1363—and who held the distinction of being an intimate friend of the Queen of England would one day come cap in hand to entreat him to buy the world's most illustrious auction house.

Born into a family of prosperous German Jewish immigrants in Pontiac, Michigan, Taubman often said he could never shake the uncanny feeling that someday he might lose everything, as his father had done during the Depression. The traumatic loss of his family's money, combined with a penchant for commercial innovation and social adventure, created in him a consuming desire to attain wealth and success—a compulsion that was imperceptible to those who knew him as a chubby youth with an awkward stutter.

Adolph Alfred Taubman was the youngest of four children born to Fannie Esther Blumstein and Philip Taubman, childhood sweethearts who had settled in America shortly after World War I. His birth certificate stated that he entered the world at three in the morning on January 31, 1924, but until he was seventy-eight—and his lawyers were trying to convince a federal judge not to send a man of such advanced years to gaol—he claimed to be a year younger than that document indicated.*

Philip Taubman worked hard to support his young family. Strong-willed and self-reliant, he laboured in orchards and fruit farms in the Michigan lake country, then founded a construction company to build custom-designed houses for the managers and workers of General Motors factories. Business flourished and Philip was on his way to achieving his American Dream when the Depression hit Detroit at a moment when he was most overextend-

---

* Asked to explain the discrepancy, Taubman suggested that his mother may have delayed obtaining his certificate until he was four and fibbed about the year of his birth in order to get him out of the house and into kindergarten early. The certificate's registration date is February 2, 1924, however—three days after he was born at home, at 635 South Saginaw in downtown Pontiac. Vanity about his age seems a more plausible explanation.

ed. The reversal of fortune sent him back to the farm to resume the drudgery of picking fruit for a living—a cruel twist of fate that shattered his ambitions and made a profound impression on his youngest son.

Alfred was eleven when his father was obliged to sell the comfortable house he had built for his family in Pontiac. Philip had taken a part-time job tending an orchard in nearby Sylvan Lake, and the Taubmans moved into a house that was little more than a shack built for migrant workers.

Philip fought to maintain his dignity and good name in the community during that difficult time. Alfred recalled that his father took pride in paying all the subcontractors who had worked for him. "His father worked fifteen years to pay off every debt from the Depression," a family friend recalled. "He never stiffed anyone, and that sense of honour stuck with Alfred."[10]

The most important thing in life, Philip Taubman told his children, was having a good reputation. It was a lesson his youngest son would take to heart.

Growing up in the shadow of his domineering father, Alfred struggled to overcome numerous challenges at school. He was left-handed, but his teachers forced him to write with his right hand. He also spoke with a stutter, misspelled words and had difficulty reading. Today his symptoms would be diagnosed as dyslexia, but for years Taubman suffered the humiliation of being made to sit at the front of the class. "He was teased by other kids who thought he was just a plain, dumb kid," recalled Dan Murphy, an Oakland County executive who sat next to him in Latin class at Pontiac Central High School.[11]

Overweight and uninterested in sports, Alfred had the prodigious girth of a well-fed German burgher even as a young boy, and he endured ridicule from his schoolmates. In recalling the woes that afflicted his childhood he remembered with lingering anger and sorrow that he was perceived as a "fat, homely, dumb Jew."[12]

The anti-Semitism Taubman encountered as a child was rampant in suburban Detroit during the twenties and thirties. Its most outspoken advocate was Henry Ford, Sr., the founder of the Ford Motor Company, whose privately owned newspaper, the *Dearborn*

Independent, ran a ninety-one-part series of incendiary articles in the early 1920s that he published collectively in a book entitled *The International Jew: The World's Foremost Problem.* "If there is one quality that attracts Jews, it is power," the book stated, echoing Ford's complaint that "moneylenders" had tried to wrest control of his company during an economic down-turn. "Wherever the seat of power may be, thither they swarm obsequiously."*[13]

Henry Ford's fame ensured a wide distribution for the book during Alfred's formative years. For a while, a complimentary paper-bound copy could be found in the glove compartment of every new Ford car.

Taubman was brought up in an observant Orthodox home. Fannie kept kosher and Alfred and his brothers, Lester and Sam, accompanied their father to synagogue every Friday evening. Alfred was proud of his heritage but left his yarmulke at home when he went to school, where he was heckled with ethnic slurs that contributed to his feeling of being an outsider.

Attending art class was one of his few solaces. Given a chance to put aside his frustration with the written word, he learned to express himself through drawing and channelled his exceptional visual intelligence into sketches of houses. His talent as a draftsman gave him confidence, and he dreamed of becoming an architect.

He got his first taste of the retail business at twelve when he took a weekend-and-evening job at Diem's, a shoe store on Main Street in Pontiac, where he proved to be a gifted and charismatic salesman. He developed a knack for guessing the exact shoe size of his customers and appealed to the ladies' vanity by suggesting a half size smaller.

Taubman also had a precocious understanding of how the physical layout of a store could seduce the public into buying. He noticed that passersby often stopped to admire shoes in the window at Diem's but resisted walking through the front door—a phenomenon he would later define as "threshold resistance."

---

* Ford issued a formal letter of apology to the Jewish people in 1927, apologizing for the articles in the *Dearborn Independent* and for publishing *The International Jew.* But many questioned the sincerity of the automaker, who went on to accept the Grand Cross of the German Eagle from Hitler's Nazi government in 1938, after the book became a best-seller in Germany.

The aspiring architect sensed that the problem lay in the placement of the front door, which was set back ten feet from the sidewalk behind a U-shaped window display. He advised the owner, Irving Diem, to move the door to the sidewalk. With some trepidation Diem followed his teenage clerk's suggestion and was impressed when the new configuration began attracting more customers into the store.

Al's ability to break down threshold resistance would become the key to his success. It was a form of creative thinking that he excelled at, and one that was an extension of his instincts as a salesman. He understood the intangible barriers that make the public hesitate to venture forth into unfamiliar or intimidating surroundings, and was able to come up with practical solutions to abstract problems that baffled more logical minds. It was a gift he would rely upon for designing crowd-pleasing shopping centres, and one that he would later deploy to erode the elitist atmosphere that prevailed at Sotheby's, which kept many potential clients away.

Taubman embraced the American work ethic and was proud to be a U.S. citizen. As Hitler came to prominence in Europe, the teenager dropped the awkward first name of Adolph—as he had been called since infancy—and switched to Alfred, but he kept the initial. Even in his late sixties he would growl, "None of your business," if a stranger had the temerity to enquire what the A. stood for in "A. Alfred Taubman."[14]

Upon leaving school in 1942 he joined the U.S. Army Air Corps and served his country during World War II by creating maps of enemy territory in the South Pacific. He was stationed in Papua New Guinea and came close to death with a three-month bout of malaria.

After receiving an honourable discharge from the army at twenty-one he enrolled at the University of Michigan's College of Architecture and Urban Planning. It was only then that he learned that his acute learning problem had a name—dyslexia—a disability that would permanently inhibit his capacity to read and leave him confused between left and right. His family teased him about his propensity for mixing up stories and getting details back to front, and he was embarrassed to show anyone his handwriting for fear they would discover his rudimentary spelling. But he had learned to keep his fears and confusion to himself.

Taubman's disability did little to inhibit his growing self-confidence. The gifted salesman was learning to sell his own charm and ebullient personality. By the time he reached college, Taubman had transformed himself from an unsure and picked-on child into a funny, popular guy who exuded an air of assurance. An instinctive survivor, he had learned to bury the humiliations of his childhood through sheer force of will and had emerged with a positive outlook and an ability to deliver jokes that amused his growing circle of friends.

Still penniless, however, Taubman funded his studies by selling flower corsages and shoes to his college contemporaries. Selling shoes gave the amorous former serviceman a chance to meet women. He convinced the owner of a store in Ann Arbor to lend him shoe samples, then persuaded the sorority mothers to let him ply his wares. While the girls were eating dinner, Taubman arranged the shoes on the steps up to their bedrooms and stood waiting with a clipboard and a smile, ready to tempt them with the latest fashions.

He flattered and cajoled his customers and usually wound up with a date and dozens of orders, which he delivered the following day like a resourceful Prince Charming with slippers to fit every stepsister and sorority Cinderella. With shoes and flowers as commodities, Taubman was learning about profit margins and how to set commission rates lessons he would later apply on a grander scale at Sotheby's.

Taubman never finished his studies. With a $5,000 loan from the lo-cal Manufacturer's Bank the twenty-six-year-old started his own construction firm in Oak Park, a Detroit suburb, and persuaded his father to come out of retirement to join him as his first business partner. Their first project was a bridal salon in Detroit, which Taubman designed, and soon he was busy constructing everything from bowling alleys to strip malls.

His innovative store designs attracted the attention of Max Fisher, a leading Michigan oil and property baron, who commissioned him to design a prototype for his Speedway 79 gas stations. Fisher's patronage was a spur to Taubman's ambitions. Speedway 79s began appearing across the Midwest and the project became a gold mine when Fisher granted him a contract to build two hundred stations, providing him with the resources he needed to fund the next step in his career.

As millions of Americans migrated to the suburbs after the end of World War II, vast fortunes were made by developers who specialized in constructing houses. But Al Taubman had another idea. He saw hordes of middle-class families moving out of big cities like Detroit into three-bedroom suburban houses and recognized a new opportunity;

They all needed somewhere to shop.

The outskirts of Detroit were already littered with ugly strip malls that had little to recommend them except convenience. Taubman considered the aspirations of prosperous suburbanites and envisioned a new kind of retail emporium—a large, luxurious indoor mall with an exciting variety of upscale stores where the public could shop, eat and even catch a movie.

With a stockpile of cash and borrowed money, he built and designed his first regional shopping centre, Southland, in Hayward, California, in 1964, which was an immediate success. Soon he was designing, building, owning and operating shopping malls all over the country, ploughing the profits from one centre into the construction of a larger one.

Taubman's shopping centres seemed to spring up everywhere, always larger, always more lavish, devouring corn patches and wheat fields. As his malls became more prolific, he became known as a trendsetter in the industry. His centres were the first to offer fountains, waterfalls, shrubbery, restaurants, elevators and prestigious "anchor" stores such as Neiman Marcus, which attracted deep-pocketed shoppers.

The Michigan mogul became legendary in the business world for his unrelenting attention to detail. He was a strict landlord who set rules for everything—from the kind of merchandise stores could sell to what their workers were permitted to wear. And he forbade tenants to paste Visa, MasterCard and AmEx decals to their windows. They had to be neatly mounted on a hanging piece of Lucite, exactly to his specifications.

If retailers failed to comply with his demands, they were given a

hard time. Taubman terminated the leases of stores that failed to generate enough income to meet his expectations. And he acquired a reputation for being brutally tough but honest, the latter attribute making
him something of an anomaly in the real-estate industry.

Taubman's vast, sprawling malls would help shape life in America,
for better and worse, for decades to come. By the early eighties his
shopping centres encircled Detroit, and he was widely blamed for
accelerating the city's decline. But he gave the buying public what they
wanted. Since his days of selling shoes at Diem's in Pontiac, Taubman
had developed a sophisticated understanding of customer behaviour
and a flair for maximizing the commercial potential of his properties.
A purchase, he liked to say, is often secondary to the shopping experience. Consequently, he designed his malls for what he called "fanta-
sy, fun and entertainment."[15]

At the grand opening of his Fair Oaks Mall in Fairfax, Virginia, in
1980, ballet dancers pirouetted through the bedding department,
mimes cavorted among the handbags and opera stars belted out arias.
Visitors to the juniors' department at the Hecht Co. store encountered
the Sheiks of Dixie playing "When the Saints Go Marching In," while
other mall-goers admired the five-tiered fountains and novel glass elevators in the main atrium. The local press marvelled that there were
7,725 parking spaces and 1·4 million square feet of leaseable space, all
of which appeared to be rented.

"They are toy garden cities," the novelist Joan Didion wrote of the
new shopping centres, "in which no one lives but everyone consumes,
profound equalizers, the perfect fusion of the profit motive and the
egalitarian idea."[16]

By the early eighties, Taubman had firmly established himself as
the preeminent developer of giant malls in America. But he craved
more. He wanted to reinvent himself as a man of taste, while adding
substantially to his fortune, which *Forbes* magazine estimated in 1983
at a tidy $500 million. With typical bravado, Taubman claimed that he
had no real interest in buying Sotheby's. They needed him, he
implied, more than he needed them. But nobody who knew Al
Taubman and sensed the scale of his ambition believed that for a
minute.

2

Social Climbing

JOHN MARION WAS INTRIGUED by the urgency in David Westmorland's voice. The earl was calling from the Bahamas to report on his promising conversation with David Metcalfe, and urged Sotheby's New York chairman to set up a meeting in New York as soon as possible with an obscure real-estate mogul named Taubman who collected important modern pictures.

"Apparently he's just done a billion-dollar deal in California," Westmorland said, excitedly. "With any luck, he's the answer to our problems."[1]

Marion had never heard of Alfred Taubman and had no clue where he lived. "All David gave me was a phone number starting with area code 313," he recalled. "Frankly, I didn't even know where 313 is. So I waited till about noon, thinking it must be California."[2]

When he finally dialled the number, Marion was put through to Taubman's longtime attorney and confidant Jeffrey H. Miro. "By the way, where are you?" Sotheby's chairman asked, after introducing himself.

"Detroit," Miro replied.

Marion smarted. If only he'd known, he could have gotten the ball rolling two hours earlier. Laying on the charm, he explained that his distinguished colleague Lord Westmorland had just informed him that Mr. Taubman was willing to consider the notion of purchasing Sotheby's.

"Oh, I don't think he'd be interested," Miro told him, bluntly.

"Well I would enjoy meeting him," Marion replied, without missing a beat. "Why don't you have him come by? I'll show him around the gallery, and let's see what he thinks of it."[3]

A few days later Marion was nervously pacing the grey carpet of his third-floor office at Sotheby's in anticipation of Taubman's imminent arrival. Westmorland had already been to see Taubman in Detroit and reported that the mogul seemed unconvinced that Sotheby's would be a sound investment. With the company's future at stake, Marion—the firm's legendary American auctioneer and a born salesman—planned to pull out all the stops. On the wall facing the chair he expected Taubman to occupy, Marion had hung a painting that he hoped would grab the Detroit tycoon's attention. It was *Classic Landscape*, a 1931 masterpiece by the Precisionist artist Charles Sheeler, which presented an idealized panorama of the Ford Motor Plant in River Rouge, Michigan.

Marion's opening stratagem worked like a charm. Taubman was settling into his chair when he suddenly jumped up. "That painting!" he exclaimed excitedly. "I almost bought that painting! It was offered to me!"

"Golly gee!" Marion replied, playing dumb. "Is that *Detroit*?" He explained that *Classic Landscape* was the star lot of an upcoming sale of American paintings and was expected to fetch up to $950,000 at auction.*[4]

In his next effort to hook the big fish, Marion led Taubman on a tour of Sotheby's four-story York Avenue premises. As they wandered through each of the expert departments, Marion was excited to observe a gleam in the multimillionaire's eye as he chatted with the firm's in-house experts as they pored over exquisite Chinese porcelains, ancient Roman statuary, Kandinsky gouaches and clocks from the golden age of Louis XIV.

"*Nobody* knew who he was," Marion recalled.

Saving the best till last, Marion invited Taubman to step into a small storage room crammed with Impressionist paintings that were

---

* Sotheby Parke Bernet sold Charles Sheeler's *Classic Landscape* on June 2, 1983, for $1·87 *million*, the highest price that had ever been paid at auction for a twentieth-century American painting.

due to be auctioned the following week. "They were just stacked there like an embarrassment of riches," Marion remembered.[5]

Taubman's taste ran mostly to midcentury modernists including Jackson Pollock, but he recognized that he was in the presence of works of exceptional quality. Marion explained that all sixteen paintings seven by Degas, three by Monet, two each by Cézanne and Manet and one by Corot were from the legendary collection of the Havemeyer family. None of the pictures had been seen by the public in more than fifty years, he explained, a distinction that made them all the more valuable.

The burly tycoon was suddenly like a little boy in a candy store as he examined Degas' *The Café Concert*, a gouache-and-pastel from the late 1870s, showing a young woman singing to a festive audience in a brilliantly lit café. That painting, he learned, was expected to reach as much as $2 million. He was also drawn to another Degas: *Waiting*, a pastel on paper from 1882 depicting a young ballerina awaiting an audition, which was expected to fetch as much as $1.75 million. These glorious pictures were due to be auctioned off as part of Sotheby's upcoming sale of Impressionist and modern paintings on May 18, 1983.

"Maybe you'd like to come to the sale?" Marion asked, casually. "Sure," Taubman replied with a grin.[6]

WHEN AL AND JUDY TAUBMAN showed up for Sotheby's black-tie evening spring auction of Impressionist and modern paintings, they were escorted to seats that John Marion had set aside for them in the front now. The courtship between Taubman and the auction house was still a closely guarded secret, although the mogul had quietly started buying up chunks of Sotheby's stock at the end of April.

The room was packed, partly due to feverish interest in the sixteen Havemeyer pictures and in other first-rate works of art in the sale by Monet, Klee, Picasso, Léger and Renoir. News of the magnificent lineup of museum-quality paintings had prompted twenty-five thousand visitors to file through the company's York Avenue galleries the weekend before the sale—the largest number in the firm's history.

Nevertheless, many of Sotheby's staffers were feeling jittery. The art market was still in the grip of a recession that had dragged on for two years, and some executives feared that the company's ongoing bitter struggle with Swid and Cogan might cast a pall over the proceedings.

John Marion was feeling confident. Earlier that day he had received a call from his senior colleagues in London, wishing him the very best of luck.

"I have a feeling I'm not just going to sell the pictures tonight," Marion replied. "I'm going to sell the *company*."7

The excitement of the crowd was palpable from the moment Marion rose to the podium to take up his gavel at seven o'clock. "There was an electricity about the room," he marvelled. "The bids were absolutely crackling, like rifle shots coming: Barn! Barn! Barn! People started applauding the first time we hit a million. And I said, 'We're going to go there a *lot* of times tonight.'"8

Fifteen minutes into the sale, Edgar Degas' *Waiting,* the pastel portrait of a young ballerina, fetched \$3.74 million setting a record for an Impressionist work sold at auction. Using a prearranged signal, Norton Simon, the Californian industrialist, had kept his hand on his chin to indicate his willingness to continue bidding. He dropped that pensive pose only when Marion had brought down the hammer on his winning bid.

Further applause came when Degas' *Café Concert* went for \$3.4 million to a mystery telephone bidder and when Cézanne's glorious *Vase of Flowers* from 1885 sold for \$2.09 million to Eugene Thaw, a prominent New York dealer.

Once Marion had knocked down the sixteen Havemeyer pictures for a remarkable total of \$16.8 million, he went on to sell a further eighty items including Matisse's *Woman in a Fur,* which the actor Jack Nichol-son purchased for \$430,000. By the end of the evening, Marion had auctioned off ninety-six artworks in two hours and ten minutes, for a grand total of \$37.4 million—a world record for an art auction.

"I think we had the wealth of the Western world represented either in this room or on the telephones," Marion told the *New York*

Times immediately after the sale.[9] Twenty years later, he was still savouring the triumph. "It was the most exciting auction I've ever seen," he told me. "Just wonderful. It was one of those magical evenings, and after being beaten up for a few years it was very, very welcome."[10]

The wildly successful sale also sent a powerful message to collectors and dealers that New York had replaced London as the international centre of the art market. It would also be remembered as the night the recession in the art market ended, and when the rollicking era of the big-spending eighties really began.

Witnessing the euphoria around him, Taubman realized that he had stumbled into a unique opportunity at precisely the right moment. Owning Sotheby's would not only be a great investment. It would also be a lot of fun.

THE THREAT of Cogan and Swid's hostile takeover had been temporarily averted, thanks to some deft lobbying by Sotheby's board. Fearing a disaster, they had rustled up an army of distinguished allies including Sir Edward Heath, the former prime minister, to plead their case to Britain's secretary of trade, Lord Cockfield.

Sotheby's enthusiastic embrace of Taubman raised many eyebrows in the art world. What was the difference, some asked uncharitably, between this vulgar American mall mogul and a couple of fast-talking corporate raiders from New York? There was little doubt that if Taubman had tried to buy Sotheby's six months earlier—before Swid and Cogan's unwelcome assault—he would have received a similar rebuff. A brash midwesterner with a Florida tan, an omnipresent cigar and an ex-beauty-queen wife was possibly not the saviour that Sotheby's board would have chosen if given their druthers. But their desperation to be rid of Swid and Cogan made Taubman's good timing and fistfuls of cash irresistible.

On September 19, with the full endorsement of the board, a deal was quickly accepted and Sotheby's slipped into American ownership in October for the princely sum of $139 million. Taubman's personal investment was $38.5 million.

"Creative financing is a hobby of mine—I enjoy it," he told Rita

Reif of the *New York Times* who believed, like many perspicacious followers of the art market and the stock exchange, that he had paid a ludicrous sum for a company that had lost $5 million the previous year.[11]

Taubman intended to have a good time proving them wrong. Sotheby's was infinitely more captivating than any real-estate deal, and he was thrilled to be the new proprietor of a place steeped in rich history and tradition. Miraculously, the former stuttering, dyslexic, pudgy schoolboy now found himself on top of the world, and he and his beautiful wife were poised to become the king and queen of Sotheby's.

"It wasn't a big investment," Max Fisher observed. "But for Al, it was a very romantic one."[12]

A FEW DAYS after gaining control of Sotheby's, Taubman clambered onto the roof of the London headquarters. Gingerly, he negotiated a forest of skylights and chimneys, pausing to get a good look at the confusing jumble of buildings below. His childhood fascination with architecture was unabated, and he was itching to use his retail design skills to improve what was known in the shopping-centre business as "flow."

Flow was notably lacking at 34–35 New Bond Street. Over the years, the firm had expanded into seventeen adjacent town houses that had been cobbled together, creating a hodgepodge of different levels, hallways, superfluous stairways and unutilized courtyards. It was a daunting task to make sense of the bizarre jumble of auction rooms, cramped offices, basements packed with works of art, twisting staircases and a perpetual jostle of staff and clients, but Taubman relished the challenge.

"There's a marvellous quaintness about the building which I wouldn't want to change," he told a reporter. "I think I can physically try to change the space, have less passages, without changing the wonderful ambiance of the building."[13]

Taubman's quest for a pleasing architectural flow was emblematic of the way he wanted the business to run. "My background is as a planner," he explained, "so I want to find a way to communicate better in the company. I look at the memos and I can get a sense of what's needed. The greater the paper, the less conversation. I believe in more conversation and less paper."[14]

The mogul had grand plans for the auction firm. It would henceforth be called simply Sotheby's, rather than Sotheby Parke Bernet—a change that would apply to the firm's fifty-seven offices around the world. "We shall regard ourselves as one international company," Taubman declared.[15]

"There is no intention of changing Sotheby's in any way that would question the integrity of its very great name and its ability to be the greatest auction house in the world," he added piously.[16]

Besides anointing himself as chairman and chief executive officer of the newly formed Sotheby's Holdings, Inc., Taubman had stacked his board with a dazzling array of international names. Keenly aware that the auction business thrived on social and business connections, he had carefully recruited a glamorous group to add lustre to the image of the recently ailing house. With illustrious names in the front of the catalogue, Taubman believed, business was sure to follow. And if the prestigious association also meant being besieged with party invitations for the chairman and his wife, so much the better.

SINCE MARRYING the glamorous Judy Mazor in the summer of 1982, Taubman had been swept up into a dizzying round of parties with a steady stream of dukes, princesses and sundry foreign potentates.

"Another evening of social climbing," he quipped lightheartedly when he ran into a friend on the beachfront-mansion cocktail party circuit in Southampton.[17]

The American tycoon was impressed by his wife's seemingly inexhaustible supply of titled European friends, but he became frustrated when the conversation invariably reverted to French, the language of continental high society.

"Al doesn't speak French," the friend noted. "Sometimes he can barely handle English with his dyslexia."[18]

On such vexing occasions, Taubman made jokes at his own expense, loud enough to embarrass his chic, multilingual wife.

"Judy!" he exclaimed more than once, "Why do I have to have dinner with people whose names I can't pronounce?"[19]

The couple's social capital had soared dramatically since the purchase of Sotheby's. Every prominent citizen in Paris, London, New York, Southampton and Palm Beach suddenly seemed eager to befriend the all-American Big Al, whose plain talk and refusal to put on airs won him plenty of fans.

As the Taubmans found themselves travelling in more exalted circles, Judy and Al—or Alfred, as he was now known—were becoming increasingly selective about whom they spent time with.

One sunny weekend in the fall of 1983, they were entertaining a large group of houseguests at their mansion in Palm Beach. One guest had asked if she could bring her friend John Hale, an English historian who was in town to deliver a lecture.

Being an unassuming, modest fellow, Professor Sir John Hale neglected to inform his American hosts of his impressive art-world credentials: He was a former chairman of the board of trustees of London's National Gallery; a trustee of the Victoria and Albert Museum; a fellow of the Royal Society of Arts; and also a fellow of the British Academy.

Remarkably, Sir John was also professor of Italian at University College in London; chairman of the British Society for Renaissance Studies; a fellow at the Harvard Centre for Renaissance Studies at I Tatti, Berenson's old villa outside Florence; a best-selling author at work on his definitive, prizewinning book *Civilization of Europe in the Renaissance;* and a recent recipient of the title Commendatore dell'Ordine al Merito from the Italian government in recognition of his services to Italian culture. The world-renowned scholar was also too discreet to mention that he was shortly to be knighted by the Queen.

Unaware of his considerable accomplishments and imminent knight-hood, the Taubmans were polite but clearly unimpressed by their academic British houseguest.

Three weeks later, on November 23, 1983, the couple were in London to attend a reception at the Royal Academy of Art for the opening of *The Genius of Venice 1500-1600,* an exhibition that critics hailed as one of the best historical art shows in living memory. As they mingled with the black-tie crowd, the Taubmans were enraptured when Queen Elizabeth II entered the gallery, accompanied by her distinguished escort for the evening, a scholarly Englishman who had masterminded the exhibition.

"Who's that with the Queen?" Taubman whispered. "He looks familiar. Don't we know him?"

"He was just staying with us in Palm Beach," Judy replied. "What's his name?" Taubman asked, blankly.[20]

The Michigan mogul's pulse was racing. He had been longing to meet the Queen of England and believed he had stumbled on a great opportunity: Professor Hale and Her Majesty had paused in front of Titian's great masterpiece of 1576, *The Flaying of Marsyas,* a gruesome canvas depicting Apollo skinning alive the satyr Marsyas. Also in the picture, to the right, loomed another of Apollo's victims: Midas, the Phrygian king with the golden touch, whom the angry god had given ass' ears.

Determined to seize the moment, Taubman stepped forward, breaking the invisible line of protocol around the sovereign. "I felt this huge hand on my shoulder," Sir John remembered afterward.

"John! How are you?" Taubman bellowed. "It's so good to see you again!"

Hale was mortified. Was this cheerfully brazen American *really* trying to cadge an introduction to the Queen? Didn't he know that he was committing a breach of royal etiquette?

"I'm preoccupied at the moment," Hale replied graciously. "But I'd love to catch up with you later."

3

Dede Brooks

AL TAUBMAN WAS captivated by Dede Brooks from the very beginning.

"I was quite impressed with her," he told me, recalling their first encounter, in a little glass-walled office on the third floor of Sotheby's in New York in the late autumn of 1983. "I didn't consider her beautiful or anything," he said with typical bluntness. "She had no feminine allure. But I found her to be very bright, and she wanted very badly to work very hard to be successful.

"Dede was the only one I saw around there that had that kind of energy," he continued. "I've always tried to get people around me with that kind of energy—it's an instinct to find people who want to make things happen."[1]

Brooks' talent and ambition were unmistakable: Six feet tall and avidly competitive, she took delight in overtaking younger male athletes by running—not jogging—around the reservoir in Central Park each morning before she arrived to put in a ten-hour day at Sotheby's. After only three years with the company she had risen to the powerful position of executive vice president of finance for North America.

Known for her sharp intellect, the thirty-three-year-old financial whiz was said to be capable of calculating auction totals faster than Sotheby's computers. Taubman was impressed to learn that she had a banker's unsentimental understanding of the changes that were necessary to transform Sotheby's into a more efficient, viable business. From observing her interaction with the firm's art experts he was also struck by her ability to explain complex business ideas in layman's terms—a gift that made her unique at Sotheby's.

Brooks' strengths played well to Taubman's insecurities. The brainy ex-banker was more adept at number crunching, deal making and negotiating than he had ever been, despite his prodigious success. And she was endowed with an innate WASP confidence that he found compelling.

She kept him entertained by cracking jokes, telling self-deprecating stories and making cheeky comments during meetings. Few could pull off such high jinks in the intimidating presence of Al Taubman, but her winning sense of humour and aura of effectiveness allowed Brooks to get away with showing scant deference to her superiors. Taubman could be quick-tempered and a bully, but his fear of confrontation left him defenceless around strong women who were unafraid to contradict him.

After a short time in Brooks' company, Sotheby's new chairman was smitten. His impressions were bolstered when he sent his new spokes-man, Christopher Tennyson, to New York in the spring of 1984 to conduct a comprehensive review of Sotheby's communications department. After interviewing a wide cross-section of the New York staff, Tennyson came away with a ringing endorsement.

"They all love Dede Brooks," he told Taubman. "She clearly understands the experts and has a reverence for them that is really spectacular." Twenty years later, Tennyson's opinion was unchanged. "Dede was a champion of the experts *and* a brilliant finance person," he told me. "She had support from every camp. And she was terrific, no question."[2]

Taubman admired Brooks' ability to make tough business decisions and appreciated her efforts to transform Sotheby's New York into a more professional operation. The Michigan tycoon and the former Long Island debutante could hardly have sprung from more dissimilar back-grounds. But Taubman recognized in her a steely determination and voracious appetite for success that was curiously similar to his own.

Diana Noyes Dwyer—known since childhood as Dede—was born on the North Shore of Long Island on September 12, 1950, the third child and oldest girl of six children born to Mary and Martin Dwyer, Jr. The family lived in Laurel Hollow, a village near Oyster Bay, in a large, rambling stone house on the water with a breathtaking view of Cold Spring Harbor and the Long Island Sound.

The Dwyers would later sell the house to John Lennon of the Boatels, who installed a sensory-deprivation tank in the attic that helped him to kick his addiction to drugs before he was killed in 1980. The free-love Liverpudlian was attracted to the house, Brooks recalled, because "it reminded him of an English country cottage."[3]

Blond and blue-eyed, Dede was born into privileged circumstances. Her mother, Mary Thompson, attended Green Vale, the private school favoured by Long Island's leading families, where her friends and fellow classmates included Gloria Vanderbilt, the railroad heiress, and Bobby Pennoyer, a grandson of the financier J. P. Morgan. Daniel P. Davison, another eminently patrician boy in Mary's class, would grow up to become the chairman of the U.S. Trust Company and the American chairman of Christie's auction house.*

Mary Thompson married Martin Dwyer, Jr., a strapping Irish-American alumnus of Montclair Academy who had graduated from Yale in the class of 1944. Martin also came from fine American stock. Through his mother, he was a direct descendant of John Alden, a founder of Plymouth colony who sailed to America on the *Mayflower* in 1620. Brooks and her five siblings adored their father, who idolized Joe Kennedy, another ambitious Irish-American who was determined that his children achieve great success in life. Big Marty, as his family called him, was a senior partner at the largest law firm on Long Island. Friends noted that Dede inherited her father's competitiveness, his tenacity and dedication to hard work as well as his ready wit and hearty laugh.

Brooks grew up in a sporty, boisterous household. She and her

---

* By a curious twist of fate, Davison would later be compelled to give a sworn deposition to counsel for plaintiffs in a class-action suit against Sotheby's and Christie's, regarding his earliest suspicions concerning the illegal conduct of Mary's eldest daughter, Dede Brooks.

siblings "fought a lot," she recalled, "but also had a lot of fun together."[4]

"My parents were extremely loving, but placed high expectations upon all of their children, particularly the oldest three," recalled Elinor Dwyer McKenna, Dede's younger sister. "My older brothers were strong athletes and good students, and life revolved around their sports schedules. The best way to secure my parents' attention was to compete in school and on the sports field, and we all did."[5]

As the oldest girl in a brood of six children, Dede Brooks listened intently when her father convinced her that she could compete and win just like her two older brothers, Andy and Martin Dwyer III. "I believed him," she said. "My father always gave me the feeling that I could do whatever I set my mind to."[6]

Brooks later ascribed some of her success in business to the tough treatment she received from Marty and Andy. "I think women with older brothers have an advantage," she observed, "because they beat on you so much as you're growing up, you have to be able to handle it."[7]

Like many daughters with two older brothers, Dede created her role within the family by being extremely efficient, organized and depend-able. "By the age of eleven she could have easily run the entire house-hold," Elinor noted.

Dede attended Green Vale School, like her mother. And when she went on to study at Miss Porter's School in Farmington, Connecticut, in 1965, she became the fourth generation of her family to attend the prestigious academy for girls, whose most famous alumna was Jacqueline Kennedy Onassis.

The Dwyers spent their summers in Mantoloking, a resort on the New Jersey shore where Big Marty had summered as a child. It seemed a life of unalloyed good fortune until the summer of 1967, when the family received tragic news: Martin Dwyer III, Dede's beloved oldest brother, had been killed in a motorcycle accident in Biarritz. He had just completed his sophomore year at Yale.

"The happy world as we knew it disappeared in that moment," Elinor recalled. "My parents had to find a way to function because they still had five children to raise under the age of eighteen. Both my mother and father turned to Dede for strength and support in coping with our terrible loss."⁸ To help her shattered parents, Dede ministered to the emotional needs of her youngest siblings, the ten-year-old Elinor and Henry, five, an experience that helped to meld her powerful instinct to nurture those in need.

One year after the funeral, Dede went to Smith College in Massachusetts, where she remained for a year until transferring to Yale in the fall of 1969. There, she met and married Michael Brooks, a handsome ex—Yale hockey player and all-around athlete, who had commanded a Navy boat in the Mekong Delta during the Vietnam war.

While still in college, Brooks fell gravely ill. At first her doctors diagnosed her with appendicitis, but while performing an appendectomy they discovered she was suffering from acute peritonitis and Crohn's disease, a chronic digestive condition marked by a painful inflammation of the intestines that required several rounds of excruciating surgery. The persistent ailment nearly killed Dede, Mary Dwyer recalled, but "she would not give in to it."⁹

Brooks later acknowledged that her bouts with Crohn's disease and the agonizing loss of her brother were life-changing experiences that framed her perspective on surviving seemingly unendurable troubles with the support of a loving family and friends. Those personal traumas also appear to have informed the two extremes of her complex character: a toughness verging on ruthlessness that was seemingly at odds with her nurturing and compassionate side.

After graduation, Dede joined Citibank, starting in the rigorous lending division training program, and excelling as one of the firm's first female lending officers. Five years later she took a leave of absence to spend more time with her infant daughter, Carter.

But she craved a new challenge.

WHEN A FRESH-FACED, confident Dede Brooks walked into the clubby Madison Avenue offices of Sotheby Parke Bernet looking for a part-time job in the finance department in October 1979, she was told nothing was available.

"Well you don't have to *pay* me," Brooks told Fred Scholtz, the chief operating officer. "I just want to work three mornings a week."[10]

Astonished by her pluck, Scholtz promised to check her references and give her a call, "It's hard to turn down a skilled worker at no pay," he noted wryly.[11]

Scholtz invited Brooks to become his part-time assistant. "I didn't pay her, at least not for a while," he recalled. "And then she became so valuable it was ridiculous not to pay her."[12]

No task seemed to faze the ambitious young assistant, who shared a cramped office with her new boss on the second floor of Sotheby's premises at 980 Madison Avenue, across the street from the Carlyle hotel. Her first assignment was to chase down clients who had failed to pay their bills on time. It was a chore that other Yale graduates might find demeaning, but Brooks accomplished the assignment with startling efficiency and charm.

"Dede was knocking on doors up and down Park Avenue to get the money," Scholtz said, admiringly. "She was perfectly willing to do that. She had tremendous energy and discipline and she was just an incredible worker. And very intelligent."[13]

Brooks' arrival at Sotheby's coincided with a period of exhilarating prosperity in the art world. A few days after joining the firm she witnessed the historic moment when a packed salesroom broke into spontaneous applause as John Marion, the firm's golden-throated auctioneer, brought down the gavel for Frederic Edwin Church's 1861 masterpiece, *The Icebergs,* at a record $2.5 million. Church's glorious depiction of a floating mountain of ice and a green translucent cave had just become the most expensive painting ever sold in the United States.

Dede Brooks was fascinated by the rapid-fire dynamic of the auction process. The bidding for *Icebergs* had opened at $500,000, then quickly escalated to $2 million, with two prospective buyers bidding furiously by telephone until one finally dropped out.

The successful sale, Brooks learned, entitled Sotheby's to collect a 10 percent "buyer's premium" as well as a 10 percent "seller's commission." The premium was a nonnegotiable surcharge paid by the winning bidder on top of the highest bid (known as the "hammer price"), whereas the seller's commission was a variable rate that was negotiated up front between the auction house and the potential consigner. The standard rate was 10 percent. But if Sotheby's was eager to win the consignment, the firm often agreed to slash the commission rate to as low as 2 percent or even—in rare cases—zero in order to convince the seller to consign at Sotheby's rather than at the hated rival establishment, Christie's.

For *Icebergs,* the premium and commission came to a total of $500,000. It was an incredible sum, Brooks marvelled, for a painting that had sold in exactly three minutes and forty-five seconds.

Coming from a world of sophisticated accounting systems at Citibank, Brooks was shocked by the antiquated and haphazard way business records were kept at Sotheby's. "There were situations that would make a chief executive's hair stand on end," she recalled. "When I arrived, there was a director of personnel who had no idea whether there were seven hundred or one thousand people on the payroll and didn't really care. And there were millions of dollars in accounts receivable where we did not know who owed us the money."[14]

Brooks discovered that Sotheby's was dominated by its loose confederation of autonomous experts, many of whom had never been required to balance a budget. "The firm's system of training produced experts, not businesspeople," she remembered, "but it was experts who made all of the decisions about business-getting, negotiating terms and marketing and public relations for their own areas. There was little real communication either between the various expert areas or with staff in the support areas."[15]

When appointed head of financial planning, Brooks set out to encourage the experts to approach their specialist areas as independent businesses. "Gee, if you keep taking in property and giving away the costs of travelling exhibitions or colour photography for your catalogue or advertising, you're going to run out of money," a colleague said, mimicking Brooks' attempts to drum rudimentary business lessons into the heads of some of the fine-art experts.[16]

Gregarious and informal, Brooks succeeded in making herself

indispensable to Sotheby's specialists. "They were just shovelling all these things at her that they didn't like to do, and she would willingly do it," recalled Susan Alexander, who had been brought in to run the personnel department. "So they *loved* her for that."[17]

Through Brooks, many experts came to realize that the financial, marketing and advertising departments could actually help them as opposed to being obstacles to getting business done.

"Dede was very accessible," Alexander recalled, "and she made herself very, very appreciated and valued by the expert staff, and also by the nonexpert staff—like the people who worked in client accounting—who had very much felt like second-class citizens at Sotheby's."[18]

In order to encourage efficiency, Brooks and Scholtz assigned a business manager to every specialist department with the goal of helping the experts to formulate their business plan for each year. "We tried to get everyone thinking forward, rather than just the next sale," Scholtz recalled.[19]

John Marion noticed that Brooks was becoming invaluable to the company. "Dede's very smart, very aggressive, very personable and she has a great ability to put deals together," he observed. "A lot of experts haven't got the practical sense that God gave a goose. They know all about the property for sale. But to sit down and put together a financial agreement with a client, with everything from loans to commission rates and sliding scales and all that stuff .... It takes a separate set of talents that a lot of the experts don't have.

"Dede was able to help them get property," he added, "and that always makes you more desirable to the experts. And she did that in a very good way. She's really a smart lady."[20]

Brooks recognized that the experts were the backbone of the business, and that winning their confidence was the key to gaining power at Sotheby's. She also learned that Taubman had purchased the company with the understanding that the specialists were the firm's most valuable resource.

Sotheby's new chairman admired Brooks' initiatives for making the experts more accountable for the success of their departments. In May 1984 he granted her wish by promoting her to the newly created position of executive vice president in charge of expert operations for the U.S. company.

With Taubman rooting for her, the dazzling trajectory of Brooks' career at Sotheby's had truly begun.

4

Tough and Exacting

IN DEBATING WHETHER to buy Sotheby's, Taubman had observed what he called "a unique marketing opportunity": a chance to transform the 240-year-old company from a highfalutin "wholesale" operation that sold mostly to dealers into a full-service, sophisticated "retail" business capable of offering private collectors everything from financial services and insurance to restoration, storage and art education.[1]

The potential upside of this business plan was enormous. Dealers of fine art, furniture and jewellery had always been the biggest buyers at Christie's and Sotheby's, and still accounted for more than two-thirds of the companies' salesroom purchases in London and New York. They were always on the lookout for some undervalued masterpiece and were usually able to pick things up inexpensively at auction. They then resold their purchases at marked—up retail prices to their private collectors, many of whom felt intimidated by the auction houses and preferred to buy from knowledgeable and reliable dealers instead.

Under the shrewd tutelage of Peter Wilson, Sotheby's and Christie's had already begun attracting a few wealthy individual buyers with the lure of glamorous black-tie evening auctions for major sales. But Taubman believed that Sotheby's could be effectively marketed to a vast untapped constituency: the tens of thousands of investors around the world with newly minted stock-market fortunes who had never seen the inside of a salesroom.

All that was required, Taubman believed, was to convince moneyed folk that Sotheby's was the most exciting and congenial place to buy fine art, furniture, rugs and jewellery, and that acquiring beautiful objects could improve the quality of their life and social status.

By targeting private collectors directly, Sotheby's could eliminate the dealers from the equation and reap far greater profits. A Wall Street fat cat who was willing to pay $100,000 for a Louis XVI commode in a fancy antique shop on Madison Avenue was likely to pay the same price—if not more—amid the heated excitement of an auction salesroom, competing with other red-blooded collectors. With only dealers in the room, the same object might fetch only $50,000.

If Sotheby's could also persuade potential consigners—widows, divorcées and executors of major estates—that far higher prices could be achieved by selling at auction, they might be tempted to abandon the dealers altogether. Such a switch in allegiance would enable Taubman to transform Sotheby's into the ultimate prize: "a retail business without inventory."[2] Or, as his lawyer Jeff Miro jokingly dubbed it, "a cash machine."

Taubman had taken the official title of chairman and chief executive officer of Sotheby's Holdings, Inc., but he had neither the time nor inclination to run Sotheby's on a day-to-day basis. Finding a suitable CEO to run the worldwide company was no easy task, however. Nobody at the firm had the crucial mixture of sharp business skills and management experience necessary to lead a complex global company with more than fifteen hundred employees. Dede Brooks showed great promise, but she was too unseasoned to assume such an important role.

After interviewing several candidates, Taubman settled on Michael Ainslie, a Tennessee-born Harvard MBA who was president of the National Trust for Historic Preservation. Tall, attractive and eminently respectable, the forty-one-year-old Ainslie exuded a confident patrician air that made him seem the perfect choice to lead Sotheby's.

Like his new colleague Dede Brooks, Ainslie believed in Taubman's strategy of cultivating private collectors. Shortly after his arrival at Sotheby's in July 1984, he got a taste of the chairman's emphasis on retail solutions to business challenges when Taubman summoned him into a meeting with Brooks, John Marion and Jim Lally, the president of Sotheby's North America, and began peppering them with the kind of provocative questions he asked his shopping-mall executives:

"Where are we going wrong with our customers? How can we give them better services? What's keeping collectors away? Why do they feel intimidated? What can we do to make them feel more welcome?"

Ainslie was spurred into action by Taubman's line of questioning. "Alfred had this idea of 'threshold resistance,'" he recalled. In Sotheby's case, he decided, the problem boiled down to a blunt reality: "People don't want to come in our door, because we make them feel stupid."[3]

The new CEO saw the off-putting arrogance exuded by some of Sotheby's specialists as a reasonable reaction to a nettlesome problem: Too much of their time was being wasted on small consignments that did little to improve the firm's bottom line. "The experts were processing so many lots," he recalled, "that they didn't have time to spend with individual clients explaining the difference between this piece of furniture and *that* piece of furniture, or whatever."

Ainslie discovered that each individual lot consigned to Sotheby's generated an astonishing total of twenty-seven pieces of paper, from receipts and invoices to lot tags and notices to clients. The huge amount of paperwork convinced Ainslie to make a sweeping executive decision: "We are going to stop selling things that are under a thousand dollars," he told his new colleagues.

Exceptions could be made if the object in question was consigned as part of a larger estate. But now it was official: Sotheby's was no longer in the business of selling inexpensive lots.*

"The whole strategy," Ainslie explained, "was to free up the experts so they could deal with clients—real clients, who hung things on the walls!"[4]

---

* The decision to scrap the sale of inexpensive objects was a boon for smaller auction houses, which prospered on the crumbs that Sotheby's left behind in pursuing the top of the market.

The new CEO understood that Sotheby's illustrated catalogues of
upcoming works for sale were among the firm's most important and
far-reaching marketing tools, and he worked closely with Taubman
to explore ways to make the glossy publications more precisely
geared to the needs of private collectors.

Ainslie found Taubman to be a tough and exacting boss, especially when it came to matters concerning Sotheby's image. The tycoon
somehow found time to examine a catalogue for every single one of
the five hundred auctions the firm held each year around the world,
and he was liable to raise hell if he was unhappy with the layout or
choice of pictures.

"Alfred would constantly call me," Ainslie recalled. "He would
have looked in a catalogue for a sale in, say, Amsterdam, and he
would see a photograph on page 212 and complain that he didn't like
the way we had shot a group of chairs. Or there would be a piece of
jewellery, and he didn't like the way the light was shining on the
object."[5] The chairman also cast his critical gaze over all of Christie's
catalogues, and complained bitterly if he thought that the rival firm
was doing a better job.

Ainslie was quickly learning what shopping-mall executives and
tenants had known for years: that Alfred Taubman was a perfection-
ist who paid an almost excruciating amount of attention to detail.

"Frankly, he was a real pain in the neck," Ainslie remembered,
"because nobody else noticed it. But he really cared. Frequently he
was right, but not all of the time."[6]

As a Harvard MBA, the new CEO was incredulous that Taubman
never seemed to spend any time analyzing Sotheby's balance sheet,
clearly preferring to leave such matters in more capable hands.
"Alfred is completely dyslexic," Ainslie noted. "He has no interest
and no capacity for numbers. He never asked me about margins and
costs. But he does know—and loves—art."

Taubman, he concluded, was almost entirely "a visual person.
Dede is the opposite—a numbers-driven person."[7]

The chairman also seemed preoccupied with socializing as a
means to win business for Sotheby's. "All he ever wanted to know
was who was at that dinner last night," Ainslie remembered, "and

why was Christie's so much more active socially than we were."

Most of all, the languid Tennessean was struck by the ferocity of Taubman's competitive spirit. "He was, I would have to say, *obsessed* with beating Christie's," Ainslie noted. "And he was the most difficult when we lost a big consignment to them. We'd have to do almost an *interrogation* to figure out why Christie's got something and we didn't."[8]

Taubman seemed perennially fixated on market share—the much-ballyhooed statistic indicating which firm—Sotheby's or Christie's—had achieved the biggest sales figures for the season.

"We were significantly bigger than Christie's," Ainslie recalled, "and that was one of the things that Alfred was very concerned about, and something he really focused me and our management time on achieving."*[9]

Competition between the two firms was never fiercer than when a major multimillion-dollar estate came up for grabs. Auctioneers were obliged to be vigilant in looking out for fresh opportunities, and to be ready to dispense condolence notes, calls and flowers as they turned to the obituary pages each morning, eagerly anticipating the news that some rich collector had gone to his or her great reward.

When the eccentric American-born heiress Florence Gould died at her sumptuous villa on the French Riviera in February 1983 at the age of eighty-seven, she left most of her $124 million fortune to a charitable foundation to promote what she called "Franco-American amity." Like elegant vultures circling some delectable prey, Christie's and Sotheby's swooped down a few days after her demise to begin picking over her worldly goods.

Gould was famous on the Côte d'Azur for her trademark blue sunglasses and the double strand of large egg-shaped pearls that graced her neck even on casual morning shopping trips. Extravagant and fun-loving, she was the widow of Frank Gould and daughter-in-law of Jay Gould, the nineteenth-century railroad magnate. Florence was also a passionate art collector, and had amassed an assortment of

---

* During Ainslie's era, Sotheby's held between 55 and 60 percent of the overall market share, while Christie's held 40 to 45 percent.

major works by Cézanne, Courbet, Gauguin, Manet, Monet, Renoir, Toulouse-Lautrec and Vuillard, among others.

While ransacking her grand apartment in Paris and her Cannes villa, the auctioneers discovered incredible troves of precious jewels, furniture, fine art and silver. Sotheby's and Christie's briskly marshalled rival teams of experts to catalogue her treasures and drew up elaborate illustrated proposals for executors of the will in hopes of snagging the prestigious and hopefully lucrative contract to dispose of Mrs. Gould's treasures.

In the end it was Christie's, with its aggressive, well-run jewellery department led by François Curiel—a neat, diminutive Frenchman with a knack for publicity—who won the opportunity to auction off the Gould jewels at the firm's Park Avenue salesroom in the spring of 1984.

It was heralded as the biggest single-owner jewellery sale in history. In order to drum up interest, Christie's held a series of glamorous cocktail parties in six cities, including Manhattan, where *le tout* New York came to marvel at the widow's finery.

"The Shah of Iran once said her collection was the only one in the world which could rival his," Curiel told *Women's Wear Daily*. "When I went to her home after she died, to make an appraisal, I found these beautiful diamond lapel clips in her shoe closet. Most people would wear them on their lapels, but she was so in love with jewellery that she even wore them on her shoes."[10]

The April auction was deemed a huge success. The star lot was a sapphire-and-diamond necklace with a 114-carat sapphire centrepiece known as the Blue Princess, which had once belonged to an Indian maharaja. After some frantic bidding it was sold to an anonymous American for $1.32 million. By the end of the evening Curiel had brought down his gavel on 86 pieces from the American widow's collection for an incredible $8.1 million.

It was practically unheard of for the executors of an estate to engage the services of *both* rival auctioneers. But Sotheby's was entrusted with the task of auctioning off Mrs. Gould's collection of antique French furniture, English silver, decorative objects and four thousand books.

The real prize Christie's and Sotheby's were vying for, however, was Mrs. Gould's remarkable collection of Impressionist and Postimpressionist paintings. The finest picture was van Gogh's *Landscape with Rising Sun,* an exquisite depiction of a wheat field ablaze with sunlight that captured the view from the artist's window while he was confined to a lunatic asylum at St.-Rémy in 1889.

In trying to win the plum consignment, the two auction houses wrote up lengthy proposals for the Gould trustees, estimating the collection to be worth more than $25 million. Sotheby's proposal offered an unprecedented series of concessions, starting with an offer to show the pictures in London, Switzerland and Japan as well as New York, so that plenty of potential buyers could see them. The firm also offered to slash its seller's commission to zero—a crucial bargaining point that was matched by Christie's.

The smaller company was prepared to match all of Sotheby's proposed concessions until it came down to one significant stumbling block: Christie's was unable to duplicate Sotheby's offer of holding a single-owner sale in New York in April 1985. Inconveniently, Christie's was embarking on a major expansion of its Park Avenue salesroom, and the firm could not guarantee that the construction work would be completed on time.

Sotheby's had won the Gould pictures by a mere whisker. Making the most of its opportunity, the firm invested a record sum of $ 1 million in promotion to attract first-time buyers, lavishing the money on international advertising, insurance, invitations, catalogues and nonstop parties, which proceeded at a giddy pace. Prospective bidders were lured with back-to-back breakfasts, boardroom lunches, full-bar cocktail parties and intimate dinners.

A few days before the auction, Sotheby's threw a champagne bash for an invited crowd of two thousand guests—an event that was hailed as one of the most glittering social occasions of the New York spring season. The April 24 black-tie sale attracted such luminaries as Bianca Jagger, Lucille Ball, Ann Getty, Baron Hans Heinrich Thyssen-Bornemisza and the Greek shipping magnate Stavros Niarchos, and clusters of armed security guards.

High rollers and executors for the Gould estate were invited to sit in the seven glass-fronted balcony boxes overlooking the salesroom, rather like those at the opera, where their champagne glasses were topped up by tuxedoed waiters.

In the space of a single hour, John Marion brought his gavel down on fifty-five pictures that sold for a grand total of $32.6 million, superseding the previous record for a single-session sale of a collection, which had been set by Christie's in London the previous summer when the Duke of Devonshire's old-master drawings had sold for $28 million. Only three of the Gould pictures failed to find buyers, and *Landscape with Rising Sun* was sold to an anonymous collector for a staggering $9.9 million.

The success of the Gould sale confirmed the impression that auction prices were rising by leaps and bounds, proof of a robust art market that was riding high on the much-vaunted Reagan–Thatcher economic boom.

Kenneth Friedman, the publisher of the *Art Economist*, noted that there was a logical explanation for the rash of extravagant prices being paid at auction: "If America has over one million millionaires," he told the *New York Times* after the Gould sale, "there are plenty of multimillionaires and these people can afford to pay ridiculous prices for things that they value."[11]

EVER SINCE Taubman's purchase of Sotheby's there had been considerable unrest in the art world over the creative and aggressive financing deals the company was offering to attract new business. Imaginative marketing and leveraging had long been cornerstones of Taubman's success in the real-estate business, and he had begun to push Sotheby's into areas of high finance that its rival Christie's and art dealers were reluctant to explore.

From their earliest conversations, Dede Brooks and Alfred Taubman had agreed that a promising way to attract spectacular consignments—and new customers—was to offer sellers a financial incentive in the form of an "advance," a loan against the low estimate of the item they wished to consign.

As the art market started to boom, Sotheby's responded by expanding its financial-services program, which became a major source of revenue for the company.

Another incentive Sotheby's offered sellers was the "guarantee," a binding contract that obliged the auction house to pay an agreed sum to the seller even if the piece should fail to sell at auction. Given the risk involved, the firm usually committed to such deals only when it felt that there was a strong market for the work being consigned and that the offer of a guarantee could really clinch the deal.

The deep-pocketed braggadocio of Sotheby's new range of financial incentives was making Christie's directors extremely nervous. Christopher Burge, the president of Christie's in America, expressed concern about potential conflicts if the auction house should be perceived as a bank—a notion that also troubled some executives at Sotheby's. Furthermore, he explained, there were qualms about the financial risks for the auction house if the market should decline precipitously.

"We are obviously aware of what our competitors are doing and we have no plans to finance," Burge told the *New York Times*. 'But we are watching it."[12]

5

Borrowed Glamour

WHILE DEDE BROOKS and Michael Ainslie were labouring to put Sotheby's on a sound operational footing, Taubman assumed a more ambassadorial role, circling the globe in his private jet and sallying forth most nights and weekends to sup, drink, shake hands and exchange air kisses wherever vast wealth and major collections were to be found.

The art world had long served as a ladder for social adventure for those with newer fortunes, but few had ever scaled to such giddy heights in so short a time, or with such sterling success, as Judy and Al Taubman. With her stupendous beauty and his leviathan wealth, the duo had become bona fide social celebrities.

They had set out to conquer New York, a city that worshiped money and power, and had become the greatest new act in town. Writing with the unassailable authority of the *New York Times,* the society columnist John Duka noted that "Judy Taubman, the wife of A. Alfred Taubman, the owner of Sotheby's, is the odds-on favourite to become the city's top hostess."[1]

Holding gracious suppers at home was a crucial component of the couple's new ambassadorial existence. And Al and Judy had all the trappings to make a splash in each of the four places where they owned homes: Manhattan, Palm Beach, Detroit and Southampton, where they had acquired a palatial beach house that was a two-minute stroll down the beach from the Southampton Bathing Corporation.

The Taubmans were unwelcome at the club, which had few Jewish members, but nobody could dispute that Al and Judy's chef served *much* better food and that they were able to attract a far more lively, cultivated and amusing gathering of mostly European guests.

Judy had infinitely improved the quality of her husband's life, and everyone agreed that he could never have pulled off his acquisition of Sotheby's—or achieved such a rapid social ascent—without her help.

"Alfred was already a well-known tycoon, but he was not propelling himself socially in New York," Boaz Mazor, his brother-in-law, remembered. "But when he married a beautiful wife, there were more dinners, receptions. Judy started to mix people socially, and people were inviting them everywhere."

In no time, he recalled, the couple were flying on their private plane to India and Argentina with Jerry Zipkin, the tart-tongued socialite, major-league gossip and self-proclaimed social arbiter who was the reigning Best Friend and walker of First Lady Nancy Reagan.

"It actually takes a year, if you have the money and power, to make a lot of friends," Mazor observed sagely. "And they did. They had all the possibilities. Judy was beautiful and charming, and everyone wants to meet an attractive couple. And they were *a very* attractive couple." [2]

Al Taubman had met Judith Mazor in February 1982 on a blind date orchestrated by David Metcalfe, the godson of the Duke of Windsor who had also encouraged the mogul to pursue Sotheby's. Friends who knew of Taubman's amorous exploits as a freewheeling bachelor were stunned when he suddenly announced he was getting married to Judy on June 17, 1982, only four months after their first date. He was fifty-eight, and she was thirty-eight.

"She gave me a deadline," Taubman confided to a friend. "If I didn't marry her, I would never see her again. And I couldn't think of life without her." [3]

Judy described it as a match made in heaven. "From the beginning we were soul mates," she recalled. "Passionate about art, we travelled the world, exploring different civilizations, visited museums, and made friends everywhere we went." [4]

The lovely Mrs. Taubman called her portly husband "Puss," short for Pussy Cat, and everyone who saw them together realized that he adored her.

Shortly after Taubman acquired Sotheby's, the couple attended an elegant dinner party in their honour at the home of a stylish Park Avenue hostess. "There was a bowl of peaches on the table," a fellow guest recalled, "and Al said, 'Judy, why don't you show them what you can do with a peach?'"

"Judy was a gorgeous, ravishing creature," the guest, a New York socialite, continued. "She took a peach and massaged it with her hands, and after a couple of minutes she held a perfect, unbruised peach in one hand, and a handful of crumpled peach skin in the other hand."

Dazzled by the performance everyone had just witnessed, the socialite's wealthy husband breathlessly issued a challenge: "I bet you can't do that again."

Without hesitation, Judy took another peach and performed the same miracle. In anyone else's hands, the unfurling of a piece of fruit would be an unremarkable occurrence. When performed by the stunning former beauty queen, however, it was a uniquely erotic experience that left many husbands panting for more.

"All the men were mesmerized, and all the women were *so depressed*," the socialite recalled. "We realized we were in the presence of a real pro. Lord knows what else she could do with those hands."[5]

Twenty years later, the socialite's husband declared it was a party trick from which he had never quite recovered.

Judy Taubman was not merely a novelty act. She was intelligent, fluent in seven languages and a walking encyclopaedia on eighteenth-century history and decorative arts. In a short time she had accrued an impressive collection of Italian drawings and French furniture as well as a cache of exceptional antique jewellery, which proved she had a sophisticated eye.

She was also remarkably up-to-date on the lineage of the great families of Europe, a useful point of reference at a time when thousands of titled Europeans were invading New York as visiting bankers or dilettantes. Judy had a talent for making introductions and for fostering relationships with folks who owned castlesful of eminently saleable objects and financiers willing to bid for them at auction. It was a skill that both she and her husband accomplished with remarkable grace and charm, for they understood that being socially accepted was extremely good for business.

After an exhausting round of cocktail parties and dinners in their honour, the Taubmans had officially established their arrival in New York society in September 1984, when they threw a lavish gala at Sotheby's to benefit the Metropolitan Museum of Art.

By then, Judy had already established herself as the darling of the couture world. She had even appeared on the cover of *Town & Country* in May 1984, wearing a diaphanous white robe and looking radiant as she embraced Très *grand personnage*, a gleaming bronze statue created by Jean Arp, the French Surrealist.

Inside the magazine, a lavish ten-page spread of photographs by Norman Parkinson showed her to full dramatic effect as she struck poses around her husband's Palm Beach mansion, wearing the latest fashions designed by Arnold Scaasi, Claude Montana and Jackie Rogers.

The mesmerizing images that stuck in most people's minds, however, were three poolside shots of a heavily bejewelled Mrs. T. wearing skimpy white bathing suits that revealed her considerable charms to devastating effect. In one double-page image, she appeared to rise mermaidlike from the glistening pool, laden with gold and crystal jewellery by David Webb, exuding a look of breathless elation.

When the magazine hit the newsstand, ripped-out pages showing the exceptionally trim, forty-year-old Mrs. A. Alfred Taubman in the almost-altogether began adorning Sotheby's staff bulletin boards, from the Impressionist department to the loading dock, where they were particularly cherished.

"All the experts put her up as a pin-up, like garage mechanics," one executive recalled, chuckling.[6]

Some questioned how the bathing beauty could possibly swim, given the tremendous weight of the giant emeralds and diamonds adorning her person. "The jewellery would have rendered even an Olympic swimmer unseaworthy," an irreverent Sotheby's staffer joked.[7]

Judy Taubman's magazine debut as the queen of Sotheby's did nothing to deter customers from buying or selling at the auction house. Ardent art fans swarmed to cocktail receptions on York Avenue, hoping for a glimpse of the delectable Mrs. T. and her mogul husband.

Everyone, it seemed new money and old money—was intrigued by Manhattan's new power couple, whose gilded glory threatened to eclipse even that of Donald and Ivana Trump. One of the most sought-after invitations in New York was a stiff, engraved summons to dine at the Taubmans' sumptuous duplex residence.

Judy had overseen the decoration of the Fifth Avenue apartment, which her devoted-Modernist husband professed to love. When Mr. Taubman asked the butler to turn up the lights, he was told they could not be made any brighter because Mrs. Taubman insisted on low-wattage bulbs to protect all the multimillion-dollar paintings and her personal collection of Old Master drawings.

Downstairs in the third-floor drawing room, among the serious French and Italian furniture, humidifiers belched out a cool mist night and day and air conditioners droned ceaselessly. "It has the effect of a dungeon," a maid noted wryly, adding that Mrs. T's strict rules for the preservation of valuable objects would occasionally drive her husband to distraction. When he asked one of the maids to turn off the air conditioner, she shook her head.

"We can't turn if off, Mr. Taubman," she replied. "It's for the furniture."

"When I die, I want to come back as a piece of furniture or a painting," he quipped. "You get better treatment around here!"[8]

The Taubmans' four magnificent houses in America were like stage sets for the nonstop drama of winning business and expanding Sotheby's prestige. With Judy's help, the mogul scored the amazing coup of appointing Her Royal Highness the Infanta Dona Pilar de Borbón to Sotheby's Advisory Board in March 1985.

The Spanish infanta, also known as the Duchess of Badajoz, was the elder sister of King Juan Carlos of Spain. The profitable alliance introduced Al and Judy Taubman to a world of shooting weekends on ancestral Spanish estates, which enabled them to forge new friendships and cultivate grandees who might have a splendid Velazquez or Zurbaran in the attic that they wished to sell.

Some wondered if the giddy excitement of consorting with the nobility was going to Al's head. Alexis Gregory, a New Yorker who had invested $1 million in the purchase of Sotheby's, flew to London for a board meeting in June 1985 and was alarmed to find Alfred Taubman and Michael Ainslie dressed in their tailcoats and top hats for Royal As-cot, which they were planning to attend after the meeting.

"God help me," Gregory exclaimed upon seeing their elaborate garb. "I've lost all my money!"[9]

TAUBMAN WAS DOING plenty of hobnobbing, but he was also keeping his eye on the ball. When Sotheby's and Christie's announced their estimated totals for the season ending on August 31, 1985, he was happy to learn Sotheby's was way ahead, with sales of $642 million—a welcome increase of more than 17 percent over the $548 million achieved for the 1983—84 season. Christie's totals were also the highest in their history, but the smaller firm had crept up by less than 8 percent, from $442 million to $475.9 million, over the same period.

The results were encouraging, but Taubman had set his sights on capturing a larger share of the global art market. In an interview with Rita Reif of the *New York Times,* he noted that some $25 billion was spent worldwide every year on art and sundry collectibles. Sotheby's and Christie's, he observed, accounted for merely $1 billion. There was clearly room for growth.

Wherever he travelled, Taubman actively persuaded his fellow nouveaux riches to invest in works of art, just as they did with stocks and bonds on Wall Street. His strategy really began to pay off by the spring of 1985, when prodigious fortunes were being made overnight on the New York, London and Tokyo stock exchanges.

As his reputation as a retail genius blossomed, Taubman was invited by the nation's top business schools to lecture on the secrets of his success. He explained his theory that art was a commodity to be traded like any other.

"There is more similarity in a precious painting by Degas and a frosted mug of root beer than you ever thought possible," he told audiences at Harvard and the Wharton School in the fall of 1984. The common denominator, he said, was in creating new markets by offering "a better value, a more exciting environment."

"A unique creative idea," he added, "can win new markets where there is no perceptible need for new goods and services."[10]

Word that the chairman of Sotheby's was equating Impressionist paintings with soda pop caused a giant kerfuffle when his words were quoted in the *Wall Street Journal* and the *New York Times*. The minor scandal inspired snobs to scoff at the brazen vulgarity of the upstart, and to complain bitterly that he was turning a respectable 241-year-old auction house into an art department store and a bank.

His detractors were wasting their time complaining. Taubman had his finger on the pulse of the eighties. Sotheby's new wave of collectors included bond traders, arbitragers and freshly minted billionaires who were intrigued by reports of soaring art prices. Some arrived for auctions in their tuxedos and wing collars, bringing along their trophy wives in Christian Lacroix pouf dresses to experience the frisson of the marketplace and to participate in the competitive ritual display of wealth. Serious contenders occupied reserved seats in the salesroom and sat clutching their catalogues with one hand, bracing themselves to raise their numbered paddles to make a bid. Others preferred to place bids more discreetly from their stretch limousines or airplanes.

Prices for fine art were leaping through the roof, fuelled in part by Taubman's retail initiatives and ready credit, expanding the universe of buyers and sellers and turning art into a more liquid commodity. At some financial institutions, including Citibank, it had become de rigueur to consider art not only for its aesthetic and sentimental value, but also for its borrowing power. Paintings by Bonnard, Caravaggio, Monet, Picasso and Van Dyck were viewed as instruments of high finance—a scenario that would most surely have startled their creators.

Leveraging was a highly controversial topic in the art world—for art dealers, financiers and most particularly for Sotheby's direct rival, Christie's. Some cautioned that the practice of treating artworks as collateral by auction houses and banks could result in an inflation of prices that could have disastrous implications for lenders and investors.

The old guard complained bitterly that Taubman was transforming Sotheby's into a stock exchange for collectibles. Eugene V. Thaw, a respected dealer, noted with dismay that art, when collateralized, "becomes a commodity like pork bellies or wheat."[11] Investors who acquired purely for investment purposes, he warned, could get an unpleasant surprise if they were forced to sell at the wrong time.

AS NASDAQ fortunes soared, the eighties were emerging as an era of borrowed glamour. Prosperous first- and second-generation Americans found themselves yearning for the dignified trappings of wealth and history—an impulse that reached its apotheosis with the opening in 1985 of the popular exhibition *Treasure Houses of Great Britain* at the National Gallery in Washington. Ignited with a lust for authenticity, people with new money longed to acquire other people's eighteenth-and nineteenth-century family portraits to adorn the artfully distressed, rag-rolled walls of their newly constructed mansions in Bel Air, Grosse Pointe, Palm Beach, Greenwich and East Hampton.

The thirst for ancestral trappings seemed unquenchable. Many indigent aristocrats had inherited paintings, furniture and jewels they were prepared to sell for the right price, and Taubman was eager for Sotheby's to help them do just that.

Dealers who felt they were losing ground resented Sotheby's pursuit of their clients. But there was little they could do about it. Sellers were delighted by the stratospheric sums achieved at blockbuster auction sales, and collectors enjoyed buying in a public marketplace adorned by famous people.

"Alfred Taubman realized that Sotheby's was inefficiently run and got the funding to correct it," Richard Feigen, a prominent art dealer, observed in 1985. "Now Sotheby's is in a position to dominate the whole art if not the auction field. I think Sotheby's will put other auctioneers out of business, and I hope not us dealers, too."[12]

6

Etonians Behaving Badly

AT A MOMENT when Sotheby's star was conspicuously rising, Christie's was receiving a thrashing in the international press. Embarrassing papers filed in connection with a court hearing in July 1985 revealed that Lord Bathurst, the new chairman of Christie's International and former president of Christie's New York, had lied about the results of a disappointing sale in 1981 when he claimed that two paintings—a van Gogh and a Gauguin—had sold for $2.1 million and $1.3 million, respectively.

The truth, Bathurst admitted in a sworn affidavit, was that both paintings had been "bought in"—the auction house euphemism for unsold—because there had been no bids for either picture above the "reserve," the secret minimum price agreed to with the consigner before the sale.

The reason he had lied, Bathurst said, was to try "to contain the possible negative impact on the art market."[1] Many cynics, however, believed that the English aristocrat had merely been trying to protect the reputation of his own auction house.

The regrettable falsehood had come to light as part of a $10 million lawsuit brought against Christie's by Dimitry Jodidio, a Lausanne-based art dealer, who had consigned eight important Impressionist paintings to Christie's for its major spring Impressionist sale in New York on May 19, 1981. After the auction, he was dismayed to learn that only one of the eight pictures had actually sold—a portrait by Edgar Degas of Eugène Manet, the younger brother of the painter Édouard Manet—which had fetched

$2.2 million, more than double the previous record for a Degas at auction.

In his lawsuit, Jodidio accused Christie's of "wrongful conduct, negligence and breach of their fiduciary duty."[2] He attempted to collect damages, claiming that the auction house had given him inflated estimates for his paintings, but a New York judge dismissed the case, opining that it was not a matter for a court of law to assess the fair market value for works of art.

Unfortunately for Christie's, Jodidio's allegations of impropriety had inspired a related investigation by the Department of Consumer Affairs for New York City, led by its crusading commissioner, Angelo J. Aponte. Christie's agreed to pay an $80,000 fine as part of an out-of-court settlement with the department, and Bathurst voluntarily agreed to give up his license to conduct auctions in New York for two years.

When the press seized upon the exciting story of fraud and deception at the famous auction house, Christie's was faced with a public-relations nightmare that threatened to undermine its credibility as a public company. Scrambling to present a dignified face to the world, John A. Floyd, Bathurst's predecessor as chairman of Christie's International, issued a statement from London declaring that the board took "the gravest view" of Bathurst's "erroneous statement."[3] Floyd also described the incident as an "isolated lapse from the high standards of conduct that Christie's employ." What had taken place, he noted piously, "was not Christie's policy and would certainly not happen in the future."[4]

Floyd's words were sensibly tailored for public consumption, but they were somewhat disingenuous. The tall, handsome, genial and occasionally abrasive sixty-two-year-old Englishman had learned of the deception shortly after the sale when Bathurst telephoned him in London to give him the results and to explain that he had misled the press over the unsold pictures. Floyd appeared to be untroubled by the news at the time. "He seemed reasonably relaxed," Bathurst recalled later.[5]

John Floyd, or Jo, as he was known, also held a license to conduct auctions in Manhattan, but city officials did not seek punitive

action against him on the grounds that he may possibly have learned
of Bathurst's deception days or even weeks after the disastrous auction. Nobody at Christie's doubted for a minute that Floyd would
have been informed of the transgression within a few hours, if not
minutes, of its occurrence. But the company's resilient longtime
chairman succeeded in escaping an awkward scandal unscathed—just
as he had in the past.

Known for being aloof and remote, Floyd was a tall, imposing
man with shoe-polish-black hair that was oiled back over his large,
square head. He was a former Head Boy at Eton, and still conveyed
a tremendous sense of authority that left many of his underlings in
awe when in his presence. He had that grand "marbles-in-his-mouth
English voice," an American colleague noted.[6]

Bowing to pressure from Floyd and his businesslike deputy, Guy
Hannen, Bathurst stepped down as international chairman and
chairman of Christie's London on July 19, 1985. "David felt obliged
to resign," Philip Hook, a friend and fellow paintings expert
recalled. "Many of his colleagues considered that he paid an unfair
price for an action universally acknowledged to have been motivated by enthusiasm rather than duplicity."[7]

Christopher Burge, the third Old Etonian Englishman involved
in the scandal, was the president of Christie's in New York.
Famously charismatic, he was a respected connoisseur who enjoyed
reading French novels in the original, and he was one of the firm's
star auctioneers. It was therefore embarrassing that he was compelled by the Department of Consumer Affairs to surrender his auctioneer's license for four months when it was discovered that he had
been aware of Bathurst's deception but had done nothing to report
it.

Bathurst later recalled that he had actually elbowed his way
through a crowd of reporters to first consult with Burge about
whether he should lie to the press and say that the two paintings had
sold. He, Bathurst recalled, encouraged him to do so (an account
emphatically denied by Burge when asked by the author).

It was not the first time—or the last—that Christie's officials
would be accused of having contemporaneous knowledge of the

nefarious actions of senior colleagues but failing to take any corrective action.

The Bathurst—Jodidio scandal had come close to destroying
Christie's ability to do business in New York—a threat that would
have had grave consequences for the London-based firm. "We were
seeking not only the licenses of Mr. Bathurst and Mr. Burge, but
the license of Christie's auction house," Aponte explained. "The
fact that the auction house took no corrective action after it
learned about the misrepresentation, we felt, made the house cul-
pable."

Perennially fortunate in such awkward situations, Christie's received a special dispensation—an amnesty, of sorts—when the
Department of Consumer Affairs announced its decision not to
revoke the firm's license to conduct auctions in Manhattan. The
department had taken into account Christie's important role in
New York business and the international art market.

"We intend to keep New York City competitive international-
ly," Commissioner Aponte told the *New York Times*. "I think the
settlement sends a very clear signal to the art world that they are
going to have to clean up their act."[8]

THE BATHURST-JODIDIO matter had a vexing corollary for
both Christie's and Sotheby's Extensive press coverage of the scandal gave disgruntled dealers an opportunity to voice their disquiet
over what they regarded as other dubious salesroom practices.

Art auctions could be confusing even for seasoned dealers and
collectors, who often complained that it was unclear—even after the
auctioneer had brought down his gavel—whether an object had
actually sold. There were many reasons for confusion. No
announcement was made if something failed to sell. And there was
usually no clear indication if it *did* sell. Quite simply, it was up to
the individual auctioneer to decide how to handle it. Some shouted
"Sold!" or called out the buyer's name, or a pseudonym. If no bids
were forthcoming at sales in London, the auctioneer often called out
a fictitious name—"Carruthers," or "Pickering"—creating the false
impression that the lot had found a buyer.

Robert Woolley, a masterly auctioneer at Sotheby's in Manhattan, had a habit of saying "fair warning" when the bidding petered out before it hit the reserve. He then called out the price of the final bid, brought down his gavel and said nothing further. Woolley was simply observing common salesroom practices, but such rituals left many people in the salesroom scratching their heads.

"I think that is a major problem," Commissioner Aponte told the *New York Times*. "We are taking a hard look at the inadequacy of the law and how we can improve it, and whether an announcement should be made when the gavel falls in terms of whether or not a sale has taken place."[9]

Auctioneers groaned at the prospect of municipal officials imposing restrictions on the theatrical magic of the salesroom. Announcing unsold items had "never been practiced," Mitchell Zuckerman, a senior vice president at Sotheby's, noted, "because it can interrupt the rhythm of the auction."[10]

The dealers' discontent centred mostly on Christie's and Sotheby's use of secret reserves, which they felt allowed the wicked auction houses to deceive the public by permitting the auctioneer to rapidly call out a series of opening bids known as "chandelier bids," even though nobody in the salesroom was bidding.

Fending off the criticism, Christie's and Sotheby's claimed that chandelier bids were performed "on behalf of the seller" in order to generate interest in the salesroom, hoping that the genuine bids that followed would far exceed the consigner's desired minimum price. Frustrated dealers argued that the practice encouraged unwitting bidders into believing that they were competing against other would-be buyers, and that it therefore created artificially high prices.

Several influential art-world figures, including Richard Feigen, an outspoken dealer on Manhattan's Upper East Side, railed against the secrecy of reserve prices and demanded that they should be made public or dispensed with altogether.

One week after the scandal broke, Commissioner Aponte warned that he was considering whether to make it compulsory for

New York auction houses to disclose reserve prices. He also revealed that he was pondering whether to force them to reveal the identities of telephone bidders and sellers.

Sotheby's and Christie's were aghast to learn of Aponte's new regulatory notions, which they feared would send their customers fleeing to dealers to conduct their transactions in private. Aponte's proposals could also impinge on their ability to create public interest in major sales, with their usual breathless talk of "anonymous sellers" and "mystery bidders" and "record prices."

As a gifted marketer and frequent bidder himself, Alfred Taubman recognized that uncertainty played a potent role in the drama of live auctions, which often inspired well-heeled members of the audience to bid far higher than they had planned to because they were caught up in the competitive thrill of the moment. To rob the process of its mystery, he believed, could spell disaster. "God help us if we ever take the theatre out of the auction business," he said. "It would be an awfully boring world."[11]

The brouhaha over Bathurst's lie and resignation had a crippling impact on Christie's. After the scandal broke, the firm's share price tumbled on the London Stock Exchange from 263 pence on July 8 to 211 pence by the end of August, wiping off more than £14 million ($20 million) from the market value of the company.

Morale at Christie's sank even lower in the autumn of 1985 when the press reported that the auction house had failed to recognize a valuable Gainsborough portrait that had slipped through its hands at a sale held at its South Kensington branch in February. The catalogue entry for lot number 207, an unframed picture of a plump, bewigged gentleman, listed the artist as "unknown." The firm had estimated the painting would fetch between £100 and £200, and it was finally knocked down at £800—quite a bargain, considering that a properly attributed work by England's most celebrated eighteenth-century portraitist had recently sold at Sotheby's for £90,000 ($139,442). The error was particularly humiliating for Christie's since the company prided itself on the great superiority of its expertise in Old Masters.

Compared with its Americanized, fiendishly efficient rival,

Sotheby's, Christie's was a remarkably anachronistic, hidebound institution in the mid-eighties. Pay was absurdly low, and there was prejudice against self-promotion and "foreigners," especially Americans. Announcements and press releases sent from London to Christie's offices in Geneva, Monte Carlo, Amsterdam, Rome, Paris and New York were addressed to; "All Provincial Offices"—a telling reflection of Christie's imperious world view.

That Christie's managed to turn a profit was largely due to the tremendous knowledge of its Old Masters Department and the conservative business impulses of its senior directors, most notably Guy Hannen. Christie's could also boast of having unrivalled connections with every duke, earl, marquis, viscount and baronet in the land who owned a stately home filled with paintings, tapestries, furniture, carpets and jewels that might need to be sold off to defray the cost of England's exorbitant estate tax.

The company's familiarity with the landed gentry was partly clue to the provenance of its own aristocratic directors. But for all of their high birth and fine connections, none of Christie's senior management had the financial and leadership skills necessary for the urgent task of transforming Christie's into the aggressive modern firm it needed to become in order to compete successfully against Sotheby's.

Lord Bathurst possessed the necessary talent, but the Jodidio quagmire scuttled all hopes of his being able to lead Christie's into the future.

He did manage, however, to discover and anoint the man who could. To the surprise of his colleagues, he chose Christopher Davidge, a young executive who was running White Brothers, the catalogue-printing division of Christie's. It was an ingenious move.

At first glance, the thirty-nine-year-old printer seemed an improbable choice to run an auction house. He had virtually no knowledge of nor any interest in—works of art. But Bathurst recognized his implacable ambition and saw that he possessed the businesslike authority to be able to give a complacent firm like Christie's the kick it so urgently needed.

During his nineteen years at White's, Davidge had transformed the printing house from a modest five-man operation to a successful international business that was a boon for Christie's. The heads of expert departments (or "technical" departments as they were known at Christie's) who had depended on him to produce their catalogues could not fail to be impressed by his formidable drive and talent.

Whether he would fit in at Christie's was another matter. Davidge had grown up in a government housing project in North London, the son of lower-middle-class parents who had worked at Christie's in lowly administrative positions. He had left school at sixteen and was acutely aware of coming from a very different background from that of his new colleagues. King Street was a veritable house of lords who spent weekends shooting at their family estates—a notable contrast to Davidge's humble roots and perfunctory education.

When he was offered the King Street job, Davidge sought advice from Guy Hannen, Christie's deputy chairman, who had known his father and grandfather. "Well, Davidge, it's like horse breeding," Hannen told him. "Every now and again the thoroughbreds get too refined and you need to bring in an old brood mare to give some toughness to the breed. I see you as the old brood mare."[12]

Davidge professed to be amused by the put-down, but he would later repeat the story as an illustration of the condescension he received from Christie's privileged directors.

During his years at White Brothers, Davidge had been in and out of Christie's headquarters on King Street on an almost weekly basis, delivering catalogues at first, then visiting experts to collect copy and photo-graphs for the galleys. His frequent visits had given him an understanding of the inner workings of the company and a clear perspective on its idiosyncrasies and shortcomings.

When he officially arrived to take charge of King Street in the spring of 1985, Davidge recalled, Christie's was "like the Conservative party, full of pomposity, arrogance, filled with people from a narrow social circle, who were not commercially aware. They recognized that the place needed a manager but wanted to limit my involvement to below stairs."[13]

Behind his back, he was referred to as "the butler." It was a slur he could never quite shake.

Davidge set out to drag Christie's into the twentieth century. Taubman's businesslike approach at Sotheby's, he discovered, was putting tremendous pressure on his new colleagues, who were finding it tough to adjust to the fiery competition spurred by the regime change at the rival firm.

"It wasn't so much the style of Sotheby's that changed," Davidge noted. "It was the fact that it wasn't being run by the people who had been at school with the people running Christie's, who therefore knew how it worked. Now it was American, and it wasn't WASP America; it was Detroit property money. So that made things a bit shaky in terms of how we would attack the future, our future."[14]

To show he meant business, Davidge toured Christie's every Monday morning at eight-thirty, and fired off memos about what needed to be painted, cleaned up or reorganized. When the work habits of junior staff failed to meet with his high standards, they were sent to his old stomping ground at White Brothers to be given a lesson on how a firm should really be run.

During his first week on the job, Davidge was incredulous to discover that the amount of warehouse space, the number of secretaries and even the size of each department's advertising budget were awarded according to "how senior you were in the company, not where the income was coming from."[15]

Years later, many art-world veterans would feel nostalgic for the good old days before reform was deemed necessary. "The auction houses were nice, rather cosy, gentlemanly, undynamic businesses in the seventies," Henry Wyndham recalled. "Then the competition hotted up. Alfred Taubman bought Sotheby's and the whole game changed. This became a theatrical, dynamic, big-money sexy business. And Davidge realized that if Christie's was going to survive they had to sharpen up their act.[16]

"Suddenly the fuddy experts had to look at their budgets," Wyndham added. "He made it a more professional game. I'm not saying that it's a *better* game, or a nicer place to work. But he made it a more professional game."[17]

By an intriguing coincidence, Davidge's opportunity to take

charge of the running of Christie's King Street in the spring of 1985 coincided with the promotion of another dynamic and promising auction executive, Dede Brooks at Sotheby's, who had been assigned the similarly important strategic job of running Sotheby's New York as its chief operating officer.

So far, they had not met. But their oddly parallel destinies would entwine with profound consequences.

CHRISTOPHER DAVIDGE'S remarkable career at Christie's had begun rather precociously in the autumn of 1953, when he was merely eight years old. For one day the eager, blue-eyed schoolboy was enlisted to help the venerable London auction house move back into its headquarters in St. James' at 8 King Street, which had been rebuilt because of bomb damage sustained in World War II. Chosen for his diminutive size, young Davidge was given the task of wedging himself into a small passenger elevator crammed with office equipment, and he was enthralled at the prospect of receiving a handsome reward for his efforts.

"The elevator was loaded up and I would have to push the button," he recalled. "I got sixpence for every trip."[18]

Born in London at the end of the war on August 23, 1945, into a family of proud but woefully underpaid Christie's employees, Davidge longed for considerably more than a pat on the head and a silver six-pence. While growing up he was convinced that the last thing he wanted to do with his life was to work for the snobbish auction house that he felt had treated his family with disdain.

His grandfather Wilfred Davidge had joined the firm in 1904 at the age of twelve, after the wife of a Christie's partner spotted him singing in a church choir. Taking a shine to the plump little urchin, she arranged to get him a job as a trainee porter at Christie's. Wilfred worked hard and rose to become the firm's senior cashier, but earned a modest weekly wage for the privilege of counting the thousands of pounds that tweed-suited English dukes and bejewelled countesses blithely paid for their whimsical Boldini sketches and Titian masterpieces. When Wilfred died of a sudden heart attack at his desk on King Street at the age of forty-one, two Christie's officials paid a visit to Eva, his widow, to express their condolences.

The firm did not grant pensions to its employees at the time, but the tragic circumstances inspired Christie's partners to offer her a stipend of thirty-five shillings a week. Christie's also offered to employ her seventeen-year-old son, Roy Davidge, who left school immediately and went to work at Christie's in 1932 to help support his family. While working in the Decorative Arts Department he met Olive Fowle, a pretty, independent-minded girl from a good family who was working as a secretary to one of the senior partners.

Olive's marriage to Roy Davidge brought little peace to her family. Her well-to-do father and mother were scandalized that their beautiful daughter was marrying beneath her social rank to a mere Christie's clerk with limited financial prospects. When she defied them by marrying the man she loved, she was disinherited—an act of cruelty prompted by an unforgiving English class system. The episode informed the bitter, Dickensian view of class politics that Olive Davidge would impart to her only child, who would spend most of his adult life trying to restore the money and social status she had lost. Roy went on to become a beloved character at Christie's, respected by those who laboured with him in below-stairs jobs and later by the firm's invariably aloof, aristocratic directors.

Growing up in Maida Vale, Davidge was adamant that he would never fall into the trap of working at Christie's like his father and grand-father. "The chap next door who worked as a butcher's assistant earned more than my father," he recalled.[19]

Davidge hated school and paid scant attention to his lessons at St. Marylebone Grammar School, preferring sports. His best friend in school was Jason Miller,* a bright, sensitive lad who was working toward his goal of attending Oxford University. A mutual friend recalled that Jason came home one day to discover that his mother had committed suicide. He reached out for support to his friend Christopher, who brought him home to stay with his parents in Maida Vale.

---

* Not his real name.

Olive Davidge consoled the distraught teenager, lavishing more affection and tenderness on him than she had ever shown toward her own son. If Christopher was jealous, he kept his feelings to himself. But his world was rent asunder when his mother suddenly announced that she was leaving her husband, Roy, to take up with the teenage Jason.

In later years Davidge would profess to be untroubled by his mother's enduring romance with his closest childhood friend, but some believed otherwise. "Although he always said how proud he is of his mother, inside there is great pain," Olga Davidge, Christopher's second wife, observed.[20]

When Christopher left St. Marylebone Grammar at sixteen with only two "O" levels, his father urged him to follow in his footsteps and take a job at Christie's. But Davidge had other ideas. Eager to establish his independence, he began his working life selling men's shirts on weekends in London's rough-and-tumble street market in Petticoat Lane, where he and a group of friends from school had started helping out on holidays and weekends the year before. "Quite frankly," he recalled, "I was earning more money than my father was making all week at Christie's."[21] Trading in shirts gave him a taste for what he called "the hustle and bustle of business dealings," and the brash street smarts he acquired as a teenager would later prove indispensable to the entrepreneurial Davidge.[22]

Petticoat Lane offered only seasonal employment and Roy craved a more stable and respectable career for his only son. To appease him, the cocky teenager agreed to go for an interview at Christie's with Guy Hannen, who was then a senior director at the firm.

"He talked about how his grandfather had been at Christie's and so had mine and how wonderful it would be if I worked there," Davidge recalled. "I listened to all of this, and toward the end of the interview he said, 'Well, do you have any questions to ask me?' And I said, 'You haven't offered me any great future. I can see there's a future if you are the grandson of one of the partners, but as the grandson of a clerk, I don't see any future.'

"The interview came to an abrupt stop," Davidge recalled, "and he told my father that I was the most arrogant young man he'd ever met."[23]

Three years later, Roy tried again. As luck would have it, Christie's had recently acquired White Brothers, which was looking for trainees. Roy saw it as a great opportunity for his son to enter the lucrative printing business while working for Christie's and threatened to evict him from the family flat unless he took the job. When the twenty-one-year-old joined White Brothers in January 1966 on a three-month trial basis, his first tasks were to load and stack paper and help out with the guillotine used for cutting paper. "Roy was extremely proud of him," recalled Ray Perman, a colleague who had helped to negotiate Christie's acquisition of White's.[24]

Davidge would often bump into Roy at Christie's headquarters on King Street while making deliveries or dropping by to collect catalogue copy to be laid out for the presses, and came to develop a closeness and affection for his father that had been absent for much of his childhood. Roy took an active interest in his son's career, but Olive preferred to leave him to his own devices. "By then I'd moved on," she recalled. "I have a very peculiar feeling about how parents should behave. We had a very good friendship, but Christopher did what he wanted to. So long as he was doing okay, that was okay with me. As far as I was concerned, he was a very good son."[25]

After thirty-four years at Christie's, Roy had risen to become company secretary, a responsible position that involved running the day-to-day administrative operations at King Street from a second-floor office overlooking Duke Street St. James'. Co-workers remembered him as an amiable, military presence. "He was a red-faced man with a handlebar moustache," said Christopher Wood, a Christie's paintings expert at the time. "We called him the Wing Commander, because he *looked* like one."[26]

Davidge would later complain that his father was poorly paid and that he endured cavalier treatment from the firm's aristocratic partners, but Roy's friends and colleagues disputed that impression. "*Nobody* was paid well, including the directors," John Herbert recalled, "but Roy never appeared bitter. He never grumbled, and it's quite unfair to say that they were impoverished. He was absolutely trustworthy and perfectly happy in his job."

"Roy was liked by *everybody* at Christie's," Ray Perman noted. "I think Chris tried to ingratiate himself by saying he came from a deprived background.27

Roy's colleagues were stunned when he died suddenly in 1967 at the age of fifty-one. Like his father, Wilfred, before him, he had suffered a fatal heart attack while still in the employ of Christie's. "It was quite a shock, because there hadn't been any sign of illness, except for his red face," recalled Anthony du Boulay, the head of Christie's Ceramics department, who occupied the office next door.28 Roy had known that high blood pressure ran in the family, but never paid attention to his diet or curtailed his enthusiastic consumption of beer. "He never looked after himself in that way at all," du Boulay noted sadly.29

Christopher would regret that his father did not live long enough to witness his subsequent glory days at Christie's. The year after Roy's death he married Susan, a warm, extroverted and vivacious Jewish girl with a slender figure and dark hair, who was slightly shorter than her diminutive bridegroom.

Sue's parents were active in their local synagogue, and his bride was keen to keep the Jewish traditions. Davidge happily agreed to convert to Judaism and study Hebrew before the wedding in order to please his new in-laws. "He changed *religions* to marry Sue," Ray Perman noted.30

In a noble effort to prove himself worthy as a prospective son-in-law, the twenty-four-year-old Davidge also underwent the harrowing ritual of adult circumcision. "Oh God, that was a painful experience for him," de Boulay recalled.31

Chris' friends regarded Sue Davidge as an ideal wife. She was loving, supportive and perennially concerned that her husband worked too hard. The couple settled down in Finchley in North London, and Sue would later bear him a son and a daughter, Paul and Alexis.

Wedding bells sounded again the following year when Davidge's mother married his best friend, Jason—a circumstance that befuddled his colleagues at White's no less than his conversion to Judaism.

"I hear Chris calls him Daddy now," a colleague joked. Davidge claimed to find nothing unusual about the union, however. "My mother is a very special lady. Very intellectual. My best friend is an English teacher," he told a reporter later, as if that explained everything.[32]

At White's, Christopher proved to be dynamic and energetic. By twenty-three he was a company director, and at twenty-seven he became the firm's managing director. His rise coincided with a period in which the printing business expanded rapidly as Christie's prospered and the firm's catalogues went from being mere text descriptions of objects offered for sale to having lavish photographic illustrations.

Davidge was blessed with an innate capacity for order and efficiency, and he took pride in thoroughly reorganizing White's to handle the stepped-up production. When Christie's opened its New York sales-room in 1977, he was faced with the challenge of producing catalogues for the new Manhattan outpost on Park Avenue.

Eager to accomplish his goal of printing all of Park Avenue's auction catalogues in London, Davidge made the extraordinary sacrifice of flying to New York forty times a year—every week during the spring and autumn auction seasons—in order to gather text for the catalogues and transparencies for the illustrations. He kept up this punishing schedule from 1976 until 1983, flying to New York every Wednesday and staying until Saturday, to the increasing frustration and annoyance of Sue, who was left at home caring for their two small children.

Davidge pushed himself to the limit of his capacities and expected his colleagues to perform similar miracles. "He was a man to be avoided at all costs because he was extremely efficient and a real taskmaster," a former Christie's clerk recalled. "When he made deadlines, everyone had to adhere to them. It was always said by the older members of the staff, 'That's the sort of chap we need running *this* company.'"[33]

7

The Golden Hamster

LIKE HIS METICULOUSLY coiffed mother, Christopher Davidge was fastidious about his appearance. He enjoyed defying the image of the printer as an ink-stained labourer by showing up for work at White Brothers in immaculately tailored—if somewhat shiny—suits with rainbow-coloured satin linings and boldly striped hand-made shirts from Hong Kong. With his blond hair invariably blow-dried into a bouffant, he exuded the confident air of a ring-master.

Davidge was revered at White's by a cadre of loyal and egregiously underpaid staffers including Doreen Edwards, who ran the firm's catalogue subscription system. Mrs. Edwards admired his ambition and doted on the young printer as if he were her own son.

Melinda Marcuse, an American working at Christie's catalogue department in New York, was riveted by her first glimpse of Christopher Davidge when she flew to London in April 1982 to pay a visit to White Brothers' printing plant on Langley Lane. "He came into Doreen's office, went behind her desk, pulled open her drawer and took out a can of hair spray and sprayed his helmet hairdo," she recalled, giggling.[1]

Marcuse was not alone in being struck by Davidge's keen attention to his appearance. On his weekly trips to Manhattan, he occasionally stayed with Ray Perman, the cheerful Cockney lad from Lambeth who had risen from a mere catalogue boy at King Street to become managing director of Christie's New York. One of the perks of Perman's job was the use of a two-bedroom apartment above Christie's on the eighteenth floor of the Delmonico Hotel on Park Avenue, where he and his future wife, Bev, frequently entertained colleagues visiting from London. When Davidge first appeared on his doorstep, Perman was struck by his guest's impeccably colour-coordinated ensemble—a track suit, luggage and sneakers with matching stripes that he had chosen for the flight from London.

The following morning, Perman was fascinated to discover that Davidge had attached a snakelike contraption with an adjustable mirror to the guest bathroom mirror, carefully positioned to offer a 360-degree view of the beholder's hairdo. Gazing upon this miraculous portable device, he realized that he had stumbled upon the secret of Davidge's perfectly teased coif.

That evening, Perman noticed a startled expression on his girlfriend's face as she greeted him at the door. Entering the apartment, he was astonished to find Christopher Davidge sitting on the living room sofa, wearing only a carefully ironed shirt and tie, with a towel strategically draped across his lap. "I thought, 'This is very odd,'" Perman recalled, "so I said, 'Where are your trousers?'"

With no hint of embarrassment, Davidge explained that it was his custom to remain bare legged until just before leaving the house because he hated to muss the neat crease in his trousers. Stunned by this sartorial exactitude, Perman realized that the reason he had never seen Davidge sit during a business meeting was because he dreaded wreaking havoc on his neatly pressed suits. "He'd always stand with his legs fully extended, so he didn't crease the knee," Perman marvelled.[2]

When a wag at Christie's nicknamed Davidge the Golden Hamster on account of his plump cheeks and golden bouffant, the name stuck. "He was always perfect," Perman recalled, "not a hair out of place, with his silk suits. That was him. He looked as if he'd stepped from a tailor's window."[3]

WHILE DROPPING into King Street in the course of his peregrinations for White's, Davidge had witnessed the furore that erupted in the spring of 1975 when London's two leading auction houses announced their plans to start charging buyers a commission—a practice that had previously existed only at auction houses on the Continent.

On Friday, May 30, 1975, Christie's held a press conference to drop the bombshell that it would begin levying a 10 percent buyer's premium on all purchases beginning that September. Three days later on Monday, June 2, Sotheby's declared it would do the same— a move that sparked a firestorm of anger from dismayed collectors and outraged dealers, who openly accused the two auction houses of collusion.

The suspicious timing of the rival firms' announcements inflamed the long-standing resentments of dealers over the rising power, arrogance and greed of Sotheby's and Christie's, prompting the biggest auction scandal that had ever hit London, which was then the centre of the international art world.

Although a mere printer at the time, Davidge watched in fascination as his elegant bosses at Christie's attempted to sidestep allegations of impropriety.

Since the eighteenth century the two leading auction houses had derived their income from acting as agents for the seller, who was charged a percentage of the sum paid by the winning bidder at auction. By 1975, seller's commissions at both firms had risen to 14 percent, a rate that many consigners considered to be extortionate.

The news that Sotheby's and Christie's also intended to extract a fee from buyers was particularly galling to the trade. A 10 percent premium, the dealers feared, would seriously cut into their profits.

Prior to the drama in London, the auction houses' fortunes had been on a two-year roller coaster. A decision by OPEC countries in 1973 to quadruple the price of oil had squeezed the economies of most Western nations, prompting a serious decline in spending. Britain's annual inflation rate was approaching 27 percent, and London's stock exchange had fallen to an all-time low. Interest rates soared to 13 percent, and the Labour government had decreed a three-day workweek on British industry.

"It's a time of horrible uncertainty," Jo Floyd told the *Daily*

Telegraph. "We are not insulated against an international depression. So one must be cautious. Obviously, we are fighting the same desperate battle against inflation and expenses as everyone else."[4]

As it turned out, Floyd had it on excellent authority that the fortunes and morale of Sotheby's were in similar disarray. One of his closest friends was David Westmorland, Sotheby's deputy chairman, whom he often chatted with at White's, the elegant gentleman's club on St. James' Street. "Jo and David had lunch together all the time," noted Charlie Hindlip,* a Christie's director who would later become chairman. "They were exact contemporaries at school and the oldest of friends."[5]

The amiable Lord Westmorland had joined Sotheby's in 1965. As one of the Queen's closest friends, he was extraordinarily well connected in British society. Floyd, a handsome, imposing figure at six-feet-four who exuded a discreet courtierlike charm, was similarly sought after in the gilded drawing rooms of duchesses and earls. He was a godfather to Lady Diana Spencer, whose family enjoyed close ties to the royal family long before she became Princess of Wales.

Floyd presided as chairman when Christie's directors gathered in their elegant second-floor boardroom on King Street to discuss the firm's perilous finances in the early spring of 1975. Though, hitherto, auctioneers had earned their income through charging a commission to the seller, it seemed clear that the only solution to their financial plight was to adopt the practice of rival auctioneers on the Continent, by charging both buyers and sellers.

Anthony du Boulay, the firm's Ceramics expert, had discovered after losing several collections to the Continental auctioneers that the income European firms gained by charging buyers gave them a distinct competitive advantage over their British counterparts.

"I found out that when things got tough, the Continental auctioneers just offered to cut their sellers' commission in order to win

---

* Charlie Hindlip, formerly known as the Honourable Charles Allsopp, inherited the title Lord Hindlip of Hindlip in 1993 upon the death of his father. In the hope of avoiding confusion, I will refer to him throughout as Hindlip, not Allsopp.

business," du Boulay recalled, "and I thought, 'If we're going to win business from Europe, we need to follow their example.'"[6]

Du Boulay urged his fellow directors to consider the advantages of such a scheme. If Christie's were to begin charging a buyer's premium in London, it too could reduce its seller's commission to win consignments from its rivals while gaining greater profits by charging both sellers and buyers.

Du Boulay's suggestion was welcomed by Jo Floyd and Guy Hannen, who spent several weeks pondering its financial ramifications. At the next board meeting, the issue of the buyer's premium was on the top of the agenda. Realizing that Floyd and Hannen had already decided that it was imperative to go ahead, several Christie's directors wondered out loud whether Sotheby's, the firm's arch competitor, would follow suit.

"Officially, we were told that Sotheby's had no agreement or obligation to go into it too," recalled du Boulay, who nevertheless suspected that Floyd had already discussed the matter with his friendly rival at Sotheby's, Lord Westmorland.[7]

"Jo said, 'I don't think we need to worry too much what they're going to do,'" du Boulay recalled wryly, "but what he said to David Westmorland and what David said to him, I have no idea. He was very discreet. In my own mind, I have no doubt that they *did* have a chat. But Jo never categorically said that he had."[8]

In an effort to appease the dealers before formally announcing the premium, Floyd sent letters to the Society of London Art Dealers and the British Antique Dealers Association—the country's two leading trade organizations—urging them to give the new charge "a fair trial."[9]

Floyd's letters failed to have any conciliatory effect and did nothing to stem the roar of outrage from dealers.

I WAS FIRST OF ALL AMAZED, then I was absolutely *furious*," recalled Sir Hugh Leggatt, a prominent Old Masters dealer and a former chairman of the Society of London Art Dealers. "I went round to see Jo Floyd, then I went round to see Peter Wilson, and I had extremely disagreeable meetings with them, too."

The encounter with Wilson, he recalled, "was *vicious*. I was furious, he was furious. And I called him every name under the sun. I
wasn't as rude to Jo Floyd, but it was quite useless to try and budge
him. They both said they needed the money, and I said I thought it
was absolutely appalling."

Sir Hugh was vexed that Sotheby's and Christie's appeared to
have reached an agreement in secret, but he was positively seething
at what he perceived as the two firms' rampant greed in seeking a
larger slice of the art business. "I was outraged that they should try
and pull a fast one on all the buyers," he recalled. "They were taking commissions both ways, and I thought that was monstrous."[10]

Determined to battle the dreaded premium, the Society of
London Art Dealers and the British Antique Dealers Association
hired legal counsel, who informed them that if the dealers could
prove that Sotheby's and Christie's had violated the Restrictive
Trade Practices Act by illegally colluding over the premium, they
would have an excellent chance of being able to persuade the Office
of Fair Trading to impose an injunction that would force Sotheby's
and Christie's to cease charging the buyer's premium.

After some foot-dragging, the two dealers' organizations applied
to the High Court in July 1979 for an interlocutory injunction to
prevent the auction houses from charging the premium. Their peti-
tion was declined, but a London judge responded by setting a date
of September 1981 for the trial of dealers versus the auction houses.

While lawyers for the dealers were struggling to build a case,
they received an unexpected bonanza when they learned that
Christopher Wood, a Christie's paintings expert and board member
who had left the firm to become a dealer, had physical evidence to
prove that collusion had indeed taken place between Sotheby's and
Christie's in 1975. To the lawyers' amazement, Wood described an
informal meeting he had attended at Christie's in May 1975 at
which Jo Floyd had confided to his fellow directors that a secret
agreement had been made between Sotheby's and Christie's to
introduce the controversial charge.

"We were informed that Christie's was going to bring in a ten-
percent premium the following week, and that Sotheby's would fol-

low suit," Wood recalled. "There's no doubt whatever that there was collusion between Sotheby's and Christie's in 1975, but it was all rather quietly and discreetly done in private conversations, behind closed doors."[11]

No official record had been kept of Floyd's revelation to the board, Wood remembered, because he had spoken at an informal conclave. But unbeknownst to Floyd and his fellow directors, the young director had gone home that night and written up the incident in his diary.

To back up his extraordinary claims, Wood showed the lawyers his 1975 journal containing the contemporaneous handwritten account.

News of Wood's secret diary caused a sensation among the tiny circle of dealers and auctioneers who learned of its existence. "Everyone giggled at the thought of Christopher rather pretentiously keeping a diary," a former Christie's director recalled. "But there was one slightly uneasy moment when it was felt that there might be some *written* evidence about collusion in the form of his diaries."[12]

Christopher Davidge was intrigued to learn of Wood's secret evidence, and suspected that the auctioneer-turned-dealer's decision to come forward was motivated by a sense of revenge.

"It was pretty well known that Christopher Wood had kept a diary," Davidge recalled. "I was also aware that he had never really been accepted by his peer group in Christie's and had effectively been cold-shouldered out of the firm."[13] The fact that Floyd and Westmorland had gotten together over the premium, Davidge recalled, was "talked about fairly openly,"[14] though it did not go beyond the small group of people in the know.

THE POTENT COMBINATION of collusion, secret written evidence and revenge was one that Davidge would not forget. Nor did it escape his attention that Jo Floyd, who appeared to have been the link to Sotheby's in the conspiracy, seemed to be surviving the scandal without any personal legal vulnerability.

By the Autumn of 1981, the dealers' legal expenses had risen to £150,000 ($293,536). So it was galling for them to learn that the maximum penalty Sotheby's and Christie's would have to pay if found guilty of collusion was a fine of £2,000 ($3,913). "It was like a rap over the knuckles," said John Baskett, a former chairman of the Society of London Art Dealers. "The whole thing was a bit of a farce."[15]

The dealers' heroic effort to take Sotheby's and Christie's to court over collusion had always seemed faintly absurd since it was the premium itself—not the alleged conspiracy—that posed a challenge to their livelihoods.

"I think if there *was* conspiracy, then it was in a charming, bumbling, inept way, rather than anything devilish," Baskett noted. "We weren't particularly interested in hauling them through the courts and having them found guilty, because it had obviously been an informal decision between Jo Floyd and David Westmorland, and discussed in their club. I don't think they thought they were doing anything wrong at the time. They were both very nice people. And it seemed a pity just to satisfy the newspapers to do all that, unless we were going to achieve the result of stopping the buyer's premium."[16]

A few days before the trial was due to begin, Sotheby's requested an emergency meeting with Christie's and the dealers to try to reach a resolution before becoming embroiled in an expensive and embarrassing court case. "They obviously didn't want the trial to take place, for reasons of publicity," John Baskett noted.[17]

At Sotheby's insistence the parties to the litigation convened at Claridge's, the elegant Mayfair hotel, on Tuesday, September 29, 1981, for a dramatic showdown that stretched until four o'clock in the morning. "It was a bit like a Whitehall farce," John Baskett recalled. "People were in different rooms and we were all walking along corridors and passing one another in the early hours of the morning. I thought the whole thing was most bizarre."[18]

The matter was finally resolved when the plaintiffs agreed to drop their lawsuit against Sotheby's and Christie's and the two auction houses agreed to pay a total of £75,000 ($146,768) toward the dealers' legal costs to date of £150,000.

"It was a conclusion which was unsatisfactory to everyone,

which is always what you expect with a compromise," Richard Crewdson, a solicitor for the dealers, noted.[19]

That the case against Sotheby's and Christie's had ended in a whimper was hardly surprising, given that the laws in Britain regarding collusion were extraordinarily mild compared to those in the United States, where violations of the Sherman Antitrust Act were punished with severe criminal and civil penalties. In 1974, the year before the alleged conspiracy over the buyer's premium in London, the United States Congress had passed a bill upgrading violations of the Sherman act from mere misdemeanours to felonies, with maximum prison terms for participants in illegal conspiracies rising from one year to three.

Twenty years later, when Sotheby's and Christie's were writing out checks for $512 million in civil fines in the United States for a conspiracy deliberately carried out by their executives, they would long for the days when a dispute over illicit auction house collusion could be settled for a mere £75,000.

THE OSTENSIBLY FIERCE rivalry between Sotheby's and Christie's was a relatively recent phenomenon. Founded in London in 1744 and 1766, respectively, the two leading auction houses had a history of cordial relations until the 1950s, when Peter Wilson had seized the reins of power and begun operating in full-battle mode, paving the way for the ferocious competitiveness of Alfred Taubman.

Taubman was proud that the great British auction house he controlled had been founded thirty-two years before the Continental Congress adopted the Declaration of Independence in Philadelphia in 1776. Sotheby's had started on a humble scale in rented rooms in London, but it had quickly prospered to become an indelible fixture in the cultural life of the British capital. Writing in 1849, the novelist William Thackeray irreverently described the London auction rooms as "full of snobs and odious, bombazine women."[20] By the time Taubman took possession of the company some 134 years later, the profusion of widows' weeds was gone, but the snobbery had survived intact.

Sotheby's was founded by Samuel Baker, a London book dealer whose portrait as a plump-cheeked gentleman in a powdered bob wig and greengage frock coat now hangs behind the front desk of the company's London headquarters on New Bond Street. His first recorded auction, on March 11, 1744, was of the library of one Sir John Stanley, comprising "Several Hundred Scarce and Valuable Books in all Branches of Polite Literature," which fetched £826 when sold in the Great Room of the Exeter Exchange in the Strand.[21]

Christie's, which considered itself the more socially superior firm, was founded by James Christie, a thirty-six-year-old midshipman who resigned his naval commission to become an auctioneer. His first sale, on December 5, 1766, included several bales of hay and "a large quantity of Madeira and high Flavour'd Claret, late the Property of Noble Personage (Deceas'd)."[22] Christie constructed a salesroom in the garden of his town house in Pall Mall, which rapidly became a fashionable gathering place for Georgian society.

Unlike his father, who had eked out a meagre living beating out the mattresses of the rich, James Christie thrived in elevated company. Witty, elegant, handsome and persuasive—it was said that he could sell fog to a Londoner—Christie was a friend and patron of the leading artists of the day. Thomas Gainsborough, his next-door neighbour in Pall Mall, painted the formal portrait of Christie—in a dignified brown frock coat and leaning on a gilded frame—that now hangs in the Getty Museum in Los Angeles.

The Americanization of Sotheby's under Taubman's aegis had injected a sense of corporate warfare unimaginable to the frock-coated gentlemen of yore. For Sotheby's, Christie's was the enemy that must be beaten, and vice versa. The competition between the two firms occasionally resulted in ludicrous situations, as in the case of Leslie and Leigh Keno, the affable identical twins who are both experts in American furniture and now stars of the American version of the *Antiques Roadshow*.

During the mid-eighties, Leigh was working at Christie's, Leslie at Sotheby's. Although extremely close, the twins were forced to sharpen their competitive skills with each other as corporate rivals.

"We just learned to talk about fishing, cars and girls, and to talk about antiques only in very general terms," Leigh Keno recalled.[23]

The twins' identical looks occasionally resulted in perplexing mix-ups. When Leigh showed up one afternoon at a Round Hill Road estate in Greenwich, Connecticut, a lady greeted him at the door, looking puzzled.

"She said, 'Did you forget something?'" he recalled. "It turned out she'd called Sotheby's and Christie's, and Leslie had been there earlier. And we both happened to be wearing a blue blazer and the same grey pants."[24]

Shortly afterward, Leslie Keno dropped by Christie's one day and was mortified when Christopher Burge, the rival auction house's chairman at the time, walked up to him and began discussing confidential details of an upcoming sale. "I said, 'Wait! Don't tell me any more—I'm Leslie,'" he recalled, laughing.[25]

Fierce competition had become part of the auction-house culture, particularly in the United States, where punitive antitrust laws outlawed improper discussions of terms. It was a legal reality that most senior American auction-house executives were keenly aware of, but one of which the Brits were often curiously oblivious.

Lord Carrington

THE ONE THING you must remember," Jo Floyd told Lord Carrington when the statesman succeeded him as chairman of Christie's in July 1988, "is that we and Sotheby's are competitors and there must be no collusion, otherwise there will be trouble."[1] Having weathered a scandal that had dragged on for six years after an alleged conspiracy over the introduction of the buyer's premium, Floyd knew whereof he spoke.

Peter Carrington was widely regarded as an ideal choice for the chairmanship of Christie's. He was the best Britain had to offer: educated at Eton and Sandhurst, his curriculum vitae including posts as defence secretary and foreign secretary, chairman of the Conservative party and secretary-general of NATO.

During his years in Mrs. Thatcher's cabinet, Carrington had struck up a friendship with the Earl of Gowrie, the tousle-haired Dublin-born poet who served as arts minister from 1983 to 1985. Known as Grey Gowrie from his name, Alexander Patrick Greysteil Hore-Ruthven, he had caused a minor rumpus when he abruptly resigned from the government in September 1985 to go to work for Sotheby's, declaring that his official salary was insufficient for him to live on in central London.

The two close friends, Carrington and Gowrie, were now official rivals in their powerful positions as chairman of Sotheby's U.K. and chairman of Christie's worldwide, respectively, but they continued to meet socially at dinners, shooting weekends and country-house parties.

Gowrie was taken aback when his American boss, Alfred Taubman, strolled into his office at Sotheby's in London in 1988 and gave him a stern warning about U.S. competition law.

"It's said that you're much too friendly with Carrington," Taubman told Gowrie.

"Don't be so silly," Gowrie replied. "We don't talk about *business*. I've known Carrington much better—and for longer—than practically everyone at Sotheby's. He was a great mentor and encourager of me in my political life, and I've remained extremely close and very fond of him."

"Well you'll have to be careful," Taubman warned, "because that sort of stuff is criminal with us in the United States."[2]

Gowrie was offended by the suggestion that his friendship with the Christie's chairman was impermissible. "I was rather angry about it," he recalled later. "I felt there was a sort of cultural difference here—that Alfred thought that most human intercourse would be about business issues."

At Sotheby's, and in the real-estate industry, Taubman had earned a reputation as a tough-talking straight shooter with a stolid, midwestern, patriotic respect for the law. Gowrie, for one, perceived him as tough but honourable. "I had no experience at Sotheby's which suggested that Alfred was peculiar in his ethics at all," he noted.[3]

Taubman refused to cut corners. He stubbornly insisted on paying New York State tax for valuable objects he purchased in Manhattan, even though he could easily avoid it by having the item shipped to one of his many out-of-state homes. And he insisted on paying customs dues for expensive items he brought into the United States on his private jet—something that other businessmen with their own aircraft often tried to avoid. "Alfred is a legal hypochondriac," Pamela Gross, his assistant at the time, observed. "He doesn't go to the *bathroom* unless his lawyer tells him it's okay."[4]

DEDE BROOKS and Christopher Davidge were thriving under the encouragement and tutelage of their respective chairmen. In January 1987, Taubman had appointed Brooks as president of Sotheby's

USA, making her the first woman to lead a major auction house.

Brooks was rewarded handsomely for her efforts. The thirty-seven-year old received $405,000 in salary and bonuses in 1987, and she was awarded options on 150,000 shares of common stock at $3 a share before Sotheby's went public again in May 1988, with an offering of 22 percent of its stock at $18 a share. Business was booming, and Taubman was thrilled. When he took the company public in the spring of 1988, he sold 3·1 million shares of Class A common stock for a total of $52·5 million—a handy return on the investment he had made five years earlier.

It was a thrilling time to be involved with either of the world's two leading auction houses, which had begun to attract international media attention in 1987—the first year that Sotheby's and Christie's sales totals crossed the $1 billion threshold. The great two-ring circus had begun in earnest with a memorable evening at Christie's in London in the spring.

In a stunning coup, Christie's had won the chance to auction van Gogh's *Sunflowers,* the celebrated depiction of fourteen sunflowers aglow in yellow against a background of yellows and oranges. It had hung at the National Gallery in Trafalgar Square since 1959, on loan, but after decades of delighting the public it was about to become available to the highest bidder. The painting had been completed in Arles in January 1889, a month before the artist sliced off his ear and sent it to a prostitute, and eighteen months before he rested his easel against a haystack and ended his tormented life with a single gunshot on July 27, 1890, at the age of thirty-seven.

Van Gogh's coffin had been covered with sunflowers—a detail that Christie's press department was careful to point out to reporters. In order to show *Sunflowers* to as many potential bidders as possible, the firm sent it on a three-week tour to Tokyo, Zurich and New York City before the auction. It was allocated its own seat on the various airplanes that transported it, and had been insured with Lloyds of London at a cost of £100,000, which Christie's had agreed to absorb.

The March 30, 1989, sale had been scheduled to coincide with the 134th anniversary of van Gogh's birth. After its whirlwind international tour, Christie's raised the painting's presale estimate to $16 million. A massive international press campaign had been launched, and more than thirty articles appeared in the British and American press proclaiming that *Sunflowers* was expected to break all previous records for a work of art. The painting had also been on view at Christie's on King Street, in a tiny room that could only be entered through a guarded security grille.

The hype and hoopla proved effective. Charlie Hindlip, the chairman of Christie's London, presided as auctioneer at the historic sale, which commenced on a Monday night at seven-thirty. A black-tie audience of 1,500 souls had been crammed into four auction rooms, with five hundred bidders and curious observers squeezed into the main auction room, and an overflow of six hundred watching on closed-circuit TV in adjoining rooms. Eleven telephone lines were opened to bidders on five continents.

The bidding for *Sunflowers* opened at £5 million, or $8 million. After less than sixty seconds it had shot to $19.2 million. The remaining contenders were at the end of four telephones, conveying their instructions to Christie's staff members dressed in formal black. There were smatterings of applause as the bidding was raised in increments of £500,000 ($800,000).

Finally, it was down to two telephone bidders. After a total of four and a half minutes of frantic activity, the losing underbidder withdrew at £22.5 million. Hindlip's gavel fell, and the room burst into wild applause. The electronic scoreboard above the rostrum spelled out the remarkable figures: £24,750,000, or $36,292,500, or 228,150,000 French francs, or 54,675,000 Swiss francs. The board simply could not cope, Geraldine Norman of the London *Times* noted, with the 5.5 billion yen.

After adding the 10 percent buyer's premium of $3.62 million, the final cost for the mystery buyer was a staggering $39,921,750. The mystery buyer of *Sunflowers* was described merely as "an anonymous foreign collector bidding on the telephone," which turned out to be a Japanese insurance company.[5]

Sunflowers was the highlight of the sale of Impressionist and Modern paintings, which totalled $62 million, establishing a record

for an auction held at Christie's. After the sale, the firm celebrated
the victory with a party in honour of the artist—who was believed to
have sold only one painting during his tragically short lifetime—with
a cake decorated with a replica of the painting.

Charlie Hindlip, the auctioneer, had enjoyed himself immensely.
"It was like skiing down a perfect piste in absolutely perfect weather," he said afterward.[6]

Many people in the art world were flabbergasted by the news of
Christie's $39.9 million triumph. "I feel like a fossil, awakened in
another era," declared Philippe de Montebello, the director of the
Metropolitan Museum of Art. "The commission alone paid to
Christie's exceeds the Metropolitan's total art purchase funds for a
year. Therefore I feel so removed from this phenomenon that I can
only watch in amazement."[7]

After nearly three decades of playing second fiddle to Sotheby's
in the area of Impressionist paintings, Christie's was pulling ahead.
The record sale was a crucial shot in the arm at a moment when
Christie's was battling takeover rumours and still reeling from the
boardroom scandals that had led to Lord Bathurst's departure two
years earlier.

Sunflowers was being sold by the descendants of Sir Alfred Chester
Beatty, an old Christie's client. To Davidge's dismay, the firm came
perilously close to losing the consignment to its auction rival. At the
last minute, he recalled, "A young *Sunflowers* beneficiary made an
argument to his family elders that Sotheby's was where the market
was, and I found it hard to disagree. Fortunately, old family ties prevailed. But a whole different scene was emerging in America."[8]

He was keenly aware that Christie's had become stagnant and
complacent, and that it was relying too much on its past reputation.

"Christie's needed to be equal to survive," Davidge recalled.[9] In
failing to win high-value consignments, he noted, the London-based
firm was in danger of being little better than the traditionally minor-
league, London-based auction firms Bonhams or Phillips.

Very soon, Christie's would become unprofitable and—even
worse—uncompetitive. Davidge's goal was to at least be equal to
Sotheby's. But to his mortification and that of his colleagues, he

learned that Sotheby's was being offered major consignments without Christie's even being consulted.

One galling example was Sotheby's coup in winning the opportunity to sell van Gogh's *Irises* in the fall of 1987. Sotheby's victory was especially disturbing for Davidge since Christie's had created a new world record in March by selling *Sunflowers* for $39.9 million. When *Irises* came on the block at Sotheby's in New York—shortly after the stock market's Black Monday—it sold for $53.9 million—breaking Christie's recent record for the highest sum ever achieved for a work of art at auction.

TV cameras, reporters and paparazzi from all over the world converged on the sale as if it were the Olympics. Fine-art auctions had suddenly become exciting world-media events, never more so than when Sotheby's held its first Russian avant-garde sale in Moscow in September 1988, an event that received global coverage, predating the collapse of the Soviet Union.

Sotheby's conspicuous string of successes since the 1950s had elicited profound apathy at Christie's. "I'll tell you how it used to be in the boardroom on a morning when we found out that Sotheby's had won something major," a Christie's director recalled. "We'd look at each other, there'd be a silence and someone might say: 'Ah well, that's Sotheby's sort of thing.'"[10]

Such apathy was no longer permitted at Christie's under the newly aggressive leadership of Carrington and Davidge. With the nobleman's full support, Davidge sensed that he could achieve great things.

"The attitude at Christie's toward Davidge was one of total fear," a Christie's insider recalled. With the protection of Lord Carrington—the most impressive and genuine aristocrat of anyone at Christie's—Davidge's power was absolute. "Davidge and Carrington perceived Christie's to be ridden with the worst kind of languid English gentlemanliness," the insider recalled, "and these were the very first candidates for the chop.[11]

Davidge playfully tyrannized Christie's top management, who were never quite sure where they stood in his estimation. Christie's New York operations were being run by a triumvirate of François

Curiel, Stephen Lash and Christopher Burge, who rarely agreed on anything. Curiel ascribed much of the awkwardness in their relations to Davidge's knack for sowing dissent.

"He told Christopher Burge, 'Lash doesn't like you,'" Curiel recalled, "and he told Stephen Lash, 'Burge doesn't like you.' And it was so that we all had to depend on Davidge. He was *very* manipulative."[12]

DEDE BROOKS was given an opportunity to really prove her mettle in the spring of 1988 when she personally orchestrated the massive sale of 10,000 items from the estate of Andy Warhol, which were sold at the firm's York Avenue headquarters in 2,525 lots over a ten-day period from April 23 to May 3.

"It is certainly the greatest challenge we have ever had in mounting a sale," Brooks observed at the time. "The logistics were mind-boggling."[13]

Sotheby's presale estimate for the collection was between $9·7 million and $13·3 million. "The potential for enormous crowds is there," Brooks observed. Sotheby's entire New York staff of 440 was roped in to help, and visitors were asked to limit their browsing of the collection to an hour and a half.

The items that inspired the most frenzied bidding were highly unusual for a Sotheby's sale. On the grey-carpeted stage, where Monets and Renoirs were usually displayed, there appeared a vast pile of cookie jars: a Humpty Dumpty, a plump panda, a frowning tramp and a laughing lamb. In a mere twenty minutes, 175 cookie jars, estimated at $7,000 before the auction, were snapped up for a staggering total of $247,830.

The sale had been expected to bring $16 million and wound up fetching $25·3 million. The proceeds from the auction—after Sotheby's 10 percent seller's commission—went to the Andy Warhol Foundation for the Visual Arts. The well-run auction proved Brooks' ability to marshal the entire company to achieve a task of labyrinthine complexity, and elicited further admiration from her champion, Taubman.

Sotheby's and Christie's were going from strength to strength each season, and their aggressive expansion was causing mounting unrest in the art world, a culture once dominated by dealers and based on secrecy and gentlemanly handshakes. Dede Brooks, the former banker, embodied the new auction ethos. "Sotheby's and Christie's are the only real big businesses in the art world," she told the *New York Times* in 1989. "We function as a stock exchange of the art market."[14]

As the two auction houses became more and more competitive with each other, sellers who knew that Sotheby's and Christie's could be played off against each other learned to drive tougher bargains. Hard-nosed, sophisticated sellers demanded cash in advance, and guarantees, which had become commonplace at Sotheby's, at stratospheric levels.

In 1989, the *Daily Telegraph* reported that Sotheby's had guaranteed the estate of the Campbell's Soup heir John T. Dorrance $110 million for his paintings after a prominent New York dealer offered the beneficiaries of his estate $100 million in cash. Christie's, which frequently protested that it disapproved of such things, had declined to get involved. It was the largest guarantee in Sotheby's history, and the expensive gamble paid off handsomely. The Dorrance pictures sold in October 1989 for $123·4 million, providing a giant windfall for Sotheby's.

Having withstood a torrent of abuse from Christie's on the subject of Sotheby's practice of giving guarantees, Sotheby's was furious when the London-based auction house admitted in March 1990 that it had changed its mind and had begun offering them, too.

"During the past twelve months or so, we have in certain cases found it difficult to compete without offering guarantees," Davidge acknowledged, explaining that Christie's was simply responding to a demand from executors and trustees of major estates. Christie's had no choice but to match the kinds of financial inducements offered by Sotheby's, he noted, to stay competitive.[15]

Brooks was full of scorn. "I find it hypocritical after the public criticism Christie's has levelled at us for our practice of giving guarantees," Brooks told the *New York Times*.[16]

Christie's had guaranteed five paintings from the estate of Robert

Lehmann that were to be sold in New York on May 15. The presale estimate for the Lehmann pictures was $40 million to $60 million. Davidge declined to reveal the size of the guarantee, but acknowledged that it was between the high and low estimates. The collection included an 1888 self-portrait by van Gogh and portraits of women by Modigliani, Renoir and Kees van Dongen.

Christie's had won the pictures over fierce competition from Sotheby's—which had also offered a guarantee—and from the prominent New York dealer William Acquavella, who offered to buy the five paintings outright. The most important and valuable was the van Gogh, which Christie's expected to fetch between $20 million and $30 million.

Davidge defended Christie's past criticism. "We stand by what we have always said," he told the *New York Times*. "Guarantees are not the proper business of the auction process. We do not believe they should be offered. However, we do have an ability to give a guarantee and still maintain professional standards that people expect from us."[17]

Dede Brooks could not resist making a gibe when she heard of Davidge's sentiments. "I find it hard to believe they are going to be giving guarantees if they don't believe they should be doing it," she quipped.[18]

Christie's acquiescence came at a time when the art market was in the midst of an unprecedented boom. When Michael Ainslie had arrived at Sotheby's in 1984, sales were $500 million worldwide. By 1989 they were $3·1 *billion*. Much of that growth had to do with the wild spending patterns of the Japanese.

In May 1990, Ryoei Saito, the seventy-four-year-old chairman of the Japanese Daishowa Paper Company, stunned the art world when he paid $82·5 million for van Gogh's portrait of Dr. Gachet and $78·1 million for Renoir's *Au Moulin de la Galette*. In doing so, he broke the record for any work of art sold at auction.

THE ART WORLD experienced the first major jolt of a collapsing economy on the night of Tuesday, November 6, 1990, when 55 percent of the contemporary art on offer at Sotheby's went unsold, including pieces by Andy Warhol, Roy Lichtenstein, Cy Twombly, Mark Rothko and Jean Dubuffet. Robert Rauschenberg's *Third Time Painting* sold for a mere $3·1 million to a private European collector, considerably less than its presale estimate of $4 million to $5 million. Sotheby's had predicted that the evening sale would fetch between $39 million and $52 million. Instead, it brought only $19·8 million.

Expectations of an art market collapse had proliferated since the June 1990 auctions in London, where nearly 50 percent of the work on offer failed to sell. It was a shocking reverse after five years of a nonstop boom, when contemporary art auction prices had more than doubled each year.

Christie's sale of contemporary art the following night did not fare much better. Just over half of the fifty-eight lots sold for a total of $36·7 million, compared with Christie's presale estimate of $47·7 million to $65·4 million.

Sotheby's experienced a further catastrophe when thirteen out of thirty-five works from Henry Ford II's art collection failed to sell in New York on November 12. The auction house had guaranteed the automotive heir's estate more than $50 million for the paintings, which fetched only a paltry $30·4 million. The following day, Sotheby's stock tumbled again, dipping close to its fifty-two-week low of 8/8 in heavy trading. After the Ford debacle, Sotheby's announced that it was planning to find new owners for the unsold works privately after the major New York Impressionist and Modern sales were over. The firm estimated it would lose $5 million on the guarantee, which would certainly make a dent in its roughly $112 million in pretax earnings to date for 1990.

After two weeks of dismal sales, Brooks was promoted from president of Sotheby's North America to president and chief executive of Sotheby's operations in North and South America. With little choice in the matter, she vowed to conduct "a more conservative policy" on guarantees in the future.[19]

WHEN LORD CARRINGTON announced Christie's half-yearly results in November 1991, a seismic groan was heard throughout the art world. Sales were down by 60 percent to a mere $494 million, and pretax profit had shrunk to $5·2 million, one-thirteenth of the already abysmal figure for the previous year.

Things were even worse at Sotheby's. The firm's pretax earnings for the same period had withered by a similar 92 percent, but its sales were down 66 percent. The shift indicated an alarming trend: Christie's was clearly gaining market share and was practically neck-and-neck with its hated archrival, with 48 percent to Sotheby's 52 percent. Market analysts noted that this represented a gain for Christie's of five market points to Sotheby's detriment since 1989. The lethal combination of Carrington and Davidge was beginning to work wonders.

Amid all the grim news of the market's collapse, there was at least some stray comedy. The *Sun,* a popular British tabloid, had fun at Lord Gowrie's expense when it discovered that Sotheby's London chairman had been frequenting a massage parlour in Camden Town during his lunch breaks. The scandal was all the more ignominious for Gowrie when it was revealed that he had been receiving what was euphemistically referred to as "hand relief."[20]

Some inquiring minds wondered why, having taken the trouble to go all the way to Camden Town, he had availed himself only of a helping hand. Taubman roared with laughter over his friend's humiliations in the press. "When I hired him, I told him you must take matters into your *own* hands," he joked. "Grey's a really hands-on manager.'"[21]

The *Daily Telegraph* took delight in reminding its readers that "massage has important therapeutic value in the relief of tension and stress. As chairman of Sotheby's, with particular expertise in the field of modern painting, he may well be going through a stressful period as poor mad Americans and sad Japanese slowly begin to discover they have been throwing away billions of pounds on the hideous rubbish which is still called 'modern art.'"[22]

As sales failed to pick up in 1992, it became clear that desperate measures were necessary to revive Sotheby's and Christie's fortunes. Both houses suffered financially from the art-market crash, which had been worsened considerably with the worldwide recession that followed the Gulf War. Back in 1989, Sotheby's auction sales had reached an all-time high of $2.9 billion. In 1992 they dropped to a mere $1.1 billion. Over the same period, auction revenues had plunged from $410 million to $201.1 million. Equally, earnings per share had dwindled from $1.96 to a mere 7 cents. In the heyday of 1989, Sotheby's net profit had been a robust $113 million, but after a precipitous slide to $13 million in 1991, it was now an abject $3.9 million—a drop of nearly $110 million in two years, and a woeful return on 1992's $1 billion of sales. Since 1990, the firm's stock price had slunk from around $37 to $9.

Both firms were holding independent internal discussions over ways to improve revenues. The most obvious solution seemed to be to raise the buyer's premium, but there was concern that raising the premium at a time of a global recession might alienate both buyers and sellers.

EARLY IN 1992, Jo Floyd went to see Christopher Davidge at Christie's. He was planning to step down as a nonexecutive director of Christie's board in May, after forty-six years with Christie's, and he wanted to give him a piece of advice.

Davidge had already met with Floyd's financial advisor, David Chaplin of Hambros, who had inquired about Davidge's projections for the future value of Christie's shares. Chaplin explained that the nearly 2 percent of Christie's owned by the Floyd family represented almost the entire wealth of the family, and that Jo was planning to create various trusts for his two daughters and grandchildren.

The CEO felt obliged to give Chaplin and Floyd a rather pessimistic view of the future. The art market was still weathering tough times, and Christie's share value was painfully low.

While meeting with Davidge, Jo Floyd attributed Christie's meagre profits to what he called the "absurd" competition with Sotheby's.

"Not only is it both eroding commission income *and* increasing expenses," Floyd told Davidge. "If you want my opinion, you should put out feelers to Sotheby's and explore ways of helping both companies to be more successful. It just makes sense. It's a tried and tested path that's been going on for more than a hundred years!"[23]

9

Pink Slips

LORD CARRINGTON had been eager to step down as Christie's chairman for nearly a year, but all the candidates he proposed as his successor had been rejected by his senior colleagues. The chief naysayer was Lord Hindlip, who invariably complained they were "not one of us"—a put-down which Davidge interpreted to mean that they had not been to Eton.

"This fixation on Eton instead of ability is terribly irritating," Lord Carrington told Davidge, who suspected that Hindlip was also shooting down Carrington's younger candidates because he was angling for Christie's chairmanship when the next candidate's term ended.[1]

Davidge admired Carrington and was aghast at the thought of his departure from Christie's. "He was a gentleman in every sense of the word," Davidge noted. "Behind a charming exterior is a very intelligent, worldly and very wise man."[2]

One afternoon in the early spring of 1992, Davidge was called down to the first-floor office of Lord Carrington, who seemed excited. He explained that he had just met with Jo Floyd who had proposed Anthony Tennant, the chairman of Guinness, the Anglo-Irish brewing behemoth, as a potential candidate for Christie's next chairman. Floyd and Tennant, it turned out, were both members of Boodle's, the gentleman's club in St. James' Street, and had briefly overlapped at Eton.

"I don't know him," Carrington told Davidge, "but Jo tells me he's planning to step down as chairman of Guinness at the end of this year."[3] On Floyd's recommendation, Carrington had already spoken to Charles Hambro, the chairman of Hambros, Christie's bank, who told him that Tennant seemed an excellent choice. Just to be sure, he promised to check with his colleague Sir Chips Keswick, who worked more closely with Christie's on a day-to-day basis.

The following day, Davidge spoke with Keswick, who assured him that Tennant was a perfect fit for Christie's. He had international business experience, great contacts and a good reputation in the City. "I'm told he also collects modern British paintings," Keswick said. "Charlie Hambro's talked to him, and he seems interested. Why don't I arrange for you to meet him?"[4]

Davidge was relieved to hear that a suitable candidate had finally been identified. Encouraged by the endorsement of Christie's bankers he went to see Tennant at Guinness' offices in Portman Square. He arrived full of great expectations, but an hour in Tennant's presence left him feeling despondent.

"I took an instant dislike to him," Davidge recalled. "He appeared to have the perfect CV for Christie's, but he was arrogant, self-opinionated and totally charmless."[5]

To his surprise, the sixty-one-year-old businessman peppered him with questions about Sotheby's: "What kind of contact do you have with the competition?" "Who at Christie's knows senior people at Sotheby's?" "What do you know about Taubman?"[6]

Feeling defensive, Davidge said he had never met any senior directors of Sotheby's. He had been brought up to avoid contact with the rival firm and pointed out that it was crucial to be seen to be in fierce competition with Sotheby's, because any friendly contact could be misinterpreted. To prove his point, Davidge began describing the allegations of conspiracy that had erupted in 1975 when Christie's and Sotheby's had introduced the buyer's premium within three days of each other.

"I know all about that," Tennant said, brushing him aside. "In my opinion, there should be contact with Sotheby's. At least at chairman level."[7]

Davidge came away from his first encounter with Tennant in a quandary. Tennant had seemed so smug and self-satisfied. But Davidge felt under pressure to settle on a suitable candidate quickly. "I genuinely felt I must put my own feelings behind me in the interest of Christie's," he recalled.[8]

As Floyd had hoped, Christie's directors felt they could not object to the appointment of Tennant, who seemed a paragon of excellent connections and business savoir faire. Acting on a nod from Davidge, Tennant wrote to Lord Carrington on May 18, 1992, to confirm that he would be happy to accept his invitation to succeed him as Christie's chairman. "I'm sure it will be an exciting and stimulating job," he wrote, "and, without any doubt—as you say—great fun. I am greatly looking forward to it."[9]

Tennant's reputation as a brilliant businessman seemed auspicious in what remained an awkward moment in Christie's fortunes. He was credited with rescuing Guinness from one of London's worst financial scandals in decades. His predecessor at Guinness, Sir Ernest Saunders, had resigned amid allegations that he had directed a vast, illegal scheme to drive up the firm's stock price during a 1986 takeover bid. Under Tennant's stewardship, Guinness had gone from strength to strength.

Even if he did lack charm, Davidge thought, Tennant might at least be able to come up with some ingenious scheme to restore Christie's profitability.

JOHN BLOCK, the head of Sotheby's Jewellery Department in New York, was in Geneva in May 1992 when he ran into François Curiel, his counterpart at Christie's. Following his usual custom, Curiel had stopped in at Sotheby's to check out the competition, and the two friendly rivals struck up a conversation. "We were commiserating about the state of affairs of the auction business and the economy," Block recalled, "and we were saying that we were considering different ways to get back into profitability."

"I don't remember who said it first," Block said. "We were considering raising the buyer's premium, and I think he said, or I said, 'Yeah, we were considering the same thing.'"[10] (When asked for comment, Curiel has denied having any recollection of this conversation and has stated unequivocally that he made no attempt to fix prices.)

On his return to New York, Block testified in court, he confided to Dede Brooks that he had met with Curiel, and that the Frenchman had told him Christie's was also debating whether to raise the buyer's premium. Block recalled later that, although the two men's conversation could be considered to be teetering on the brink of breaching American antitrust laws, Brooks did not warn him to avoid talking to anyone at Christie's about pricing.

In late July Curiel and John Block were back in Geneva to round up material for their fall jewellery sales and the two rivals met up again. Curiel told Block he had apprised Chris Davidge of their previous conversation about the buyer's premium in the spring, and the two jewellery experts confided that their respective firms were now in active, serious discussions about raising the premium. Coming away from their meeting, Block realized that Curiel's confession was useful market intelligence.

"I looked at it as an insight into the enemy camp," he recalled later.[11] On his return to New York, Block reported his conversation to Brooks, who seemed intrigued but somewhat sceptical.

ON SEPTEMBER 17, 1992, Christie's officially announced that Sir Anthony Tennant would succeed Lord Carrington as the chairman of Christie's International. It was agreed that the sixty-one-year-old businessman would join the board in January as a prelude to replacing Lord Carrington as chairman in May 1993.

Like Carrington, Tennant would keep an office at Christie's but work for the auction house only on a part-time basis. He was planning to remain active as a senior advisor to Morgan Stanley and to serve on the boards of Forte, Guardian Royal Exchange and the British Stock Exchange.

Speaking to the press about Tennant's appointment, Davidge seemed excited at the prospect of having a partner with financial expertise on board who could offer help in marketing and international branding. "Sir Anthony's arrival will give us a clear corporate business identity as a firm not confined to the auction business,"

Davidge told the *Daily Telegraph*. "Any plans we may have will mature with the guidance of a man of stature in the City."[12]

SOTHEBY'S TOOK the art world by surprise on November 2, 1992, when it announced an increase in its buyer's premium. After seventeen years of charging a flat 10 percent on all auction purchases, the firm was raising its rate to 15 percent on the first $50,000 (£30,000) of the hammer price, and 10 percent on anything above that threshold. The new rates would be effective from January 1, 1993.

In announcing the higher rate, Michael Ainslie reported an increased third-quarter loss of $7·7 million. He defended the hike by pointing out that "people, space, cataloguing and related marketing" accounted for 85 percent of the firm's costs.[13] The only alternative, he noted, was to close offices and reduce staff.

Angry dealers accused Sotheby's of unnecessary expansionism and bloated expenses, noting that the firm had expanded from eighteen offices in 1975 to eighty-eight by 1992.

"What the hell have they spent their money on to have to change the premium?" one dealer asked in an interview with the *Independent* of London. "There's no risk. They don't buy works. The only way is overheads. The staff is bigger than they need."[14]

Speculation was rife over whether Christie's would follow suit. "I cannot believe it," Otto Naumann, an Old Masters dealer, told the *Independent* of London. "If Sotheby's goes to 15 percent, and Christie's doesn't, Sotheby's should get ready for a whopping great loss."[15]

Both auction houses had responded to the economic downturn with pink slips and slashed costs. Christie's had cut 120 jobs, including the heads of departments for Islamic Art, Silver and Clocks and Watches. Sales in traditional areas like English furniture and Old Masters paintings, however, remained virtually unaffected.

On December 17, Davidge announced his intention to reduce Christie's 1,360 workforce further by eliminating sixty mostly administrative jobs in Europe. "We haven't operated as efficiently as I would like on the world stage," he told the *New York Times*.[16]

When asked how Christie's was planning to act in response to Sotheby's recent announcement regarding the buyer's premium, Davidge seemed circumspect. "It's been a source of constant discussion," he told Carol Vogel of the *Times*. "But we're in a different position from Sotheby's. Since they did it first, we have had time to discuss the matter all over the world to see what the benefits are. There is certainly popular reaction for us not to increase the buyer's premium, but I don't want to create a situation where we are not competitive."[17]

Everyone at Sotheby's was beginning to get nervous, and John Block contacted Curiel to find out what was going on. "I called François," Block remembered, "and I said, 'Do you guys still have plans to adjust your rates?' And he said, 'Well, we haven't had our board meeting yet, but I think we will after we have that meeting.'"[18]

Block was pleased to hear it. "I took it from what he said that he thought they would raise the premium," he recalled.[19]

Sotheby's announcement was the subject of heated discussion when Christie's board convened at 8 King Street later in December. Davidge strongly opposed matching Sotheby's new rates, arguing that the fragile market needed buyers. "This is not the time to be charging them more," he warned.[20] But Davidge failed to persuade his fellow board members. Anthony Tennant had been invited to attend the meeting as chairman-elect and was clearly unconvinced by Davidge's reasoning. He proposed that Christie's should immediately increase its charges in line with Sotheby's. "We were all a little scared of him," Davidge recalled.[21]

After holding out for seven weeks, Christie's finally announced on December 22, 1992, that it was planning to match Sotheby's recent raise in the buyer's premium. The only difference was that Christie's new rates would take effect on March 1, 1993.

"In the end, we really had no choice," Christopher Davidge told the *New York Times*. "Internally we really were hoping we wouldn't have to raise the buyer's premium at all, but in the end we felt it was important to be competing with Sotheby's on a level playing field."[22]

FROM HIS CRITICAL REMARKS at his first Christie's board

meeting, it was clear that Tennant was highly opinionated and a force to be reckoned with.

Sir Anthony was descended from a wealthy and illustrious clan of Scottish entrepreneurs who started out as humble farmers in Ayrshire.

The family came into wealth when an ancestor, Charles Tennant, invented bleaching powder in 1799, giving rise to a flourishing business that Charles' grandson, the first Lord Glenconner, turned into a vast fortune. Raised in a world of privilege, Anthony served as a commander in the Scots Guards in Malaya before going on to read history at Trinity College, Cambridge.

Instead of following his father into the world of finance, he took a job in advertising at Mather and Crowther, a precursor of Ogilvy & Mather. By the age of twenty-nine he had become a director, overseeing successful advertising campaigns for Schweppes ("The secret of Sch ... ") and J. Sainsbury ("Good food costs less at Sainsbury's").

Proud of his noble lineage, Tennant exuded a patrician air even as a junior executive. Tom Jago, a former colleague, recalled that while working on a campaign for Shell Industrial Lubricants the two drove up to Corby, a working-class steel town in Northamptonshire, in Tennant's Hillman Minx.

"He stopped at a bus queue in the pouring rain," Jago recalled, "and said, 'Can you tell me the way to the steelworks?' And nobody moved a muscle. They never even looked at us. So as Anthony wound up his window, he said, 'Well, it's your *livelihood*, my good people,' then sailed off, quite lordly."[23]

Tennant was a talented businessman, but not universally liked. "He's a bit of a cold fish, quite self-satisfied," a colleague recalled. Others found him pleasant. "He was perfectly amiable," Jago observed. "He had a taste for schoolboy humour—slipping on bananas, that sort of thing."[24]

While chairman and chief executive of Guinness, Tennant doubled the firm's profits by focusing on its core products and jettisoning less remunerative subsidiaries. He was knighted by the Queen at Buckingham Palace in June in recognition of his success in transforming the fortunes of Guinness—a feat that had also earned him the distinction of Chevalier of the French Légion d'Honneur in 1991. He left Guinness with an annual pension of £500,000 ($757,750).

As Christie's chairman, Tennant was expected to focus on business-getting for the company, which required his presence at a marathon of social events. He was also expected to deal with the City and oversee compliance with the laws that restricted a public company.

IN SEPTEMBER 1992, Tennant had begun familiarizing himself with Christie's operations, strategies and key clients. From the very beginning, he was critical of practices he believed were contributing to Christie's poor financial performance. Tennant was frustrated that Sotheby's and Christie's frequently waived commissions down to zero on large high-volume consignments. And he complained about Christie's habit of giving away loans without charging interest and the company's failure to charge appropriately for guarantees.

As a newcomer and outsider, Tennant observed that with such long-established practices in place at both Christie's and Sotheby's, it was no wonder that neither company was very profitable. He was proud of his reputation for creating shareholder value at Guinness, and determined to prove that he could achieve the same for Christie's.

10

Breakfast in Mayfair

September 1992

YOU'RE ALFRED TAUBMAN, aren't you?" "Yes," the American
replied, staring blankly at the elegant, bespectacled figure who had
just made his way across a crowded gallery at the Royal Academy of
Art in London to introduce himself.

"I'm Anthony Tennant," the Englishman announced in a languid,
aristocratic accent. "As you may have heard, I'm going to become
chairman of Christie's next year."

"Congratulations," Taubman said, shaking his hand. "I wish you
all the luck."

"You wouldn't mind if I called, would you?" Tennant asked, "and
maybe we could get together?"

"Fine," Taubman replied, blithely.[1]

Tennant thanked him, said good night and turned to join the
throng of departing dinner guests.

"What does this guy want?" Taubman asked himself as he wandered across the Royal Academy's anterior courtyard and ventured
into Piccadilly to find his car and driver.

"He was obviously curious," Taubman told me later. "I wasn't
curious. He struck me as a tall, rather attractive English gentleman.
Nothing extraordinary. But he had very strange glasses," he added,
chuckling, "like two big windshields."[2]

A few weeks later, Tennant called Taubman's New York office to
inquire when he was planning to be back in London. Would it be
possible, he asked, for Mr. Taubman to set aside an hour or so for a
private chat?

Always delighted to make the acquaintance of a titled Englishman, Taubman invited his new rival to breakfast at his London pied-à-terre, which was conveniently close to Tennant's new office at Christie's in St. James'.

"We both felt it didn't make any sense to do it in a public place," Taubman told me. "Not that we were doing anything wrong. But someone might surmise that we were doing something like merging."[3]

LONDON WAS SWATHED in a dense, blinding fog when Sir Anthony Tennant pulled up in front of a five-story redbrick Edwardian mansion in South Audley Street at 8:30 A.M. on Wednesday, February 3, 1993. Stepping out into the cold morning air from a chauffeur-driven black Mercedes, he approached the grandiose double doors at the side-street entrance, studied the polished brass intercom and rang the bell for Flat 2.

A Filipino maid answered and buzzed him in. When the tiny elevator opened on the second floor, the larger-than-life presence of Alfred Taubman was waiting to greet him, freshly shaven and dapperly dressed in a tweed suit.

"Good to see you, Sir Anthony," Taubman said, giving him a vigorous handshake.

"Call me Tony," Tennant protested as he followed his host into a small, comfortable drawing room adorned with mostly British antiques, paintings and sporting prints. A uniformed maid brought the two men a hearty English breakfast of scrambled eggs and bacon.

"We had the most enormous breakfasts," Tennant later recalled with a wry smile.[4]

Taubman got a kick out of entertaining the British nobility at his Mayfair flat—a two-minute walk from Park Lane and a stone's throw from Harry's Bar, the high-priced hangout for international café society, which was one of Judy and Alfred Taubman's favourite restaurants. The couple had bought the two-bedroom apartment in January 1986 as a base for their expanding social life in London and as a stopover for their frequent transatlantic forays for shooting weekends at England's great country estates.

After a cheerful preamble about the shooting season, Taubman and Tennant settled into a discussion of the woeful state of the international art market. The Englishman described himself as a novice in the auction world who was trying to learn the business and looking for ways to make it more profitable.

"Well, I must applaud your appointment to Christie's," Taubman said. "They could certainly use someone of your background." "How do you mean?" Tennant asked.

"They clearly haven't been focusing on the bottom line under Lord Carrington," Taubman replied, unable to resist an opportunity to take a jab at the competition. "I understand you brought great shareholder value at Guinness. Maybe you can shake Christie's up a bit."[5]

Delighted to have a captive audience, Taubman opined that Lord Carrington and Christopher Davidge were incompetent businessmen who were doing a lousy job of providing value for Christie's stockholders. He launched into a blistering attack about Christie's business tactics. It had recently come to his attention, he noted indignantly, that Christie's experts had been openly disparaging the authenticity of multimillion-dollar works of art coming up for sale at Sotheby's. Such vicious talk was prompted not by scholarly concern, he complained, but by a cynical desire to undermine confidence in Sotheby's expertise and to sabotage its sales.

"When Christie's goes out and dogs one of our paintings verbally by saying, 'It's not this, it's not that,' *of course* it's not going to do well at auction," Taubman said bitterly. "This kind of bad-mouthing is a really bad practice and it hurts the entire industry. Both houses should respect each other's expertise. Because that's all we have."[6] Tennant was taken aback by Taubman's passion on the subject and promised to look into the matter. Registering his English guest's polite look of concern across the breakfast table, the tycoon could hardly believe his good luck. It was his nature to bully, criticize and deliver unsolicited advice, and he had never had an opportunity to discuss such issues with Christie's soon-to-retire chairman Lord Carrington, whom he had met once only to shake his hand at a shooting party at Blenheim Palace.

Scarcely pausing to draw breath, Taubman denounced what he considered an outrage that had been perpetrated the previous summer. When Christie's announced its end-of-season results in July 1992, it claimed to have increased its worldwide market share over a two-year period from 43 to 49 percent—its highest ratio against Sotheby's since the 1950s. Scrutiny of Christie's published financial statements, however, revealed that the firm had artificially inflated its lacklustre auction totals for 1992 by including the results of its private-treaty sales. Christie's sales figures for this normally unheralded category had been particularly robust that year due to the firm's role in negotiating the sale of Holbein's *Lady with a Squirrel*, a painting consigned by the Marquess of Cholmondeley, to London's National Gallery in April for £10 million. "It was a totally unfair comparison," Taubman bellowed. "If we had included private-treaty sales, we would have had sixty percent to your forty percent."[7]

After an hour of being bullied and beguiled by Taubman, the Englishman proposed they should get together in April, when he was planning to be in New York. He encouraged Taubman to come prepared for their next meeting with specific examples of Christie's infractions, and he promised to address each issue one by one.

Tennant was startled by Taubman's brash charm and belligerence, but the American's virulent attacks upon the competence and reliability of senior management at Christie's—most notably Davidge and Hindlip—squared with Tennant's low opinion of the business instincts and abilities of his new colleagues. On that subject, at least, they had plenty in common.

As he stepped out to the cool winter morning, Tennant was pleased with himself for starting a dialogue with Sotheby's chairman. The fog, he noticed, was beginning to lift.

FEW DAYS after Taubman's return from his jaunt to London in early 1993, Michael Ainslie went to see him at his Fifth Avenue office to deliver an audacious proposal. The chief executive arrived at the mogul's thirty-eighth-floor master-of-the-universe aerie overlooking Central Park knowing that there was only a slender chance that his boss would accept the prospectus he had secretly been working on for months. But after more than two years of slogging through a brutal recession, he was feeling restless and had decided that nine years of being at Taubman's beck and call was enough.

"Frankly, it was not easy," Ainslie noted. "He is not an easy man to work for. It was a very difficult relationship, particularly in the latter years."[8]

After withstanding a barrage of what he considered unfair criticism, complaints and demands from Brooks and Taubman, Ainslie had decided he would remain at Sotheby's only if he could run his own show. Emboldened by the cash bonanza he had gained from selling off large chunks of stock since the company had gone public in 1988, he had surreptitiously lined up a group of interested investors backed by First Boston to try to convince Taubman to sell his controlling stake in Sotheby's.

The generous offer, Ainslie explained, involved paying Taubman $15 for each of his 17.9 million shares—which would give him a profit of more than $53 million over Sotheby's current stock price. It would also allow him to walk away from the company with a tidy $268 million.

Taubman was taken aback. He told Ainslie he would consider the proposal over the weekend, but he had already made up his mind. On Monday, he called to inform him that he had absolutely no intention of relinquishing his controlling interest in Sotheby's.

"Fine, that's your choice," Ainslie replied, wearily. "It's been a good nine years. You've made a lot of money. I've made some money, and I am going to leave the company. I really don't choose to stay."

"I'm sorry you feel that way, Michael," Taubman said. "Is there anyone at Sotheby's who you think is capable of running the company when you leave?"[9]

"There's only one person—Dede Brooks," Ainslie replied. "But she has some problems, because she's not trusted or respected in other parts of the company outside New York."

"What do you mean by that?" Taubman asked, testily.

"Those are strong words, but they're well chosen," Ainslie replied calmly. "Dede's been extremely critical of the rest of the company during this recession. She's been saying that London isn't cutting costs quickly enough and that they're not doing as good a job as we are in New York."[10]

Barbed comments like those, he noted, had hardly endeared Brooks to Sotheby's London staff. "But Dede is very bright and capable," Ainslie conceded. "She's running a good business in New York, and she knows how to make money. She's very aggressive, very good with clients and very effective."[11]

After an elaborate discussion, Taubman and Ainslie agreed to expand Brooks' duties by making her head of Sotheby's auction business worldwide, with a trial period of up to one year to see whether she could build support for herself in Europe and Asia. If she succeeded, Taubman would invite her to take over as CEO of Sotheby's Holdings, Inc., the umbrella company that included the firm's real-estate and financing divisions.

In the meantime, the two men agreed that Ainslie would remain in his position for the time being and that Brooks would continue reporting to Ainslie, whom she openly despised.

MICHAEL BROOKS was excited for his wife when she came home with the news that Taubman had offered her a huge promotion. But he was incredulous when she explained that the job would require a lot of international travel and she would have to sacrifice more of her life to Sotheby's.

"I didn't think there were any more hours in the day you could work!" he joked.

"Mike, it won't be so bad," she told him. "I'll just have to start my day at six A.M. talking to my colleagues abroad instead of eight-thirty or ntne."[12]

The forty-three-year-old certainly had her work cut out for her. Beginning officially on April 1, 1993, she was to become responsible for overseeing more than 550 auctions a year in thirty-six countries, striking deals with major clients and bringing in business on a global basis. Furthermore, she was expected to accomplish all this at a time when the art world was showing only feeble signs of emerging from a prolonged recession.

The grim statistics spoke for themselves: Sotheby's pretax profits had tumbled from $105 million in 1989 to a mere $6.5 million in 1992—a year in which Christie's had been nearly twice as profitable in Europe. Under Christopher Davidge's increasingly tough leadership, Christie's had consistently outperformed Sotheby's in London since 1988, and the rival firm was clearly on a winning streak. Brooks was determined to reverse the trend and declared her intention to begin spending 30 percent of her time in London.

Seizing the bull by the horns, she flew to the British capital at the end of March to brief the firm's 583 London staff on her vision for improving efficiency and raising profits. She insisted that there was "nothing bad" in store for her new colleagues and promised she was not planning an Americanization of Sotheby's in Europe.

Seasoned experts nevertheless began quaking as Thunderstorm Dede hit town. Those who survived the axe wielded by her eager deputy, Roger Faxon, were bombarded with Brooks' "gushograms"—faxes of praise for jobs well done. The English staff also found themselves having to adjust to unfamiliar buzzwords like "leadership," "teamwork" and "role models."

Brooks sought to improve the combative working relationship between Sotheby's American and European staffs by pointing out that the experts in New York and Europe had been wasting too much of their time and energy competing with each other. Sotheby's was a worldwide corporation, she reminded them, and it was important to unite as one company to focus on beating the real competition: Christie's.

BY A CURIOUS TWIST OF FATE, the unexpected announcement of Dede Brooks' promotion to her new global job at Sotheby's had coincided almost exactly with the official elevation of Christopher Davidge to his new status as chief executive officer of Christie's International.

Lord Carrington had taken everyone by surprise during one of his last board meetings as Christie's chairman on January 10, 1993, by suddenly proposing that Davidge should be awarded the title of CEO—a newly created position at Christie's that would theoretically give him equal authority to that of the firm's chairman-elect, Sir Anthony Tennant. Carrington later revealed that he had made his decision without discussing the matter with anyone, including Davidge.

"Tennant was furious and tried to raise an objection," Davidge recalled with a chuckle, "but Carrington very stylishly ignored him and put it to the vote."[13]

The motion was unanimously approved, to take effect in March.

Carrington later explained to Davidge that he had forced through his promotion as CEO in order to prevent Tennant from running rough-shod over him and possibly forcing him out of the company.

"You don't deserve that," Carrington told Davidge. "And Christie's needs you far more than Tennant."[14]

In appointing Davidge to the new role of chief executive of Christie's International, Carrington was transferring real power to his tireless protégé. Chairmen of Christie's had traditionally also acted as the firm's chief executive. Carrington's decision to grant Davidge worldwide status was in line with his own desire to return to politics and a vote of confidence in Davidge's leadership abilities. It also signalled the end of an era in which important company decisions were made by committee at a snail's pace.

"It was probably the right decision at the time," Charlie Hindlip admitted ruefully. "Davidge was incredibly hardworking. He had a Napoleonic streak, but I don't think he had a grand design. He's more Mussolini, really. He made things run on time."[15]

Like Dede Brooks at Sotheby's, Christopher Davidge devoted most of his waking hours to his career with Christie's, to the exasperation of his spouse. The stress of his frantic travels had taken a severe toll on his first wife, Sue, and on their marriage. "She said she would have preferred for me to have a mistress than to work for Christie's," Davidge recalled, "because she could compete with a mistress but didn't know how to compete with Christie's."[16]

When the marriage broke up, Davidge moved out of the house in North London that he had shared with Sue and their two children

and into a rented flat in South Kensington. He blamed himself entirely for the rupture.

"I used to work seven days a week," Davidge admitted. "I sacri-
ficed my first family."[17] Feeling utterly dejected by the failure of his
marriage, Davidge forbore dating women for six months.

All that changed, however, when Olga Visiascheva, a ravishing
blond former model from St. Petersburg, Russia, strode into his
office to inquire whether Christie's might be interested in selling art
in her native country.

"Sotheby's had just had their first successful auction in Moscow
selling Russian art," Olga recalled. "I thought, 'Hmm, Christie's has-
n't done it, so surely they're going to follow the market.'"[18]

The daughter of a Russian admiral, Visiascheva had fled the Com-
munist regime and had briefly been married to an American doctor.
She had little art expertise. But she spoke fluent English and Russian
and wanted Christie's to hire her as a coordinator and interpreter to
liaise with the emerging art market in Moscow and St. Petersburg.
There was an opportunity to capitalize on all the deep-pocketed
black-market millionaires who were hungry for paintings to adorn
the walls of their newly built dachas. As usual, Sotheby's had pio-
neered by making the first move. Christie's was waiting to see if the
rival firm's enterprise was successful before committing money to a
commercial venture in a country that was still awash in political
instability and struggling through perestroika.

Davidge had received a letter from the young Russian with a copy
of her résumé attached. He was unprepared for the gorgeous creature
who arrived wearing high heels and a Thierry Mugler dress. At thirty-one, she was eleven years his junior. And he was bowled over by
Olga's beauty and brains.

A few days later, she received a letter from Davidge. "I have tried
to telephone you but without an answer," he wrote. "If you could be
free for lunch or dinner in the near future, please phone me at the
office number above."

Excited about the prospect of a job, Olga called Davidge and
noticed that he sounded awkward. "What about dinner on Friday?"
he asked. "Fine," Olga replied.

After hanging up, she began to dread the prospect. "He was so formal on the telephone," she recalled. "I thought, 'My God, this is going to be a boring dinner.' But I had to go. I wanted to find a job."[19]

The evening was not at all what she had expected. To Olga's amazement, she found Davidge to be charming and self-deprecating. As she listened to the Englishman describing his difficult childhood and his ambition to transform Christie's into the world's leading auction house, she began to find herself strangely attracted.

The attraction was clearly mutual, even though Olga was not his usual type. The diminutive blond, blue-eyed Davidge had always had a hankering for short, dark-haired women. But Olga was precisely the opposite. She also had a fabulous figure and a habit of wearing pretty powder blue or pink suits that flattered her creamy complexion. Olga Visiascheva did not get the job at Christie's. But she gained a husband.

After the breakup of his marriage, Davidge had turned over his house to Sue and their two children. Olga spent the night with Davidge, and as he left his apartment first early the next morning on a business trip, he asked her to close the door firmly behind her when she left. When he returned several days later, he found his apartment in disarray. He feared he had been burgled, but it turned out that Olga had not left.

When Davidge told his mother that the beautiful Olga had moved in, Olive was concerned for her son.

"Be careful," she warned him. "You don't know anything about her background!"[20]

But Davidge was besotted. He decided it would be a good idea for him and Olga to have a place of their own in London, and found the perfect flat at Georgian House, an apartment building around the corner from Christie's in fashionable St. James'. He also persuaded Christie's directors to let him have the grand apartment at a modest rent.

On weekends, Olga and Chris retreated to Farthings, a postwar cottage in the village of Hawkhurst, on the Kentish Weald. "It's a charming little house, with a lovely established garden," Olga noted.[21] The couple had fallen in love with the glorious view of a valley in front of the house, and Christopher had sold some of his Christie's stock options in 1990 to raise £205,000 to buy the property.

Like Sue, Olga quickly grew disenchanted with her husband's long hours at work and his frequent absences. When he was in London, Davidge normally got to his desk by 7:15 A.M. and worked for twelve hours before taking Olga out to dinner at some expensive restaurant. For more than four months a year he was travelling, visiting the firm's seventy-eight offices around the world and monitoring the hiring, firing and progress of the company's 1,300 employees.

During a three-week period in the spring of 1993, he travelled to Brazil, Argentina, Amsterdam, Paris, Geneva, Tokyo, Hong Kong, Singapore and twice to New York. A reporter at the *New Straits Times* in Singapore asked if he ever took a break. "You'll have to have a word with Mrs. Davidge," he replied. "Even on holiday, I spend most of my time on the phone or the fax. Christie's gets under your skin. It would be easier for a wife to cope with a mistress than with Christie's."[22]

The recycled remark, first ascribed to his first wife, angered his second: "I wouldn't say that," Olga said. "I found mistresses more difficult to cope with."[23]

Davidge's steady stream of hotel romances with secretaries and obliging art experts was the stuff of legend at Christie's. It was a droit-du-seigneur diversion known as "fishing in the company pond," which he shared with other married male colleagues.[24]

The strains in the Davidges' marriage were obvious to everyone who spoke with Olga, who complained that she often felt lonely, stranded in the couple's flat around the corner from Christie's with their young daughter. "Olga sat for years on end, knowing no one, in that flat while Chris was flying around the world," the wife of one of Christie's directors recalled.[25] "I didn't know half the time if she was telling the truth," an English friend recalled. "She used to say that Chris hit her. And I did see her with a black eye once."[26]

Davidge later acknowledged the fisticuffs, but insisted he was never the instigator. "Olga was violent throughout our marriage," he told a friend. "She has scars on her face and body from fights as an adult with her sister. A common form of attack was to spit in my face and attempt to knee me in the groin. She once pushed me down the stairs at Farthings. Most of her rages were brought about by her extreme jealousy."[27]

Davidge's colleagues suspected that he travelled so extensively partly to avoid the strife of his home life. When little Sasha Davidge was born in June 1990, her parents were thrilled with their baby girl. Blond and blue-eyed, she was the spitting image of her father, who proudly pushed her in a pram around St. James'. When the baby was just two months old, however, tragedy struck after a visit to the doctor for her first vaccination.

A single shot of DPT, the triple vaccine routinely administered to infants wards off diphtheria, pertussis and tetanus, and had devastating repercussions. Little Sasha cried day and night for two months. When her tears finally ceased, a pediatrician determined that the baby had stopped developing mentally and physically and that she was showing early signs of autism.

"Our daughter was disabled by vaccination," Olga said later, fighting tears. "It brain-damaged our child."[28] Sasha would not learn to walk until she was two or speak until she was four and a half.

Olga blamed her husband for their daughter's problems. She consulted a biochemist who told her that Sasha's immune system had probably been compromised at birth because she had been exposed to German measles.

The whole thing was Christopher's fault, Olga declared. She claimed that while she was pregnant in the autumn of 1989, her husband had pressured her to have tea with his former assistant, a well-connected English lady whose father was a prominent London lawyer.

"Christopher said the reason I had to go was because she's the daughter of an establishment person," Olga recalled. "He felt he was an up-coming managing director and it was important to him that I went."[29]

A few days later, the hostess telephoned Olga to warn her that she had discovered that her son had the measles, a common contagious eruptive disease that can produce congenital defects in infants born to mothers infected during the first three months of pregnancy. "I happened to be eight weeks pregnant," Olga recalled, "which is the most dangerous time." German measles, she noted, "can lead to brain damage, blindness and nervous-system damage. And Sasha does have all those issues."

"Sasha," she concluded harshly, "was disabled because of Christopher."[30]

Davidge was understandably upset by the suggestion that he had been responsible for his daughter's predicament. "Olga's doctor told me that in his opinion it was the fact that Olga refused to eat sensibly during her pregnancy," Davidge told a friend. "She was concerned not to lose her figure. Of course, Olga rejected this possibility."[31]

Devastated by what had befallen her daughter, Olga noticed that her husband seemed heartbroken and profoundly concerned at first. But he then threw himself back into his working life and resumed his heavy travel schedule.

"Christopher ignored it," Olga recalled bitterly. "He thought about business."[32]

ANTHONY TENNANT arrived for his second breakfast meeting with Alfred Taubman at 8:30 A.M. on April Fools' Day, 1993. This time, they met at Taubman's apartment in New York. Sotheby's chairman led his guest into a formal dining room graced by an exquisite Canaletto of eighteenth-century Venice. In this exalted setting they breakfasted on smoked salmon and scrambled eggs prepared by his private chef.

Before Tennant could take his first bite, Taubman began barraging his guest with a long litany of complaints.

"Christie's has some business practices which I believe are way out of line," Taubman declared, indignantly.

"What's troubling you?" Tennant asked.

Taubman began by criticizing Christie's practice of offering interest-free, non-recourse loans* to potential consigners, which he

---

* loans that give, in case of default, the right of recourse against the work of art only.

referred to contemptuously as "Christie's guarantees." "Non-recourse loans are just guarantees without *calling* them guarantees," Taubman told him, "and they should be disclosed in Christie's catalogues."

Under American law, he explained, auction houses were obliged to disclose if they had any financial interest in an object for sale. This was usually done by making some kind of indication in the catalogue, such as a black dot next to the listing of the lot in question.

"From what I understand, Christie's is breaking the law," Taubman growled. The questionable practice, he argued, gave Christie's an unfair competitive advantage, but it was ultimately an unprofitable one for the auction house that Sotheby's had no intention of adopting.

To back up his assault on "Christie's guarantees," Taubman handed Tennant a list of eleven deals that Dede Brooks had dictated to his secretary. In each case, Taubman told him, Christie's had offered clients interest-free, non-recourse loans as a way to win business. The Englishman thanked him for the list and promised to look into the matter upon his return to London.

After breakfast, the two men moved into Taubman's study to smoke cigars. "Christie's has been trying to poach some of Sotheby's experts," he told Tennant, maintaining his indignant tone. The two rivals, he explained, had a long tradition of refraining from hiring staff way from the competition. But that cardinal rule seemed to be breaking down. Taubman railed against Christie's cavalier attitude, explaining that such defections harmed company morale and should not be tolerated.

While he still had Tennant's attention, Taubman claimed that an unnamed source at Christie's had been making disparaging comments to the *Wall Street Journal* about a staff change at Sotheby's. Quite simply, he declared, it was disrespectful for Christie's to be commenting on Sotheby's internal affairs. To prove his point, he handed Tennant a copy of the offending article from the *Journal* which contained speculation about the reasons why Kevin Bousquette, a partner of Henry Kravis at KKR, had been hired at Sotheby's.

The two chairmen also discussed how to handle the nettlesome subject of market share. Both men agreed that the practice of comparing sales results with the rival firm led to an antagonistic relationship between the two houses, and that it encouraged the press to report on the auction firms in adversarial terms.

"All this trumpeting of market share seems fairly pointless to me," Tennant observed dryly. Every time that Christie's or Sotheby's boasted to the press or to clients about market share, he noted, the competition between the two firms was ratcheted up unnecessarily. If both firms kept up the current crazy practice of giving zero-percent commissions in order to win business way from each other, and giving away valuable concessions, neither house would ever make a proper profit. There had to be another solution.

Tennant's oblique reference to the subject of adjusting auction commissions made Taubman nervous. He warned the Englishman they needed to be careful to avoid any discussion that might violate American antitrust laws.

"You and I must never talk about price," he told Tennant, staring at his rival through a cloud of postprandial cigar smoke. "I'm happy to discuss issues of mutual concern. But there's no way I would ever break the law. In the United States, we have this statute called the Sherman Anti-trust Act, which means we're not allowed to ..."

"I know what it is," Tennant said, interrupting him.

"Good, so we're clear on that," Taubman said. "I wouldn't feel comfortable going ahead unless we had that understanding."[33]

After touching on a further litany of complaints during their forty-five-minute breakfast, Taubman climbed into his chauffeur-driven limousine for the eight-block ride down Fifth Avenue to his office at Fifty-sixth Street, just in time for his monthly pedicure and manicure.

With Anthony Tennant's aristocratic background, distinguished track record in business and interest in country sports such as shooting and fishing, Christie's chairman was just the kind of Englishman Taubman enjoyed spending country weekends with. But he had no intention of cultivating Tennant's acquaintance outside their discreet breakfast meetings.

"This was our competitor," Taubman told me later. "I never lost sight of that, I can assure you. When I looked at him, he was the guy we were going to *kill*, financially. So he was not my friend, and I didn't expect him to be."[34]

SINCE MOVING into his plush new fourth-floor office at Christie's in January 1993, Tennant had begun conducting closed-door meetings
with company directors and heads of specialist departments, making detailed inquiries about their business performance without informing Davidge of his intentions or conclusions.

The snub made Davidge become nervous. Excluding him from the information-gathering process was hardly conducive to establishing a good working relationship, he told himself. Tennant was clearly pursuing his own agenda, and seemed intent on assuming a more executive position than his predecessor, Lord Carrington.

Davidge was beginning to regret his acquiescence in the hiring of Tennant. "Not only was he disloyal about me behind my back," he recalled, "but also about Charlie Hindlip, Christopher Burge and Noël Annesley, among others. I cannot remember him having a good word to say about anyone."[35]

Out of loyalty to Davidge, a few senior executives who had been summoned to meet with Tennant went to see him afterward to volunteer the topics they had discussed. David Tyler, the group finance director, and his deputy, Peter Blythe, approached Davidge in late March to ask if he was aware that Tennant was asking questions about specific competing offers that Christie's and Sotheby's had made to potential consigners during the past year. The questions were so detailed that Tyler and Blythe assumed Davidge had provided Sir Anthony with the privileged information. After all, the only three people at Christie's who knew the exact terms on such a wide range of deals were Tyler, Blythe and Davidge himself.

"How do you want us to answer him?" they asked.

Davidge was dumbfounded. In listening to Tyler and Blythe, he recognized a pattern from other colleagues' reports of their conversations with the chairman-elect. He told his colleagues that he had *not*

provided the details of such deals to Tennant but said that he would
speak with him. Tennant's knowledge of such specific confidential
information could only mean one thing. He must be receiving high-
level intelligence from someone at Sotheby's. But how? And from
whom?

Eager to find out, Davidge arranged a meeting with Tennant.
When challenged, Tennant blithely recounted the history of his
meetings with Sotheby's chairman. After a chance meeting at the
Royal Academy, he told Davidge, Taubman had congratulated him
on being appointed to Christie's and said that he had welcomed a
businessman coming to the firm.

Tennant also told Davidge that he had met Taubman at his
London flat. "The art was *not* very good," he noted, scathingly. "I
have better pictures." He joked that Taubman had been unable to
remember the names of the artists whose paintings hung on his walls.
"He needs a card for each one," Tennant reported. "Even with a crib
sheet he cannot pronounce the artists' names correctly."[36]

Tennant explained that Taubman had given him a handwritten
list of eleven competitive deals which proved that Christie's were
lousy deal makers. Each of the offers listed, Tennant noted, involved
the kinds of loans that Taubman referred to as "Christie's guarantees."

Echoing Taubman's complaints, Tennant railed against Christie's
practice of offering consigners non-recourse advances on zero-commission deals, which meant that the auction house was out of pocket if the object failed to sell. "These deals are totally irresponsible,"
Tennant told Davidge. "They're high risk with no financial benefit.[37]

To prove his point, Tennant handed him Taubman's list of deals.
Davidge studied the piece of paper with keen interest. The handwritten document purported to show the terms that Sotheby's and
Christie's had offered to sellers to try to win their business. The first
item referred to an assortment of seventy-nine paintings collected by
Gloria and Richard Manney, whose company, the Mediators, was in
bankruptcy proceedings. Estimated at $4 million to $6 million, sixty-
two of the seventy-nine pictures had sold at Christie's in May 1992
for $3·34 million.

According to the document, Christie's had won the consignment by offering a $3 million non-recourse loan with a zero seller's commission. Davidge knew this was wrong. In fact, he recalled, Christie's had actually offered a $1 million, full-recourse loan, with no commission. Reading further, he noticed that Sotheby's had overestimated several offers Christie's had made on major pieces of property.

"I can assure you these figures aren't accurate," Davidge told Tennant. "I suggest you leave this with me and I'll get back to you with the facts."[38]

"Very well," Tennant replied. "Let's see what you can come up with."

Davidge was irritated by Tennant's imperious, sceptical tone, which implied that he found Davidge to be incompetent. Suppressing his anger, he warned Tennant that Taubman was just trying to rock the boat at Christie's, and said he did not appreciate the American's efforts to negatively influence the future chairman against his new colleagues.

Tennant was unimpressed by Davidge's protestations. It was crucial, he told him, to have a top-level dialogue with Sotheby's to discuss industry practices.

Controversially, Davidge later recalled that Tennant told him Christie's needed to establish new commission rates in order to make a reasonable profit, and the most practical way to go about it was to have a quiet word with Sotheby's to hammer out an agreement beneficial to both firms.

Davidge also recalled that he was amazed when Tennant revealed that he had been briefed on the advantages of getting together with Sotheby's by Jo Floyd in 1992, before Tennant agreed to take the job at Christie's.

When asked for comment, Tennant rejected the suggestion that he advocated getting together to with Sotheby's to fix prices, and also denied that Floyd advised him to do so.

Furthermore, Davidge claimed that when he tried to caution Tennant about the dangers of discussing auction commissions with the competition, Tennant told him it was too late. He had spoken to Taubman before Sotheby's announcement of an increase to the buyer's premium in 1992, and the two had agreed that the next increase in charges would be announced by Christie's first.

Davidge recalled that he had no way of verifying Tennant's extravagant claim. It was possible that Tennant was exaggerating the extent of his discussions with Taubman in order to bully him into action. Whatever the case, Davidge recalled, Tennant was making it clear that he saw his reluctance to enter a working dialogue with Sotheby's as a sign of weakness.

"You're wet behind the ears," Tennant told him. "This is a practice followed by many international businesses. If you don't like it, you should consider whether you have the skills to run an international business or merely the ability to run a small auction company."[39]

To prove his point, Davidge recalled, Tennant described the profitable relationship he had established in the international drinks business with Bernard Arnault, the chairman of LVMH Moët Hennessy—Louis Vuitton, the world's leading luxury-goods company. Guinness was strong in the whiskey and gin business, Tennant explained, while LVMH was strong in champagne and cognac. By joining forces, they had gained a greater strength in the marketplace and had shared in the profits as partners in joint ventures in more than twenty countries around the world.

"He said they had split the world up into brandy-cognac or whiskey as the lead drink for each country," Davidge recalled. "An example he gave me was whiskey in Japan and brandy in Taiwan. They were to be priced differently, depending on the country."*[40]

Davidge was stunned by Tennant's descriptions of his dealings in the drinks business. Christie's new chairman, he recalled, was clearly serious about working discreetly, but closely, with Sotheby's.

"I've done all the groundwork," Tennant told him. "It's up to you to carry it out."[41]

---

* Tennant ridiculed Davidge's subsequent speculation that Tennant may have engaged in price-fixing in the drinks business. "The idea that we rigged prices is nonsense," Tennant said, referring to the joint ventures between LVMH and Guinness. "We charged what we could get away with in any market, and we shared in the profits because we were partners. We didn't market champagne, and they didn't market whiskey. There was nothing improper. In fact it would be crazy not to do it."

11

Levels of Competition

DAVIDGE'S HEAD was spinning when he emerged from his meeting with Tennant. In a panic, he sought the advice of a European businessman friend and confided that he was thinking of resigning.

"Don't be so hasty," the confidant said after listening to Davidge's recent account of his conversation with Tennant in April 1993. "Let him meet with Taubman again to see if he's bluffing, then ask him to give you a written report of what they've agreed to. That way, you're protected."[1]

Davidge liked the idea of obtaining written documentation to establish Tennant's request—which sounded illegal—and decided to heed his friend's advice. He knew that getting Sir Anthony to write a memo summarizing his meeting with Taubman would be easy. The new chairman was always jotting notes to himself and dispensing memos to his colleagues with the fervour of an evangelical pamphleteer.

Davidge was amused by one of Tennant's eccentricities. When walking around the office he always kept a pen in the front breast pocket of his suits. "I've never seen anyone except *schoolboys* put their pens in their jacket pocket," Davidge recalled.[2]

The pen that Tennant took with him wherever he went was a gold Cross ballpoint with a harp logo at the top—the logo of Guinness—the company whose profitability he had so ingeniously transformed by entering into a close working relationship with LVMH. The success of that scheme had earned him a knighthood.

If he proved successful at restoring Christie's fortunes, he could surely earn even greater accolades.

EAGER TO EXONERATE HIMSELF from the charge of incompetence, Davidge faxed his preliminary findings concerning the errors in Sotheby's eleven-deal list to Tennant, who was enjoying an extended Easter vacation at his country estate in Hampshire.

In a four-page fax dated April 8, Davidge sent a copy of the list Tennant had given him, with two pages of Davidge's handwritten corrections to show that the details provided by Sotheby's were in many cases way off the mark. "I have a lot of background information on most of the deals which I would rather give to you personally," Davidge wrote.[3]

When he returned to London, Tennant went to see Davidge to make sure he understood all the information Davidge had given him. "Thanks for these figures," he said. "I'm going to discuss these with Taubman when I see him again at the end of the month."

Davidge was alarmed to learn that Tennant was planning another rendezvous with Sotheby's chairman. "It worries me that you're meeting with Mr. Taubman," he warned him. "You're new to this business, and I don't think you understand that we've traditionally kept Sotheby's at arm's length."

"Nonsense," Tennant replied. "In my experience, a close relationship with one's competitor is to everyone's advantage. It takes out a level of competition which is unnecessary."[4]

Still steamed about the welter of criticisms, Davidge took the new chairman by surprise on April 16 by presenting him with a sixty-page briefing book that he had compiled in order to refute Taubman's various allegations and complaints.

The none-too-brief briefing book included responses to allegations of poaching, making inappropriate comments to the press regarding Sotheby's market share, "Christie's guarantees" and breaking contracts.

On the hot topic of Christie's failure to disclose its non-recourse loans, Davidge explained that he had asked the firm's general counsel, Patty Hambrecht, to look into the matter to find out if Christie's was somehow violating American law by failing to identify guaranteed lots.

In response, Hambrecht had sent him an e-mail via Irmgard Pickering, his assistant, explaining that the matter had been taken care of: "One could argue that we had guaranteed a minimum price—which must be disclosed," Hambrecht wrote. "We agreed that it would be better to make some catalogue disclosure, which has now been done. It appears under 'Info for Prospective Sellers' in the front of the catalogue and says that sometimes advances are only secured by the property offered for sale."[5]

Davidge had rounded up a handful of documents showing that Sotheby's had exaggerated its market share in proposals the firm had prepared for potential consigners, which clients had passed on to Christie's. He also noted that the bad-mouthing Taubman was complaining about was not limited to Christie's. Davidge told him he had heard that a senior director of Sotheby's had been spreading a rumour that Lord Carrington had been asked to step down as Christie's chairman because a group of major shareholders were dissatisfied with his performance because he was not commercially minded.

"It's a travesty," Davidge told Tennant. "You're getting a biased view of Christie's tactics. I'm going to give you some facts of my own."[6]

To prove his assertion that Sotheby's was trying to home in on deals already signed with Christie's, Davidge showed Tennant a letter that the rival firm had sent to the executor of the estate of the Countess of Lovelace, whose collections included fine silver, paintings and valuable books.

"*Everybody* knew that the Countess of Lovelace's estate was going to be sold by Christie's," Davidge told Tennant, "but Sotheby's still wrote to her executor and tried to break up the agreement to sell at Christie's."[7]

The offending letter, Davidge told Tennant, had been sent in December 1992 by Timothy Sammons, a director of Sotheby's in London, stating that Sotheby's would be "delighted to undertake the sales entirely without commission."[8]

"This is a spoiling tactic," Davidge told Tennant. "Sotheby's knew

we'd already quoted a commission rate of six percent."[9] The countess' estate was not the largest to come up that season, he noted, but
that was hardly the point. "It's a competitive world," Davidge
warned. "We can't afford to lose business."[10]

Responding to Taubman's assertion that Christie's had improper-
ly included private-treaty sales in its auction results for 1992, Davidge
pointed out that he had already told the press that Christie's would
not combine the two different results in the future. "I don't think it
does the industry any good to have the bickering we did last year,"
he said.[11]

Davidge was prepared to admit that including private sales had
been misleading. But he refused to accept the suggestion that
Christie's was alone in manipulating sales results.

"Sotheby's uses market share statistics and distorts them as well,"
he told Tennant.[12] To prove his point, Davidge produced copies of
Sotheby's proposals that had fallen into Christie's hands, which
showed that Sotheby's had flagrantly exaggerated its market share
while trying to win business. One such item was a 1989 proposal for
the Hunt Collection, an impressive assemblage of antiquities. The
document contained some disparaging remarks that Davidge had
underlined and handed to Tennant in a pile of similar rebuttals.

"Christie's is, in modern times, lagging behind Sotheby's in this
collecting area," the proposal read. "Ms. Nugee's expertise, particularly with respect to Greek vases, seems somewhat questionable. We
understand that she was primarily responsible for cataloguing a sale
on January 10, 1987, in which three major Greek vases were withdrawn for authenticity reasons."[13]

Personal attacks of this sort were outrageous, Davidge said.

"You seem to be under the impression that Christie's is the guilty
party and Sotheby's is innocent," Davidge said. "I don't condone this
kind of behaviour, but it's pretty much the way both companies
operate.[14] You should be aware of Sotheby's business practices," he
added. "I don't think they're correct."[15]

Davidge also pointed out that he had recently become aware of a
controversial new practice at Sotheby's. The rival firm was offering
to make substantial financial contributions to a charity of the poten-

tial consigner's choice as a tactic for winning business. To prove his point, Davidge showed Tennant a copy of a letter Sotheby's had sent to the Commissioners and Chairman of the Presidential Commission on Good Government for the Republic of the Philippines, who were planning to dispose of treasures left behind by the country's deposed leader Ferdinand Marcos and his wife, Imelda.

The letter was from Lord Gowrie, chairman of Sotheby's in London, who had written to the Philippine government officials in January 1993 to state that Sotheby's would be prepared to make a charitable contribution of $200,000 to the people of the Philippines if the sale should fetch more than $12 million.

Davidge explained that Christie's now felt obliged to match Sotheby's new tactic of offering to make charitable contributions to win business. "This is another example of weakening our income stream," Tennant observed. "Do we *have* to continue making charitable contributions?"[16]

"Maybe you should mention this to Taubman," Davidge said.

A GENTLE BREEZE was blowing from the northwest and the sky was cloudy when Sir Anthony Tennant showed up at Alfred Taubman's London flat for another breakfast of smoked salmon and scrambled eggs on April 30, 1993. Hoping to set Taubman's mind at rest—and to preempt another lecture—Tennant told him that Christie's had taken steps to ensure that the firm would stop making disparaging comments about Sotheby's in the press, in written proposals and in remarks to clients. Even so, he admitted, that goal would be especially difficult to achieve since it involved more than five hundred people—the number of people working at Christie's in London at the time. He also reassured his host that Christie's would cease making claims to the press about market share.

Going over the various subjects they had discussed in their previous conversations, Tennant summarized the topics they had already agreed upon: From September 1993, neither Christie's nor Sotheby's would give any "straight" guarantees—the kind where the auction house did not get to share in the proceeds if the winning bid exceeded the guarantee price promised to the consigner. Both firms would also abandon the practice of making advances on single lots, and they would no longer make any loans to sellers below the prime rate, known in England as the London Interbank Offered Rate, or LIBOR.

Dealers, or "trade" *vendors,* would be given a rate of no better than 5 percent, and they would be obliged to pay their own insurance costs, while trade *buyers* would be offered no more than ninety days' credit.

Furthermore, Tennant noted, it was agreed that the two firms would no longer pay more than 1 percent in introductory commissions to third parties when the deal in question involved a zero seller's commission. Nor would they make any offers to sellers who were already under contract with the rival auction house, although he insisted that Christie's did not do that anyway. Finally, he noted, Christie's would cease making charitable contributions if it saw that Sotheby's had stopped doing so.

"Christopher Davidge now knows of these conversations," Tennant told Taubman, referring to their power breakfasts. "Perhaps Dede Brooks should know, too. Otherwise no one?"[17]

Taubman agreed that their discussions should be kept private, and reminded Tennant that Sotheby's would like to return to the traditional agreement of not poaching each other's employees.

Turning to the subject of the list Taubman had given him at their last meeting, Tennant pulled out a slip of paper on which he had jotted down a summary of Davidge's objections: "You gave me a list of eleven specific deals," he told Taubman. "Only two out of eleven were right. Several were full-recourse loan offers and several loans included interest." The issue of Christie's failing to report its non-recourse loans was now moot, he explained, because an ordinary loan could not be construed as a guarentee on the auction price. "What you call the Christie's guarantee is now identified in our own Conditions of Sale in the catalogues."[18]

Taubman appeared confused. "Let me get this straight. Are you planning to stop doing 'Christie's guarantees'?"

"I did not mean that," Tennant replied, firmly. "We're still going to do them."[19]

Still steamed up on the subject, Taubman launched into more invective about "Christie's guarantees," hoping to convince Tennant that non-recourse, no-interest deals were a bad policy.

As a case in point, Taubman cited the recent negotiations over the estate of Rudolf Nureyev, the great Russian ballet star who had fled to the West penniless in 1961 and died a multimillionaire at the age of fifty-four in January 1993 after a tragic battle with AIDS. By the end of his remarkable life, the dancer had acquired a total of seven homes: in Paris, London, Monaco and New York; on an island off Italy's Amalfi coast; a 550-acre farm in Virginia and a Caribbean retreat in St. Barth's. He had been a passionate art collector, and his houses were filled with treasures.

Sotheby's and Christie's had competed fiercely for the estate, keenly aware of the marquee value of his name. Among the highlights of the collection was *Satan Starting from the Touch of Ithuriel's Lance,* by Johann Heinrich Fuseli, which Christie's expected to fetch between $500,000 and $700,000. Other, less intrinsically valuable objects were priceless on account of their provenance. Nureyev had owned two mustard-coloured couches that had belonged to Maria Callas, who, like the impetuous Russian, was known in France as a *monstre sacré.* The proceeds from the estate were earmarked for two charities, the Rudolph Nureyev Foundation in the United States and the Ballet Promotion Foundation in Liechtenstein, which he had set up to help dancers, promote classical ballet and fund medical research. Lord Rothschild was the head trustee.

"Jacob Rothschild tells me that Christie's promised the Nureyev estate a nonrefundable, non-recourse loan," Taubman told Tennant. "This kind of deal makes no economic sense. It gives you all the risk of a guarantee with no upside benefit."

According to the calculations of Sotheby's financial experts, Taubman explained, Christie's would have a tough time making a profit. "You'll barely break even at eight million dollars," the mogul remarked. "And you'll have to do ten million to make even a very small profit."*

---

* The contents of Nureyev's Manhattan apartment were sold by Christie's in January 1995 for $7.9 million; a pair of his ballet slippers fetched $9,200.

"That's crazy," Tennant said. "I'll have to take this up with Davidge."

"You do that," Taubman said. "He may also be interested to know that when Sotheby's gives a guarantee, we *always* insist on sharing the upside with the client."[20]

Turning to the delicate matter of auction commissions, Tennant urged Sotheby's chairman to agree that something must be done to make the auction business more profitable. "We're getting killed on our bottom line," Tennant told Taubman. "I feel it's time to increase pricing."

"I agree," Taubman replied. "But it's your turn to go first this time. We took the risk on the buyer's premium."[21]

TENNANT WAS FEELING EXULTANT after his meeting with Taubman. When his black Mercedes dropped him off at Christie's, he headed directly to Davidge's office on the fourth floor. Disappointed to learn that the CEO was in a meeting, Tennant penned an upbeat note on Christie's stationery: "Chris, I had a good breakfast. I will make a date in your diary to give you a thorough debrief."[22]

While the details were still fresh in his memory, Tennant retired to his own office and closed the door. Taking out a blue-ink pen, he jotted down all the details he could recall from his conversation with Taubman. After memorializing the various routine topics they had discussed, he jotted down his own musings about pricing.

"A schedule exists," Tennant wrote, referring to the official, but rarely implemented, scale of sellers' commissions already in place at both firms. "We should get back to it—15 percent downwards, on a sliding scale." To Tennant, the economic advantages of making sellers' commissions nonnegotiable were obvious. With $1 billion in sales, he calculated, Sotheby's and Christie's could easily be making more than $50 million a year in profits.

Anticipating Davidge's nervousness about American antitrust laws, he sought to assure him that there was nothing to worry about. "A hundred industries, banks, etc., all do it without talking about it," he wrote. "It is easier for us than for people dealing in goods that can be priced exactly. With a sliding scale based on value, there should be no problem because you cannot price-fix a unique object."

After setting down his pen, Tennant read over the last sentence and decided to insert one word. Pleased with the result, he read it back to himself aloud:

"There should be no *legal* problem."[23]

Later that day, he strode into Davidge's office. "First of all, I want you to know that I had a *very* good meeting," Tennant said, grinning.[24]

He told Davidge that Michael Ainslie was expected to step down as Sotheby's worldwide CEO within the next few months and that Dede Brooks would be succeeding him. The two chairmen had agreed that Davidge and Brooks should get together to hammer out the details of the various subjects the two chairmen had discussed, Tennant explained, and told him that he had given Davidge's home telephone number to Taubman for Brooks to call. "I understood from Tennant that Dede was to telephone me when her new appointment had been confirmed," Davidge recalled.[25]

The two chairmen would now step back, Tennant explained, but stay in touch in order to monitor the two executives' progress, and intervene only if necessary.

Tennant was proud of what he had accomplished. As he had suspected, the CEO looked uncomfortable when Tennant explained that he and Taubman had agreed that it was time to raise pricing.

Davidge knew from speaking to Patty Hambrecht, Christie's general counsel, that price-fixing was merely a civil offence in Britain, but that in the United States it was considered a serious crime. Tennant and Taubman's agreement that prices should be raised sounded dangerously close to being unlawful.

"This seems unnecessary," Davidge told Tennant. "Sotheby's and Christie's always follow each other's commission increases anyway. We can raise commissions without having to put our reputation at risk."[26]

Tennant seemed unimpressed with Davidge's protestations and reminded him of his responsibility to Christie's shareholders to boost the company's fortunes.

Before leaving the room, he warned Davidge to keep his mouth shut about the meetings between the two firms' chairmen and the proposed discussions between the two CEOs.

"Obviously, this is a sensitive matter," he told Davidge.[27] "It's in everyone's best interests if only you and I know about this. And that's the way it should be at Sotheby's. Only Taubman and Mrs. Brooks should know."[28] "I think it would be wise to keep it to the four of us.[29]

"Very well," Davidge replied. "I won't mention this to anybody."

CHRISTOPHER DAVIDGE had no intention of keeping his promise. He was concerned about the possible ramifications of being a party to the shenanigans being organized by Tennant, he recalled, and he decided to meet with his discreet European business friend for more advice.

"Do you know if your colleagues would support such an arrangement?" the friend asked.

"I don't really know," Davidge said. "But if I tell them about it, I don't trust them not to go directly to Tennant, who told me to keep it to myself."[30]

Uncertain of how to proceed next, Davidge began to fear that Tennant was right to question his abilities as a leader. It would break his heart to leave Christie's, he told himself, because he felt he was just getting into the job and had a clear idea about future strategy.

"I genuinely did not know what my own position was," Davidge recalled, "and I was very uncomfortable for Christie's reputation." Having witnessed the outrage that had erupted when Sotheby's and Christie's had introduced the buyer's premium a few days apart, he feared that the London art dealers in particular could make life tough for Christie's, partly out of revenge for what had occurred in 1975.

In order to protect himself from possible recriminations, Davidge decided to speak individually to his three most senior colleagues— Christopher Burge, Charlie Hindlip and François Curiel—who between them represented the main countries in which Christie's did business, with the exception of Hong Kong and the Far East, of which Davidge had recently become chairman.

"I believed the best form of safety was to tell my senior colleagues so they were just as responsible as I was," Davidge admitted later.[31]

Eager to avoid incurring the chairman's wrath, he decided he would omit any mention of Tennant and Taubman's discussions. Slippery as ever, he also hoped to shift the blame by telling his colleagues that getting together with Sotheby's to raise pricing was all Dede Brooks' idea.

Nevertheless, he was unsure if it was wise to get into bed with Sotheby's. He resolved not to try to sell his colleagues on the idea, but merely to gauge their reactions.

He predicted that Burge would probably object. Curiel, he recalled later, had been saying for the past year that he had wanted to reach an understanding with John Block at Sotheby's that, at a minimum, could be applied to the two firms' jewellery departments worldwide. (Curiel has firmly denied telling Davidge that he wanted to reach an understanding with Block and has no recollection that Davidge consulted him before arranging to meet with Brooks.) Davidge was uncertain about how Hindlip would react, but he guessed that he would probably be against the idea of colluding with Sotheby's over commissions.

If his predictions turned out to be right, Davidge decided, he would be able to confront Tennant armed with the objections of a couple of Old Etonians like Burge and Hindlip. Their support would at least give him the confidence to stand up to the new chairman.

First, he went to see Charlie Hindlip, the chairman of Christie's U.K., who was an expert on Old Master paintings and English furniture, and head of business-getting in England. Behind closed doors in Hindlip's office on King Street, Davidge asked what he thought about the idea of getting together with Dede Brooks to discuss the notion of creating a new set of nonnegotiable seller's commissions as a way to revive profits.

"I said, 'You've got to do it, but I wouldn't discuss it with Sotheby's,'" Hindlip recalled. Hatching an illegal scheme was unnecessary, he believed, "because Sotheby's would have fallen in line with us anyway." Furthermore, "'The risk was always that if you found out, you're in trouble.'"

If Christie's went ahead with new nonnegotiable rates and Sotheby's failed to follow, Christie's, with its higher rates, would lose business to its rival. If so, Christie's could revert to its current pricing schedule six months later. "It could have cost us 4 million pounds," Hindlip estimated. "But that was a great deal less than the eventual loss."

Hindlip doubted that Davidge would follow his advice, "but I didn't think he would talk to Sotheby's."[32]

Next, Davidge went to see Christopher Burge, who was head of Christie's Impressionist and Modern picture departments worldwide and president and CEO of Christie's America. The cultured Englishman was also in charge of business-getting in North and South America and spent much of his time cultivating major American clients and their lawyers.

Burge was initially reluctant to get together with Sotheby's to discuss commissions, Davidge controversially recalled later, but after giving the matter some thought he changed his mind and said, "Let's do it right away. I'm sick of losing consignments."[33] (When asked for comment, Burge, too, stated he had no knowledge of Davidge's price-fixing arrangements with Brooks.)

Davidge recalled that he asked Burge if Dede Brooks could be trusted. Burge had known her for years from serving with her on the board of the Frick Art Reference Library, and he had formed a favourable impression. He told Davidge that Brooks was extremely competitive but essentially trustworthy.

Heaving a sigh, Burge explained that he hated the way the art world was going. He lamented the demise of the great old-time collectors, who had built up relationships with auction experts based on a shared love for their respective collecting passions. "The new collectors are mostly just buying trophies," Burge observed.[34] He disliked having to deal with increasing numbers of lawyers acting on behalf of estates who invariably had neither knowledge of art nor any loyalty to past relationships with the deceased collector.

"These days, it's all about the *deal*," Burge observed, glumly. "Maybe if there was no more deal making of this kind, the business would revert to its more civilized practices."[35]

"I remember being very sad for Christopher," Davidge said, recalling their conversation.[36]

By consulting with his colleagues, Davidge reasoned he had ensured their complicity and silence. If he should ever land in trouble for discussing commission changes with Sotheby's, he could threaten to reveal that he had carried out the scheme with their approval. They knew he was perfectly capable of such a cutthroat tactic. Davidge had an ingenious way of presenting the truth to his advantage; he had the street smarts of a lad who had begun his professional life selling shirts on Petticoat Lane.

A catalogue publishing executive involved with another auction house, not Sotheby's, who entered negotiations with Davidge to merge their two firms' printing operations, offered a colourful assessment: "You'd be crazy to trust him," the Cockney printer said, laughing. "As we say in my part of London, 'He's as slippery as a jellied eel in a bucket of snot.'"[37]

TEN MINUTES after Tennant had left the breakfast table at nine-thirty on April 30, 1993, Taubman was in his car, headed for London's Hatfield airport. His pilot and crew were preparing for a ten-thirty A.M. takeoff, bound for Detroit, and he was planning to attend an evening reception for honorary-degree recipients at the University of Michigan.

On his way to the airport, he asked his driver to make a stop at Sotheby's on New Bond Street. He wanted to talk to Dede Brooks, who was still in town after the previous day's board meeting, where she had dazzled the board with her plans to improve efficiency and streamline the worldwide business.

Brooks had proposed creating a new, global management committee that would report to her and meet once a month to work on sales strategy, sales locations, pricing, press and marketing strategies. She had also come up with the novel idea of appointing handpicked executives to take on worldwide nonexpert positions for finance, press relations, general counsel, human resources and business development.

When Taubman arrived at Sotheby's that Friday morning,

Brooks was in the middle of back-to-back interviews with the BBC and *Women's Wear Daily* to discuss her new role as the first woman to head an international auction company. She recalled that he sent word he would like to see her.

Taubman loved the old-fashioned second-floor room overlooking New Bond Street that served as his office when he was in London. Unlike his immaculate headquarters in New York and Bloomfield Hills, both custom-designed by Michael Graves, the room was modestly sized and slightly shabby, with faded red silk on the walls, tatty burgundy-coloured curtains fraying at the edges and a large nineteenth-century desk supported by creaky floorboards that sloped toward the middle of the room.

While the *WWD* photographer was setting up lights to take her picture, she recalled, Brooks slipped away to have a quick word with Taubman, who had told her that he had just met with Christie's chairman to discuss auction industry practices.*

"He and I got along very well together," Taubman told Brooks, "and I can see working with him. We agreed that we are both killing each other on the bottom line, and it's time to do something about it."[38]

Taubman explained that he and Tennant had agreed on a number of subjects, and that they had left it that Brooks should get together with Christopher Davidge in order to go forward and implement them, and in some cases actually work out the details.

"He and I feel that it's time to increase pricing," Taubman told Brooks, "and I told him it was *their* turn to go first."[39]

Brooks would later remember that the details of how to handle commission rates were left up in the air. "Mr. Taubman told me that they'd agreed to raise pricing," Brooks remembered, "not necessarily how."[40]

"Don't tell anyone else about this," Taubman warned Brooks.

"Fine, I won't tell anyone," she replied.[41]

Brooks had every intention of keeping the secret to herself. The scheme Taubman was proposing was risky, she recalled, but she felt

---

* Taubman has strongly denied that this conversation took place.

that taking such action was justified. "It was illegal," she acknowledged later, "but I didn't think it was harming our clients."

Brooks felt that Sotheby's was entitled to be paid properly for its efforts. "We were extremely concerned about our financial results," she recalled, "and we saw ourselves in a sort of death struggle with Christie's in terms of the direction the business was headed in. I felt that we gave incredible service to our clients, and I didn't feel that the clients were paying us fairly for it."

She was well versed in America's stringent antitrust laws and was under no illusion that she was signing onto a scheme that involved breaking the law.

"I was nervous about it," she recalled, "but I agreed to do it willingly."[42]

APRIL 30, 1993, was a stressful day for Dede Brooks. She was confident that she could handle the enormous challenges and responsibilities of running a global business. But another, more personal, subject was weighing on her mind.

The day before, her brother Andy Dwyer had been forced to resign as president and chief executive officer of their family-controlled, publicly traded company, JWP, amid allegations of financial improprieties and a plummeting stock price.

Dwyer's fall from grace was fairly spectacular. Since 1978, he had transformed Jamaica Water Properties from a $40 million water utility into a technical-services company with reported revenues of $3·6 billion in 1991. Now Wall Street analysts were noting that the company seemed to be teetering on the verge of bankruptcy.

On top of its fiscal woes, JWP was facing a class-action lawsuit filed with a federal court in White Plains, New York, which accused the firm and its senior management, including Andy Dwyer, of crooked accounting practices that had resulted in several write-downs and restructuring charges in 1992. According to the lawsuit, the defendants had created "an illusion of profitability."[43]

As a director and major shareholder in JWP, Dede Brooks had lost millions of dollars as a result of her brother's alleged crimes and faulty corporate governance. "It was catastrophic for Dede financially," a colleague noted.[44] Before the stock had started to tumble in 1992, he recalled, Brooks' personal stake in JWP had been worth between $20 and $30 million. Now it was virtually worthless.

Remarkably, just as Andy Dwyer was facing the threat of criminal and civil prosecution over accounting irregularities at JWP, his sister Dede was steeling herself to meet with Christopher Davidge to engage in an illegal dialogue to fix prices. True to her rivalrous nature, Brooks was still fiercely competitive with her older brother. After years in Andy's shadow, Dede Brooks was emerging as a rising star of Sotheby's world-wide operations. And she was determined to prove she was capable of becoming the successful one in the family.

AUCTION COMMISSIONS were one of the leading topics of discussion when Sotheby's directors convened for a board meeting in October 1993. The company's chief financial officer, Kevin Bousquette, commented that while the new buyer's premium appeared to be having some positive effect, it was being offset by a further erosion of the vendor's commission.

In order to win business during the seemingly inexorable slump in the art market, Sotheby's was obliged to offer more and more zero-commission deals and enormous guarantees, accompanied by concessions ranging from waived charges for insurance, transportation and catalogue costs to elaborate touring exhibitions and hardbound single-owner catalogues.

Brooks noted that several factors had contributed to this disturbing trend. There had been a change in the mixture of sales. Non-Impressionist paintings and jewellery were booming, but those were areas where consigners usually insisted on paying no commission. Simultaneously, there seemed to be a slump in decorative arts, where the auction house usually received its full sales commission. The rise in the buyer's premium in January 1993 seemed to have emboldened dealers and other sellers to demand zero-percent seller's commissions, with the argument that Sotheby's was already receiving additional compensation from buyers.

Brooks warned that it would be a major challenge for management to prevent any further erosion from taking place in 1994.

* * *

WHILE THE ART MARKET remained in the doldrums, Christopher Davidge was working toward his ambitious goal of catching up with Sotheby's, which had long maintained a record of much higher revenues and profits and a larger network of revenue-generating outposts around the world.

Since becoming CEO in March, he had travelled extensively in Asia with the intention of building up Christie's business in the Far East. The firm lagged far behind Sotheby's, which had been holding successful sales in Hong Kong since 1973.

Asia, Davidge believed, would dominate the art market in the twenty-first century, with the Chinese in the lead. Preparing for the inevitable end of the worldwide economic recession, he wanted Christie's to be ready to cash in on what he predicted would be a new wave of collectors and collecting. To that end, he had been spending time in Shanghai exploring the sociopolitical networks of mainland China. The experience left him feeling exhilarated. "One of the things I enjoy about the Chinese is their attitude to business," he told Geraldine Norman, the salesroom correspondent for the *Independent*. "They get straight down to it, cutting out the preambles. Their directness reminds me of working the London markets."[45]

Davidge wore his working-class background as a badge of pride. But his constant references to his lowly roots suggested a gnawing insecurity and a need to remind himself and others of his extraordinary success in making the leap from barrow boy to global CEO. Since getting the top job, Davidge's colleagues noticed, the former printing executive had become woefully self-aggrandizing.

Intolerant of dissenting opinions, he ran Christie's with a rod of iron and seemed delighted with his own power. His extravagant expense account was a subject of much discussion among his coworkers, who resented his frequent $7,750 round-trip excursions to New York on the Concorde and his predilection for flying British Airways first class to all other foreign destinations.

"Chris was terribly self-important," Lady Hindlip noted, "and he always had a chip on his shoulder. He really was chippy."[46]

"The chippy side of Chris always felt that he was a great, accomplished man and he wasn't appreciated in England because they're all snobs," Lord Hindlip observed. "I think he felt that when he went to America, he would be accepted and his true value would be perceived. But he suddenly realized that he was far less interesting in America.

"He was frankly a boring little man with no sense of humour," Hindlip noted cheerfully. "All he had to offer in the way of conversation about Christie's was details of its printing presses—not very much fun. But in Asia, he found a continent where by turning up in first class surrounded by very expensive suitcases and people bowing and saying, 'Ah, Mr. Davidge-San,' he was the big cheese."

Being short, Hindlip added cattily, "he was more their level. And he was much happier and more relaxed there." Joking aside, Hindlip admitted that Davidge's decision to invest in the Far East was shrewd and farsighted. "He caught up with Sotheby's, and they'd been there long before us," Hindlip conceded. "He deserves a bit of credit for that."[47]

Davidge's mandate for Christie's expansion into South America proved to be less rewarding. Wealthy Latin Americans preferred to buy Latin American art in New York, where Sotheby's and Christie's wooed them with extravagant competing parties with dancing and South American dishes prepared in their honour.

"The Latin American expansion was completely cuckoo—idiotic and quixotic," Lord Hindlip observed. "He saw himself as conquering South America—sort of the Simon Bolivar of the auction world."

Until Davidge's great rise at Christie's, the firm had traditionally been run by art experts, and many of the older staff were contemptuous of Davidge's all-business worldview. The popular opinion among art experts at Christie's was that their CEO was a philistine. "Chris is just not interested in works of art," Hindlip complained. "He just doesn't get it." Davidge's failure to correctly pronounce the names of famous artists like Vuillard, Bonnard and van Gogh frequently sent his London colleagues into paroxysms of laughter behind his back.

"He *always* got the names wrong," Hindlip recalled, giggling.

"And he was very bad at English, too. He'd say things like, 'He's really not creditable.' Well, we all knew what he *meant*. But he was peppered with malapropisms."[48]

Davidge laid no claim to being a connoisseur. "I've never been attracted to Christie's because of the art side," he admitted to *a Sunday Telegraph* reporter in the spring of 1993. "But I love dealing with people."[49]

The claim that Christie's new CEO enjoyed human interaction came as something of a surprise to some of his London co-workers. Davidge had developed a reputation for ruthlessness and was becoming increasingly isolated from many of his colleagues.

"Chris was a remote, distant, dictatorial figure," Ed Dolman, his successor, recalled. Rather than descending to mingle with the crowds in the salesroom during auctions, Davidge preferred to watch from a closed-circuit TV screen in his upstairs office. He also abstained from private views. "Chris never came to Christie's openings because he didn't really know anybody," Lady Hindlip noted.[50]

Always rather formal and aloof in the office, he expected Christie's staff to address him respectfully as "Mr. Davidge" or by his initials, "CMD." Meanwhile, Lord Hindlip was greeted as "Charlie" by everyone at Christie's, including the porters.

"Davidge makes *everybody* feel uncomfortable," Hindlip observed. "He's the most disquieting person. There's no real humanity there. He has an ability, in my case, to make one hate oneself, or certainly feel enormously less of oneself. Davidge is *worm* factor of ten."[51]

BY THE AUTUMN OF 1993, Anthony Tennant was becoming agitated that Davidge had not heard from Brooks. When, he wondered, was Sotheby's going to announce her new position as CEO of Sotheby's Holdings? And when could she and Davidge start talking about ways to trim the intense competition between the two firms?

Davidge was eager to find a way to increase revenues. During the summer of 1993, he struck upon the idea of "signalling" to Sotheby's that Christie's was contemplating a switch to nonnegotiable commissions. He decided to start by choosing a few smaller departments

and declaring a new policy that seller's commissions were nonnegotiable for those categories, with exceptions only for VIPs.

But though it seemed a good idea at the time, the scheme was
never carried out. The only way to synchronize auction commissions, Davidge realized, was to speak to Dede Brooks.

WITHIN DAYS of the official announcement in November that she
would be succeeding Michael Ainslie as CEO of Sotheby's Holdings
the following spring, Brooks picked up the telephone to call Christopher Davidge at his London flat.

"It's Dede Brooks," she said. "I guess you've been expecting this
call."

"Exactly," Davidge replied. "When can we get together?"[52]

They agreed to meet for dinner at the Stafford, a small and discreet hotel near Green Park that was redolent of eighteenth-century
London.

Davidge greeted Brooks in the bar with a formal handshake. The
two archrivals had met only twice before—once at the London home
of Godfrey Barker, a leading art-world journalist, and once briefly
when Christie's and Sotheby's were trying to form a joint lobbying
agreement for trade initiatives in Switzerland. With the awkwardness
of illicit lovers, the competitors sidled off into the Pink Room, an
intimate private dining room.

"I think both of us were very nervous at the outset," Davidge
recalled. "Obviously, we both knew that this meeting had far-reaching consequences and instinctively we knew it shouldn't be taking
place." Also, he noted, "I'd been in the company for twenty-five
years or so, and one didn't talk to Sotheby's, certainly not at my
level."[53]

Brooks was quietly trying to get the measure of her opponent. "I
had never really spent any time with Davidge," she recalled, "so I did-
n't at that point trust him." She told Davidge that she felt strange
about meeting with him but said she was doing so partly out of loyalty to her chairman, Alfred Taubman.

"Are you concerned about what we're being asked to do?" he
asked. "Not really," Brooks replied.[54]

Davidge took comfort from Brooks' nonchalance, figuring that as an American she must be aware of the risks involved. "The fact that she was not concerned impressed me," he recalled later.[55]

The two auction executives discussed the dispiriting state of the art market, which appeared to be slowly recovering from the doldrums of 1990. Davidge touched on all the items on his mental agenda in order to establish whether Brooks had been briefed by Taubman in the same way he had by Tennant.

"We talked generally about guarantees and zero commission on commission rates," Davidge recalled, "and about bad-mouthing, or being disrespectful to each other in the press."[56] Both agreed that a policy of limiting disparaging comments was fine in theory, but was probably impractical. "With all of our colleagues all over the world it might be a little difficult at times to control everybody," Brooks noted.[57]

They agreed that their two companies should stop boasting to the press about market share, and discussed the notion of establishing a guarantee formula for splitting the difference between the guarantee price and the overage when a work of art sold for more than the guarantee price. "You have much more experience on guarantees," Davidge told Brooks. "I think you should handle that."[58]

The two executives finally got around to the subject of commissions. "I have to tell you I'm a bit upset," Brooks told Davidge. "Mr. Taubman assured me that Christie's was going to go first. I thought you would have changed your pricing schedule by now."[59]

"Well I'm sorry to disappoint you," Davidge said. "But I thought that you and I should work together to come up with the best solution for changing our pricing. After all, we just raised the buyer's premium last December. We need to be careful about timing."[60]

"Well, we ought to do it," Brooks said. "We can work on it together."[61]

Something had to be done to improve profitability. "I think we're all concerned about the bottom line," Brooks said. "We're killing each other, so we should find a way so we get paid fairly for what we do so we can provide a decent return to our shareholders."[62]

As they rose from dinner, Davidge and Brooks agreed to meet the following month.

Their next encounter came much sooner than they expected. A few days later, they bumped into each other at the airport in Zurich. Both were in town with experts from their respective auction houses to pitch for the estate of Jacques Koerfer, a well-known collector and former chairman of BMW.

Careful to avoid creating any suspicion, the two executives acted as if they had never met.

DAVIDGE HAD HURRIED home after the meeting at the Stafford Hotel. Amid a blaze of candles on the dining room table, he took painstaking notes from their conversation in order to create a record of all the matters they had touched upon. The next day, he called Tennant to tell him the good news that Brooks seemed to be fully aware of the topics the two chairmen had discussed in April.

"I'm pleased we're on the same page," Tennant told him. "If you meet with her again, will you keep me informed?"

"Of course," Davidge replied.[63]

Brooks also rang Taubman to report on her meeting with Davidge.

"We got on pretty well, considering that we're very different people," she said. "He and I are going to work together to put all these things together."

"Good," Taubman replied. "I'm glad we're making some progress."[64]

NOTWITHSTANDING THE FIERCE rivalry between Sotheby's and Christie's, there were numerous occasions when it was considered acceptable for the two firms to confer on matters of industry practice.

While Bill Ruprecht was head of Sotheby's Marketing Department in 1993, he was intrigued by a proposal from a firm called Centrox for Sotheby's and Christie's to pool their auction catalogues and sales results into a central database. It was envisaged as a useful resource for auction-house experts and private dealers to refer to when trying to estimate the market value for a work of art, and as a means of tailoring information sent to clients about exciting lots in upcoming sales.

Keen on pursuing the idea, Ruprecht met several times during the fall of 1993 with senior Christie's executives, including Patty Hambrecht, to discuss the potential advantages of such a scheme. Both firms had outside lawyers in attendance to monitor the proceedings to ensure that none of their discussions or potential agreements could be construed as collusive.

"We did that under the minute-by-minute oversight of antitrust counsel," Ruprecht recalled. "They were in every meeting we had together with Christie's."[65]

The directors of both companies knew that such supervised colloquiums were taking place. But neither Davidge nor Brooks was taking such precautions because they were trying to circumvent the law.

12

Abysmal Results

DEDE BROOKS' EFFORTS to overhaul Sotheby's business in London were under way by the autumn of 1993, but she was sensitive to criticism that the firm was becoming too American. Hoping to restore some missing Britishness, she initiated a search for an Englishman with strong social connections who could drum up new business from the country-house set. With any luck, such a person could help her achieve her goal of overtaking Christie's lead in the British capital.

"The view in London was that we didn't have strong enough English old-family representation on the board," she recalled, "and that we really needed someone at the top."[1]

Rumours had been swirling for months that Lord Gowrie, the chairman of Sotheby's U.K., was ready to relinquish his duties, which had become mostly ceremonial since the arrival of Brooks' sharp-eyed, businesslike deputy, Roger Faxon. For several months, Brooks had been trying to recruit Henry Wyndham, a paintings expert with an impeccable pedigree and aristocratic connections who had left Christie's to become a private art dealer. The exceedingly tall Wyndham—six-foot-eight in his scarlet socks—seemed an ideal candidate. But after numerous interviews, and much wooing, he had decided to turn down Sotheby's offer.

"What are we going to *do*?" Brooks asked Grey Gowrie, who agreed to review a list that a search firm had drawn up of likely prospects among the British Establishment.[2] Gowrie's eyes lit up when he saw the name of Lord Camoys, with whom he had shared a room at Oxford.

Thomas Stonor, the seventh Lord Camoys known to friends and colleagues as Tommy had recently retired as deputy chairman of Barclays de Zoete Wedd, a merchant bank. The fifty-three-year-old earl had recently been appointed as a lord-in-waiting to the Queen— a position that involved representing the sovereign at weddings, funerals and other state occasions—an encouraging indication that he moved in the highest international circles. He also lived in splendour at Stonor Park, his country seat in Oxfordshire, which had been in the family for eight hundred years. Owning one of the largest country houses in Europe seemed a perfect calling card for a prospective member of Sotheby's illustrious board who would be expected to persuade fellow estate owners to consign their finer chattels to Sotheby's.

At Brooks' instigation and Taubman's invitation, Tommy Camoys joined Sotheby's board at the end of October 1993 as deputy chairman of Sotheby's Holdings, a newly created position that reflected the firm's great expectations of the noble lord.

Having declined Sotheby's offer of employment, Henry Wyndham suddenly changed his mind and agreed to join the firm as chairman of Sotheby's U.K. The unfailingly gracious and politic Englishman proved to be a superb auctioneer and a formidable business-getter.

The quick-tempered Camoys, however, turned out to be an unfortunate choice for Sotheby's. "The man is just scary," a Sotheby's director recalled. "I've never seen anyone with such a short fuse."[3]

DAVIDGE AND BROOKS got together again in December at 17B Three Kings Yard, a comfortable two-bedroom flat that Sotheby's had rented for Brooks' use during her frequent trips to London. The conspirators had agreed that it was unwise to meet in public. Davidge's flat was out of the question because it was located in the same block as Christie's. It would arouse suspicion if Brooks was seen entering the building. But her new pied-à-terre was tucked away in a quiet corner of Mayfair behind Claridge's hotel. With virtually no street traffic, the undistinguished 1960s three-story beige-brick building was a discreet location for conspiring to fix auction commissions.

After climbing a single flight of steep steps to Brooks' duplex apartment, Davidge discovered an unpretentious, simply furnished living room. The two CEOs immediately got down to the substance of the issues they had touched on at the Stafford: vendors' commissions, market share, guarantees, trade commissions, introductory commissions, contractual property, Alfred Taubman, Michael Ainslie, poaching staff, British VAT (Value Added Tax) and the possibility of holding auctions in France.

On the subject of market share, Davidge and Brooks agreed that both Christie's and Sotheby's should cease giving worldwide market-share figures to the press. Echoing Tennant's sentiments on the subject, Davidge opined that constant references to market share were making the two companies unnecessarily competitive with each other. Even so, he and Brooks acknowledged, there was nothing that would stop enterprising journalists from calculating market-share figures by themselves.

Turning to guarantees, Brooks and Davidge decided to adopt a sliding scale for guarantees. The greater the risk involved, the higher the percentage on the overage earned by the auction house.

They also agreed to abolish the practice of giving interest-free advances and single-lot advances. Davidge asked how Brooks felt about "Christie's guarantees," which Taubman had objected to. "I don't care how you treat that," she told him. "That's your business."[4]

"It's a nonissue now anyway," Davidge explained. "We now indicate in our catalogues if we have a financial involvement in certain lots."[5]

Turning to commissions, Davidge told Brooks that Anthony Tennant had been pressuring him to come to an agreement with her over a new pricing structure that could be implemented by both firms by the end of the year.

"It's just not realistic," he told Brooks. "We've just raised the buyer's premium in January. If we try raising commissions again in this soft market, everyone—our clients, the dealers and the press—is going to give us hell for trying to gouge them when they're struggling themselves."[6]

Davidge and Brooks agreed to spend some time examining the best way to raise prices, how to make them binding and how any change would affect their existing pricing schedules. Both auction houses already charged seller's commissions ranging from 6 to 15 percent, and sellers were becoming increasingly persistent in demanding zero-commission deals.

"I really feel strongly that we ought to try to come up with a new seller's commission so consigners actually pay for all the services we give them," Brooks said.[7]

"I agree," Davidge replied, "but it will only work if we make it non-negotiable."

Brooks agreed. "It would be easier to change the buyer's premium," she observed. "But the vendor's commission is the way I think we should go."[8]

When it came to poaching experts, it was decided, they would no longer attempt to entice staff away from each other's companies. But they acknowledged that nothing could stop employees from approaching the rival firm directly if they wanted to.

Next, they discussed the fact that a handful of big clients who bought at both Christie's and Sotheby's routinely failed to pay on a timely basis for goods they purchased. It was a tricky issue because both companies had allowed the situation to drift for years. The two CEOs agreed to work closely together to identify the most difficult and unreliable clients who failed to pay their bills on time and put pressure on them to meet their financial obligations. If that failed, the two firms would make a pact to ban those clients from trading at either auction house until their invoices were paid in full.

Brooks pointed out that it would be futile to try to force one particularly canny international dealer based in Switzerland, into such an arrangement because he never paid his bills on time. "He just takes as much time as he chooses to take," Brooks observed later. "Expecting him ever to pay interest is impossible."[9]

Getting around to the subject of their chairmen, Davidge told Brooks he was appalled by the number of inaccuracies in the eleven-deal list that Taubman had passed on to Tennant. Brooks blamed Michael Ainslie as the likely source for the incorrect information and promised that with her appointment as CEO the situation would change. "Michael doesn't understand the business," she complained.[10] "But he's leaving Sotheby's, and I'm going to be in charge of the company. Alfred will be getting his information from me.[11]

"Alfred is an amazing man," she continued. "He's incredibly passionate about Sotheby's. But he's not involved in the day-to-day running of the business. He's prone to listening to gossip, and he sometimes has a hard time separating truth from fiction."[12]

After meeting with Brooks, Davidge took out a legal pad and jotted down a couple of pages of notes summarizing their conversation. He wanted to give Tennant a detailed report of the topics and conclusions he and Brooks had reached, and thought it wise to keep a record of their discussions in case of any unforeseen repercussions.

Brooks later remarked that Davidge never seemed to be taking notes when they met. "Once or twice, he had a lined piece of paper with three or four things written in pencil that he wanted to touch on," Brooks recalled, "but not notes or anything I would characterize as an agenda."[13]

Unlike Davidge, who kept extraordinarily detailed records of their secret meetings, Brooks rarely kept notes. Colleagues observed that Brooks had an extraordinary head for details and could usually recall specific pieces of information several years later.

"I never kept records," Brooks said. "I just wasn't a note taker."[14]

After her meeting with Davidge, Brooks recalled, she rang Taubman to tell him that she felt she was making progress. "We've actually agreed on a guarantee formula," she told him, "and we're working on pricing and all the other issues we agreed to take a look at."[15]

Davidge recalled that he also went to Anthony Tennant to report on the discussions. "The majority of the things I discussed with Dede can be phased in now," he told Christie's chairman. "But we can't do anything about making any changes to the vendor's commission straight away. But we can keep talking about it."

"I understand what you're saying," Tennant told Davidge. "But I'm disappointed."[16]

EARLY IN JANUARY 1994, Tennant mentioned to Davidge that he was planning a trip to New York and said he was planning to meet with Taubman at his office on Fifth Avenue. Were there any new developments, he asked, in the discussions with Mrs. Brooks? Davidge immediately gave her a call. They both agreed that it was a bad idea. A private meeting between the chairmen of Sotheby's and Christie's was liable to arouse the suspicion of Taubman's new assistant, Melinda Marcuse, who had previously worked at Christie's.

The bright, spirited Melinda—a tall, zany blonde—had been running Taubman's New York office since March 1993. She had assumed the responsibility of scheduling all his appointments and social engagements, which involved making sure that his pilots, his flight crew, chauffeurs, butlers, housekeepers and chefs were in the right place at the right time to do his bidding. She was completely unfazed by Tennant's meetings with Taubman, who told her that Christie's chairman was eager to discuss topics of mutual interest in the auction industry.

"Tony Tennant here," the Englishman said when he called Marcuse to make an appointment. "Might your boss have some time to see me?"[17]

All of their get-togethers were at Tennant's instigation. "We never called *him*," Marcuse told me. "He always called us, unless I was returning his call.[18]

Christie's chairman showed up at Taubman's baronial offices on the thirty-eighth floor of 712 Fifth Avenue in New York on January 12, 1994. Nestled behind Harry Winston, the jewellers, the building was one of the tycoon's largest construction projects. Tennant left after receiving the grand tour, having stayed for no more than thirty minutes. Taubman seemed mystified by his visit.

"I don't know why the hell he keeps coming back," he told Marcuse. "We talk about the same thing, and he doesn't get it done!"[19]

His constant refrain, he told her, was that Sotheby's and Christie's should avoid bad-mouthing each other in the press and avoid harping on market share. "I also encouraged him to get more involved with holding auctions in Paris," Taubman noted. "I think it's very important to the industry for foreign auction companies to be allowed to sell in France."[20]

"We should cooperate as an industry," he added. "Because we *are* the industry."[21]

SINCE LEARNING that she would soon be getting Michael Ainslie's job, Brooks had made no effort to conceal her feelings of contempt toward her soon-to-be ex-boss. By chipping away at Taubman's confidence in Ainslie, and using every opportunity to put him down, she had hastened the departure of the man who had stood in the way of her path to success.

Brooks had always inspired admiration and affection from many of the staff. But as she gained power, she was developing a reputation as a tyrant. No one doubted that Brooks cared deeply about Sotheby's. But her quick temper and controlling nature frequently made life irksome for those under her thumb. When Ainslie unofficially ceded control of Sotheby's Holdings to Brooks in January 1994, she wasted no time in getting rid of his loyal assistant, Christine Chauvin, who had observed that the relationship between Brooks and Ainslie was "always one of a certain combat."[22]

The abrupt firing came as a shock to Chauvin. Brooks had assured her of a secure future at Sotheby's after Ainslie's departure. "She offered me the moon, and then from one day to another it wasn't there anymore," Chauvin said, recalling her bewilderment. An elegant, dignified Frenchwoman who had begun her fourteen-year career at Sotheby's as the trusted right hand to Peter Wilson, Chauvin was determined to register her outrage at the upstart who had summarily fired her.

Shortly after being let go, she called Brooks' office to schedule a formal appointment. "I went back to see her," Chauvin recalled, "and I gave her a piece of my mind. I said, 'Number one, you don't handle people right.' She was flabbergasted that anyone would dare question her, but she apologized. She said, 'I'm sorry. I guess my hate for Michael was transposed to whoever was close to him.'"23

SIR ANTHONY TENNANT had the great misfortune of having to follow in the footsteps of his popular predecessor. "Peter Carrington charmed everyone, remembered everyone's name, even knew the names of the doormen," an art-world observer noted. "He made wonderful speeches, and people *adored* him."24

By contrast, a Christie's director recalled, "Tennant knew hardly anybody. He was a very cold, conceited person."25

With each new insult and put-down from Tennant, Davidge regretted that he had been largely responsible for recruiting him. "Tennant was about as inappropriate as a chairman of Christie's could be," Davidge lamented. Traditionally, Christie's chairmen were welcomed to the firm's offices worldwide as an excuse to invite local collectors and dealers to preview auction exhibitions and drum up business.

"Without exception, not one office invited him back," Davidge said.

"He was a complete disaster, and I cannot recall one single decision he made that contributed positively to Christie's."26

Part of the problem was that Tennant could spare an average of only half a day weekly to attend to Christie's business. His directorships of other boards and his duties as a senior advisor to Morgan Stanley kept him preoccupied with high-stakes deals that captured his interest and imagination far more than did Christie's. And as a mostly absent non-executive chairman, he had little to do with the running of the company.

"I had no authority over Davidge," Tennant recalled. "And I suppose I should never have taken the job on those terms. He did whatever he wanted to do, and didn't inform me. So I never participated in any single conversation about a client. Or a client's business. I was more of a flag carrier than anything else. And all the time I was there I had more important things to do."

There was one notable exception.

Early in 1994, Tennant received a call from Meshulam Riklis, an

Israeli-born American financier, who was in the midst of divorcing his young wife, Pia Zadora, the actress, singer and former *Penthouse* centre-fold who had starred so memorably in the movies *Butterfly* and *Santa Claus Conquers the Martians*. The corporate raider's financially troubled company, the McCrory Corp., was in the midst of bankruptcy proceedings, and he needed cash to pay a large divorce settlement.

Riklis told Tennant he was planning to sell twenty-two Impressionist, Modern and contemporary artworks from his collection, many of which were hanging at Pickfair, his mansion in Beverly Hills, which had been built for the silent-movie stars Douglas Fairbanks, Jr., and Mary Pickford.

Sotheby's had already made an attractive financial offer, Riklis explained, and had estimated the paintings to be worth roughly $30 million. But based on their friendship, he told Tennant, he was willing to consign the collection through Christie's if Tennant was prepared to match Sotheby's offer.

Excited at the prospect of winning his first big multimillion-dollar consignment for Christie's, Tennant urged his colleagues to accept Riklis' proposal. It was an error that would cost the firm dearly. Christopher Burge, the chairman of Christie's North America, was dismayed to learn that many of the pictures had already been offered privately to major collectors, and were not "fresh to the market." Christie's nevertheless accepted the consignment and set high estimates. Claude Monet's *The Red Boat* was listed in Christie's catalogue with a high estimate of $7 million; Picasso's *Seated Woman* was estimated at $5 million to $7 million; and Jackson Pollock's *Number 22* at $2 million to $3 million.

Riklis was also given a whopping $15 million advance and a zero-percent seller's commission deal. Christie's agreed to pay for all packing and shipping costs, customs duties and catalogue expenses. His pictures were also featured in a separate, single-owner catalogue—a rare honour usually offered only for collections of exceptional quality.

The Riklis deal was a debacle. Fourteen of the twenty-two works consigned by the financier were included in Christie's Impressionist and Modern sale in New York on May 10, 1994, with a presale estimate of $19 million to $25 million. When they came up for auction, however, only six of the paintings were sold, all under or within their presale estimates with a disappointing total of $6·5 million. A week later in the firm's contemporary sale, Pollock's *Number 22*, which was advertised as being worth as much as $3 million, sold for a mere $1·7 million.

"Tennant did the deal and we ended up losing over $12 million," Davidge recalled. "Of course, he blamed Burge."[27]

RIKLIS' PAINTINGS were not the only items to bomb at Christie's R that night. More than half of the artworks being offered failed to sell, including Paul Cézanne's *Still Life with Open Drawer*, which had been estimated at $4 million to $5 million, and Gino Severini's 1914 abstract depiction of a woman peering over a balcony, expected to bring $2·5 million to $3.5 million.

"One interpretation is the market has slipped further down," said Michael Findlay, head of Christie's Impressionist and Modern Art Department.[28] The last time that so many artworks had gone unsold, art world observers noted, was in 1981.

Sotheby's had an even worse sale the following night, when a Venetian landscape by Monet that was expected to fetch between $7 million and $8 million failed to sell. The following week, in its contemporary sale, Sotheby's was unable to find a buyer for Jasper Johns' *Highway*, a colourful abstract painting from 1959. Before the sale, experts had predicted it would fetch the highest price for a work by a living artist since Willem de Kooning's *Interchange*, which had sold for $11·5 million in 1989 at the height of the boom market.

Highway, a dazzling eruption of reds, pale blues and yellows, was expected to fetch $8 million. A large guarantee had been given to the consigners, Peter Brant, the newsprint manufacturer and owner of *Interview* magazine, and his wife, Sandy. Bids rose quickly from $5 million to $7·2 million, at which point Lucy Mitchell-Innes, the auctioneer, whispered, "Passed," provoking much nervous chatter among the audience.

The mood before the auction had been one of bubbly excitement because the quality of the art was nearly as high as it had been during the boom of 1989. After the sale, there was much hand-wringing about the slow recovery of the market. "It's a recovery where you go forward two or three steps and then take a step back," Dede Brooks told the Associated Press.[29]

Monet's Venetian landscape and *Highway* had been featured on the covers of Sotheby's Impressionist and contemporary catalogues, respectively. That neither sold was a bitter blow.

Christie's was doing no better. At the firm's contemporary sale, thirty-two of seventy-six works failed to sell. Art dealers blamed the disaster at Christie's on unrealistically high estimates that failed to take into account increasing pessimism about the world economy and rising interest rates.

The combined total for the major New York evening sales of contemporary, Impressionist and Modern art at Christie's and Sotheby's that season was $135 million, compared with $162 million the previous fall and $144 million a year earlier. And profits continued to dwindle.

AS CEO OF SOTHEBY'S HOLDINGS, Brooks had new responsibilities that included coordinating lobbying efforts with Christie's. She no longer felt shy about letting her colleagues know that she was in touch with Davidge on policy matters of mutual benefit to both companies. In June, Brooks was in London and putting on her coat to leave for the day when Susan Alexander, head of personnel for Sotheby's worldwide, popped into her office to say hello.

"What are you up to this evening?" Alexander asked.

"I'm going to meet Christopher Davidge of Christie's for a drink," Brooks replied.

"Why?" Alexander asked, astonished.

"Well, I just think it's a good idea for me to size up the competition and get a sense of who my opposite number is," Brooks said. "Michael Ainslie's problem was that he never had any personal sense of who he was competing with. I think this will be a good thing for the company."[30]

Alexander came away from their brief exchange marveling at further proof of Brooks' tenacity and fierce competitiveness.

"I thought they'd never met," she recalled.[31]

MORE THAN A YEAR had passed since Tennant and Taubman's momentous breakfast meeting on April 30, 1993, but almost none of the "agreements" that the Englishman had faithfully recorded on paper had been carried out. Competition between Sotheby's and Christie's was just as stiff as ever. Both firms were still fighting to win major consignments, offering to slash seller's commissions to zero and advancing every other conceivable financial inducement.

The abysmal results for the spring 1994 sales convinced the conspirators, however, that something must be done to boost profits. After meeting for cocktails with Davidge, Brooks felt it was time to enact some of the agreements they had been discussing since their dinner at the Stafford.

In Sotheby's London boardroom on June 22, Brooks announced that she and her senior colleagues had concluded that Sotheby's should no longer offer interest-free advances and that they should immediately abandon the practice of offering to make a donation to a charity of the consigner's choice in order to win business. She also stated that the firm would no longer offer introductory commissions in excess of 1 percent on zero-percent-seller's-commission deals, and no nonrefundable advances, unless in the form of a guarantee with a significant upside potential.

Brooks explained that this new positioning was likely to have a negative short-term impact, but that it was necessary for the company's long-term benefit. "With all these pressures on costs, we need to be especially sensitive to being paid for what we do," Brooks told the board.

"It doesn't make sense for us to pursue items irrespective of financial consequence."

"We may have to lose some market share to Christie's," she added, still giving no indication that she knew Davidge was planning to exact similar measures at the rival firm, "but at least we'll be more profitable."[32] If Sotheby's ceased making interest-free loans, she noted, the firm's earnings per share could increase by as much as two cents.

BROOKS AND DAVIDGE got together again at the end of the summer of 1994 to go over their options. 'We had a discussion about whether to increase the vendor's commission or the buyer's premium," Brooks recalled.[33] "Davidge was always of a mind that we should change the vendor's commission schedule that we already had, to a nonnegotiable commission. And I agreed with him, because philosophically I agreed that we were working on behalf of the sellers.

"On the other hand," she continued, "the buyer's premium was much easier to change. But Davidge was very concerned that if we increased the buyer's premium in London—which was an incredibly important market for both houses—the expected increase in the Value Added Tax would make the buyer's premium get as high as 20 percent. And he had a serious problem with that."[34]

"So, we had a philosophical conversation," she added, "and it looked like we were moving in the direction of the nonnegotiable vendor's commission.[35]

13

A Bolt of Lightening

EARLY IN JANUARY 1995 Lord Camoys approached Dede Brooks, she claimed, with what he thought was exciting news. He had run into his old friend Anthony Tennant, and the two men had agreed that it would be a splendid idea if they could sit down with Brooks and Davidge to discuss commission rates. Brooks made these inflammatory statements in court.

Sir Anthony Tennant, when asked for comment, described them later as "nonsense", however. He added, "I bumped into Camoys at our club, but we certainly didn't have any discussion of any meetings." (Lord Camoys has declined to be interviewed for this book.)

In court, Brooks professed to be horrified. The rendezvous Camoys was proposing was totally unnecessary because she already knew of Christie's intentions from Davidge. But what really concerned her was the danger of widening the small circle of players already privy to the conspiracy.

"Under no circumstance should we have such a meeting!" she claimed to have told Camoys flatly.[1]

Brooks recalled later, she then spoke with Christopher Davidge as well to convey her concern: "Could you tell Tennant please *not* talk to Camoys about us getting together?"[2]

Brooks had lobbied hard to persuade Sotheby's board to hire Lord Camoys, against the strong objections of some of her senior colleagues in New York. But within a few weeks of his arrival, Brooks realized that the choice had been a mistake.

"He was a thorn in everyone's side, including my own," Brooks admitted. "He drove me crazy, but I didn't have to deal with him very much."[3]

Camoys had been highly effective in the world of merchant banking, but he seemed to be having trouble adjusting to the auction business. "Tommy was a very successful and highly intelligent man," Henry Wyndham noted. "And to make the transition from that business to Sotheby's was a difficult one. We are a very quirky business," he added. "We're not dealing in widgets. Everything is an individual work of art.

"You're dealing with sophisticated experts," he continued. "Some of them have artistic temperaments but they're great people and very honourable and dedicated to their jobs, and their fields. I imagine it's rather different from dealing with merchant bankers."[4]

SIR ANTHONY TENNANT was not winning any popularity contests at Christie's, either.

Ever since the Riklis sale, there had been a growing consensus at Christie's that Sir Anthony's tenure as chairman was not a wild success. "Tennant was a terrible stuffed shirt—very pompous," Charlie Hindlip observed. "He's deaf, too, which is not his fault, poor chap. But he didn't get along with *anybody*."[7]

"Why on earth Chris wanted Tennant in the first place, I'll never know," Hindlip continued. "Tennant is like that old maxim—the only way you can become a member of a club is to get in before anyone knows who you are. That way, they don't blackball you."[8]

The traditional role of Christie's chairmen was to bring in business by exerting charm upon a vast network of personal contacts. Filling that job requirement seemed to be something of a challenge for the present incumbent. "The problem was, Tennant knew *nobody*," Hindlip lamented.[9]

Having borne the brunt of much of Tennant's ill humour and criticism, Davidge was delighted by the sniping behind the chairman's back. "It was being openly discussed internally and externally what a bad appointment it was," he recalled.[10] Encouraged by his colleagues, Davidge went to see Sir Chips Keswick of Hambros, Christie's bankers, to ask whether the firm was likely to suffer any problems with the City and with stockholders if Christie's decided not to extend Tennant's contract for another three years when it expired in the spring of 1996.

Keswick admitted that he had relied upon the endorsement of his own boss, Lord Hambro, who was a personal friend of Tennant, and upon the fact that Tennant had been recommended by Christie's venerable former chairman, Jo Floyd.

According to Davidge, Keswick promised to assist Davidge in thwarting Tennant's second term as chairman.

STEPHEN LASH had been feeling suspicious for months. By the third week of January 1995, the grey-haired, bespectacled head of Christie's Trusts and Estates Department was beginning to panic.

"I couldn't confirm categorically that I knew, but only that I detected some 'smoke' suggesting 'fire,'" Lash wrote to himself in a memo dated January 21, 1995."[11]

Lash recalled that his first inkling that Chris Davidge and Dede Brooks might be having inappropriate discussions was when he observed them together in Manila in August 1994. Accompanied by other executives and teams of experts from Sotheby's and Christie's, the two CEOs had been in town to meet with Philippine officials about the possibility of appraising and auctioning off millions of dollars of artwork and jewellery that had been left behind by President Ferdinand Marcos and his wife, Imelda, when they fled the country.*

With not much to go on in the way of evidence except his own nervous instincts, Lash feared that three of his colleagues on the trip to Manila—Patty Hambrecht, François Curiel and Christopher Burge—were aware of the two CEOs' shenanigans but were deliberately acting as if they knew nothing. In one of his jottings, he summed up the troika of Hambrecht, Curiel and Burge as "3 monkeys"—an apparent reference to the monkeys in the Japanese proverb who profess to Hear No Evil, See No Evil, and Speak No Evil.

Committing his thoughts to paper was a deeply ingrained habit

* To Lash's dismay Sotheby's, not Christie's, received the go-ahead to auction the Marcoses' spoils. But the Philippine authorities ultimately decided not to proceed with the sale.

for Lash. "He can't blow his nose without a memo," noted Phillips "Pete" Hathaway, who worked for Lash at Christie's in the late 1970s.[12] His January 21 memo was the first of more than three dozen pages of notes that the cautious executive would keep as a record of his fears that Christie's and Sotheby's CEOs were somehow violating American anti-trust laws.

A veteran of the auction world, Lash had developed an early taste for collecting while growing up in Boston. He was fascinated by steamships, and had bought his first painting of 1 he *Queen Mary* in 1967 for $35 from a junk shop in Alston, Massachusets. That purchase led him to collect three models of the *Queen Mary* and several of the *Normandie. By* the 1990s, he had accrued a prodigious array of steamship artefacts from the golden era of passenger liners, from 1890 to the mid-1950s. And he was the proud owner of more than two hundred transatlantic steamship models, paintings, posters and books.

Meticulous by nature, he kept detailed records of his collections. The tall, well-tailored Lash prided himself upon his ability to walk up and down Park and Fifth avenues and point to each grand duplex, triplex or penthouse apartment and recite the names of its multimillionaire occupants and their attorneys, and whether they were likely to consign their collection to Christie's—or, God forbid, Sotheby's— upon their death, divorce or bankruptcy.

"He can't tell you what's on the walls," a Christie's painting expert noted, tartly. "But he knows who they are and who their lawyer is."[13]

Lash's London colleagues were amused by the social capital Lash felt he had gained by marrying Wendy Lehman, a feisty, wisecracking New York heiress whose father had been adopted in infancy by Herbert H. Lehman, a scion of the great Jewish banking family that spawned Shearson Lehman American Express. Proud of the illustrious connection, Lash never tired of pointing out that his wife's grandfather had been governor of New York and had served in the U.S. Senate—details that he insisted should be included in his official Christie's bio.

"I've actually heard him say at parties, 'Hi, I'm Stephen Lash,

Wendy Lehman Lash's husband,'" Charlie Hindlip recalled, giggling.[14]

After detecting an unseemly familiarity between Davidge and Brooks in Manila, Lash had his suspicions further aroused in January 1995 during negotiations for two important estates: that of Jean Stralem, a New York philanthropist who had died the year before, and of Georgia Colin, the widow of Ralph Colin, a prominent New York lawyer who had founded the Art Dealers Association of America.

The news that Sotheby's had won Stralem was a bitter blow to Christie's, and to Stephen Lash in particular. "I think Christie's thought they could get both because of their relationship with Stralem," Brooks noted.[15]

Lash had barely participated the negotiations, but he suspected that the Stralem collection had wound up at Sotheby's due to some devilish pact between Brooks and Davidge. He decided to share his anti-trust suspicions with his friend Danny Davison, a former chairman of Christie's New York who was still on the board of Christie's International.

Davison instinctively felt that Davidge could not be trusted. "He was cagey, capable and energetic," he noted, "and I had a good deal of admiration for his abilities. But he was an evil fellow, there's no question about that."[16]

When Lash confided his suspicions, Davison suggested raising the matter with Lord Carrington, who had the authority to confront Davidge. If Lash's suspicions were true, Davison told him, he would feel obliged to resign from Christie's board. The two men agreed to reconvene over breakfast at the Stafford Hotel in London on January 23.

FOR LASH, the notion of the two rival CEOs having illicit communications was all the more disquieting since he happened to live in the same building as Brooks—an elegant Seventy-ninth Street co-op on Manhattan's Upper East Side.

Brooks realized that suspicion, might be aroused if Davidge was spotted entering or leaving her apartment. But she convinced herself that there was no real reason for concern. "It wasn't the ideal place," she said, "but it was no more risky than anywhere else. Eighty or ninety percent of what Christopher Davidge and I talked about was totally legitimate, and all our colleagues knew we were meeting about lobbying."[17]

Early in January 1995, Davidge and Brooks got together briefly at Brooks' apartment. He explained that he had asked Christie's finance department to calculate the likely financial windfall for Christie's and Sotheby's if both firms were to adopt the identical vendor's commissions the two had previously discussed, which involved a sliding scale from 10 percent to 2 percent for the most expensive lots.

According to his colleagues' calculations, Davidge explained, Christie's would probably gain a profit of between $12 million and $15 million during a full year of the new commissions, while Sotheby's, with its higher turnover, would be likely to gain $18 million.

After meeting with Davidge, Brooks recalled, she rang Alfred Taubman to give him the encouraging news that Christie's was planning to adopt a new scale of nonnegotiable vendor's commissions.

WHEN CHRISTIE'S BOARD met at King Street on January 23, 1995, David Tyler presented a review of the results for the previous year. Sales had increased by 13 percent in 1994, but profits were at a standstill, largely because of continued pressure on the vendor's commission.

The higher sales figures for 1994 reflected the salutary effect of three lots in particular: an Assyrian relief from the seventh century B.C. that had unexpectedly sold for $12·8 million, after lying ignored for decades in the snack bar at Canford School in Dorset;* the Leonardo Codex, which had sold in New York to Bill Gates for $30·8 million; and the Fabergé Imperial Winter Egg, which had fetched an astonishing $5·5 million at Christie's Geneva in November.

* The Assyrian relief was bought by Shinji Shumei Kai, a Japanese Buddhist group, which planned to transport it into the mountains of Shiga Prefecture.

Christie's performance was improving globally, Tyler noted, but the firm was still trailing Sotheby's with less than 45 percent of the U.S. market share.

Seizing the moment, Davidge officially proposed to raise Christie's revenues by introducing a new sliding scale of nonnegotiable vendor's commissions. To quell any doubts, he argued that the company could feel justified in adjusting its rates. Christie's fame continued to spread worldwide, but the firm was not being properly compensated for the extraordinary services it provided to sellers. It was time for Christie's to end the unprofitable practice of working for the vendor for nothing. He suggested that the company should take prompt action and announce the changes after the board's next meeting in March, to take effect on September 1 in time for the firm's fall sales.

Danny Davison warned the board that the firm should be careful about how it went about introducing a new set of commissions. "From personal experience," he told the board, "I can tell you that an American antitrust inquiry is a bloody nuisance. It takes up a great deal of executive time and a great deal of legal expense."[18]

Just as Davidge had predicted, the board expressed enthusiasm but asked for a more detailed, comprehensive proposal to be forwarded to them before the next meeting on March 7.

David Tyler and Peter Blythe quickly drew up financial estimates for the proposed changes and Michael Hockney, the marketing director, drafted a press announcement and a list of hypothetical potential questions and answers regarding the changes, which was to be distributed to all of Christie's offices worldwide.

"Obviously, a change in our vendor's commission raised a lot of questions about how they would be applied, why we were doing it and when they would come into force," Davidge recalled. "So I was anxious that the company would have the questions and our corporate responses if they spoke to clients or spoke to the press."[19]

Davidge had agreed to show Dede Brooks all the materials to make sure she was in agreement and he felt under enormous pressure to get everything ready in time for Christie's board meeting in March, where he hoped to persuade the firm's directors to agree to the new fixed commissions.

DEDE BROOKS had just returned to her office after an amusing lunch at Le Cirque with Jerry Zipkin, the acerbic New York socialite, when she received an urgent telephone call from Davidge.

"I need to see you right away," he told her, calling from London.

"I'm going to Detroit tomorrow," she replied, glancing at her calendar for Wednesday, February 8, 1995. "I don't see how I can meet with you."

"Can I see you early in the morning?" Davidge asked.[20] "I'll take the Concorde. Can you meet me at the airport?"

"If it's *that* important, I will," Brooks said.[21]

"He made such a huge deal of it," she remembered later.[22]

The following morning, after a late night celebrating her husband's birthday, Brooks drove to JFK to meet Davidge, who arrived on the Concorde at 9:25 A.M.

As they had agreed the day before, she picked up Christie's CEO in her dark green Lexus outside the British Airlines terminal. The furtive duo then headed for the short-term parking lot across the street, where they moved to the backseat of the car so Davidge could show her the top-secret documents he had brought with him.

Davidge pulled out a draft of the Christie's press release announcing a new, nonnegotiable vendor's commission that he planned to propose to Christie's directors.

"Do you have a problem with it?" he asked nervously.

"No," Brooks replied. "It looks good to me."[23]

The only surprise was that Christie's proposed price schedule made no accommodation for dealers, who traditionally received a lower, wholesale rate. Other than that, she assured him, Sotheby's would be able to match its rival's new rate structure. The change would have to be ratified by Sotheby's board, but she did not foresee a problem. "I'm sure there will be some changes," she said, "but nothing very significant."[24]

---

* Taubman later vehemently denied that Brooks had told him of her meeting with Davidge at JFK. "There was *no* communication regarding any of this," he told me.

Pleased with her response, Davidge showed Brooks the list of hypothetical questions and answers that had been drawn up with the intention of distributing them to Christie's offices around the world.

"I want you to see this, because it indicates how we're planning to present the commission change to our clients," Davidge told Brooks. "Let me know if you have any observations, or if you think there might be any difficulties with these questions and answers."[25]

Sitting in the back of Brooks' luxury car at JFK, Davidge and Brooks read aloud each of the written responses, which included one no-table gem:

Q: Isn't this the age-old tactic of trying to increase profits through price-fixing? Do you have any antitrust concerns?
A: We are instituting a new policy which we believe to be fair-er and more straightforward than in the past.

A stickler for detail might argue that the answer did not address the question. But the co-conspirators were satisfied with the Q&A. Davidge explained that he intended to present the changes to Christie's directors in time for the next board meeting, four weeks later.

After an hour, Brooks drove Davidge back to the British Airways terminal, where he caught the 12:30 P.M. Concorde flight back to London. When he returned to Christie's the following morning, Davidge explained his absence to colleagues by saying he had been at the dentist.

WHEN BROOKS ARRIVED in Michigan, she recalled, she alerted Taubman that she had met with Davidge and that Christie's was planning to announce its new pricing schedule in March. "I don't remember what his words were," she said later. "I think he was just pleased it was happening."[26]

The following morning, during a fifteen-minute break between the annual Audit and Compensation Committee meeting and the full board, eight of the firm's directors posed for a photo that was to be included in the company's 1994 annual report. In the picture,

Taubman sits in the centre, with a contented smile, while Dede sits
to his right with her head cocked to one side, grinning at the camera.

Brooks had plenty of reasons to feel jubilant. She was excited that
the wheels were finally in motion for a scheme that promised to
boost Sotheby's annual profits by as much as $18 million.
Furthermore, she had just received the delightful news from Max
Fisher that the Audit and Compensation Committee had decided
that morning to award her a generous 200,000 stock options, which
had an earnings potential of $3·5 million over a five-year period.

Brooks' spirits were buoyant even though she had received a
scolding from Fisher. The eighty-six-year-old Michigan oilman had
commended her on doing an excellent job, but had criticized her for
being "trigger-happy." Too often, he warned, she made important
decisions without consulting the board and tended to surround herself with "yes people," which compromised "bench strength."[27]

Brooks was not about to let Fisher's reprimand dampen her spirits. She took the board by surprise by delivering an impassioned spiel
in favour of introducing a new set of nonnegotiable vendor's commissions. "We'll hold fast, with no discounts—what we want is profits," Brooks told the board. "We'll compete on service, not on price.
If we lose consignments, we lose them. Let Christie's buy market
share, but it would be crazy for them to undercut us and beat their
own brains out."[28]

Brooks' new tack was a dramatic turnaround. She had always
advocated raising the buyer's premium in previous board meetings.
To explain her radical new position, Brooks noted that Sotheby's
was achieving woefully inadequate financial returns considering the
extraordinary level of service the firm was providing to its clients.
Raising the buyer's premium would be a mistake because of the
British government's threat to begin charging Value Added Tax on
top of it. A hike in the premium, she told the board, was likely to
inspire mutiny among buyers in Europe. Kevin Bousquette informed
the board that if they decided to go ahead with the change to the seller's commission Brooks was proposing, the earliest that such a rate
could be implemented would be September.

To Brooks' delight, her fellow directors agreed that there was a need to rationalize Sotheby's business in order to ensure that the firm was paid for its efforts for sellers. It was left that Brooks would meet with her top management team to produce a detailed study on the proposed change, and that she would report back at the next board meeting in April.

The plan was beginning to fall into place.

MICHAEL AINSLIE had been present at the board meeting but had opted out of the group photograph. After eleven years of involvement with Sotheby's, he had decided to step down officially from the board at the shareholders' annual meeting in June.

For all their fights behind closed doors, Ainslie had always held Taubman in high regard and he believed that their parting in 1994 had been amicable. But when the Taubmans threw a black-tie ball in Palm Beach on February 3 to celebrate Alfred's seventieth birthday and neglected to invite Ainslie and his wife, Suzanne, Sotheby's former CEO was chagrined. The abrupt fall from grace was especially poignant for the Ainslies, who had met at the party for Taubman's sixtieth.

Taubman's apparent lack of appreciation for his efforts left a stinging impression. "He had made six hundred million dollars on the back of my work," Ainslie said, "and we weren't invited to that big party. It was a very clear signal that he wanted nothing to do with us."[29]

In turning his back on Ainslie, Taubman had squarely placed his confidence in Dede Brooks, who could do no wrong in his eyes.

AFTER RETURNING to London from his airport rendezvous with Brooks, Davidge recalled, he told Tennant the good news that Brooks foresaw no problems in convincing her board to adopt a similar schedule. Tennant's response, he remembered, was:

"Finally, that is good, excellent. We now wait on Sotheby's."[30]

When Christie's board met at King Street on March 7, Davidge showed his fellow directors a blow-up slide of the press announcement he intended to unleash two days later. As expected, the board voted unanimously to adopt the new schedule. They also agreed that the firm would have to honour all existing contracts with sellers who had already been promised favourable commission rates for sales scheduled to take place after September 1, 1995, when the new rates went into effect.

At the same meeting, finance director David Tyler explained that Christie's had recently switched to an "undeviating policy" requiring an upside participation for all guarantees given by Christie's. The company directors were fully aware that the upside policy was one that Sotheby's had been exercising profitably for years. What nobody in the room knew except for Tennant and Davidge was that the decision for Christie's to follow Sotheby's long-established lead had been prompted by bullying from Alfred Taubman.

In light of the top-secret plans for the new pricing schedule, Davidge announced, Christie's staff should be instructed not to discuss the proposed new rates with anyone outside the company. Tennant seconded his suggestion, emphasizing that discretion was vital.

ON MARCH 9, Brooks was chairing a meeting of the International Executive Committee in London when her assistant burst into the room with a press release from Christie's headed "Christie's International PLC Announces Change in Auction Charges to Sellers." The new tariff came in the form of a two-page announcement accompanied by a chart outlining the new rates, with a sliding scale based on the hammer price.

"The purpose of this new policy," Davidge was quoted saying, "is to provide a clear, equitable and nonnegotiable scale of charges to our clients."[31]

Brooks was overjoyed. "I was thrilled," she admitted later. "I was delighted that it actually had happened."[32]

The news came like a bolt of lightning, and had an almost surreal quality. The agenda for Sotheby's Management Committee meeting included a discussion of Brooks' recent proposal to Sotheby's board about switching to a nonnegotiable vendor's commission.

"Everyone was astonished," Susan Alexander recalled. "The

coincidence of us meeting and having these issues part of our agenda—and recognizing that the people from Christie's must have had some kind of similar meeting within the last few days.... It was amazing."[33]

Her London colleagues were equally astonished.

"I was absolutely flabbergasted—couldn't believe it," Henry Wyndham recalled. "And Christie's terms were *nonnegotiable*. That was the key underlying factor."

Trying to digest the news, the group broke into a lively discussion of how Sotheby's should respond. "We were divided," Wyndham said. "A lot of people thought we should follow. My first reaction was not to bother. I was of the view that we should take advantage of the fact that we'd be more competitive. Then I got persuaded that it actually made more sense to follow. The general feeling was, after debating it, that it was much more sensible, bearing in mind that our vendor's commission was disappearing in the competition. So it seemed like the best thing to do."

Despite the bizarre timing, nobody suspected that Christie's new rates were the result of an illegal conspiracy.

"There was no inkling," Wyndham recalled. "Not an iota of an inkling."[34]

In casting their minds back to that pivotal meeting, Brooks' colleagues remembered that her face betrayed no sign of having any prior knowledge of Christie's announcement.

"There was nobody in that room who was more shocked than Dede," Bill Ruprecht recalled. "She asked everybody to go around the table and specifically speak to what they thought about this, and indicate what they felt about whether or not we should pursue a similar pricing strategy."[35]

In hindsight, Brooks' colleagues realized that there *was* something slightly unusual about Brooks' behaviour. Their CEO was usually opinionated, decisive and assertive. But on this occasion she seemed eager to solicit her fellow executives' views.

"That was the most bizarre thing of that meeting," Susan Alexander recalled. "At the time, I was naive enough to think that maybe Dede had finally realized the importance of letting other people express their opinions in meetings. I thought, 'Maybe she's turning over a new leaf."[36]

The Sotheby's managers noticed that the same old 10 percent commission rate would continue to apply for goods that sold for less than $100,000. But in New York, Christie's would continue to charge up to 20 percent for goods that sold below $7,500. Only property that sold for $5 million or more qualified for the lowest commission rate of 2 percent.

For sellers, the only saving grace of the new tariff was that it offered clients the reward of lower commission rates the more they consigned to Christie's within a calendar year. Under the new policy, each seller's commission rate would be calculated on the value of property he or she sold within twelve months, rather than the old consignment-by-consignment arrangement that still applied at Sotheby's. This novelty, which Davidge proudly referred to as a "volume discount feature," was likely to offer comfort only to the very rich.

Shortly after Christie's press release arrived at Sotheby's, a copy was faxed to Alfred Taubman's office on Fifth Avenue, where it arrived at about 4:30 A.M. New York time. Later that day, Brooks called her boss to make sure he had heard the good news.

"They did it!" she told Taubman. "Christie's actually came out with an announcement on their price increase!"

"Congratulations," he replied.[37]

14

Deception

GODFREY BARKER WAS ASLEEP in a hotel room at Brussels airport on March 9 when he was jolted awake by an early-morning telephone call from Chris Davidge. "I have some important news," Christie's CEO told the *Daily Telegraph* salesroom correspondent. "We've just announced a new schedule of seller's commissions, and I wanted you to be one of the first to know."[1]

Startled by this revelation, Barker fumbled for a pen as Davidge recited the new rates.

Like every other self-respecting art-world journalist, Barker was on his way to Maastricht for the annual art fair that drew thousands of prosperous Europeans and a smattering of wealthy Americans. As soon as Barker reached the press room in Maastricht, he telephoned Dede Brooks to ask about Sotheby's intentions.

"Are you going to be following Christie's new tariff?" Barker asked. "What new tariff?" Brooks replied, feigning surprise.[2]

Reading from his pad of paper, Barker gallantly spent fifteen minutes dictating Christie's new rates into the telephone, one by one. Brooks professed to be utterly astonished and told Barker that she thought it would probably take several weeks for Sotheby's to decide how to respond.

Brooks kept up a marvellous act of expressing amazement. When she received a call later that day from Alexandra Peers of the *Wall Street Journal*, she acted again as if she were hearing the news of Christie's press release for the very first time. (Five years later, the two journalists compared notes and realized that she had lied to them both.)

That Dede Brooks was able to avoid suspicion about her collusive talks with Chris Davidge is something of a miracle. Among her colleagues, Brooks was notorious for her inability to keep a secret. But on this occasion, Brooks knew that it was crucial to keep it to herself. Her career, her reputation and her company's future were at stake.

CHRISTIE'S NEW TARIFF of charges had been faxed to journalists all over the world, and there were reports in the world's leading newspapers the following day. Anthony Tennant, who was anxious to be seen to be the master of ceremonies in announcing the change, attempted to make the new rates sound as if Christie's was doing the buying public a favour. "The new structure offers vendors clarity and simplicity," he told the *Daily Telegraph*. "It is fair to clients and will benefit the company."[3] Many in the art world were stunned that it was Christie's—always the more traditional, cautious firm—that had shown some innovation.

"When we announced this nonnegotiable commission," a former Christie's expert recalled, "the thing that staggered us was that Christie's had announced it *first*. It was just unheard of! We *never* took the lead in anything."[4]

WHEN BROOKS RETURNED from London, she met briefly with Marjorie Stone, Sotheby's chief in-house counsel. Stone suggested bringing in Irving Sher, an antitrust lawyer from Weil, Gotshal, the firm's outside legal counsel, to meet with senior staff before Sotheby's made any changes to its own commission structure.

Brooks tried to distance herself from Weil, Gotshal's directives in order to avoid having to respond to any direct questions from the lawyers about her contact with Chris Davidge. "I remember being removed from the discussion as much as possible," she recalled.[5] By keeping the truth to herself, Brooks had already begun to mislead Sotheby's lawyers.

When the *New York Times* asked her to comment on how Sotheby's planned to respond, Brooks professed to be undecided. "We're still analyzing the matter," she told Carol Vogel of the *Times* a week after Christie's announcement, "and we will be doing some more work before making any recommendations to the board."[6]

Since returning to New York, Brooks had made a point of meeting individually with the head of each department at Sotheby's in order to canvass their opinions.

"How do you feel about Christie's changing its commissions?" she asked Pete Hathaway, the head of Sotheby's European Furniture Department in New York.

"God, Dede, I think it's incredibly greedy," Hathaway replied.

"But Pete, we could make so much money if we follow suit," she told him.[7]

Brooks also called in the business managers for each of the firm's five biggest departments and gave them the task of assessing what the financial impact would be if Sotheby's were to match Christie's new rates. After a week of painstaking financial analysis that required many late nights and considerable head scratching, they assembled for a meeting in Brooks' office to present her with figures they had been working on for seven days.

After listening to their submissions, Brooks flew into a rage. "How do you expect me to make a decision based on information like this?" she asked, screaming.[8]

Many art experts and executives who lacked Kevin Bousquette's grasp of the financial imperative for Sotheby's to follow earnestly believed that if the firm decided *not* to match Christie's new price structure, sellers would balk at Christie's new rates and bring all their business to Sotheby's.

Christie's announcement had come at a moment when both auction houses were busy collecting consignments for their fall sales. "Here at Sotheby's," an executive recalled, "we said, 'All we need to do is hold out for the next six months and we'll get every single consignment. Then we could capitulate at just a modestly different scale so there would be some distinction. And we'd still have a competitive edge.'"[9]

That strategy already seemed to be under way when it emerged that Sotheby's had won a major jewellery consignment by delaying its response to Christie's new rates. The collection belonged to a member of the secretive Alghanim family, one of the wealthiest and most powerful dynasties in Kuwait.

Dede Brooks and John Block, the head of Sotheby's Jewellery Department, had secured the plum consignment by promising the family a zero-percent seller's commission for a sale that was scheduled to take place that fall.* Sotheby's had scored a tactical advantage. Having already announced its new nonnegotiable minimum of 2 percent, Christie's was unable to match Sotheby's offer. "Christie's made an effort to get it away from us," an employee recalled, "but Dede and John convinced the consigner."[10]

Sotheby's also offered the family a single-owner catalogue, which was designed with a white cover graced with a diamond fringe necklace. The top lot was an enormous, 6·7-carat, heart-shaped deep-blue diamond that was expected to fetch as much as $3 million.

Christopher Davidge was furious when he learned that Sotheby's had won the Alghanim consignment because of the delay in matching Christie's new nonnegotiable rates. He began to fear that Brooks was double-crossing him.

AT ELEVEN O'CLOCK on Wednesday morning, March 29, Sotheby's board participated in a conference call to discuss the firm's revenue strategy in light of Christie's announcement.

"From looking at Christie's results," Brooks told the board, "you can see that they had to change their pricing. And it certainly appears that Sotheby's *has* to do likewise."[11]

An ideal solution, she suggested, would be for Sotheby's to follow the scheme recently announced by Christie's—perhaps exactly—although Sotheby's still needed to decide whether it wanted to match the annual aggregation aspect of the rival firm's new structure.

After an hour of discussion, Sotheby's board voted unanimously to make the firm's commission structure identical to the one proposed by Christie's, with a few final details to be discussed and approved by the board's executive committee, which was composed

---

* The consignment, Magnificent Jewellery from a Private Collection, sold at Sotheby's New York for $9,249,025 on October 25, 1995.

of Brooks, Taubman and Max Fisher. Brooks had delivered a bravura performance, and everything seemed to be working out nicely.

Before making any public announcement, Brooks called Davidge to alert him that Sotheby's was indeed planning to go ahead with matching Christie's rates, with minor changes.

On the morning of Thursday, April 13, 1995, Sotheby's announced its own new seller's commission rates, which were strikingly similar to Christie's with a few cosmetic exceptions. Christie's new rates were effective as of September 1, 1995; Sotheby's were to become effective on September 5.

Brooks' quote in the press release sounded as if Sotheby's alone had dreamed up the idea of changing vendor's commissions: "We have been reviewing our commission structure in response to the increased internationalization of our business and the sophisticated global marketing services expected by our sellers around the world," she said. "After careful consideration of the alternatives, as well as the increasingly competitive nature of our business, we have designed a new commission structure for sellers around the world. It recognizes our clients' past patronage and allows us to remain competitive in this challenging business environment."[12]

There was no mention in Sotheby's press release that its new rates were nonnegotiable, but when journalists called from all over the world to ask, they were told that this was indeed the case.

ELEVEN DAYS after Sotheby's reciprocal announcement, Anthony Tennant and Tommy Camoys ran into each other during a lunch at Spink, a prestigious dealership in coins, medals and Oriental art with premises next door to Christie's, which the auction house had acquired at Davidge's instigation in 1993.

Over lunch, the two men discussed their respective firms' recent pricing announcements. Camoys voiced his concern that now, in the absence of competition on pricing, both firms would be forced to inflate their estimates on works of art in order to win business—a dangerous practice that could lead to unrealistic expectations, high reserves and many unsold lots.

Camoys confided that Sotheby's board had unanimously agreed

that the firm should adopt Christie's new rates, and that Sotheby's would have gone first if Christie's had not. He told Tennant that some Sotheby's board members were worried that if they did match Christie's rates, Sotheby's might be accused of collusion and that an inquiry by the U.S. Justice Department could tie up a lot of senior management's time.

The deputy chairman also observed that Sotheby's American directors were concerned about market share, despite their protestations to the contrary. "Maybe we shouldn't both chase the same big stuff every time," Tennant wrote—a notation that would create a considerable scandal when it came to light.[13]

TWO WEEKS after Sotheby's published its new rates, Christie's revised its pricing schedule on April 30 to match Sotheby's lower rate for museums.

Already exultant over their victory in successfully introducing the new rates, Davidge and Tennant were delighted when Christie's board approved enormous pay increases for its CEO and chairman on May 11, two months after the announcement of the new fixed rates. Davidge received a giant raise of 39 percent, sending his annual salary soaring to £317,000 ($500,000), a boon that gave him an extra £1,700 a week.

Tennant's more modest compensation went up by 35 percent to £108,000 ($170,000), a sum that was £38,000 ($60,000) more than his esteemed predecessor, Lord Carrington, had been earning in 1993.

Newspaper reports of Davidge's and Tennant's giant pay raises prompted Nigel Griffiths, the shadow consumer affairs minister in the House of Commons, to complain that this was "another case of bosses producing second-division results being paid premier-league salaries."[14]

WHEN BROOKS and Davidge met again at her flat in Three Kings Yard on June 28, 1995, Davidge proposed that Christie's and Sotheby's should impose a new policy of refusing to grant the usual concessions made to big-league sellers such as waiving expenses for catalogue illustrations, shipping and insurance charges.

"I think that would be a really bad mistake," Brooks told him. "I can't agree to that."[15] She explained that she was leaving it up to the managing directors of the U.S. and European divisions of Sotheby's to decide how they wanted to handle concessions. "I don't think we should take away the right of negotiating expenses from the art specialists," Brooks said. "We're already taking away their ability to negotiate commissions."[16]

"One of the reasons that people like working at Sotheby's," she added, "is that they have some autonomy, with the ability to negotiate, which for a lot of them is a fun part of their job. My feeling is that you don't want to make it so they don't have any ability to make decisions themselves."[17]

After returning to New York, Brooks compiled a detailed three-page memo to Sotheby's worldwide staff explaining how the new rates would apply to Sotheby's transactions beginning in September. These new rates, she told them, were *minimum* commissions that could not be waived or reduced. To reassure Davidge that this was indeed Sotheby's new policy, Brooks faxed a draft copy of her memo to her co-conspirator. He added the fax—which showed it had been sent from Sotheby's executive office in New York on the morning of July 13, 1995—to the burgeoning pile of potentially incriminating documents he was keeping under lock and key.

SINCE ANNOUNCING SOTHEBY'S NEW RATES, Brooks had been asking her senior colleagues to compile "grandfather" lists of clients who had preexisting deals with Sotheby's for sales occurring after September 5, 1995. Such deals would have to remain unaffected by the new pricing change.

In late July, Brooks and Davidge met at her London fiat, this time to exchange their respective firms' top-secret grandfather lists. Sotheby's eight pages included the estates of Jerry Zipkin, the Manhattan socialite, whose estate sale was scheduled for December 1995; the Comte de Paris, whose furniture, paintings and jewellery were to be sold in Monaco in December; and Seema Boesky, the former wife of the disgraced financier Ivan F. Boesky, who was planning to sell Impressionist works from her collection.

After handing over Christie's lists, Davidge pressed a plain sealed envelope into Brooks' hand, explaining that it contained information about a highly confidential deal at Christie's which he could not reveal to her at the time for political reasons. He also assured her that the name of Christie's mystery client would become apparent a few months later.

Brooks promised not to open the mysterious envelope.

CHARLIE HINDLIP was already aware that Davidge and Brooks were meeting frequently, but he was shocked when he learned that the CEO was exchanging grandfather lists with Sotheby's.

"There were moments when Davidge fell into terrible rages because of the things he said Dede had done or had been indiscreet with," Lord Hindlip recalled, "which led one to believe pretty clearly that some in-depth conversations were taking place."[18] Even so, Hindlip recalled, Davidge was never specific about where, when and what he was discussing with Brooks.

Frequent meetings were one thing. But discussing individual client deals with the competition? The very idea made Hindlip furious. "All it told me was that Davidge had been damned indiscreet," he recalled. "I think it's *incredibly* dangerous to discuss the intimate details of your deals with a client, with the chief executive of the opposite auction house."[19]

The notion of exchanging lists, Hindlip observed, was "another of the stupidities of the Great Davidge Plot."[20]

A FEW DAYS after meeting in secret with Christopher Davidge to exchange confidential documents, Dede Brooks fired a popular employee at Sotheby's because her husband had taken a job with Christie's.

Laura Whitman, a bright, dedicated twenty-nine-year-old cataloguer in Chinese Painting, had all of the talent and potential to become a top expert in her field. Her new husband was Paul Prevost, a thirty-one-year-old expert in American Furniture.

Brooks told Whitman that Sotheby's wished the newlyweds well, but explained that her husband's new job would put them both in an untenable position. As a business-getter at Christie's, Prevost would be privy to confidential information including negotiations with clients, meetings with lawyers for estates and secret reserve prices. Whitman's job also gave her privileged access to all kinds of information that Christie's would love to get their hands on. How could the newlyweds possibly navigate the conflict of interest?

"I just think this is an impossible situation," Brooks told Whitman's bereaved colleagues. "It's not an effort to hurt anybody. But you've got to understand that this is a business where the privacy of information about what we're doing is so critical."[21] It was advice she had neglected to dispense to herself.

DEDE BROOKS had been exactly right when she told Christopher Davidge that Sotheby's experts were frustrated over the new virtually identical vendor's commissions offered by the two firms. Their frustration was exacerbated by the fact that they were now expected to hand over much of the negotiation process for big deals to the suits upstairs.

"A lot of people were really upset, and I was one of them," recalled Pete Hathaway, who was director of Sotheby's European Furniture department in New York. "Suddenly, if a consignment was worth over a hundred thousand dollars you had to get help from the executive floor. The clients were often friends of yours whom you'd known for twenty years, and suddenly you had to report it. We did what we were told, but it felt like a slap in the face."[22]

Brooks increasingly began to insert herself into the deal-making process in the firm's most high-profile areas, starting with Impressionist Paintings and later in Contemporary. Her urge to exert control over all of Sotheby's big deals was another manifestation of her competitive nature. In her early days at the company, Brooks had been a compassion-ate, sensitive boss who enjoyed helping experts win deals. She was uniquely gifted at teaching them the art of the deal, and helping them to consider all of the financial vehicles and negotiating tactics available to them. But as she had grown more powerful, Brooks wanted to run every aspect of Sotheby's, which included competing with the firm's own experts to win business.

"Dede's main criticism of Michael Ainslie as CEO was that he never did any business development and didn't bring in big deals," Susan Alexander recalled, "so when she became CEO she wanted very much to do both sides of things."[23]

Consequently, Alexander noted, "the experts felt extremely usurped by her."[24]

Christopher Davidge enjoyed manipulating events in the background, allowing experts and superb auctioneers like Charlie Hindlip, Christopher Burge and François Curiel to receive the glory. But Brooks wanted to be seen to be a public personality and a visible deal maker.

"This is a business that gives you access to wealth and power unlike almost any in existence," Bill Ruprecht observed. With the board's approval, Brooks had arranged a time-share arrangement for a private plane—a Gulfstream IV, like the one owned by Alfred Taubman. "Dede controlled access to the plane," another Sotheby's executive recalled. "In those go-go days, so many of our key clients were wandering around in private jets. And Dede's ability to navigate in that community was helped by having the plane."[25]

As Sotheby's global CEO, with a Gulfstream IV at her disposal, Brooks had the wherewithal to be a "player" in the league of Henry Kravis, Ron Perelman and Steve Wynn, the Las Vegas entrepreneur, who had a prodigious collection of Impressionist paintings. In the banter of high-stakes deal making, she was able to make exotic suggestions:

"Oh, you want to go play golf in Pebble Beach?" "You want me to fly the picture out to Vegas, Steve?"

It was the language of high-stakes, glamorous, international deal making that Brooks excelled at. "In the Ping-Pong, in the dance of a deal, she's the most agile person I've ever met," Ruprecht noted.[26]

As Brooks increasingly dominated the negotiations with top clients, two of the firm's biggest business-getters, David Nash and Lucy Mitchell-Innes, a husband and wife who headed the Impressionist and Contemporary Departments, respectively, began to feel that in Brooks' mind they had become practically irrelevant to the deal-making process. To their horror, Brooks had begun sizing up pictures and spouting estimates to clients, without having any training or expertise in the fine arts.

"This drove the experts crazy," Susan Alexander recounted, "particularly Lucy and David."[27] As a world-class expert and business-getter, Nash was appalled by Brooks' desire to handle the negotiations for every major deal. "I enjoyed working with her until she essentially took over my job," David Nash said. "After that, I didn't enjoy it."[28]

"I hadn't *planned* on leaving," Mitchell-Innes recalled. "Basically there wasn't anything I could have done. Dede wanted David and me *out*."[29]

The announcement of Mitchell-Innes' departure was greeted with astonishment and anger by many of her colleagues, who squarely blamed Brooks for the departure of one of the art world's most luminous and talented players. "If Dede's relationship with Lucy and David had not been so fraught by that point, I believe that Lucy would have been willing to try to figure out another solution," Susan Alexander observed.[30]

"Dede had so eroded their level of trust in her," she added.[31]

Brooks was blamed for what many saw as a catastrophic piece of mismanagement.

"I don't think she had any understanding of the chain of events she created," Bill Ruprecht noted. "She didn't particularly think that those bad things that happened had anything to do with what she precipitated."[32]

15

Remarkable Improvements

ON SEPTEMBER 1, 1995—the same day that Christie's new commissions officially went into effect—the firm's highly effective general counsel in New York, Patty Hambrecht, was promoted to the position of managing director of Christie's North and South America.

Hambrecht's appointment stunned many in the art world. The decision to promote her had been made by Davidge, who was greatly enamoured of the glamorous, attractive lawyer. He was eager to change Christie's stuffy, male-dominated British image, and relished the prospect of pitting Hambrecht against Dede Brooks.

As Sotheby's worldwide CEO, Brooks was already ahead in the game, but the two successful female executive executives had much in common. Both were in their mid-forties and had graduated from Yale. They also both had strong financial backgrounds—Brooks at Citibank, Hambrecht as a litigator and mergers-and-acquisitions attorney at the Wall Street law firm Hughes Hubbard & Reed. Both were also married to successful bankers.

Auction-goers who previously had no knowledge of Hambrecht's existence started to pay attention when the petite dynamo was seen bidding on behalf of Microsoft chairman Bill Gates, the richest man in the world, when he paid $30.8 million for the Leonardo Codex at Christie's in December 1994. Hambrecht had made the connection with Gates through a friend at Hughes Hubbard, and the result had been a major coup for Christie's.

Exceedingly bright and soignée, Patty Hambrecht was known for her mordant wit and low tolerance for fools. "When people ask why I got into the auction business, I like to say, 'It's in my blood.'" she said. "My parents were antiques dealers in New Orleans; my mother ran the estate part of the business, and my father, the furniture. I went to my first auction in London in 1959; it was at Christie's, and I was six years old."[1]

Davidge and Hambrecht enjoyed each other's company and occasionally attended the ballet together. Many of their colleagues interpreted their closeness as a passionate office romance.

"They had a very flirtatious relationship," recalled Todd Merrill, a former Christie's PR director, "and she was his absolute favourite." Hambrecht, he recalled admiringly, was "the most dramatic, flamboyant, best-dressed woman at either Christie's or Sotheby's. The woman was *decked* with jewellery—amethysts, turquoise and diamonds. On a daily basis, she would walk into Christie's in a Givenchy suit, with four-inch-long rocks dropping to her shoulders, and carry it off. She was always just off to Cap Ferrat for the weekend, living the auction-house life to the hilt. She added colour and style at Christie's, where a lot of people wore the same shirt and suit every day."[2]

Not everybody welcomed the dynamic duo of Davidge and Hambrecht. "They were very small and yapped a lot," a Christie's director noted.[3]

With her personal style and flair, Hambrecht was an effective ambassador for the company. "It's a profession that values beauty and customer service," she told *Town & Country* in an article that compared Hambrecht and Brooks. "As a woman who has run a household, I'm concerned with how I look and how my house looks. I can speak knowledgeably about what good customer service is. The business tends to play to a woman's strengths."[4]

Christie's experts were taken aback by Hambrecht's penchant for conducting brisk meetings while attending to her beauty rituals. Fernando Gutierrez, the head of the Latin America department, recalled that during his sessions with Christie's glamorous managing director she was invariably "brushing her hair, putting on lipstick or mascara, putting on her shoes and running down to the elevator to catch a limo.

"That's Patty as an administrator," he added wryly.[5]

TAUBMAN CALLED BROOKS sounding angry in September 1995 when Christie's announced it was planning to sell jewels from the magnificent collection of Princess Salimah Aga Khan at an auction to be held in Geneva on November 13. Brooks shared his dismay.

"We were extremely upset that Christie's had gotten this deal because it was an incredibly important jewellery collection," she recalled. The fact that Taubman knew the princess, she added, "made it even more painful that she had given her collection to Christie's."[6]

Brooks doubted that Christie's was planning to charge the princess a seller's commission, but she did not recall seeing any reference to the princess' sale on the grandfather lists Davidge had given her in July. She guessed that this deal must be the one that Davidge was referring to when he passed her a sealed envelope in July.

"Well, why don't you open it?" Taubman asked.

"No, I gave my word that I wouldn't," Brooks replied, piously.[7]

Unable to resist the temptation, she opened the envelope and found a piece of paper on which Davidge had written the letters S.A.K., clearly a reference to Sally Aga Khan. The former British fashion model had recently obtained a divorce from her husband of twenty-five years, Prince Karim Aga Khan, the Geneva-based spiritual leader of Ismaili Muslims.

The beautiful princess, the former Sally Croker-Poole, was said to have gained $85 million from her divorce from the British-born Karim—K to his friends—who was one of the world's richest men. They had married with great fanfare in Paris, with Princess Margaret as the guest of honour, but had mostly lived apart for nearly two decades. Sally still lived in a magnificent $25 million house in Geneva and had recently bought a $3.8 million luxury flat overlooking Hyde Park in London. She planned to sell 261 items from her vast collection of jewels against the will of the Aga Khan, who had instigated a legal battle to prevent her from selling the jewels.

"The negotiations at that time were very sensitive," Davidge recalled, "and I didn't want to let Sotheby's know there was a chance of a sale."[8] In an unusual arrangement, the princess had also signed an exclusivity contract with Christie's, which prevented her from selling through any other auction house until 1999, on the understanding that Christie's would not charge her any seller's commission.

Friends of Princess Salimah were startled to learn that the princess had consigned her jewels to Christie's rather than Sotheby's, which had been courting her assiduously for years. Alfred and Judy Taubman had been friendly with the princess for more than twenty years. And the princess' closest and most loyal friend in Geneva was Ines Franck-Schwarzenbach, a woman from one of Switzerland's finest families, who worked at Sotheby's.

Franck-Schwarzenbach had been hired by the auction house in 1979 on the strength of her social network. "Ines had very good connections in Geneva," a former colleague noted. "But her most important connection was Sally Aga Khan, because they had been friends for years."[9]

The gossip in Geneva and London was that the Khans' divorce had brought the fifty-six-year-old princess under the control of an advisor, who was said to have persuaded Sally to relinquish her old friends and her past. He was said to be screening all of her calls and contacts with the outside world. And it was believed that Sally was so eager to satisfy his every whim that she had agreed to sell her jewels through Christie's, even through they had already been promised to Sotheby's through Ines.

Franck-Schwarzenbach was stunned to receive a formal letter from her lawyer in September demanding the return of any items of Sally's jewellery, without any explanation. It was a sad conclusion to more than twenty years of friendship, and many in polite society in Geneva came rallying to Ines' defence.

After the princess' collection slipped through her fingers, Franck-Schwarzenbach was fired by Simon de Pury, the chairman of Sotheby's Europe.

"Ines was quite shocked," a former colleague recalled, "because she had a good relationship and they were sharing the same office in

Geneva."[10] Competition between Sotheby's and Christie's was hardly dead.

IN JULY 1995, Sotheby's announced a tremendous coup. The firm was given the go-ahead to auction a spectacular collection of paintings

from the estate of Joseph H. Hazen, a philanthropist, film producer and attorney, who had been married to the heiress Lita Annenberg Hazen. The collection was estimated to be worth more than $30 million and was expected to be the cornerstone of its fall sales in November.

Hazen had produced numerous movie classics, such as *Barefoot in the Park* and *Sony, Wrong Number*. His art collection included several dazzling pieces, including van Gogh's *Thicket,* a lush forest landscape that the penniless, unsaleable artist had painted one month before killing him-self in 1890. The picture was estimated to sell for about $10 million. Other masterpieces in the collection included Léger's *Pipe,* a large Cubist canvas from 1918 inspired by the stylish metallic forms of early-twentieth-century weapons, which was estimated to fetch between $5 million and $7 million.

The *New York Times* reported that Christie's had competed for the collection and lost because Sotheby's had placed higher estimates on the pieces and had offered Hazen's heirs a larger guarantee. Sotheby's had also promised to showcase Hazen's collection with a splendid hardcover catalogue.

The star lot of the Hazen sale, and one of the highlights of the fall season at Sotheby's, was van Gogh's *Thicket,* which sold for $27 million; the total came to $51·8 million, giving Sotheby's a 2 percent profit on the seller's commission of $1·036 million, in addition to the buyer's premium of $5,175,000, for a total of $6·21 million.

It was certainly a more satisfactory result than during the bad old days of zero commissions.

WHILE SOME CLIENTS accepted Christie's and Sotheby's new rates without complaint, others were angry and even suspicious. Herbert Black, a Canadian multimillionaire scrap-metal dealer who owned a superb collection of English furniture and Impressionist paintings, contacted Christie's in the fall of 1995 about selling some works from his collections. He was told that he would have to pay a seller's commission of at least 2 percent in addition to charges for catalogue illustrations, insurance and transportation costs.

"It was the first time I went to deal with them that there was no flexibility," Black recalled. "I was surprised because in the past whenever I sold items both at Christie's and Sotheby's, I never paid a commission, never paid any insurance or any other miscellaneous expenses. And when I queried them on that, they said to me, 'Well, these are the current rates.'[11]

Dismayed, Black went to Sotheby's and spoke directly with Dede Brooks, who had been cultivating him for years as a major client. Black explained that he had recently built a palatial new home in Montreal to house his collection, and had decided to deaccession a few major pieces.

Brooks told him that Sotheby's would be delighted to handle the sale and explained that the company had a new set of commission rates on a sliding scale that were nonnegotiable.

"She said, 'Well, Herb, it's ten percent down to two percent,'" Black recalled, "and she actually quoted from the same hymn sheet as Christie's quoted from."

To finish the conversation, he recalled, "Dede grabbed me by the arm, looked me straight in the eye, and with a big smile said, 'And, Herb, you can't do better anywhere else.'"

"Her arrogance, and the laughter in my face, was rather embarrassing," Black recalled. "And it was obvious at that point that the two of them were colluding."

CHRISTOPHER DAVIDGE called Dede Brooks from the Lodge at Pebble Beach in California in November 1995 to discuss a series of deals for the upcoming spring 1996 season, including the negotiations for the estates of Joanne Toor Cummings, a New York philanthropist, and Lita Annenberg Hazen, a patron of scientific research and the sister of Walter H. Annenberg, one of the Metropolitan Museum of Art's biggest donors. Mrs. Hazen had died in October, a few days before works from the estate of her husband, Joseph Hazen, were auctioned at Sotheby's.

Davidge later claimed that his discussion with Brooks was part of An innocent effort to ensure that the two firms were not being lied to. "There was a recurring theme that clients and their lawyers would usually claim that either company were making more generous offers than in fact either company was," he noted. "This was potentially a major problem, so at the time Dede and I were anxious to establish mutual trust. Not to influence events."[12]

Shortly after Davidge's call to Brooks from Pebble Beach, Stephen Lash was apoplectic when Christopher Burge took him aside and asked him which estate consignment Christie's should prefer—Mrs. Hazen or Joanne Cummings? Without going into much further detail, Lash recalled, Burge explained that Davidge was seeking a "consensus."[13]

To Lash, the clear implication was that Brooks and Davidge were dividing up clients. As a trusts-and-estates expert who struggled on a daily basis to ensure that major business came to Christie's, not Sotheby's, he was mortified at the thought of the firms' two CEOs divvying up big estates on a one-for-me, one-for-you basis.

"I can't stand what seems to be going on," he whispered to Patty Hambrecht, as they huddled together in a corridor in Christie's offices on Park Avenue.

"Neither can I," she replied.

"There was no ambiguity as to what we were discussing," Lash wrote afterward in a secret memo, recording his distress.[14]

Hambrecht was also worried about the indiscreet relationship between Christie's and Sotheby's CEOs, and she decided to confront Davidge.

"As a Christie's lawyer, I must tell you that if my suspicions are correct, I must instruct you against any such actions which are illegal in the United States," she said, speaking in a stiff, formal tone to indicate that she was dead serious.

"As a friend," she added, "*please be careful*, and do not trust anyone—not least your colleagues."[15]

Davidge appreciated Hambrecht's discretion and friendly advice.

"Patty is a very intelligent lady who knows me very well," he confessed later. "Out of friendship and loyalty she did not put me on the spot with direct questions."

Even so, he noted, "I suspect she guessed what was going on."[16]

PRICE-FIXING, a rebounding economy and strong single-owner auctions had a marvellous effect on Sotheby's sales and profits for 1995. By the end of the year, the firm's auction sales had reached $1.67 billion: an increase of 25 percent over the $1.3 billion reported in 1994 and the fourth highest annual total in the firm's history.

Besides the fillip of the new vendor's commission—which had gone into effect in time for the firm's fall sales—profits were also up thanks in part to the wild success of the fifteen-day house sale of the Grand Ducal Collections of the House of Baden, the Donald and Jean Stralem Collection and the Joseph H. Hazen Collection.

"We've had the strongest year since 1990," Brooks told the *New York Times*.[17] Two of the most successful areas, she noted, were in sales of Impressionist and Modern art and jewellery. Sotheby's profits came to an encouraging $32.6 million, or 58 cents a share, a dramatic 61 percent gain from the previous year.

Sales were also up at Christie's, in the same areas. They had risen to $1.5 billion, a 17 percent increase over the $1.3 billion the firm had reported for 1994. Pretax profits rose 32 percent, from $27.5 million in 1994 to $36.3 million in 1995, and earnings per share increased to 13.5 cents per share, 36 percent up on the 9.93 cents achieved in 1994. In Christie's annual report for 1995, Sir Anthony Tennant noted that this remarkable improvement was largely the result of a 14 percent increase in auction sales and the higher revenue generated during the autumn sales "after the introduction of our new commission structure."[18]

Both auction houses had sold objects at higher prices than they had since the height of the market. "We sold 108 lots for $1 million or more this year," said David Tyler, Christie's commercial and finance director. "That's the most since 1990."[19]

With the art market already on a sharp incline, Davidge and Brooks were hopeful that a full year ahead of nonnegotiable sales commissions would do wonders for their two firms' profits. For all of their collusive conversations, the competitiveness between the two CEOs was as fierce as ever. The Englishman was content to convince Brooks that he was an ally, but he was plotting and scheming with all his might to achieve his goal of surpassing Sotheby's sales results in order to claim Sotheby's jealously guarded title of "the world's leading auction house."

To those already in on the conspiracy, Davidge bragged that his counterpart at Sotheby's, Dede Brooks, was scrambling to compete with him.

"I'm running her ragged," Davidge told Charlie Hindlip, who was aghast at what he deemed to be a vulgar expression.

"He probably read that in some corporate manual," Hindlip said with a shudder.[20]

16

First Lady

DANNY DAVISON was relaxing at his 1,200-acre farm in Norman Park, Georgia, on Sunday, January 14, 1996, when a telephone call disturbed his rustic idyll. A keen fly fisherman and an excellent shot, the former chairman of U.S. Trust and of Christie's, Inc., was in the midst of his annual two-week vacation shooting quail on his estate.

The call was from Stephen Lash, who had bad news to report. He felt he now had "strong reason" to believe that Christopher Davidge and Dede Brooks were having illegal discussions over the confidential terms the two houses were offering to their clients.

"I've seen enough smoke to suggest that there is fire," Lash told him.[1] Hearing the panic in his friend's voice, Davison cautioned him to protect his own career and to make certain that he had conclusive proof of antitrust activity before alerting anyone else to such serious allegations. Lash cited what he saw as a damning piece of evidence. In December 1995, Burge had told him that Sotheby's and Christie's were thinking of eliminating travelling exhibitions because they were proving to be costly and ineffective marketing tools. To Lash, it was clear that travelling exhibitions were yet another topic of inappropriate discussion between Davidge and Brooks.

"As far as I was concerned, this became the straw that broke the camel's back," he wrote, in a memo that he composed to remind himself of the details of his conversation with Davison. "It made me think that some smart consigner would now seek proposals from Christie's and Sotheby's and learn that neither house would then be offering travelling exhibitions."

"This, in conjunction with identical terms," he noted, "would smack of collusion."*[2]

After listening to more of Lash's concerns, Davison confided that he had attempted to raise the subject of antitrust with Tennant the previous year, and that Tennant had basically told him to "go away."[3] The chairman's brusque response, Davison told Lash, had alarmed him.

"This certainly squares with my impressions," Lash wrote afterward. "I can recall AT [Tennant] consistently referring to the need to have a quiet word with the competition in a way that appeared dead serious and committed." Such alarming comments, he observed, had "been made by Tennant over time in response to pressure on margins and the giveaway of seller's commission almost from the very day he joined Christie's."[4]

Lash told Davison that he had recently been in touch with Jim Hurlock, the chairman of White & Case, a distinguished international law firm, and he suggested setting up a conference call so the three men could discuss how to proceed next. In concluding their Sunday-morning conversation, Davison advised Lash to distance himself from such inflammatory antitrust matters since his career was at stake. As he was a retiree, Davison's was not. He offered to bring Lash's concerns to the attention of Peter Carrington. If necessary, he and Carrington could confront Davidge together.

In another secret memo after speaking with Davison, Lash fretted that he was playing with "dynamite." "If I play it wrong, I am finished," he wrote. "I am not an outside director. I am a whistle-blower."[5]

Two days later, on January 16, 1996, Davison assured Lash that he had taken the matter to the board and that everyone was on notice. He also warned Lash to stay out of it.

For Danny Davison, Lash's allegations presented a conundrum.

---

* After learning of Lash's allegation on this point, Brooks told me that she and Davidge had never made an agreement to eliminate travelling exhibitions. At issue was that Sotheby's clients who travelled to New York were often upset to learn that the pictures were out on the road. Consigners often demanded travelling exhibitions, however, and the practice was never stopped.

He had known Dede Brooks since she was a child, having been a school-mate of her mother, Mary Dwyer, at Green Vale. For the life of him, he could not understand why Brooks would do anything so patently stupid.

"Dede Brooks would be insane to do this," Davison told Lash. He added that he felt Lash was being somewhat paranoid.

"I just couldn't believe it," Davison recalled. "I thought it was possible that *lower* employees might have got involved, but I couldn't believe that these two bright people were doing this."[6]

Deeply concerned about what to do next, Lash met with Dan Pollack, a criminal defence lawyer, in his office at 114 West Forty-seventh Street on March 1, 1996. In preparation for the meeting, Lash had typed up a letter on his personal stationery to Christopher Davidge, leaving blank spaces for Brooks' name.

> March 1, 1996
> Dear Christopher,
>
> I am writing you, in strictest confidence, to register my concern about your communications with   Although, of course, I have no first-hand knowledge of those communications, I am troubled about the possibility that they may constitute collusive conduct, which is anti-competitive and possibly illegal.
>
> If your communications with   are, in fact, collusive, vis-à-vis our clients or potential clients, I urge, for your benefit, as well as for the sake of the Company, that they cease, without more. Any such conduct could have grave consequences for the Company, for you, and possibly even for the other directors.
>
> Sincerely yours, Stephen S. Lash.[7]

It was the perfect warning letter. But Lash, fearing for his job, and on advice of counsel, never sent it.

At the same time, Lash asked himself why Christie's directors in the U.K. shouldn't be required to sign a form saying that they had read the American antitrust laws. He believed that Lord Carrington, as an outside director, would be the best person to enforce such a rule. "It is hard to get this message across to Brits," he wrote, referring to the yawning divide between American and British understandings of the extreme severity of U.S. antitrust laws.[8]

DAVISON WAS DUE to step down from the board of Christie's International in May, and he was anxious to press the issue of Christie's antitrust policy before his departure. On March 5, 1996, he sent a fax on U.S. Trust Company stationery to Anthony Tennant, urging him to introduce the topic at the firm's upcoming board meeting:

> Dear Anthony,
>   I think it would be worthwhile at the meeting next week if we instruct management to circulate annually the antitrust memo which was drafted last year and sent to officers to sign. I believe it should have wider application than the U.S. offices, since U.S. law has application overseas (unfortunately) and in any event there are community laws on the subject.
>   This is particularly important in view of the fact that Christie's has such a high profile in the United States and for that matter the world. The fact that the board has paid attention to this thing should be very helpful in avoiding any future problems.
>   Sincerely, Danny[9]
>   cc: Richard Aydon
>   bcc: Stephen Lash

The relationship between Tennant and Davidge had never been particularly cordial, and now he suspected that the shrewd CEO was behind the effort to oust him as chairman.

Tennant had no real political power over Davidge, who reported directly to the board. But he had a way of expressing his displeasure that was guaranteed to make him squirm. Staff bonuses at Christmas were allocated according to a performance review by each employee's immediate superior, who in Davidge's case was Tennant.

Reviews were invariably based on a one-on-one meeting to discuss the strengths and weaknesses of each employee during the previous year, at which the individual would be informed how the points allocations would be made.

Davidge was furious when he learned that he had been awarded a piddling bonus, based on an unfavourable evaluation that Tennant had given of his job performance for 1995. He went to see Tennant to confront him and to complain that he had not been given the benefit of any discussion.

In defending his decision, Tennant explained that he was irked that Christie's had failed in 1995 in making strides toward its long-term objective of surpassing Sotheby's annual sales results by 1999. Sotheby's costs, he noted, had risen less sharply than Christie's, and its profits had risen dramatically, unlike Christie's. Sotheby's return on capital was much better, and its profit level was a staggering 75 percent above Christie's.

Davidge angrily pointed out that Dede Brooks' bonus compensation as CEO was calculated at 0.5 percent of Sotheby's profits. Tennant, however, argued that since Dede Brooks lived in New York the comparison was irrelevant.

After listening to Davidge's complaints, Tennant composed a note to the Human Resources Department summarizing their conversation. "We agreed that the increased vendor's commission had been a very significant achievement," he wrote, "but that I had played some part in this with him."[10] Afterward, he told Davidge that after reconsidering the matter, it had been decided that he should receive 43 bonus points, resulting in a $111,000 bonus. That amount, he explained, was roughly equivalent to 0.3 percent of the company's pretax profit of $36.6 million for 1995. In order to assuage Davidge's anger, Tennant assured him that his role was of great value at Christie's and noted that his continued commitment for the years ahead was "vital."[11]

WHILE PUTTING the finishing touches on Sotheby's annual report for 1995 in the last week of February 1996, Dede Brooks was called upon to sign an official document: The six-page letter was addressed to Deloitte & Touche, Sotheby's outside auditors, avowing that there had been no violations of any laws or regulations that should be considered for disclosure in the company's consolidated financial statements.

"There have been no irregularities," the text read, "involving management of employees who have significant roles in the internal control structure."[12]

By signing such a document for 1995—the year in which she had fixed prices with Christopher Davidge—Brooks was committing yet another federal offence. Curiously enough, Deloitte & Touche was the very same firm that had uncovered the financial irregularities perpetrated at JWP under the reign of Brooks' older brother, Andy Dwyer.

THE BLOCKBUSTER sale of items from the estate of Jacqueline Kennedy Onassis was perhaps the defining moment of Sotheby's glory in the late 1990s. It was certainly the event that catapulted Dede Brooks onto the world stage as a media celebrity.

"I think I should be an auctioneer," she told Al Taubman.

"Why?" he asked, clearly incredulous. "You've got plenty to do. You have a worldwide operation that needs managing, that needs it, wants it, cries for it. Why do you want to do this?"[13]

Brooks also canvassed her colleagues. Some were encouraging, others were not.

"She wanted to have complete control and complete power," Susan Alexander noted. "There was no stopping her. It was one more way to get her name and her picture out there."[14]

BROOKS LOVED conducting auctions, and several of her colleagues noticed that she seemed intoxicated with her success at the podium. The privilege of wielding the gavel for the nine sessions of the biggest sale in Sotheby's history had been awarded to the firm's seven finest auctioneers: Henry Wyndham, Bill Ruprecht, John Block, Lisa Hubbard, Simon de Pury, William Stahl and David Redden. And Brooks was scheduled to take two sales.

Exerting executive privilege, she made certain that she was

assigned to take the sales that were likely to have the most press coverage and greatest prestige. And she kicked off the bidding on April 23, 1996.

Lisa Hubbard, a seasoned expert who ran Sotheby's Jewellery Department in Hong Kong, flew especially to New York for the occasion at Brooks' request. A single mother, she brought along her young daughter for the exciting, once-in-a-lifetime experience of seeing her mommy wield the gavel for the sale of the former First Lady's costume-jewellery collection. Minutes before the sale, on the morning of Thursday, April 25, Hubbard's adrenaline was racing as she prepared to take the rostrum when suddenly Brooks walked over and informed her in a matter-of-fact fashion that she would be taking the auction instead.

"She told Lisa *right* before the session, with her daughter standing there," an indignant Sotheby's executive recalled. "And they'd flown from *Hong Kong* to do that!"[15]

Crestfallen, Hubbard and her daughter watched as Dede Brooks auctioned off all of the glamorous lots, including a triple strand of fake pearls, which had appeared in a famous 1962 photograph of a young John-John Kennedy in his mother's embrace, pulling one strand over her chin as she tossed back her head and smiled. After frenzied bidding, the faux baubles with an estimate of $700 sold to the Franklin Mint for a staggering $211,500.

Once all the major items had been sold, Brooks turned the auction over to Hubbard. "Lisa had to sit out the first hundred lots or so," an indignant Sotheby's staffer recalled. "She was essentially the relief pitcher."[16]

To Brooks' credit, the results were stunning. In the media frenzy that followed, she told reporters that the sale had set a world record for an auction exceeding its presale estimate: At $2.5 million, the sale's high estimate of $39,000 had been exceeded more than 60 times.

Newspapers and TV shows reported the outrageous prices on a daily basis: $48,000 for a lowly tape measure; $772,500 for President Kennedy's golf clubs; and a staggering $575,500 for his humidor. After four days of record-breaking sales, the Onassis auction had generated a whopping $34.5 million.

"It was the most extraordinary experience of my career," Brooks told *Town & Country,* "without any exception, without any question."[17]

The statistic Brooks was proudest of was the record sales of the 500-page catalogue, which had generated more than $4 million in gifts and profits for the Kennedy Foundation. "The most catalogues we'd ever sold before was 35,000," Brooks explained, "but for this sale we sold 115,000."

To achieve that dazzling result, Brooks had exerted merciless pressure upon a young staffer who had been assigned to oversee the catalogue sales.

"Dede would call him up at all hours—seven o'clock in the morning, two o'clock in the afternoon—to ask, 'How many copies have sold in the last two hours?'" a colleague recalled. "He was so thorough and diligent that he would sprint back and forth to her office with these spreadsheets so he could be absolutely accurate. And every time she'd see him, she'd just look at this piece of paper and crumple it up and throw it at him and say, 'That's bullshit! I know it's more than that!'"

"He became terrified and demoralized," the colleague recalled. "It was a hazing and a set of demands that were *not* manageable."[18]

Brooks already had a reputation for being tough. But in the preparations and aftermath of the Onassis sale, many of her colleagues observed that she was becoming thoroughly tyrannical. A senior executive recalled his astonishment at Brooks' cavalier behaviour after a team of staffers had worked hard to create a proposal for a major collection.

"We'd built this beautiful presentation of material," the executive recalled, "very elaborate, and people had been working in shifts for seventy hours straight to assemble the presentation materials for the deal." When he showed the proposal to Brooks twelve hours before it was due to be pitched to the client, the colleague recalled, she yelled, "This looks like shit!"

"I thought, 'Oh my God! How could she be doing this?'" the executive remembered. "It was beautiful and absolutely consistent with what we had discussed. I said, 'My God, I'm sorry you're not happy. Maybe we should change stuff.' And she said, 'Well, you should do that."

Twelve hours later, after thirty people had stayed up all night to ad-dress the various issues Brooks had criticized, the executive went back to his CEO with the material she had demanded.

"I just can't believe you did that," he told her.

"Too bad," she replied, offhandedly.

"It wasn't about the *product*," the executive noted. "It was about needing to undermine anybody's autonomous contribution. Not just mine, but the thirty people who had worked on it."[19]

Dede Brooks tended to present very different sides of personality to different divisions of the company.

"With the administrative side of the house, she would be much more violent and vocal in her criticisms," the executive said. "Dede really didn't want the art experts to see her dark side."

Lesser mortals found it hard to cope with Brooks' enormous energy, her demands and verbal abuse. "With some recreational zeal she would fuck with my head on occasion," a senior Sotheby's executive recalled. "She liked just to kick as hard as she could kick you, in order to keep you guessing, and to keep you off balance so she clearly had the upper hand."[20]

BY LATE 1995, Davidge had begun a campaign to unseat Anthony Tennant as chairman when his three-year term expired in May 1996, and it had the tacit approval of the majority of Christie's directors. The only problem was finding a suitable replacement. Lord Hindlip had all the international society contacts and charisma that Tennant had so notably lacked. But Hindlip, who had worked at Christie's for thirty-three years, was considered too quirky and irreverent for the job. As the May deadline loomed, however, he seemed the only solution.

"It was not my idea for Charlie to become chairman," Davidge grumbled regarding Hindlip's promotion. "I had to move Tennant on, and Charlie and his wife made it clear that he *had* to succeed Tennant."

Hindlip was one of the firm's star auctioneers, and one of its most prodigious business-getters. His appointment would certainly be popular with auction goers. Davidge feared that if he chose someone else for the role, Hindlip was likely to resign from Christie's in indignation, and his departure could be exploited by Tennant as an excuse to stay put. "I was between a rock and a hard place," Davidge recalled. "Lord Carrington said he could not support Charlie as chairman, as did Christopher Burge, Noël Annesley and Stephen Lash."[21]

Hambros, Christie's bankers, sought reassurances from Davidge that he would personally spend time with stockholders and their agents and not let Hindlip loose on any sensitive corporate issues. "If Chips Keswick had not been so convinced of Tennant's unsuitability for Christie's, I would not have got Charlie's appointment through," Davidge admitted. "Charlie was the lesser of two evils."[22]

Tennant's enforced departure as chairman was handled in typical gentlemanly fashion. "I have agreed to the request of my colleagues to remain on the board as a nonexecutive director," Tennant said in a statement, "to assume the chairmanship of both the Audit and the Remuneration Committees, and to continue to contribute to the development of our business strategy."[23]

Tennant was inheriting the Audit chairmanship from Danny Davison, who was due to relinquish his post as a nonexecutive director at the board meeting in May. Davison was anxious to use his limited amount of time left to compel Sir Anthony to bring up the subject of antitrust compliance at Christie's board meeting on May 20, the last one he would attend.

Davison advised Lash to drop the matter of the suspected collusion altogether and leave it in his hands. He was leaving the board and had nothing to lose by pushing the antitrust issue. On May 13, he faxed a letter to Tennant's office at Christie's in London, urging the soon-to-be ex-chairman to bring up compliance at the next meeting:

Dear Anthony,
    At the last meeting, I thought I understood that the subject of the antitrust memorandum would be brought up at the coming meeting. I'm anxious that a discussion of the memo be

put on the agenda for my last meeting. As you know, I am concerned about the problem because of our high profile in this country and the fact that there are so few real competitors. I think the problem can easily be handled in a routine way but I'm anxious to see that it is put into a routine before I depart. I appreciate your help.

Sincerely, Danny[24]

Davison sent a copy of the letter to Lash, who carefully filed it away.

DANNY DAVISON'S LETTER did the trick. When the board of Christie's International met at King Street on May 29, 1996, he and Stephen Lash were delighted to find the antitrust topic on the agenda.

The subject was addressed by Patty Hambrecht, and by Christie's in-house legal counsel Richard Aydon and Anthony Streatfeild. After some discussion, it was agreed that Christie's U.S. policy should be recirculated and signed annually, and that outside the United States an appropriately amended document should be circulated and signed.

Christopher Davidge proudly informed the board that Christie's higher profits reflected a "very substantial contribution from the new commission scale," and noted that Christie's percentage of lots sold was running at 82 percent, compared to 78 percent at Sotheby's.

When Charlie Hindlip officially succeeded Tennant at the end of the meeting, he politely thanked Sir Anthony for his contribution as chairman of the board over the past three years. Hindlip was acting like a gentleman.

17

Cheaply Framed

ONLY THREE WEEKS after Davidge had been bragging to Christie's directors about the marvellous positive effect of the new nonnegotiable commission rates upon profits, he and Dede Brooks received disturbing letters from the Office of Fair Trading announcing that "informal enquiries" were being made into possible anticompetitive practices in the auction business in violation of Britain's Fair Trading Act of 1973 and Competition Act of 1980.

"Concerns have been voiced to the Office," the letter noted, "that [the] United Kingdom's two principal Auction Houses, Sotheby's and Christie's, have set commission rates in identical terms, that previously dealers were able to negotiate the commission rates with both the Auction Houses."[1]

The letters, dated June 25, 1996, requested a reply by July 11.

Brooks referred the matter to Freshfields, Sotheby's outside counsel in London. When the topic of the O.F.T.'s inquiry was raised by Christie's board, Davidge dismissed the suggestion of impropriety as mere nonsense.

"Of *course* there was no collusion," he told his fellow directors.[2]

Like Brooks, Davidge tried to remain at arm's length from the investigation. Christie's official response was made by the firm's group financial director, David Tyler, who was sent off to meet with the O.F.T.

In preparing Sotheby's response to the allegations, Brooks participated in a transatlantic conference call with a couple of Freshfields lawyers lasting several hours in which she ridiculed the notion that any collusion had taken place. Confident that there was nothing to worry about, the prestigious British law firm submitted a twenty-five-page report on July 31 emphatically denying any wrongdoing on Sotheby's part: "Any changes in the vendors' commission rates," the letter stated, "have been a legitimate response to competitive pressures and changing conditions within the market."[3]

Brooks and Davidge nervously awaited the O.F.T.'s response.

AFTER ALL the excitement over the spring and summer sales had died down, Christie's finally got around to circulating copies of the firm's antitrust policy in order to ensure that every employee would understand American antitrust laws and realize the importance of complying with them.

The official document stated that "any type of agreement, understanding or arrangement between competitors—whether written or oral, formal or informal, express or implied—that limits competition is subject to antitrust scrutiny." Staff were told to strictly avoid any communications with a competitor regarding prices and pricing policies, terms or conditions of sale, profits, margins or costs and bidding for particular consignments.

Furthermore, Christie's employees were instructed to "immediately emphatically refuse" to discuss pricing with competitors and to "leave the meeting (or hang up the telephone)" if a competitor began discussing the subject.[4]

Among the signatories in the United States were Christopher Burge, Patty Hambrecht and Stephen Lash, all of whom had strong reasons to believe that these rules had already been violated by Davidge and Brooks.

DAVIDGE HAD added his signature to the list of executives who claimed to have read and understood Christie's antitrust policy, but he continued to meet with Sotheby's CEO. In December 1996, they got together to discuss the estate of Doris Duke, the reclusive tobacco heiress who had died in October 1993, aged eighty.

Ever since the heiress' mysterious death, Christie's and Sotheby's had been battling for the opportunity to auction off thousands of items from her vast collections. The negotiations had been delayed and complicated by an ongoing legal dispute for control of her estate, which one lawyer described as the "World Series of litigation."[5]

Determined to win the Duke consignment, Davidge went to see Brooks to try to persuade her that Sotheby's should back off from pursuing the business.

"We've already put a lot of money into this," he told her. "It's a grandfather deal for us, and we should be getting Duke."

"You need to understand something," Brooks replied. "I'm sure you've worked hard, but we're going to compete flat-out for it."

Davidge and Brooks also discussed the possibility that Sotheby's and Christie's might one day be able to hold auctions in France. "We had significant disagreement about Paris," Brooks recalled. "Sotheby's was in favour of the market opening, and Christie's was against it, so Davidge and I were in very different places on that subject."[6]

When Christopher Burge casually mentioned to Stephen Lash that Davidge and Brooks had met to talk about the "grandfathering of Duke," the nervous trust-and-estates executive was appalled to hear that the two CEOs were once again discussing the intimate details of a deal that both firms were pursuing.*[7]

BROOKS AND DAVIDGE had assiduously honoured their illegal pact to make commissions nonnegotiable since 1995. But now that the market had rebounded and major collections were up for grabs, Brooks succumbed to the temptation to renege on their deal.

Early in 1997, Davidge was dismayed to learn that Sotheby's had offered to waive its seller's commission in order to land a magnificent collection of Impressionist pictures from the estate of John Langeloth Loeb, the investment magnate who had headed Loeb Rhoades & Co., and his wife Frances Lehman Loeb, yet another wealthy relation of Wendy Lehman Lash, the well-connected wife of Stephen Lash.

The highlights of the collection included Cézanne's *Madame Cézanne au fauteuil jaune,* an austere portrait of his wife, Marie-

---

* The trustees of Doris Duke's estate ultimately shelved their auction plans.

Hortense, an oval-faced woman with an inscrutable gaze, who famously disliked her husband's paintings; Édouard Manet's magnificent *Self-Portrait,* with brush in hand; and a gorgeous Toulouse-Lautrec dancer.

Eager to win the collection, Sotheby's had agreed to give in to the Loebs' demands that they consent to drop the vendor's commission altogether. The sacrifice was enormous. Sotheby's estimated the Loeb collection to be worth $90 million, which in theory meant forgoing a desirable 2 percent commission of $1.8 million. Still, income from the buyer's premium could easily be well in excess of $10 million.*

Christie's reluctantly agreed to do the same. "As a result of Sotheby's offering zero, we offered zero," Davidge recalled. "The client told us that Sotheby's had decided to charge zero commission over any consignment in excess of $50 million."[8]

While making a presentation for the Loeb estate on February 24, 1997, Stephen Lash, Chris Davidge and Christopher Burge took a brief recess to discuss the deal in light of John Loeb, Jr.'s request that they find some way to embellish their financial offer. Lash felt confident that they could convince the Loeb heirs to select Christie's by promising to make a handsome donation to the Loeb family foundation. He was dismayed, however, when Christopher Burge told him that he had spoken privately to Davidge, who said that he and Dede Brooks had agreed that the two firms would no longer compete by making donations to foundations or charities to win specific consignments.

Alarmed by what seemed further proof of a conspiracy, Lash wrote himself a memo on February 24, noting that Davidge "had agreed with Dede Brooks that there would be no further donations to foundation/ charities."[9]

Later that day, Lash called Davidge from the New Haven train

* The Loebs' twenty-nine paintings were sold at Christie's in New York on May 12, 1997, for a total of $92.8 million, the second-largest total to date for a single-owner sale. Highlights included Cézanne's *Madame Cézanne au fauteuil jaune,* which sold for $23.1 million—the top price of the week. Édouard Manet's *Self-Portrait* went for $18.7 million, and the Toulouse-Lautrec dancer established a new auction record price for the artist at $14.5 million.

station to discuss the Loeb negotiations. They agreed that despite
Dede Brooks' promise not to make a charitable donation to win
business, Sotheby's was likely to offer to make a payment to the
Loeb Foundation in order to level the playing field. If Sotheby's
caved, they agreed, Christie's should do the same.

The carefully wrought agreements made between Brooks and
Davidge were beginning to unravel.

WHEN SOTHEBY'S and Christie's formally announced their
annual sales results for 1996 in February 1997, Christopher Davidge
was jubilant to report that Christie's had surpassed its longtime rival
for the first time since 1954 with $1.602 billion, compared with
Sotheby's $1.599 billion.

It was a trifling lead in financial terms—$21 million—but cause
for tremendous celebrations at Christie's. The firm's sales were up
by 9 percent from $1.47 billion, whereas Sotheby's 1996 sales figures
were down 5 percent from $1.67 billion in 1995.

"We did have a quiet glass of champagne," a British director of
Christie's recalled.[10]

Davidge observed that fixing seller's commissions was the best
possible device he could have engineered to Christie's benefit, and
to Sotheby's detriment.

"The culture among the experts at Sotheby's was far better suited to negotiating vendor commissions with clients," Davidge noted.
"They were overall very commercial and far more successful than
their counterparts at Christie's."

Christie's experts, he said, tended to be far more focused on scholarship. "As soon as there was any mention of reducing the vendor's
commission they had no confidence or skills to negotiate terms."[11]

"The fixed commission," he continued, "helped Christie's to
work to their strengths and took one of Sotheby's great strengths
away. Christie's market share improved immediately, and my goal
to be *equal* to Sotheby's became immediately attainable."

Many clients, he noted, began making decisions based on
expertise, often to Christie's advantage. "I do not believe anyone
understood this at the time," Davidge observed, "but Taubman's

jealously held market leadership was almost lost overnight."[12]

ALARM BELLS rang out at Sotheby's in February 1997 when a popular British news programme on Channel 4, aired an hour-long report alleging that the auction house was guilty of flaunting international smuggling laws. The programme had been masterminded by the British journalist Peter Watson, who showed film footage of Roeland Kollewijn, a Sotheby's expert in Milan, offering to smuggle an Old Master portrait by Giuseppe Nogari to London. Unbeknownst to anyone at Sotheby's, Kollewijn's technically illegal offer had been captured on tape by a hidden camera.

Watson's book, *Sotheby's: The Inside Story* described how the company had smuggled antiquities from India, Iran, Cambodia and the Mediterranean, along with other tales of alleged improper business practices.

Brooks was livid when she heard about the double threat of the TV programme and the book. She immediately flew to London and was at Sotheby's offices on New Bond Street until two A.M. planning an emergency strategy to respond to Watson's allegations. The following day, she met with British reporters to express her fury that Kollewijn, and Sotheby's, had been entrapped by Peter Watson.

"I'm more than angry, I'm outraged," she told the *Evening Standard*. "One person has used innuendo, speculation and put Sotheby's in a position where we are perceived as not taking our integrity and ethical standards seriously."[13]

"I'm calm because I'm a professional," she continued. "But I'm outraged. We had a choice: Let this thing defeat us, get angry, lash back. Or see in this an opportunity. It's an opportunity to demonstrate just how important our integrity is."

Faced with a potentially devastating problem, Brooks attempted to deflect adverse publicity from the smuggling scandal by launching a widely publicized independent review committee to look into the allegations in Watson's book. Headed by Max Fisher, the committee hired outside counsel to advise them. The mission of the review committee, Brooks explained, was to conduct an ethical inquiry into auction practices throughout the company.

"I take questions of ethics and integrity very seriously," Brooks declared. "I have lived my life that way. My name is all I have."[14]

JOHN J. GREENE, an Irish-born antitrust prosecutor with the United States Department of Justice in Manhattan, had been eyeing the world's two leading auction houses for the past few months with considerable interest after receiving a tip from a disgruntled source in the art world who was convinced that Sotheby's and Christie's had conspired to make their commission rates nonnegotiable.

Greene, a fifty-two-year-old Fordham Law graduate who had grown up in Cootehill in County Cavan before moving to the United States in 1964, was an unlikely foe for the glamorous world of the multimillion-dollar transactions, cocktail receptions and high-stakes auctions. His past courtroom triumphs included a 1991 conviction of Manischewitz, the Jersey City, New Jersey, baker accused of fixing the price on about $25 million of kosher-for-Passover matzo between 1981 and 1986.

Some who doubted his efficacy wryly referred to the federal prosecutor as "the Matzocutor."

But it was unwise to underestimate the formidable Mr. Greene. Extraordinarily persistent, he invariably won convictions. His steely resolve had been tested when he was wounded while serving as an infantry platoon leader in Vietnam, and he still walked with a slight limp from the shrapnel embedded in his knee.

Greene had received his tip on the auction-house matter while investigating dubious practices in the art world for eleven years. His original interest in the fine-art business had been spurred by a minor scandal over the sale of an unprepossessing wooden chest that was auctioned off at Christie's East, a lower-priced outpost of the firm's New York head-quarters on Park Avenue, in April 1986.

In examining the chest, a few antique dealers had been intrigued by a crucial detail that Christie's had failed to notice, which made it infinitely more valuable: The piece was etched with numbers on one side that indicated that it had once belonged to Mabel Brady Garvan, a celebrated collector who was a major benefactor of the Yale University Art Gallery.

Christie's had estimated that the chest would fetch between $1,200 and $1,800. Instead, it sold for $30,000. What subsequently sparked Greene's interest was that *a second*, private, auction took place minutes later in a van parked on New York's Upper East Side. The handful of participants were antique dealers who had made a pact not to bid against each other during Christie's auction. Among themselves, however, the bidding for the chest went up to $98,000. This secretive and highly illegal practice, known in the art world as "ring-bidding" or "knockouts," was the bane of the auction houses and of innocent sellers who wound up getting far less money than their objects were worth.

Greene had doggedly pursued the members of that cartel, and had won guilty pleas from three dealers who paid a grand total of $170,000 in criminal fines. Among those who pled guilty was a renowned furniture and art dealer, Bernard and S. Dean Levy, Inc., of Manhattan.

The Levys and their fellow conspirators were found to be in violation of the Sherman Antitrust Act, a law named after Senator John Sherman of Ohio, which was designed to outlaw any contract, scheme, deal or conspiracy to restrain trade. It was passed by the US Congress in 1890 in response to mounting outrage over the power of monopolists like John D. Rockefeller, whose Standard Oil Company controlled nearly 85 percent of all the crude oil refined in the United States.

Wielding the provisions of the Sherman Act, which carried severe penalties, John Greene had brought charges against three other antique dealers accused of similar violations in New Hampshire and Newport, Rhode Island.

Exposing rings was not easy, but sooner or later a disgruntled dealer who had failed to get the piece he was bidding for usually decided to come clean and rat on his fellow dealers in exchange for lenient treatment.

Greene declined to name the disaffected dealer who had supplied the tip regarding the auction houses, saying only that in pursuing convictions in the art world there was "an evidentiary trail from one to the other."[15]

John Greene's fiefdom was on the thirty-sixth floor at 26 Federal

208 LORDS AND LIARS

Plaza, a grim government building across from the cluster of court-houses in lower Manhattan. The government offices of the Antitrust Division were dry, humourless and uniformly beige. Etched in dull gold on glass double doors were the names of Ralph Giordano and his deputy, Phil Cody. Inside, formal posed photographs of President Bill Clinton and Attorney General Janet Reno hung on the walls, and a stiff arrangement of dried eucalyptus branches graced a side table.

In stark contrast to the executive offices of Christie's and Sotheby's, which were often hung with multimillion-dollar paint-ings, the only art on view was a lugubrious Bierstadt print of a canyon and lake, cheaply framed.

The office was humming with excitement at the prospect of pursu-ing a conviction against the world-famous auction houses. If success-ful, the investigation would be an enormous coup for the New York office of the Antitrust Division. It would also assure a promotion for the diligent John Greene. "We did have building suspicions that there were improper communications between these companies," Jim Griffin of the U.S. Department of Justice noted later. "There certain-ly appeared to be inappropriate discussions of pricing."[16]

DIANA PHILLIPS was sitting in her office at Sotheby's one morn-ing in early May when she received an urgent call from Kevin Bous-quette. As head of Sotheby's Press Department worldwide, Phillips was still handling the fallout of the *Dispatches* debacle, which she had described, rather optimistically, as the "scandal-to-end-all-scandals."

As she entered Bousquette's spacious, immaculately tidy office overlooking York Avenue, Phillips found the handsome blond chief operating officer sitting at his desk looking as white as a sheet, hold-ing an eleven-page document in his hand.

"We've been subpoenaed by the Justice Department on suspicions of colluding with Christie's on commissions," Bousquette told her.

Sotheby's sultry South African press officer burst into peals of laughter. "You've *got* to be kidding," she replied. "Nobody could be *that* stupid. Everybody knows we hate each other."

Phillips would later remember that moment of sidesplitting mirth with nostalgia.

"It was beyond my wildest dreams," she said later of the seemingly absurd news she heard that day. "This seemed completely beyond the realm of possibility."[17]

Leafing through the eleven-page subpoena, Bousquette told Phillips that it looked as if the inquiry might be more directed at the art dealers, whom the Justice Department appeared to be investigating as well.

Sure enough, Greene also subpoenaed the records of more than two dozen prominent art dealers, including Richard L. Feigen, William Acquavella, Simon Dickinson, Colnaghi, Hirschl & Adler, Robert Haboldt and Otto Naumann.

The language of the subpoena left no doubt that the Justice Department suspected some collusion between the world's two largest auction houses: It demanded the production of "all documents" created since 1992 "which relate to any communication, oral or written, conversations, discussion, meeting, formal or informal, or other contact between the Company and any other auctioneer or any of its owners, directors, officers, employees, agents or representatives concerning auctions including but not limited to (A) Consigner's commission, (B) Buyer's premiums, and (C) other conditions of sale at auction."[18]

The subpoena warned against the destruction of any of the requested materials: "Any person who withholds, alters or destroys documents demanded by this subpoena may be subject to criminal prosecution for obstruction of justice, contempt of court, or other federal criminal violations. Conviction for any of these offences is punishable by imprisonment, fines, or both."[19]

Later that day, a battalion of antitrust litigation lawyers from Weil, Gotshal came to review the subpoena and to assess its requirements and implications. They sat in a meeting with Dede Brooks, Kevin Bousquette, Mitchell Zuckerman and Rena Neville, Sotheby's general counsel.

During the meeting, Brooks was warned that the subpoena would require her to turn over all of her phone logs, diaries and all records of her communications with Christie's, which she readily agreed to do, knowing that she had no choice.

In trying to determine what might have prompted the investigation, the lawyers asked Brooks to describe her contacts with Christopher Davidge. She replied that she had met him several times to discuss legitimate industry issues, such as auction scheduling and joint lobbying agreements, but left it at that.

The antitrust lawyers raised the question of whether individual employees at Sotheby's should retain separate counsel just in case their personal interests should at some point clash with those of Sotheby's. Brooks assured the lawyers that she did not need to hire a lawyer to protect her own interests. "She felt that it would give a bad impression," Rena Neville recalled, "and that it wasn't necessary and that it wouldn't be appropriate."[20]

Once the Weil, Gotshal lawyers had left, Brooks began to worry about having to turn over records of her contacts with Davidge. She telephoned Christie's CEO at home in London to suggest they go over their calendars to make sure they were consistent about the dates of all their various meetings.

To Brooks' amazement, Davidge told her that he had not kept any calendars and reassured her that there was nothing to be consistent about. The two CEOs agreed that since a Justice Department investigation was now under way it would be reckless for them to meet again in the foreseeable future.

Since the end of 1995, Brooks and Davidge had communicated less and less. "I didn't really trust him," Brooks admitted later. "I didn't always feel he was straight with me on certain things. And I didn't see any point in meeting with him. And then after the subpoenas came, clearly I wasn't going to talk to him at that point."[21]

Brooks felt confident that the truth would never come to light because she had told no one about her price-fixing conversations with Christopher Davidge. And she believed the secret was safe with Davidge, whom she assumed had just as much to lose if he spilled the beans.

"I just didn't say anything to *anyone*," she told me later. "People knew I met with him, but I didn't share our conversations on the subject."[22]

18

Brown Shorts

WHEN A FEDERAL MARSHAL arrived at Christie's Park Avenue offices with a menacing subpoena, Patty Hambrecht placed a call to a senior partner at Skadden, Arps, Slate, Meagher & Flom, who was one of the most aggressive and experienced defence lawyers in the country. They agreed it was imperative to interview all of Christie's senior executives to see if there might be any truth to the price-fixing allegations hinted at in the subpoena. Hambrecht was in the room for Davidge's interview, which took place in New York.

The senior partner asked if Davidge had had any inkling that Sotheby's was going to follow when Christie's announced its new seller's commission structure in March 1995. Davidge assured him that he had not. After Christie's made its announcement, he told them, he had been terrified.

"I was so scared Sotheby's wasn't going to follow suit that I browned my shorts," Davidge declared.[1]

Browned his shorts? The lawyers were aghast at the vulgar expression Davidge had used to profess his innocence. They were also unconvinced. Immediately after the interview, Patty Hambrecht and the senior partner huddled for a private meeting behind closed doors. "I don't believe him," the Skadden lawyer said.

"Neither do I," Hambrecht replied.[2]

The lawyers agreed that Hambrecht would confront Davidge and question him further.

As soon as he arrived the next day, she stepped into Davidge's office and closed the door. "This is serious, Christopher," she said.

"Let me explain something to you. *If* you colluded with Sotheby's, it will be a lot better for you—and for the company—if you tell the truth now."

If the allegations were true and Davidge failed to speak up immediately, she told him, there was a distinct possibility that Sotheby's could run to the government and get amnesty, which would leave Christie's vulnerable to prosecution. And Davidge could be ruined.

He avoided giving her a direct answer.

"What would happen," he asked, "if I had a piece of paper signed by Taubman and Tennant showing that the two of them colluded over this?"

Hambrecht was speechless. She didn't believe for a second that such a document really existed. Tennant wasn't that stupid.

"Is this piece of paper real or hypothetical?" she asked.

Davidge did not reply.

"This is very serious," Hambrecht warned him. "If you've broken the law, tell me now. But I have to warn you—if you tell me you did it, I'm going to have to turn you in myself."

Again, Davidge did not reply.

"Obviously, I said it in such a way he didn't admit to it," Hambrecht recalled later.

After pleading with Davidge to come clean, she neglected to pursue the matter.

"I'm not proud of that," Hambrecht admitted later.[3]

THE SENIOR PARTNER and his colleagues at Skadden, Arps questioned all Christie's senior executives, including Christopher Burge and François Curiel. One by one, each told the lawyers that they had no knowledge of any conspiracy.

Christie's executives were asked to turn over any documents relating to contact with Sotheby's, but they produced only documents relating to the scheduling of sales. Discussions had indeed taken place between the two firms, they said, but such communications were for the benefit of buyers and were in no sense anticompetitive.

The Skadden lawyers decided that there was nothing to be concerned about. "There were no admissions of contacts of an inappropriate nature between Christie's and Sotheby's," the lawyers concluded in a secret report, "nor did any documents appear, either in the U.S. or the U.K., which contained references suggesting inappropriate contacts."[4]

Davidge later recalled that he was not concerned that he would be betrayed by the colleagues whom he had already told about the conspiracy, Christopher Burge, Charlie Hindlip and François Curiel. "We were all in it together," Davidge said, "and they knew that in return for falling on my sword if needed my contract would be paid out."[5]

As an Englishman based in London, Lord Hindlip was *not* interviewed by Skadden, Arps at the time. He was aware of Davidge's conversations with Brooks over the seller's commission, but had convinced himself that it was unimportant. "This may seem weird," he said later, "but all the original conversations were in 1993. And by 1997 a hell of a lot had gone on. The whole thing seemed to have gone away. We were absolutely not sticking to whatever agreement there *had* been. We had fixed rates, but we were busy cutting each other's throats like we always had."[6]

HAVING ACHIEVED his goal of overtaking Sotheby's sales, Davidge was determined to live the high life in New York. He longed to emulate the international James Bond life of his business idol Joe Lewis, Christie's largest shareholder, who had grown up in North London and now lived in splendour as a tax exile in Lyford Cay in the Bahamas. In November 1996, the auction executive rented a luxurious fifteenth-floor penthouse at 525 Park Avenue, a dignified pre-war building two blocks north of Christie's Fifty-ninth Street headquarters.

A decorator was hired to transform the apartment into a palace befitting a global chief executive. The 4,000-square-foot penthouse boasted a gallery, a library, three bedrooms, a maid's room and a vast drawing room and dining room connected by a winter garden. Outside was a further 1,900 square feet of wraparound terraces.

The staggering monthly rent of $32,500 was paid by Christie's.

"It was quite amazing," Olga Davidge recalled. "It was a five-million-dollar penthouse—beautiful and really very special. Christopher always knew how to take care of himself, without question."[7]

The walls of the penthouse were often adorned with multimillion-dollar paintings that Christie's had failed to sell at auction. Davidge's lordly new digs and the extravagant amount of Christie's funds expended in their refurbishment were subjects of disconcertment among his senior colleagues and their wives. Especially those who were accustomed to Christie's meagre salaries.

"It was a *complete* waste of money," Lady Hindlip recalled. "He had a *folie de grandeur*."[8]

The rumour at Christie's was that Davidge's apartment was costing the company $17,000 a month—roughly half of the actual rent.

"How can we afford to pay that for his apartment?" François Curiel asked.[9]

ON JUNE 3, 1997, the Skadden lawyers flew to London to pepper Davidge with more questions. He assured them that he had not engaged in conversations with anyone at Sotheby's about commissions, and flatly denied that he had exchanged confidential grandfather lists with the competition. The subpoena from the Department of Justice only required the production of documents that were physically in the United States, so Davidge's papers in the United Kingdom were technically outside the Antitrust Division's jurisdiction.

Nevertheless, the lawyers wanted to be on the safe side. They asked Davidge to supply copies of all of his papers relating to Sotheby's. To satisfy them, he turned over a pile of harmless documents that he kept in his sixth-floor office at Christie's in London.

He neglected to mention to the lawyers that he had amassed memos, letters and faxes from his illicit communications with Dede Brooks. But those potentially dangerous documents were safely stored under lock and key a mere hundred yards away in his flat at Georgian House.

THE EXISTENCE of the auction house subpoenas was a closely

guarded secret, known only to the lawyers and a handful of senior executives at each firm. But in early June, Carol Vogel of the *New York Times* broke the story that the Justice Department had subpoenaed Sotheby's and Christie's, and more than a dozen prominent Manhattan art dealers. Gina Talamona, a spokeswoman for the Justice Department, told the *Times* that "the Antitrust Division is looking at the possibility of anticompetitive practices in the fine-art auction industry."[10]

Adverse publicity about the subpoenas inconveniently coincided with Christie's much awaited auction of seventy-nine dresses owned by HRH Diana, Princess of Wales, for charity.

Charlie Hindlip was to be the evening's auctioneer and, as chairman, he escorted the princess when she came to New York for a cocktail reception to promote the sale. The British tabloids had a field day running stories that accused the noble lord of placing his hand on Princess Diana's derriere as he escorted her around the crowded New York showroom.

"It was very busy and lots of people were trying to meet her," the fifty-six-year-old Hindlip told the *Mirror* of London. "My role was like a rugby prop forward trying to make space through a scrum of people. I was trying to *protect* her.[11]

On that dramatic night, which foreshadowed the press scrum that preceded the princess' death a few weeks later, Olga Davidge ran into Patty Hambrecht, whom she assumed was having a romance with her estranged spouse.

"Are you all right?" Hambrecht enquired. Olga said nothing, feeling instinctively that Patty realized that the Davidges' marriage was in pieces. "I always liked Patty," Olga recalled, "even though by then I was aware that it was quite possible that things were going on between her and my husband. But it didn't matter, really."[12]

AS THE GOVERNMENT'S antitrust investigation dragged on for months, Brooks expressed impatience about the substantial resources it was draining from the company.

"If John Greene thinks that we don't compete, he ought to come and spend a day at Sotheby's," Brooks told Steve Reiss of Weil,

Gotshal, who sympathized with the CEO's frustration. "Spending time at Sotheby's," he recalled, "the fact was that there was a huge competition and animosity, frankly, between these two companies."[13]

Reiss felt confident there was little to worry about. "She was enormously invested in the fact that nothing had gone wrong," he recalled. "It wasn't simply a denial, it was vehement denial ... An extraordinarily convincing denial."[14]

DURING THE MONTH of December 1997, Christie's largest share-holder, Joe Lewis, paraded a succession of his friends in the banking world through Christie's boardroom with a view to helping Davidge form a consortium that would turn Christie's into a private company.

The idea, Charlie Hindlip recalled, was to buy the publicly traded firm, "and then it was going to be parcelled out to large stockholders with collections of art which would give them an incentive as working directors. I wasn't sure if it would work," Hindlip added, "but it was an interesting idea."[15]

Alas, there were no takers. "It was highly exhausting and ended in failure after fifteen people had stared at the ashes of Christie's and said, 'No, thank you,'" a Christie's insider recalled.[16]

Facing the prospect of new ownership, Davidge realized that some kind of a protection letter might be crucial to his survival. He was concerned that if his role in the conspiracy became known, he would be forced to resign, and that under the terms of his contract Christie's would not be obliged to pay him a penny. He sought reassurance from Charlie Hindlip.

"Chris said, 'If I have to fall on my sword, would you make sure that my contract is honoured?' And I said, 'Yes, of course.' And he said, 'Would you write me a letter to that effect?'"[17]

In a letter on Christie's stationery, dated December 1997, Hindlip wrote with an elegant, forward-leaning hand: "Dear Christopher, I am writing to reassure you that in the unlikely event that it should happen you are forced to resign your position because of the antitrust hearings in the U.S., Christie's will fully protect your position as per your contract—you need not worry but I am sure in any case there is nothing to worry about. Yours ever, Charlie."[18]

Hindlip would come to regret having written that letter. Even so, he considered it only fair that Davidge should receive a decent settlement if he had to leave Christie's. At the time, Hindlip noted, Davidge had a three-year contract at an annual salary of $480,000. If he should have to resign, he could expect a golden handshake of $1.4 million.

"I have no shame about this at all," Hindlip recalled. "I think it would have been unreasonable not to give him that severance." Davidge remained nervous about the U.S. Justice Department investigation, "but as a Brit I felt this was an American problem," he recalled. "I had Charlie's letter, so the worst that I thought could happen to me was having to resign from Christie's."[19]

AFTER NEARLY A YEAR of contending with the fallout of the embarrassing Channel 4 programme, Dede Brooks issued a memo to the firm's worldwide staff on December 16, 1997. It reported on the findings of the Independent Review Committee that had been commissioned by Sotheby's board of directors to look into all allegations of misconduct.

"As you all know," Brooks wrote, "it has been and is Company policy that employees may not violate or assist in the violation of the laws of any country in which we do business."[20] Attempting to strike a positive note, she remarked that Sotheby's had made a "commitment to take a leadership role on ethical and legal practices."[21] Three days later, Brooks made an appearance on *Wall Street Week with Louis Rukeyser,* a public broadcasting television show in the US, during which Rukeyser alluded to Sotheby's smuggling scandal in Italy.

"How honest is the art game?" Rukeyser asked.

"That scandal caused us to really relook at our business," Brooks replied. "We launched an internal review and we have been working with our independent directors and outside counsel for ten months. I am confident today that we are really setting a new level of standards in the business."

"After all," she added, "our integrity is all we have."[22]

Shortly after her appearance on *Wall Street Week,* Dede Brooks recruited her old friend Donaldson Pillsbury, a former partner at Davis
Polk & Wardwell, to join Sotheby's as the firm's in-house general
counsel. Before accepting the job in January 1998, he sought Brooks'
reassurance about the antitrust investigation that had begun the previous spring. "I wanted to be sure I wasn't stepping into a mess,"
Pillsbury recalled. "She told me that I didn't have to worry."[23]

19

Soaring Fortunes

DEDE BROOKS WAS BECOMING increasingly omnipotent as Sotheby's global CEO. The firm's fortunes were beginning to soar with the increased revenues from the seller's commission, and she appeared to have headed off the government's antitrust investigation. A long string of successes had left her chafing at having to answer to the chairman and deputy chairman of the board.

"You'd be in a room with Dede, and Max Fisher or Alfred Taubman would call," a Sotheby's executive remembered, "and she would say, 'I'll call them back.' And I thought, 'I can't believe she's doing this!'"[1]

Under company policy, every loan in excess of $10 million had to be approved by the Executive Committee of the board, which consisted of Taubman, Fisher, Jeff Miro and Brooks. In May 1998, Sotheby's Financial Services made one of the largest loans in its history to Wolfgang Flottl, an Austrian-born financier who had been buying and selling at auction for years. The loan was a whopping $240 million.

Brooks had to get permission from Max Fisher, who was in London, staying at Claridge's, "Dede was always very nervous when she had to get approval," recalled Bill Sheridan, Sotheby's chief financial officer. "She didn't like it." On their way up to Fisher's hotel room, he recounted, Dede said, "I hate getting approval from these old men who always fall asleep at meetings."[2]

"She wanted to do things herself," Sheridan added. "She thought she knew better."[3]

WHEN CHRISTOPHER DAVIDGE filed for a divorce in March 1998, Olga reached out to a powerful New Yorker whom she had never met. She dialled Sotheby's number, identified herself and asked to speak with Dede Brooks.

"I'm sorry to trouble you," Olga said in a quiet Russian voice. "But I have absolutely nobody to talk to. And I really don't know where to turn."[4]

Brooks was astonished to find herself talking to the wife of her co-conspirator.

"I didn't know anybody in New York," Olga recalled. "I didn't have a way of finding an American lawyer and out of my desperation I called Dede and asked her for a lawyer. What else was I supposed to do? I had a child who was having seizures. And I was on my own."[5]

Brooks was gracious, and agreed to help. Her assistant called Olga back a few hours later with the name and number of a divorce lawyer.

While in the throes of his bitter divorce, Davidge was rushed to the hospital in April 1998 with a severe case of rectal bleeding. "At first they thought it was colon cancer," he recalled.[6] After five days in the hospital, however, he returned to his usual punishing work schedule.

A few weeks after Davidge's trip to the hospital, Christie's announced on May 5 that François Pinault, a French billionaire investor, had paid an undisclosed sum to acquire Joe Lewis' 29 percent stake in Christie's, which instantly made him Christie's largest shareholder.

It was an extraordinary coup for the sixty-one-year-old Pinault, who had left school at sixteen to work for his father, a Brittany timber merchant. He had established his first business at twenty-seven with a $25,000 loan from his family, and by 1998, he was worth more than $7 billion. Along the way, he had accumulated a series of high-profile acquisitions through Artémis, his private investment company, whose holdings included the Château Latour vineyard; Printemps stores; Converse sneakers; Samsonite luggage; the Vail ski resort in Colorado; and a controlling interest in Gucci. A short, compact and intensely private man, Pinault lived in a seventeenth-century château at Montfort L'Aumauray, outside Paris.

His acquisition of Christie's would bring to an end 232 years of British ownership. If Christie's board decided to approve the deal proposed by Pinault, Davidge personally stood to make $3.1 million for his shares. Christie's directors could hardly refuse to accept Pinault's generous cash offer, and Artémis officially gained ownership of Christie's on June 25, 1998.

Pinault's $1.2 billion deal was certainly welcome in fiscal terms, but Davidge felt threatened. "In a way, Christie's had been *his* company," a fellow director recalled. "He'd got market share after forty-two years. And now it was in the hands of someone he'd never met, who just signed a check one day. It wasn't Chris' company anymore."[7]

Part of the problem was a language barrier. Pinault did not speak English, and Davidge had no intention of learning French. Shortly after Pinault bought Christie's, Davidge was surprised when a friend took him aside for a few words of friendly advice.

"Do you have a watertight contract?" he asked Davidge.

"Why do you ask?"

"You place too much trust in Charlie Hindlip's loyalty," the friend observed. "He was loyal while you were top dog. But now you're just another employee. Just wait. You'll see. Lord and Lady Hindlip will start cultivating Pinault and his executives, and you'll be history."[8]

At first, Christie's new owner recognized that Davidge had done a remarkable job in running the firm, and was eager to retain his services. Finding himself in demand, the Englishman renegotiated his contract on extremely favourable terms that were authorized by Patricia Barbizet, the CEO of Artémis. Davidge's yearly salary was increased on July 1, 1998, from $480,000 to $1.25 million. And his three-year contract was simultaneously extended to five years.

Davidge neglected to mention his new salary to his ex-wife. Their divorce decree was issued on June 29, 1998, two days before his giant raise.

"Christopher always made a complete secret of all financial

affairs," Olga recalled. "As far as I was concerned, I divorced a poor man."[9]

PATTY HAMBRECHT'S DISMAY, the persistent rumour that she and Christopher Davidge had been having an affair appeared on the Internet on August 24, 1998. It was the lead item in "The Royal Flush," a popular gossip column on artnet.com: "Two sources at Christie's tell us that Mrs. Christopher Davidge has reportedly named Christie's North America chief Patricia Hambrecht as an alleged co-respondent in her divorce action against her husband, Christie's International czar Christopher Davidge."[10]

The story caused much mirth and merriment when it appeared. But it was not true. Olga Davidge had *not* named Patty Hambrecht as a co-respondent for the very simple reason that she was not the petitioner. "Christopher is the one who filed for divorce," Olga recalled. "I never named Patty. That might have been the case, but as far as I'm concerned half of Christie's could have been involved."*[11]

Hambrecht was adamant that the rumours were false. When she presided over a press tour of Christie's new headquarters at Rockefeller Centre at the time the "Royal Flush" article appeared, she found herself fending off questions about her putative romance with Christie's CEO.

"It's all over the art world that you're sleeping with Christopher Davidge," a prominent art journalist told Hambrecht. "Is it true?"

"I'd rather fuck an elephant," Hambrecht replied, succinctly.[12]

Even Charlie Hindlip, who loved to gossip, did not believe the rumours were true. "Chris had affairs with lots of women who worked at Christie's," he recalled, "and he invariably told me about them. And he never said anything about Patty. A lot of people will tell you that they were found in flagrante delicto. I don't think it's true."†[† Was it true that Davidge and Hambrecht had been romantically entwined? "The answer, 'yes' to this question, when it was first raised years ago would have killed it," Davidge told a friend re-

---

* A copy of the Davidges' divorce decree identifies Christopher Davidge as the Petitioner, and Olga as his Respondent. No co-respondent is named.

cently. "'No' invites continued speculation. Sometimes I wish I had, and then it would have died as a story. But the truth is I did not."][13]

While his colleagues were debating his amorous exploits, Davidge was slowly emerging from a terrible funk. "My marriage to Olga was the single biggest mistake of my life," he told a friend. "I will pay the price till my dying day, not just financially but emotionally, too."[14]

The romantic landscape was not entirely bleak for Davidge. The amorous Englishman had begun a furtive romance with Amrita Jhaveri, a beautiful young woman from a wealthy family in Bombay who was Christie's representative in India. Jhaveri had studied in the United States and graduated from Brown University in 1991 and was regarded by all who knew her as a star.

"She's very bright," noted Pravina Mecklai, a leading art dealer in Bombay. "We thought she did wonders for Christie's in India, with the right connections to open doors for Christie's everywhere."[15]

COMBING THEIR WAY through thousands of Rolodexes, diaries and telephone logs from senior auction house staff, the federal prosecutors sought evidence of improper communications between Sotheby's and Christie's. One by one, midlevel employees at both firms were subpoenaed to appear before the grand jury to testify about their knowledge of contacts between the two auction houses. Sotheby's hired John Siffert, a respected criminal attorney, to represent the handful of staff who were called.

Pete Hathaway, the head of Sotheby's European Furniture Department in New York, was astonished when he was summoned to testify. "Most of the jurors were sound asleep and had absolutely no idea what I was talking about," Hathaway recalled.[16] He was aghast when asked to read out loud from a telephone log message he had left for Brooks on November 15, 1992, shortly after Sotheby's had announced the new hike in its buyer's premium.

"FYI—from a reliable source at Christie's," the message said, "he heard that Christie's is going to follow with the 15 percent buyer's premium. Call for details."[17]

Hathaway was asked to explain himself.

"I heard it at a cocktail party," Hathaway told the grand jury. "I *do* remember calling her office from the warehouse, but I don't know who said it."[18]

Hathaway suddenly felt very uncomfortable. "If I *was* part of a price-fixing conspiracy," he told the prosecutor, "do you honestly think I would be that *stupid* to leave a message with a secretary that was going to be carbon-copied?"[19] Several members of the grand jury burst out laughing, arousing others from slumber.

After his courtroom ordeal, Hathaway headed uptown to Sotheby's and stopped into Brooks' office. "How was it?" Brooks asked.

"It was just the worst thing in my life," Hathaway responded. "What the *hell* is going on?"

"Pete, I just want you to know that this is so trumped up, all this," Brooks told her friend, looking him straight in the eye. "I would *never* do something like that. No one in this company would *ever* do something like that."[20]

Brooks' reaction was so vehement that Hathaway believed she must be telling the truth.

Bombshell

CHRISTOPHER DAVIDGE was feeling restless as the summer of 1999 drew to a close. He had devoted nearly thirty-four years to one company and now found himself yearning for a new life, free of Christie's burdens and irksome responsibilities. While celebrating his fifty-fourth birthday on August 23 he was struck by an appalling thought. He was now three years older than his father, Roy, had been when he collapsed from a heart attack, dying, like his own father before him, after an exhausting day's work at King Street. Davidge was determined not to suffer the same fate. In contemplating early retirement, he was finally focusing his obsessive drive on his personal life. He had squandered two marriages, to Susan and Olga, by enslaving himself to his work. Now, madly in love with Amrita Jhaveri, who possessed beauty, captivating charm and a keen intellect, Davidge began for the first time to consider a life of leisure.

"I look forward to nothing more," he told a friend, "than spending the next ten years reading books in order to keep up with Amrita."[1] As well as a life of pleasure. The couple's relationship was intensely physical. "The pair of them can't keep their hands off each other on the street," the friend noted with a lascivious chuckle, "let alone anywhere else."[2]

Yearning for a second youth wasn't Davidge's only reason for wanting to quit Christie's. Intense disagreements with some of his senior colleagues had escalated to the level of war during the past year as rival factions scuffled for position before the new French owners.

Lord Hindlip found himself in a furious, protracted battle with Davidge for Pinault's trust and for control of the company. Davidge complained to all who would listen that Hindlip was incompetent.

"Charlie can be the most charming guy in the world, but at the end of the day he is very arrogant," Davidge observed. "He did not grow into the job of chairman."[3]

In the battle for supremacy with Pinault, however, Hindlip had the upper hand. He was a charismatic figurehead who excelled at all the auction-house skills that Davidge lacked. He was a superb auctioneer and was knowledgeable about all kinds of works of art. And he had an unrivalled ability to line up business through his network of social connections, which included his long-standing friendships with members of Britain's royal family.

While Davidge was contemplating his own future in the weeks surrounding his birthday, Hindlip was doing his utmost to get him fired.

"He was making the company unprofitable," Hindlip recalled later, still feisty with indignation. "He had lost touch with the staff, and he was losing people."[4]

"I wasn't really getting on with my colleagues as best as I should," Davidge admitted later, with considerable understatement. "I lost my edge and my initiative."[5]

By isolating himself in Christie's top-floor executive suites in London and Manhattan, Davidge avoided contact with most of the firm's employees and he had trouble recognizing them by sight. When Christie's held a bowling party for all of its New York staff in June, Davidge showed up wearing tight black jeans and a shiny, form-fitting black turtleneck. What made the night memorable for the staff was not his attempt at male-model attire but that he arrived so late for the morale-boosting event. Word quickly spread that the chief executive had spent the previous hour on a different floor, confusing regular patrons of Bowlmor Lanes in Greenwich Village by sauntering around, occasionally sticking out his hand and saying, "Hello, I'm Chris Davidge."[6]

The English executive had promised Pinault that he would stay at Christie's for at least a year. But he had been the master of his own fiefdom for too long and was uncomfortable under the control of Artémis. By summer 1999 his year-long obligation had expired and, under the terms of his five-year rolling contract with Christie's, he could expect a generous severance package.

"The fissures in the relationship weren't obvious to rank and file," a Christie's director noted, but the tension was "quite patently obvious" to the main board. "I think we all thought that it was just a matter of time."7

Davidge's summer of discontent had begun with a series of vexing developments in the spring. In April 1999, Patty Hambrecht had masterminded the extravagant launch of Christie's new Manhattan head-quarters in Rockefeller Centre. Some members of Christie's staff questioned the wisdom of going to the bankers for $75 million to convert a parking garage into a 315,000-square-foot, three-story colossus. But the austere corporate interior was considered a resounding success. As president of Christie's North and South America, Hambrecht was in charge of relocating five hundred employees to the new space, along with such valuable commodities as paintings by Miro, an ancient Roman nude and a snappy 1937 Alfa Romeo 2900B race car. Finally, on April 23 there was an outdoor ceremony, under a persistent drizzle, featuring a performance by the Girls Choir of Harlem in electric-blue robes, singing a musical tribute to Ella Fitzgerald, Billie Holiday and Dinah Washington. Drenched by the rain, Christopher Davidge sat stoically in the front row with Amrita Jhaveri.

But inside Christie's splendid new headquarters, many of the firm's American employees were restive and threatening to quit. Lord Hindlip was alarmed by the rumblings of discontent and told Davidge that he intended to spend four months in Manhattan to gauge the situation and determine how it could be remedied.

After a few days with his American colleagues, Hindlip realized that drastic action needed to be taken. He sat down to write Davidge a letter in June 1999 outlining his concerns about the way that the younger man was running Christie's.

"New York was an absolute shambles," Hindlip recalled. "Neither he nor Patty Hambrecht talked to anybody. They lived in a closed world." Art experts and management felt they were getting no support. "Chris always backed up Patty," he noted, "and undermined me and everybody else. Everyone wanted to leave. It was a mess, *a real* mess."[8]

The problem was not just with New York. With Davidge at the helm, Christie's International was less profitable than in 1993, when he had taken on the job of chief executive. "Chris was killing the business," Hindlip said. "His travel and Concorde trips were becoming obscene, and then they started including Amrita."[9]

Reckless spending had become part and parcel of Davidge's grandiose view of the chief executive's role—one in which the auction house's formerly autonomous art experts were treated like subordinates to an all-powerful executive. Hindlip's distaste for the new, imperial CEO was matched by the rampant dissatisfaction among the experts. Davidge had lost many of the stars among the firm's constellation of world-class specialists, including Simon Dickinson, the head of Christie's Impressionist and Modern Paintings Department, whose departure from the firm in 1995 had been a severe blow to the company's prestige and profitability.

In his June 1999 letter to Davidge, Hindlip strongly advised him to assign Patty Hambrecht a different job.

"Patty was an extremely good lawyer, a nice person, and she was clever and imaginative," Hindlip recalled. "But it became frantically apparent that she was as *bad* at being the managing director as she'd been really *good* as a lawyer."[10]

Hindlip told Davidge he believed that Hambrecht's skills might be better applied to another job within Christie's, possibly as a strategic director to help map Christie's future. Moreover, he urged him to move back to New York to run the firm's Manhattan operations himself and to use his authority to make it work. Davidge refused point-blank. "He rather rudely said that there was nothing new or original about my letter," Hindlip recalled, "and that he absolutely wasn't going to do it. He didn't want to be in New York. And anyway, he said, my days were over."[11]

Finding himself embroiled in a serious power struggle, Hindlip flew to Paris to speak to Christie's new owner. "I never had said anything remotely disloyal about Chris to Pinault," Hindlip recalled later. "I think it came as a shock to him when I did."[12]

"You've got a choice," Hindlip said. "It's either Davidge or me. I'm not staying if he does."

"I'm very sorry," the Frenchman replied, astonished. "Can't you work together?"

"No"[13]

While face-to-face with Pinault, Hindlip plucked up the courage to warn the Frenchman that in December 1997 he had written Davidge a letter to assure him that if he should have to leave Christie's for antitrust reasons, the firm would still honour his lucrative contract. It was wiser to tell Pinault now, Hindlip reasoned, rather than wait for Davidge to use the letter to blackmail him with it later by inferring that Hindlip had knowledge of the conspiracy.

"Pinault said, '*C'est stupide, mais je connais beaucoup plus stupide,*'" Hindlip recalled of his employer's remark that he'd heard of stupider things. "I couldn't have put it better myself."[14]

In delivering his ultimatum to Pinault, Hindlip knew he was taking a terrible risk. "It will probably cost you a lot of money to fire Davidge and it *won't* cost you a lot of money to get rid of me," Hindlip said blithely, "because I don't have a big contract."[15]

For good measure, Hindlip also described the chaotic state of Christie's New York operations and advised Pinault that something must be done to remove Hambrecht from the role of president of North and South America. Pinault needed little persuading.

Davidge was beginning to realize that his future at Christie's was limited. "I knew that Charlie Hindlip and Stephen Lash were complaining about Patty to Artémis as a way of undermining me," he recalled. "Artémis was expressing no confidence in Patty and was questioning her continuing in her position."[16]

Sensing that trouble was brewing in Paris, Davidge had no option but to accede to Pinault's wishes to sack Hambrecht, his friend and long-time protégée. "When Pinault bought the company the *one* person they wanted out was Patty," Hindlip remembered. "But Davidge protected her. Davidge suddenly realized that it was *his* job that was on the line. And that's the only reason why he got rid of Patty. He should have moved her aside. Getting rid of her was actually quite unfair."[17]

The fact that Hambrecht had been dismissed was kept secret in order to preserve her dignity. The *New York Times* simply reported that after eleven years with Christie's, Patty would "take a sabbatical beginning next month."[18]

While Hambrecht's career was grinding to a halt in New York, Davidge was in London, receiving reports of Hindlip's colloquy with Pinault. Davidge fought back, claiming that he had the support of Christie's board. He offered Hindlip an unappetizing choice —to step down as Christie's chairman or be fired altogether.

"Give me a month to think about it," Hindlip replied.[19]

A few days later, on July 8, Hindlip's strategic position was strengthened by the spectacular success of an auction he presided over at King Street. The collection of works of art belonging to the Austrian branch of the Rothschild family had come to Christie's due to Hindlip's long-standing relationship with the consigner, Baroness Bettina de Rothschild.

Part of the excitement surrounding the sale was that the collection had been seized by the Nazis during the German Anschluss in 1938 and had only recently been restored to the Rothschild family by the Austrian culture minister, fifty years later. Among the highlights were several outstanding Frans Hals portraits, an illuminated medieval prayer book and a Louis XVI royal commode, which was sold to the museum of Versailles for $10·9 million. Hindlip brought down the gavel on the final lot after nearly four hours at the podium, having achieved a grand total of $89·9 million. "It was one of the most successful sales in the history of auctions in Europe," he told the *New York Times* afterward. "Never before has such a cross section of the arts fetched such extraordinary sums of money in one evening."[20]

Flush from his triumph, Hindlip informed Davidge in late July that he had no intention of accepting his ultimatum. He then spoke again to Pinault, who asked if there was any way for Hindlip and Davidge to work together. "Absolutely not," Hindlip replied. "It's either him or me."

BOMBSHELL

231

"Okay," Pinault replied, wearily. "I'm going to get rid of Davidge. But I need time."[21]

EDWARD DOLMAN, the Christie's executive imported from London to take Patty Hambrecht's place in New York, was an affable, thirty-nine-year-old rugby fanatic, known as Ed, whom Davidge had been grooming for the past two years as his eventual successor. An Englishman of stout build with a tousled mop of sandy hair and a certain boyish eagerness, Dolman had joined the Furniture Department at Christie's South Kensington in 1984. "In those days if you were male you were made a porter," he recalled. "I was making an appalling annual salary of two thousand, eight hundred pounds [$4,000] a year, so I gave myself a year."[22] He stuck it out, and went on to become managing director of Christie's Europe.

In his new job, Dolman was responsible for running Christie's day-to-day operations in North and South America. He soon discovered that he had his work cut out for him. Christie's was drastically less profitable in America than it was in Europe, in striking contrast to Sotheby's. He was also dismayed to learn that more than thirty of the firm's high-ranking experts and managers in America were threatening to quit. The tactic of some members of the management team of pitting rivals against each other within the company had led to widespread alienation and disillusionment.

Within the first week of arriving in New York, Ed Dolman sat down with Christie's lawyers to go over all outstanding legal issues. The anti-trust investigation was considered so unimportant that it was fourth on the list. "They said, 'Oh, it's been going on for two years, but nothing's really come of it,'" he recalled. "[They said it was] just one of those things of being in a duopoly—there are always going to be accusations of collusion, but there's no proof at all."[23]

FEELING RELIEVED to be free of Christie's political machinations, Patty Hambrecht was enjoying a glorious summer in the Hamptons. She was still in her forties, attractive, smart and well connected, and her friends were confident that it would not be long before she landed on her feet again. *Crain's New York Business* had recently named her as one of New York's 100 Most Influential Women in Business—an accolade that had appeared in print after she had been asked to leave Christie's. Unfortunately, her idyllic respite was interrupted when a federal marshal showed up at the door of her rented beach house in Sagaponack to deliver a subpoena to testify before the grand jury in Manhattan.

"They sent a uniformed marshal, which would upset anyone," a friend noted.[24]

Under the terms of her separation agreement with Christie's, Hambrecht was obliged to support the firm's efforts to cooperate with the government's antitrust investigation. She had no choice but to truthfully answer their questions, and it was imperative that she first speak to Cliff Aronson, Christie's outside counsel.

Clifford H. Aronson was a first-rate antitrust lawyer and a partner in the leading New York firm of Skadden, Arps, Meagher & Flom. Clipped, intense and aloof, he was quite a force to be reckoned with. Hambrecht and Aronson met for an awkward interview in the second week of October at Aronson's office in Times Square.

Aronson immediately began grilling Hambrecht to find out whether she had been aware of any inappropriate contacts between the two rival firms during her years as Christie's general counsel and as president of Christie's North and South America. Having been summarily fired by Davidge, she had nothing to lose and began to unleash her suspicions.

To Aronson's dismay, Hambrecht recalled having several conversations with Davidge during the mid-nineties that gave her the impression that he had held illegal and compromising discussions with Dede Brooks on several topics, including commissions. Hambrecht also confessed that in 1997 Davidge had asked what would happen if he had a piece of paper implicating Sotheby's chairman, Alfred Taubman, in the antitrust conspiracy being investigated by the U.S. Justice Department. Hambrecht told Aronson that Davidge was a prodigious note taker and speculated that he might have kept written records of his illicit meetings with Dede Brooks. She even went so far as to suggest that he might be hiding them at Farthings, his secluded country cottage.

Hambrecht's allegations were incendiary, but she had no concrete evidence to support them. "We didn't know if what Patty was saying was necessarily the truth," Ed Dolman recalled.[25]

Armed with Hambrecht's troubling accusations, Aronson and John Donovan, a Skadden, Arps colleague, flew to London to meet with Davidge on October 20. The Englishman strenuously denied that any inappropriate contacts had taken place and pointed out that he had already turned over sheaves of documents concerning his contacts with Sotheby's. "Whenever we interviewed him, we asked for documents relevant to the investigation," Aronson recalled. "He told us that we had everything."[26]

Unconvinced, the Skadden lawyers warned Davidge that the next time he travelled to New York he might have to testify before the grand jury. They also strongly advised him to retain his own attorney.

While in London, the Skadden lawyers expanded their investigation. One of their most illuminating interviews was with Irmgard Pickering, Davidge's former assistant, who revealed that Davidge and Brooks had met several times during the critical period in 1995 when Christie's and Sotheby's were altering their commissions. She admitted that she had no specific knowledge of what had transpired between the two chief executives, but noted that Davidge had seemed "confident" when Christie's had altered its commission rates that Sotheby's would follow.

The Skadden lawyers were deeply concerned. For the past two years, everyone they interviewed at Christie's in New York had insisted there had been no conspiracy. Now that their circle of inquiry was expanding it was clear that Christie's could be in serious legal trouble.

While in London, Cliff Aronson interviewed Lord Hindlip, who was taken aback by the lawyer's questions. "I thought the antitrust stuff was dead and buried until Cliff suddenly appeared," admitted Hindlip, who had never been questioned about the possibility of illegal communications between Christie's and Sotheby's. "They didn't ask," he recalled, "because I don't think they had *a clue* there had been any."[27]

Having been assured by Pinault that Davidge was going to be

fired, Hindlip felt no obligation to hold back in rendering his account of the man he believed was ruining Christie's. To the New York lawyer's astonishment, Hindlip revealed that Davidge had intimated to him that he had conferred with Dede Brooks in 1995 about Sotheby's intentions of matching Christie's revised seller's commissions schedule. He also recalled that Davidge had indicated that he and Brooks had exchanged their respective firms' grandfather lists, and that he had been appalled by their indiscretion. To an antitrust attorney, these were horrifying revelations. They seemed to confirm Aronson's suspicions that the two CEOs had conspired to make their two firms' seller's commissions non-negotiable. Now it appeared that they had even taken steps to make sure that neither side was "cheating."

"I got the impression that I quite shook him," Hindlip recalled. "Cliff's a very good interrogator, and he didn't let on to me that he'd talked to Patty."[28]

With these staggering new revelations in hand, Aronson attempted to meet with Davidge again in November, but he refused to speak further until he had found a suitable attorney. Davidge's colleagues in New York were shocked when he failed to show up for Christie's crucial evening sales at Rockefeller Centre. On the night of November 9, Christopher Burge wielded the gavel for a thrilling auction of major Impressionist and modern works. Three anonymous bidders battled furiously for Picasso's *Nude on a Black Armchair,* a 1932 portrait of the artist's mistress Marie-Thérèse Walter slumbering with her arms stretched above her head.

Davidge's refusal to show up for the big New York evening sales in November irked his colleagues all the more since Christie's totals for the season (like those at Sotheby's) had soared to their highest records since the all-time highs of spring 1990. "His heart basically wasn't in the job," Ed Dolman recalled. "He knew he'd lost control, and he'd lost the faith and support of the company."[29]

Pinault learned of Davidge's troubling absence from Hindlip and Barbizet. The time had come, the French billionaire concluded, for Davidge to relinquish his post. The decision to compel Davidge's departure was complicated by his lifelong connection with Christie's and his impressive track record in the auction business. Davidge was vexed to learn that Hindlip had told Cliff Aronson that he suspected that Davidge had exchanged papers with Sotheby's. And he suspected that Hindlip was scheming to get him fired.

Not all of Davidge's colleagues were hostile. François Curiel had heard that Patty Hambrecht had been interviewed by Christie's anti-trust lawyers, and that she had suggested that Davidge had been involved in collusive activity with Sotheby's. When Curiel ran into him in Hong Kong, Davidge was touched that Curiel seemed genuinely concerned about his future. The Frenchman offered to help him in any way possible, and to his astonishment, Davidge relayed the entire sequence of events and told Curiel that he had handwritten notes from Tennant. But by now it seemed too late. Davidge's fate appeared to be sealed.

In the meantime, he sought the best legal representation he could find in London. He wound up choosing Lynda Martin Alegi, a bright, capable attorney at Baker & McKenzie. At their first meeting, Davidge told Alegi that he felt no animosity toward Christie's. He wanted to leave Christie's with his head held high, and just wanted to be sure he understood his legal position. Alegi responded by asking Davidge to write up a diary of the conspiracy. When he handed her a long and extensively detailed synopsis a few days later she was thunderstruck. *LAWYER*

"How did you get all this?" Alegi asked.

"From my notes," Davidge replied, showing her a file crammed with extensive notes from the conspiracy.[30] Alegi told him that in all her years of experience she had never seen such documentation.

Cliff Aronson was becoming frustrated with Davidge's repeated refusals to communicate with him directly. When he learned that Davidge had retained independent counsel, he flew to London to meet with Alegi on December 1. She explained that she was new to the case, but since the matter called for expertise in American antitrust law, she was planning to bring in a colleague in the United States.

"She did not disclose anything substantively," Aronson recalled, ruefully.[31]

* * *

IN EARLY DECEMBER, Davidge flew to Paris to meet with
François Pinault and Patricia Barbizet, the Chanel-clad CEO of
Artémis. His flight was delayed two hours due to fog, and by the
time he arrived at Barbizet's office Pinault had already left for another meeting and Barbizet was about to leave for a lunch appointment.
Cutting to the chase, Davidge told her that he no longer felt he was
the right person to be CEO of Christie's.

He also decided to drop his bombshell. The antitrust investigation
being conducted by the U.S. Department of Justice, he revealed, was
justified. It was *true* that he had met with Dede Brooks of Sotheby's
to rig the change in the seller's commission in 1995.

In making his confession to Barbizet, Davidge may have imagined
that she would share his European disdain for the absurd zealotry of
American laws. But he also saw a chance to protect himself from
future recriminations if the conspiracy should come to light after his
departure.

"I said that I had a skeleton in my cupboard which was the
antitrust inquiry in America," he recalled, "and that it was better that
they were aware of that."[32]

Davidge guessed that Barbizet already knew what he would say.
As soon as he had appointed Baker & McKenzie, he suspected,
Artémis had come to the same conclusion. He asked if they would be
prepared to make him a financial settlement in lieu of terminating his
contract.

Barbizet told him Artémis was prepared to do so, and that it
would be in addition to any monies he might receive under the terms
of his contract with Christie's. She asked him to fax her his ideas for
a suitable sum of money. In bidding him adieu, she told him that she
had enjoyed working with him, and said that she was sad for him that
after so many years he was leaving Christie's.

JOE LINKLATER, the criminal attorney whom Lynda Martin
Alegi had enlisted to help Davidge with his legal problems in the
States, was head of Baker & McKenzie's criminal practice in the
United States. Born, raised and based in Chicago, the fifty-seven-year-

old lawyer specialized in white-collar criminal cases involving complex civil litigation. He was involved in representing a key defendant in the BASF/ Hoffmann—La Roche case, the biggest antitrust case in U.S. history, in which both firms had pleaded guilty to a decade-long conspiracy to fix and inflate vitamin prices.

Linklater was on a skiing trip in Wyoming on December 10 when he spoke to Davidge for the first time, having arranged an early-morning call in order to take care of business before hitting the slopes. The nervous Englishman outlined his antitrust concerns and explained that he had kept meticulous notes of his correspondence with Christie's former chairman, Sir Anthony Tennant, and his conversations with Sotheby's CEO Dede Brooks. After listening for twenty minutes, the attorney allayed his fears by coming straight to the point.

"Mr. Davidge, I don't want to make light of your predicament," Linklater told him in a broad, assured Chicago accent, "but I rarely get calls from people in your situation who have as many options open to them. I don't give any guarantees about criminal cases, but my guess is this is going to work out fine. So we'll talk later, if that's okay."

"That's the advice I was hoping to hear," Davidge replied. "I like people who cut to the chase."[33]

Upon his return to Chicago, Linklater called Cliff Aronson in New York, hoping to receive a briefing on the government's antitrust investigation to date and to glean what information Davidge may have already divulged to Christie's lawyers. Aronson refused to play ball. Finding himself rebuffed at every turn, Linklater grew suspicious that Christie's was preparing to throw his client to the wolves.

As one of the most effective antitrust lawyers in the country, Aronson could be relied upon to be ruthless on Christie's behalf. Linklater suspected that Aronson was hoping to force Davidge into admitting his guilt in an illegal conspiracy with Sotheby's. If he could accomplish that, the New York lawyer would doubtless urge Christie's owners to make a beeline to the Justice Department to reveal their findings and apply for Christie's to be protected from prosecution under the Antitrust Division's amnesty policy.

If Christie's failed to reach the prosecutor's door before Sotheby's did, the auction house could be exposed to criminal prosecution and a massive federal fine. Stalling could destroy Christie's ability to attract consignments from nervous vendors and leave the firm vulnerable to the potential civil lawsuits that would inevitably follow. But to prove that a conspiracy had truly taken place, and that Davidge was involved, Aronson would need concrete evidence—in the form of the written notes that Patty Hambrecht suspected he was hiding at Farthings.

Before hanging up, Aronson told Linklater that he believed Davidge was withholding documents and demanded that they be turned over immediately. Linklater assured him that if his client had any papers that were relevant to the Justice Department's investigation he would make certain that Aronson received them.

LINKLATER first laid eyes on his client's trove of notes when he flew to London to meet with him for the first time on December 22. After examining Tennant's handwritten notes—which seemed to indicate that Tennant and Taubman, not Davidge and Brooks, had initiated the conspiracy—he told Davidge that he had three options. First, he could decide to take his papers back; destroying them would be a criminal act in the United States. Second, Davidge could decide not to return to the United States for the rest of his life. Linklater told him he would not recommend this option, since Davidge had a daughter living in the United States. Third, Baker & McKenzie could hold Davidge's papers in their London office and make them available to Christie's or their lawyers should the need ever arise.

Whichever option Davidge chose, Linklater explained, it was vital that any termination agreement should include a clause that protected Davidge from having to pay legal fees.

The Chicago lawyer's arrival in London coincided with a bitter fight over the terms of Davidge's severance agreement with Christie's. While the two men were sitting in Baker & McKenzie's offices poring over documents, Shona Newmark, a London colleague of Linklater's who was handling Davidge's negotiations with

Christie's over his termination agreement, came in to report that the auction house was adamant that his severance contract should include two potentially compromising clauses.

The firm was willing to pay Davidge a severance of £5 million ($8 million) in three installments, Newmark explained, but only on a couple of thorny conditions. First, that Davidge agree to state that he had committed no breach of fiduciary duty during his tenure at Christie's. Second, that Christie's could terminate his remaining severance payments if it turned out that he had been guilty of "conduct" tending to bring him-self or Christie's into "disrepute," including "breaching any regulatory requirement or requirement of law."[34]

Linklater was incredulous. From Davidge, he knew that Patricia Barbizet had already been told of his involvement in an illegal conspiracy with Sotheby's. Whether Christie's London lawyers, Stephenson Harwood, were also aware of the conspiracy was unclear. But they appeared to be setting Davidge up to sign his own death warrant.

"That's absolutely unacceptable," Linklater told Newmark, shaking his head. It was ludicrous to expect Davidge to sign a document stating that he had broken no laws when pages of proof of his guilt lay in his very hands. But Christie's lawyers refused to back down. Without those two provisions there would be no deal, and no severance.

To Linklater's further consternation he received another demand from Christie's London lawyers for all Davidge's papers relating to his contacts with Sotheby's. Linklater declined to respond, but time was running out. Another clause in Davidge's severance contract required him to turn over all Christie's documents, including copies, along with company credit cards and keys, by December 31. To fail to do so would void his $8 million settlement.

To judge from the degree of hostility emanating from Christie's attorneys, Linklater was convinced that the firm was plotting to manoeuvre Davidge into a "clawback"—legal jargon for a move that would force him into a lie to get the first instalment of his severance money; Christie's could then refuse to make additional payments and even demand their money back on the grounds that he had lied.

Linklater made a daring calculation of Christie's intentions. If Christie's could point the finger of guilt at Davidge, they might be able to win amnesty from the Justice Department. But Linklater added a twist to the formula. He reckoned that Christie's could accomplish that feat only if they obtained his notes, which were the only conclusive, physical evidence of a conspiracy. The Chicago lawyer decided that the best plan of action was to take Davidge's papers with him to the United States and deliver them on his own terms. "I was troubled that if the documents remained in England in the possession of Christie's I might not be able to get my hands on them later if I needed them," he recalled.[35]

If the papers remained in the UK, Christie's would have no obligation to hand them over to federal prosecutors in New York, because the Justice Department lacked jurisdiction over company documents that the London-based company chose to keep in Britain.

To be on the safe side, Linklater had all of Davidge's pages photocopied by a paralegal, who carefully numbered each page. "I wanted to be sure to give them to an American lawyer who was dealing with a grand jury subpoena and knew what it meant," he noted. "And I was confident that a Skadden lawyer would deal with them professionally."[36]

"I didn't have a close working relationship with Christie's or its lawyers," Linklater continued, "and I thought that some effort might be made to carve him out."[37] (In legal terms, a "carve-out" occurs when a corporation seeking amnesty from federal prosecution attempts to exclude an individual from leniency—Christie's could save itself from legal peril and leave Davidge to fend for himself.)

After several hours at Baker & McKenzie, Linklater and Davidge repaired to Christie's to continue their all-day meeting, which lasted late into the night. In discussing their options, the two men decided that the only way that Davidge could receive at least the first instalment of his $8 million severance was to sign the flawed severance contract, with its patently absurd clauses denying that illegal conduct had taken place.

Linklater did not have the benefit of a crystal ball, but he felt confident that if he could establish that Davidge had not instigated the conspiracy there might be a way to make certain that he could collect his entire settlement and avoid exposure to massive criminal or civil fines. "I felt sure, based on what I knew about the people at the top of the Anti-trust Division, that they would not carve out somebody like Chris once they knew all the facts," he recalled.[38]

ON CHRISTMAS EVE, Christopher Davidge spent most of the day in his flat in Georgian House, nervously awaiting confirmation that the paperwork for his severance contract was complete and that the first payment of $3·2 million had been made into his bank account. Once he had received word that everything was in order, he walked around the corner to his office on King Street, accompanied by Amrita.

Over a glass of champagne, he signed his resignation letter in the office of Richard Aydon, Christie's chief legal officer. Peter Blythe, group finance director, was also present, with Ed Dolman, who signed the document on behalf of Christie's.

"I felt very calm," Davidge recalled, "and convinced that this was the right outcome for both myself and Christie's."[39]

Christie's directors waited until the end of the day on Christmas Eve, when much of the world was too busy wrapping gifts to pay much attention, to alert the company's 2,200 worldwide staff by e-mail that Chris Davidge had left the firm. In an accompanying e-mail to his former colleagues, Davidge sought to convey the impression that the idea for his departure had been his alone: "On January 1st, 2000 I will have been at Christie's for precisely 34 years," he wrote, "ten of which I have spent as Chief Executive. I have now decided to step down as Chief Executive Officer and a director and to hand on my responsibilities to Edward Dolman whom I identified some time ago as a worthy successor.

"The greatest satisfaction for me," he added, "has been the recognition of Christie's as the pre-eminent auctioneer. I would like to thank all of you for helping me in this achievement."[40]

Linklater had returned to Chicago with Davidge's notes bundled under his arm, and he left a voice mail for Cliff Aronson on Christmas Eve to say that he had some important documents for him. Startled by the message, Aronson tried calling Linklater on Christmas Day from Vail, where he was on a skiing vacation. He finally caught up with him on December 27.

Finding Aronson in a hostile mood, Linklater explained that before sending him Davidge's notes he should understand some facts about the conspiracy and the nature of the documents.

"I told you I want them," Aronson snapped. "If I don't have them by tomorrow we're exercising our option under the severance agreement."[41]

Undeterred, Linklater insisted on giving a thumbnail description of the files, hoping to convince Aronson that a carve-out of Davidge would be unwarranted. A criminal conspiracy had occurred, Linklater explained, but Davidge was not the instigator. One batch of the notes had been started by Anthony Tennant, who had discussed auction commissions with Sotheby's chairman. Another file contained the agendas of Davidge's meetings with Brooks, which had been set in motion subsequent to the first meetings between Taubman and Tennant. To prove his point, Linklater read aloud from Tennant's pivotal notes from April 30.

Aronson was shocked that such documents really did exist. He was also taken aback by Linklater's interpretation of the conspiracy—that Davidge had been acting on orders from Tennant. After listening to more excerpts, Aronson demanded that Linklater send all of the documents to his home in Rye, New York, by overnight FedEx.

With deep regret, Aronson cut short his Vail vacation and caught a flight back to New York to examine Davidge's disturbing pile of papers.

THE EMPTY LONDON STREETS were still adorned with Christmas decorations when Ed Dolman made his way to his new office at Christie's on King Street. Outside, all looked merry and bright. Inside, after only four days on the job as Christie's new worldwide CEO, he faced the unfolding of the worst crisis in the firm's 233-year history. Dolman had been thrust into the top job on short notice on Christmas Eve, after spending nearly fifteen years working his way up through Christie's. He had established a reputation for affability and pragmatism and was a popular choice for CEO. But at thirty-nine he was young to be thrust into a position of such responsibility.

Now that Chris Davidge's powder keg of documents was in Christie's possession, it fell to Dolman, his successor, and to Christie's in-house counsel in New York, Jo Backer Laird, to make the decision of whether to turn them over to the Justice Department. Given the likelihood that Sotheby's had already gotten wind of Davidge's departure, there was a dangerous possibility that the rival firm might try to beat Christie's to John Greene's door and plead for amnesty at Christie's expense.

Worse still, Davidge might try to get there first and bring about the ruin of both firms. Each scenario was too nauseating to contemplate, and Dolman and Laird clearly had only one choice: to hand the documents over *immediately*.

To the twenty-five original pages that Davidge had handed to Joe Linklater, along with multiple photocopies, the Skadden lawyers added hundreds of pages of documents that they thought might be relevant to the government's investigation. They included copies of Christie's grandfather lists which they had already culled from Davidge's office in London. By the time Christie's had assembled its final package, it had swelled to nearly six hundred pages.

Aronson was charged with the urgent errand of delivering them to John Greene. But when he dialled the prosecutor's office, he was told that Greene and his boss, Ralph Giordano, were on Christmas break. To Aronson's considerable relief, Greene received the message and called back to set up an emergency summit for the following day.

At one o'clock on Wednesday, December 29, 1999, Aronson walked into the austere thirty-sixth-floor offices of the Antitrust Division at Federal Plaza in downtown Manhattan. He announced himself to the receptionist, who sat in a glass-walled booth in front of a flickering computer screen festooned with stuffed toy animals. He was shown into a small conference room adorned with Victorian prints in gold frames. But Aronson was not looking at the art. Nervous as hell, but eager to maintain his composure, he made a formal presentation of the documents to John Greene and his colleague Patricia Jannaco and explained how they had come into his possession. He then read a few passages out loud before taking his leave.

The documents were a bombshell for the prosecutors. Without them, the auction house investigation had been spinning its wheels. With them, John Greene knew he could press for a conviction.

21

Secret Guilt

HAVING MADE the momentous decision to throw Christie's to the mercy of the Justice Department, Ed Dolman and the tiny circle of people aware of the firm's predicament were obliged to wait an agonizing three weeks before learning whether the company would be accepted into the government's antitrust amnesty program. In the interim, it was imperative that the matter remain top secret. One careless whisper could jeopardize the firm's chances for leniency and bring about legal and fiscal ruin.

Cliff Aronson was summoned to Washington on January 12 for a three-o'clock meeting at the Justice Department to present Christie's case for amnesty to a roomful of officials including James M. Griffin, the head of the government's antitrust enforcement program, and his deputy, Scott Hammond. John Greene was also present, with his fellow prosecutors from New York.

The Washington officials seemed sceptical of Christie's application for amnesty. They pointed out that despite receiving a subpoena in 1997, the auction house had waited two and a half years before coming forward to confess its crime. Aronson explained that Davidge had been the perpetrator, and that his incriminating documents had come to light only after his departure from Christie's. He also noted that the decision to hand over the documents had been made by Edward Dolman, the firm's new CEO, and Jo Backer Laird, its general counsel, who had no prior knowledge of the conspiracy.

Flicking through Davidge's notes, the Washington officials noticed that they contained countless abbreviations, obscure references and few dates. Without Davidge's cooperation, it would be almost impossible to extrapolate their precise meanings, and the prosecutors would have a tough time winning convictions of Sotheby's, Dede Brooks and Alfred Taubman.

As a British citizen, Davidge could not be compelled to come to America to stand trial. Price-fixing was illegal under British law, but it was a civil, not criminal, offence in England, so he could not be extradited. Faced with this dilemma, the government lawyers pressured Christie's to do what they themselves could not do—produce Davidge.

With Christie's fate weighing on his shoulders, Aronson called Linklater on Friday, January 14, to explain that the Justice Department wanted to know whether Davidge would lend his cooperation to Christie's in its application for amnesty. Linklater replied that he would have to consult with his client first.

The following Monday, Linklater called the Skadden lawyer to propose an unpalatable deal. Christie's application for amnesty, he noted, seemed to be riding on Davidge's decision to cooperate. Could he therefore assume that Christie's would agree to waive the two punitive provisions in his client's severance contract, and not seek to renege on its promise to pay Davidge's $8 million severance in full?

"I could hear his teeth grinding," Linklater recalled, chuckling. "Yes, you can rely on that," Aronson told him.[1]

With a heavy heart, Aronson delivered the news to Dolman and Laird that Christopher Davidge was prepared to save Christie's skin if the firm would agree to make good on its promise to make him a wealthy man.

Dolman composed an e-mail to Patricia Barbizet outlining Davidge's various demands, which included Christie's paying for all his legal fees and any fines. Once the deal was approved, Aronson immediately called John Greene to confirm that Davidge was on board.

DAVIDGE'S TROVE OF EXPLOSIVE documents jump-started John Greene's moribund investigation. The prosecutor wasted no time in issuing a flurry of subpoenas in the first two weeks of January to Alfred Taubman and his various companies—the Taubman Realty Group, TaubCo Management, Inc., Taubman Centres, Inc. and the Taubman Company Limited Partnership. The subpoenas demanded the production of all his diaries, calendars, telephone bills, business and travel records from January 1992 to January 2000 relating to his responsibilities as an owner and director of Sotheby's Holdings and his contacts with representatives of any other auction house.

Upon learning of the subpoenas, Sotheby's in-house counsel Don Pillsbury conferred with the antitrust lawyers at Weil, Gotshal, trying to figure out what was going on. There seemed to be no particular cause for concern. It was common practice when prosecutors were closing an investigation to issue a final round of subpoenas in order to ensure that they had left no stone unturned. The lawyers surmised that the whole investigation was running out of steam.

"We knew that the grand jury was going to expire soon," a Sotheby's lawyer recalled, "and we thought that it would end with a whimper rather than a bang."[2]

When John Greene received the green light from Washington to grant Christie's conditional amnesty, he called Cliff Aronson at midday on January 24, 2000—exactly one month after Davidge's departure from Christie's—to deliver the news. Two days later, Aronson received a copy of the final amnesty agreement from the government, signed by Gary Spratling, the deputy assistant attorney general.

Christie's amnesty agreement was conditional upon two key clauses. First, that upon discovering the anticompetitive conduct it was reporting to the prosecutors, the firm had taken "prompt and effective action" to terminate its part in the conspiracy and come forward to report the activity. Second, that Christie's had not coerced Sotheby's to participate in the criminal activity nor had it been the originator of the conspiracy.

The stark reality, however, was that although Ed Dolman and Jo Backer Laird could genuinely be said to have had no idea that the illegal collusion existed until shortly before Christie's made its application for amnesty, there were several Christie's senior directors who had at least some reason to suspect it by 1997, and had done nothing to stop it. The list included Christie's chairman, Lord Hindlip; the deputy chairman, François Curiel; the former general counsel, Patty Hambrecht; its honorary chairman Christopher Burge; and its new American chairman, Stephen Lash.

To grant Christie's amnesty when almost the entire hierarchy of the firm may have been suspicious of the conspiracy for several years could be considered questionable. But fairness was not the government's concern. The provision in the Anti-trust Division's amnesty policy that allowed corporations to come clean even after a federal investigation had begun had yielded a bonanza of convictions since 1993, when the policy was expanded to protect such Johnny-come-lately criminals willing to grab amnesty at the expense of their co-conspirators. Previously, a price-fixer who wanted amnesty in exchange for testifying against a co-conspiring competitor was obliged to bring his information to the Antitrust Division before any investigation had begun.

Another curious aspect of the conditional amnesty afforded to Christie's was that the real originator of the conspiracy might at that stage in the investigation have been Sir Anthony Tennant of Christie's, *not* Alfred Taubman of Sotheby's—a suggestion clear to Christopher Davidge, who had not yet been given an opportunity to share this with the prosecutors. Christie's conditional amnesty seemed to be based on incomplete research.

The supreme irony was that two of the ostensible instigators and orchestrators of the conspiracy—Tennant and Davidge—were getting away scot-free, while their American counterparts at Sotheby's—Taubman and Brooks—faced ruin.

NINETEEN NINETY-NINE had been a spectacular year for Sotheby's and for Dede Brooks, who had every reason to feel proud of her accomplishments. She had been instrumental in negotiating for the firm to hold a single-owner sale of Impressionist and Modern artworks from the collection of Mr. and Mrs. John Hay Whitney—one of the greatest private art collections in America—which had fetched a staggering $128,315,600 in May. The evening auction included the sale of Cézanne's *Rideau, cruchon et compotier*—a glorious still-life composition painted by the father of modern art in 1893.

The picture had sold for $60·5 million, a record sum for a Cézanne and the fourth-highest price ever achieved for a painting sold at auction.

That same year, Sotheby's had achieved a record $49·5 million for Picasso's *Femme assise dans un jardin*, a Cubist portrait of the artist's mistress Dora Maar, which he had painted in a single day. Other triumphs included $4·04 million for a 55-carat diamond ring and $387,000 for Lou Gehrig's last baseball glove.

Even colleagues who had endured her blistering screaming fits and towering rages acknowledged that Brooks could be magnificent in business. No one in the auction world could match her extraordinary combination of talents for negotiating multimillion-dollar deals with clients, plotting the firm's global financial strategy and inspiring staff to push themselves to the limit of their capacities. Under her watch as chief executive, auction sales had skyrocketed from $1·33 billion in 1994 to $2·26 billion for 1999. She had also led the company's expansion to encompass ninety-four offices in thirty-six countries with fourteen worldwide salesrooms holding 750 auctions a year.

But suddenly, she feared that all her achievements were about to come crashing down on her head.

DEDE BROOKS ARRIVED at Sotheby's shortly after one o'clock on Friday afternoon, January 28, 2000, looking tanned and exhausted. She had just returned from an out-of-town jaunt with a group of the firm's top clients to Casa de Campo, a luxurious resort in the Dominican Republic, for a few rounds of golf at the island's famously challenging course, the Teeth of the Dog.

Her Caribbean idyll had been interrupted on Thursday evening when her friend Don Pillsbury telephoned to deliver puzzling news: Christie's lawyers had called to break off the formal joint-defence agreement they had made with Sotheby's in 1997 when the two firms received subpoenas from the Justice Department looking into possible illegal practices in the art business.

Pillsbury was concerned, but had no reason to comprehend the magnitude of the information he was imparting. Brooks, however, was thunderstruck. She was still reeling the next day when she returned to her office to face a pile of mail and messages that had accumulated in her absence. "I was in such shell shock that I hadn't slept the night before," she recalled. "I immediately figured out that something was up."[3]

Starting to panic, Brooks sensed a connection between Pillsbury's news and the abrupt departure of Christopher Davidge from Christie's a month before. "I hadn't talked to Davidge in *years,* so I had no clue why he had left Christie's," she recalled.[4].' Now, she began to fear that Davidge had been forced to leave the rival firm because of antitrust concerns and that he had somehow implicated her in an illegal conspiracy. Terrified of what might happen next, Brooks decided it was imperative to find herself a criminal attorney. But she had no idea where to start.

"I had never had a lawyer in my *life,*" she confided later, while under house arrest at her $5 million, twelve-room apartment on Manhattan's Upper East Side.[5]

Brooks' first choice for counsel was John Siffert, the shrewd and boyishly handsome fifty-two-year-old lawyer who for the past two years had been representing a slew of Sotheby's executives, art experts and secretaries who had been called before the grand jury in connection with the government's inquiry.

By a peculiar twist of fate, Siffert had already made a four-o'clock appointment with Brooks that day in order to get acquainted. Having shepherded several of her colleagues through the grand jury process, he thought it likely that she would be the next witness to be called, and thus his future client. As far as Siffert could tell, the government's antitrust investigation was running out of steam due to a lack of evidence. He fully expected Brooks to be the last Sotheby's employee to be called to testify before the grand jury before the federal prosecutors threw in the towel.

Just before Siffert's arrival, however, Brooks was chatting in her office with Susan Alexander, the director of Sotheby's human resources, when the head of the press office, Diana Phillips, interrupted with urgent news: A reporter from the *Financial Times* had called and was demanding a comment from Brooks for an explosive article due to run the following day. Phillips explained that according to the *FT,* Christie's had turned over new information to the U.S. Justice Department pertaining to the auction-house antitrust investigation and had been granted conditional amnesty from prosecution. What was Sotheby's response?

Brooks was stricken with fright, but she was careful to show no sign of alarm to her colleagues. Once they had left the room, however, she buried her face in her hands and felt as if she were being swept up in a tidal wave.

By chance, John Siffert arrived early for what he expected to be a pleasant, perfunctory meeting with Dede Brooks, along with Sotheby's in-house lawyers and outside antitrust counsel from Weil, Gotshal & Manges. To his astonishment, Brooks invited him to step into the conference room next to her office with her alone. She shut the door firmly behind them and began to weep.

Shaking with emotion and speaking through tears, Brooks unburdened herself of a guilty secret that had dogged her for the past six years. The topic was so sensitive and fraught with danger, she explained, that she had told no one about this. Not even her husband, Michael.

As Siffert listened in amazement, the forty-nine-year-old executive divulged the secret history of her illicit communications with Christopher Davidge. "I knew I could have, and should have, stopped it," Brooks admitted. "I could have said no and I didn't."[6]

Siffert was nonplussed. As a lawyer, he was paid to be sceptical. But in two years of providing counsel to members of Sotheby's staff, nothing had given him any indication that Brooks had been involved in any wrongdoing, or that any conspiracy had occurred.

"Dede was really very forthright and very troubled and immediately accepted responsibility for what she had done," Siffert recalled. "She understood this was going to result in a dramatic effect on her life and her relationship with Sotheby's."

As Siffert listened, Brooks described the topics she had discussed with Davidge. She confessed to having tried to fool herself that she had done nothing illegal.

"I had convinced myself that we didn't have an agreement, but that we had *talked,*" she recalled. "In my own mind, I never did agree

252 LORDS AND LIARS

to it verbally. I never signed anything. I never said, 'I agree to it.' So I was convinced that I wasn't really breaking the law. If you want to, you can delude yourself into thinking that nothing's going to come of it," she added. "Because when it comes down to it, how are they actually going to *prove* it?"

Without any documents to establish her guilt, Brooks felt, "It's his word versus mine, and it's an interpretation. Obviously, I was very, very scared," she recalled, "but it wasn't so clear-cut that I was going to go turn myself in the next day and say 'mea culpa.'"[8]

"We didn't spend a lot of time talking about the seller's commission," she added. "All told, before it happened, we didn't spend more than maybe an hour or two talking about it, over the months. My view was, I just wanted him to do it. There was no question that we were going to follow if he did it."

Having never had her own lawyer to turn to for advice, Brooks was unsure of the provisions of the Sherman Antitrust Act. In describing her actions, she learned for the first time that they had alarming legal ramifications.

"It wasn't until I talked to John Siffert that I realized that my conversations with Davidge amounted to an agreement," she said.[9]

Siffert could see that Brooks was in a highly emotional state. He encouraged her to get home quickly so that she could break the news to her family and think about her next move. To confess her crime immediately to either Sotheby's or the government would severely limit her options. At this point it was vital to do and say as little as possible.

John Siffert was low-key and the very model of discretion, but he had handled a colourful roster of criminal cases. As a promising young assistant United States attorney in 1977, he had successfully prosecuted "Fat Tony" Salerno on tax-evasion charges, to the exasperation of Roy Cohn, the reputed mobster's formidable attorney. Siffert had also won the first insider-trading case in 1978 and held the distinction of having represented Truman Capote in a notorious libel case against Gore Vidal. (When pressed, Siffert could perform a brilliant imitation of Capote exclaiming, "I'm not going to pay Mr. Vidal one dime."[10])

Brooks was impressed with Siffert's incisive evaluation of her legal woes and asked him to be her lawyer. He pointed out that to do so could create a serious conflict of interest. If a case should go to trial, he would be prevented from cross-examining his existing Sotheby's clients in her defence. It *might* be possible for him to represent her, he explained, but he would first need to obtain their permission. In the meantime, he promised to help her find another lawyer.

Siffert explained that it was vital for her to have independent counsel to help her reach her first decision, which would be irreversible: whether to cooperate with the government's investigation. To Brooks' horror, he warned her that if found guilty of violating the Sherman Antitrust Act she could face a huge criminal fine and spend three years in gaol.

AFTER NINETY harrowing minutes discussing her plight, Brooks and Siffert braced themselves to face Sotheby's lawyers, who had been cooling their heels outside her door. At five-thirty, the attorneys and eight senior Sotheby's executives gathered for an emergency meeting.

Entering the conference room, Brooks' colleagues were shocked to find their usually exuberant and outspoken CEO looking pale and cornered, sitting in abject silence. To their bewilderment the only words she uttered were to alert them that a potentially damaging story was expected to appear in the next day's paper. She then introduced John Siffert, who explained that he had advised his new client to say nothing further.

For those in the room with no clue of what had already transpired, the presence of Steve Reiss and Richard Davis of Weil, Gotshal, Sotheby's outside counsel, seemed to underscore the gravity of the occasion. "It was obvious there must be a meaningful six-hundred-dollar-an-hour matter to discuss," noted Bill Ruprecht, the managing director of Sotheby's North and South America.[11]

It was puzzling to most of the Sotheby's senior executives present that it was John Siffert—a high-powered criminal attorney they had never met—who ran the meeting, not the normally combative, take-charge Dede Brooks, who thrived in a crisis.

"Something clearly totally traumatic was unfolding, and we didn't have any sense of what it was," Diana Phillips recalled, "but I knew it was absolutely dire. Looking at Dede's face, I knew that something absolutely terrible had happened."[12]

Siffert quietly explained that Christie's appeared to have reached an amnesty agreement in connection with the government's antitrust investigation, and he warned that Sotheby's only response should be: "No comment." The firm's attorneys strongly disagreed. They were aghast at the serious allegations due to be made against Sotheby's in the next day's *Financial Times* and argued that it was essential for the auction house to issue an emphatic public statement declaring that no improper conduct had taken place.

Calmly, and without betraying the secret of Brooks' guilt, Siffert reiterated that Sotheby's should merely say, "No comment." He sensed an impending legal storm and knew that any denial of wrong-doing at this stage could expose Sotheby's, and Brooks, to further criminal and possible civil claims that could incur hundreds of millions of dollars in fines.

Once Brooks and her colleagues had left for the evening, Siffert stayed behind to chat with Sotheby's lawyers. Trying to decipher Siffert's opaque responses to their questions, the firm's attorneys wondered out loud whether there might be a connection between the *FT*'s call and the slew of subpoenas that Alfred Taubman and his various companies had received in the past few weeks.

"They started speculating about whether Dede knew that Taubman had done something wrong, but she wasn't involved," Siffert recalled. "Then they wanted to issue a press release saying that no *employees* had been involved. And I said that it was wiser to say, 'No comment.' I knew things they didn't know, and I was not prepared to tell them."[13]

The significance of what had just transpired was unclear to many of Brooks' colleagues, who came away thoroughly confused. "Something was wrong, but I didn't know *what*," Bill Ruprecht recalled. "I went home for the weekend thinking, 'I wonder what happened?'"[14]

Susan Alexander, who had been with Brooks when she first

learned of the *FT's* call, was equally perplexed. "It felt like stepping off a cliff," she recalled. "What struck me was 'Where did all these lawyers come from and how did they get here so fast?' We just did-n't know what we were in for," she added, "but you knew walking out of that room that life was never going to be the same."[15]

LATER THAT NIGHT in London, Robin Woodhead, Sotheby's perennially chipper CEO for Europe and Asia, ignored the blinking light on his answering machine when he returned home from dinner after a long day at the office. On the way to his country house in Dorset the following morning, he pulled into a gas station and was stopped in his tracks by the blaring headline on the front page of the *Financial Times*: CHRISTIE'S ADMITS FIXING COMMISSIONS: AUCTION HOUSE TELLS THE U.S. JUSTICE DEPARTMENT THAT IT MADE DEAL WITH SOTHEBY'S.

"I felt as if I'd been hit by a truck," he recalled.[16]

The article was ostensibly focused on Christie's admission of guilt, but the accompanying photograph on page one of Dede Brooks, Wood-head's boss, gave a clear indication that Sotheby's was now the primary target of the Justice Department's criminal investigation.

Within hours, the news had sent shudders of astonishment through-out art, financial and social circles around the globe. In Palm Beach, Florida, major players in the art world were assembling for an international art-and-antique fair when a cacophony of cell-phone calls from Europe, Asia and New York began delivering the news.

Some New York dealers expressed jubilation that the hated auc-tion houses had finally been caught red-handed, but details were frustratingly scarce. Godfrey Barker, the British journalist, became an instant art-fair celebrity when gossip circulated that he was speak-ing on the telephone to Christopher Davidge in the Bahamas. Davidge, the rumour went, was staying with Joe Lewis on Lyford Cay, luxuriating in the sunshine while the art world absorbed the jolting news.*

---

* In fact, he was travelling in Latin America. "I was in Argentina, blissfully unaware," Davidge recalled.

Jeff Miro, Taubman's longtime confidant and lawyer, had been fly-fishing in the Florida Keys on Friday afternoon when his serenity was broken by a call on his cell phone from Don Pillsbury at Sotheby's.

"We don't know what's going on," Pillsbury told him, "but Christie's has advised us that they will have to pull out of our joint defence agreement regarding antitrust."

"What are you getting at?" Miro asked.

"There's going to be a piece in the *Financial Times*," Pillsbury warned. "It has something to do with Dede and Al. Apparently Al had a meeting with Tennant."

"I'm at a loss as to what you're talking about," Miro replied. "One of his *tenants*? In which mall?"[17]

THE FOLLOWING MORNING, while on his way to the Miami airport to catch a flight back to Detroit, Miro called Dede Brooks, who had left him a message on Friday night.

"Dede, what's going on?" Miro asked. "What's this about one of Al's tenants?"

"No, not *a tenant*," Brooks replied. "*Anthony* Tennant."

"I don't know who Anthony Tennant is," Miro told her. "I'm still at a loss. Is this about the antitrust case?"

"I think Al could be in trouble," Brooks warned him. "I've been thinking about this, and I think Al ought to just sell his Sotheby's stock and get out."

"Dede, if there's trouble brewing why would Al Taubman want to walk out the door with a target on his back?" Miro replied. "I've never seen him walk away from trouble. As a company, we'll just deal with it."

"Yeah, I guess you're right," Brooks said, with uncharacteristic acquiescence.

After hanging up, Miro was bewildered. "I thought, this is more serious than Dede is letting on," he recalled. "The company must really have a problem."[18]

22

Disaster

WHILE A TALE of gothic horror had been unfolding at Sotheby's on Friday afternoon, the atmosphere in Christie's executive offices was considerably more confident and up-beat. The news of Christie's amnesty had hit the wire services, and newspapers from around the world were calling the firm's New York and London offices.

Ed Dolman addressed a group of fellow executives and warned them that trouble lay ahead: "However bad it will be for us, it will be *much* worse for Sotheby's."[1] Christie's employees worldwide were instructed not to talk to the media, and the firm's Press Department issued an opaque and carefully worded statement vetted by the lawyers: "Christie's new owner, and our new senior management, recently became aware of information relevant to the antitrust investigation being conducted by the Department of Justice. The information concerns possible conduct prior to the tenure of our new management. We immediately disclosed that information to the government. Christie's can confirm that we have been granted conditional amnesty by the Department of Justice.

"Christie's new management and new owner are committed to up-holding the standards of trust and integrity that have been the hallmark of Christie's business for over two centuries. We are cooperating fully with the Department of Justice's investigation and will continue to do so."[2]

Although emboldened by their amnesty, Christie's directors expected a firestorm the following day when the *Financial Times* hit the stands. Senior executives and experts began a hasty telephone campaign to major clients in an effort to do some damage control.

Christopher Burge, Christie's honorary chairman and the firm's star auctioneer, placed one of his first calls to Herbert Black.

"Herb, listen, I have to tell you something before you read it in the newspapers," Burge said. "We've turned over documents to the Justice Department that confirm that we had an arrangement with Sotheby's. And, er, I just felt that you'd really be upset when you'll read this, so I'd rather call you and just make peace with you now."[3]

If Burge expected a sympathetic response, he was mistaken. "How much are you going to pay me?" Black asked, point-blank. "*Pay you*?" Burge asked with a nervous laugh.

"Yes," Black replied. "With what you've just acknowledged I feel there's money owing."[4]

Immediately after hanging up from Burge, Black called his friend Chris Lovell, a prominent antitrust lawyer in New York, who had won a record $1.027 billion settlement in a price-fixing case related to the NASDAQ market.

"We have a great case," Lovell assured him. Five hours later, the New York lawyer had drafted a complaint which he faxed to Black at home in Montreal. The two men agreed the lawsuit should allude to the suspiciously identical commission rates Sotheby's and Christie's had introduced during the nineties for their buyer's and seller's commissions. "Beginning at least as early as or about January 1, 1992," Lovell wrote, "defendants agreed to cease competing with one another on the basis of price."[5]

At ten o'clock on the morning of Sunday, January 30, 2000, Lovell filed the first civil antitrust lawsuit against Christie's and Sotheby's in New York, calling for the federal court to compel the auction houses to "disgorge their ill-gotten and unlawful gains."

Black's timely lawsuit inspired others. By Tuesday, seventeen suits had been filed against Sotheby's and Christie's, and dozens more were on their way. The group of angry customers who filed suits within the first few weeks included Evelyn Frank, a New York businesswoman known as the Tugboat Empress and the Dragon Lady, whose family ran a maritime business in New York and New

Jersey. Like many of his fellow complainants, Black was unsentimental about bringing charges against the two auction houses, which had courted him so assiduously for years.

"If you break the law, you have to pay, you know what I mean?" Black told me, speaking from a cell phone from his car in Montreal. "They're not higher and above the law." Black seemed to relish the notoriety his lawsuit might bring him. "You've talked to people-what's their attitude to Mr. Black?" he asked me cheerfully. "Okay, I might have lost a few friends and made a few enemies. So be it."[6]

ON MONDAY, JANUARY 31, the first day of trading since the Financial Times revelations, there was frenzied trading on Sotheby's stock, listed as BID on the New York Stock Exchange. Shares plunged by 14.58 percent, falling by $3.50 to close at $20.50, after dipping as much as 20 percent during the day. Sensing trouble ahead, several Wall Street analysts promptly downgraded their recommendations.

Christie's, being a privately held company, did not have to weather such indignities. In order to signal an end to its role in the alleged auction house conspiracy, the London-based firm announced changes to its buyer's premiums and seller's commissions on February 7, 2000. Under the new rates, it would become more expensive to buy art at Christie's and cheaper to sell—a shrewd way of trying to win business away from Sotheby's.

Beginning on March 31, Christie's would begin charging buyers 17.5 percent on the first $80,000 of the hammer price and 10 percent above (up from the previous rate of 15 percent on the first $50,000 and 10 per-cent thereafter). The new rates for private sellers were effective immediately.

Ed Dolman, Christie's new CEO, claimed that the firm had been considering the changes for the past year. The sudden change, the firm declared, had "simply been accelerated by the recent events"—another oblique reference to the price-fixing scandal that was rocking the art world.

Later that month, Sotheby's introduced a new sliding scale of buyer's commissions, which were slightly more expensive than those at Christie's. But Sotheby's matched Christie's new seller's commissions for private sellers almost exactly. As before, Sotheby's new rate sheet included special reduced rates for dealers and museums.

After both firms had adjusted their rates, Ed Dolman reflected how extraordinarily easy it had been for Christie's to raise its commission structure and for Sotheby's to follow. "Collusion was completely unnecessary," he noted. Dolman surmised that the conspiracy had taken place because Davidge and Brooks had been, "two egos out of control, power-mad and fancying themselves as great deal makers."[7]

Henry Wyndham, Sotheby's London chairman, was similarly mystified. "I don't know why there needed to be a conversation at all," he said. "As you can see, we changed our commission and there was no need to talk.

"With a duopoly, it's like two people selling tomatoes in the street. If one person raises or lowers their prices, the other one's going to follow."[8]

As news of the auction houses' perfidy began to sink in, many people in the art business expressed a sense of outrage. "This is a spectacularly big deal for the art world," observed Victor Weiner, the executive director of the Appraisers Association of America in New York. "Anyone who had a personal relationship with an auction house in the last few years could feel betrayed. A lot of collectors are fuming mad about this."[9]

Rival auction houses were hopeful that public outrage might send some business their way. "Sotheby's and Christie's have a very tight grip on the top end of the market," noted Nick Bonham, the deputy chairman of the London auction house that bears his family's name. "It may just be that one or two people may decide to try one of the other salesrooms."[10]

To many art dealers, news that the auction houses had been caught red-handed was not a surprise. "It never for a moment occurred to me Christie's and Sotheby's hadn't come to some arrangement," said Alex Wengraf, a London dealer, who was jubilant at the fate that had befallen Sotheby's and Christie's.[11] "As far as I'm concerned, anything that hurts them is good for the trade.

They've always portrayed themselves as great institutions when really they're just dealers like the rest of us and on the whole they are less honourable than the independent dealers."[12]

THE NEWS OF CHRISTIE'S conditional amnesty deal did come as a shock to many at the company. Even senior experts had no idea of the firm's dramatic negotiations with the Justice Department, or that Davidge had been actively colluding with Brooks.

Charlie Hindlip was overjoyed at Davidge's departure, but was furious that he had gotten away with such a huge severance bonanza. "I wanted Davidge out of Christie's," he admitted. "But I think the settlement he got was *outrageous*. I feel it's wrong. He shouldn't have asked for it, and he shouldn't have been given it." Eight million dollars, he noted, was an extortionate sum "for a thoroughly unsatisfactory chief executive who had committed what in America is a criminal act."[13]

WITH STORM CLOUDS LOOMING on the horizon, Don Pillsbury advised Taubman and Brooks to hire their own legal representation. When Jeff Miro asked for a recommendation, Pillsbury suggested Scott W. Muller, an attorney with a brilliant reputation at his old firm, Davis Polk & Wardwell.

Miro felt confident about accepting Pillsbury's recommendation. In early February, Muller went to meet Taubman for the first time at a face-to-face meeting at his Fifth Avenue office. Joining Muller on the case was Robert B. Fiske, Jr., a distinguished criminal attorney who had served as U.S. attorney in the Southern District of New York during the late seventies, and as the first independent counsel in the Whitewater investigation.

The lawyers were clearly first-rate. So were their fees. Fiske's hourly rate was $650, Muller's $500. If Taubman were to be charged with a crime and the matter should come to court, the process was likely to take as long as two years—a time frame that could earn Muller and Fiske fees upward of $2 million apiece. It was an expensive gamble, Miro realized, but entirely worthwhile if they could keep Taubman out of gaol.

Having signed on to represent Sotheby's former chairman, the lawyers were concerned to learn that he had lost a lot of his mental acuity during the past year. Taubman had been razor sharp for most of life, but lately he was becoming increasingly confused and forgetful. Piecing together a case based on his failing memory was not going to be easy.

Taubman's health had taken a turn for the worse while he was summering at Meadow Beach, his house in Southampton, in July 1999. It was one of the hottest days in years, and the electricity had failed, bringing the air-conditioning to a halt. "I pleaded with Alfred not to venture out," Judy Taubman recalled, "but he wanted some fresh air. He returned shortly after—a frightening sight—like a wounded bear. Barely able to walk and looking disorientated, he slumped into a chair, totally incoherent."[14]

Neurological tests indicated he had suffered a series of strokes. Fiercely proud as usual and protective of her husband, Judy told friends that he had a temporary "heat stroke." After that incident, Taubman's personality seemed to change. The ebullient, blustery tycoon had become uncharacteristically docile.

"What the hell happened to you? You're *nice*!" Melinda Marcuse joked.

"No I'm *not*," Taubman remonstrated, laughing![15]

Taubman's feisty personality had begun to reemerge since the summer, but he remained frail. Those close to him were fearful of the repercussions for his health if the prosecutors should choose to launch criminal proceedings against him. A trial, they feared, could prove fatal.

AS THE INTERNATIONAL MEDIA continued to pry, Sotheby's and Christie's staff were ordered not to discuss the antitrust matter with anyone. Many people at Sotheby's were bewildered to learn of allegations of a conspiracy with the firm's hated archcompetitor.

"The culture here at Sotheby's is so competitive with Christie's," David Redden, vice chairman of Sotheby's North America, noted.[16] "And it's quite personal. Because if *we* don't get it, *they* get it.

"For us who compete daily with Christie's over property, the idea that you would actually talk to them and have a conversation in which you say, 'Hey, let's conspire together,' is *inconceivable*. It's so beyond the realm of reality.

"Trust is so fundamental to the way we do business," Redden continued. "Many of our clients come in knowing nothing about the objects they own. They turn them over to us absolutely on faith—that we know what we're doing, that we will look after them properly, that they won't be cheated.

"The actions that have undermined and betrayed that trust," he added gravely, "were unconscionable."

IN THE TENSE, dramatic days following Brooks' tearful confession, John Siffert prompted Brooks to recall as many specific details as she could of her meetings with Davidge, and to reconstruct the thrust of her conversations with Taubman during the conspiracy.

Brooks was distraught, but she was keeping up with her normal hectic schedule. She flew to Seattle to meet with Jeff Bezos, the founder of Amazon.com, to discuss their joint venture in sothebys.amazon.com. In the midst of other discussions involving some of her colleagues from New York, Brooks met privately with Bezos and explained that Sotheby's was in serious trouble as a result of the new developments in the government's antitrust investigation.

"I just wanted him to know, from me, that things were not good," Brooks recalled.[17]

She was in Seattle with a retinue of senior Sotheby's executives who were struck by the somewhat surreal intensity with which she was carrying on with business. "She was extremely manic, wanting to make new deals and new resolutions," Bill Ruprecht recalled. "There was an urgency and desperation about what she wanted to achieve in a couple of hours that was bewildering. I didn't understand it."[18]

ON HER RETURN to New York, Brooks hired a second lawyer, Steve Kaufman, a respected, legendary New York lawyer with an avuncular manner. Kaufman's credentials, like Siffert's, were impec-

cable. He had once been the youngest chief of the Criminal Division
in the United States Attorney's Office, and his list of clients included Michael Milken, the Aga Khan, George Steinbrenner and Frank
Sinatra.

Kaufman had never met Brooks. But by a remarkable coincidence he had also represented her brother, Andy Dwyer, back in
1992 when he was the subject of an investigation by the SEC.
Kaufman had been instrumental in resolving Andy's problems
before the matter got to court, and Andy was more than happy to
pass on a glowing recommendation to his sister.

Having no knowledge of Davidge's amnesty deal with the gov-
ernment, or of his explosive trove of incriminating documents,
Kaufman and Siffert surmised that the federal prosecutors would
have a hard time proving Brooks' guilt if a case should come to trial.
Press reports were indicating that Davidge had been excluded from
Christie's amnesty deal, and it seemed obvious that without his
cooperation, the government probably had no concrete proof of
Brooks' involvement in the conspiracy.

Nevertheless, having witnessed Brooks' emotional confession in
late January, Siffert felt certain that she would wind up choosing to
cooperate with the government rather than opting to fight a tough
case in court. "Going through a trial requires a very steely kind of
personality," he noted, "and Dede was very forthright and troubled
by what she had done."[19]

In advising Brooks of her other options, Kaufman and Siffert
pointed out that she could go directly to the Department of Justice
to try to strike the best possible deal for herself, without telling
Taubman or Sotheby's.

"Dede rejected it," recalled Siffert, praising what he perceived as
his client's high-mindedness. "She said, 'I don't want to unnecessarily hurt Sotheby's or Taubman,'" he continued. "She felt a responsibility to Sotheby's and its employees and to Taubman, who had
been decent to her throughout her career. And she thought she
would give Taubman and Sotheby's an opportunity to accept
responsibility as well. She hoped they could make a joint deal that
was best for everybody."[20]

Kaufman and Siffert scheduled a 2:45 P.M. appointment with Steve Reiss and Richie Davis, Sotheby's outside antitrust counsel, at the Weil, Gotshal lawyers' offices on the thirty-fourth floor of Trump Plaza, overlooking Central Park. The date was February 14, but their message was no valentine. In a necessarily blunt conversation, Brooks' lawyers delivered an outline of their client's version of the conspiracy. At the direction of Alfred Taubman, she had met with Christopher Davidge in 1993 and the two executives had held illegal discussions over auction commissions.

The Sotheby's lawyers were aghast to learn that a conspiracy had indeed existed, and to realize that Brooks had been lying to them for years. They were also appalled to learn that Taubman was implicated. Left with little choice, they tentatively agreed to Brooks' proposal that she, Taubman and Sotheby's—through their respective counsel—should form a joint defence agreement to try to reach a global settlement that would limit Sotheby's exposure to a serious criminal fine.

Leaving a legal morass in her wake, Brooks flew to Paris that evening in a last-ditch effort to save a major deal that seemed likely to go to Christie's. The prospective consignment was an exquisite Picasso portrait that was being offered by a French family, and it was expected to fetch somewhere in the region of $30 million.

Brooks had also made an appointment with Bernard Arnault, the chairman of LVMH Moët Hennessy—Louis Vuitton. In an earlier conversation, she and the French billionaire had discussed the fact that, during the summer of 1999, Arnault had offered Alfred Taubman an opportunity to sell his controlling 13·2 million shares in Sotheby's at $47 each—a price that would have given the American the tidy sum of $620·4 million. Taubman had refused to sell, acting on Brooks' advice that he should hold out for $100 a share—a price Arnault was unwilling to pay.

The legal travails of Sotheby's and Christie's appeared to be a bonanza for Arnault. Having failed to buy Sotheby's from Taubman the previous year, he had purchased Phillips, the London-based auction house, in November 1999 for the trifling sum of $115 million. Founded in 1796, Phillips had long been a distant third to

Sotheby's and Christie's, but with Arnault's financial muscle it suddenly had a strong potential for being able to take on the two giants, who were mired in an expensive and embarrassing scandal that was likely to drag on for years. Arnault had a powerful motive for wanting to dominate the international art market: Christie's had been purchased in 1998 by his hated archrival, François Pinault, who was said to be the richest man in France. Gleeful over the auction-house travails of his archrival, Arnault vowed to transform Phillips into a luxury company that could rival the beleaguered Sotheby's and Christie's.

Arnault confided to Brooks that he was still seriously considering the option of making a bid to purchase Sotheby's outright. Brooks warned Arnault that serious criminal allegations were being made about Sotheby's in the United States, but she tried to convince him that buying the publicly traded auction house would still be a great investment. "I said that Sotheby's was about the experts and the distribution network, the franchise all over the world and its clients," Brooks recalled. "I just wanted him to know what a great place it was, so that even if I left he should still look at the company as a possibility."[21]

WHILE STILL IN PARIS on Wednesday night, Brooks received a call from Don Pillsbury, who explained that the Audit Committee of Sotheby's board had been informed of Brooks' account of the conspiracy and that there were grave concerns about her future with the company.

Brooks was devastated, but not surprised. She realized she should probably try to get back to New York as soon as possible, but decided to spend the following day fervently pitching for the $30 million Picasso with two of her European colleagues, the London paintings expert Michel Straus and Princess Laure de Beauvau-Craon, the head of Sotheby's office in Paris.

"Little did they know it was probably one of the hardest days of my life," Brooks recalled, "because I knew at that point that things were really *bad*."[22]

Realizing that the jig was up, Brooks returned from Paris on

Thursday night to find her lawyers preparing for a showdown with the federal prosecutors the following day.

When lawyers for Brooks, Taubman and Sotheby's arrived at the Antitrust Division's office at Federal Plaza, they were shown into the large conference room—a long, windowless space festooned with cheap prints of Impressionist paintings in fake gold frames, including a Monet seascape and a van Gogh street scene. The government lawyers were so embarrassed by the cheap copies of the sort of multimillion-dollar paintings sold by Sotheby's and Christie's that they deliberately seated counsel for Brooks, Taubman and Sotheby's with their backs to the offending pictures.

"I didn't select the art," John Greene assured me later.[23]

Steve Reiss kicked off a fraught two-hour-long meeting with John Greene and Ralph Giordano by explaining that Sotheby's was seeking to enter a corporate guilty plea that would spare Brooks and Taubman from prosecution as individuals. Greene remained impassive in his chair as groups of lawyers for the various parties filed in and out of the room, taking turns to try to win him over. The Weil, Gotshal lawyers were taken aback that Giordano, John Greene's boss, sat at the meeting with his cowboy boots up on the table, chomping an unlit cigar.

When it came time for Siffert and Kaufman to make their presentation on Brooks' behalf, they were treading on thin ice. Relying on speculation that Christie's had carved Christopher Davidge out of its amnesty deal, Siffert earnestly told the prosecutor that Brooks was prepared to deliver incriminating testimony to implicate Davidge in a criminal conspiracy.

If Greene was wildly amused by the spectacle of Brooks' counsel making a solemn promise to deliver a witness whom he already had in his pocket, he at least had the good grace not to laugh out loud. Little did they realize that the prosecutor was counting on Davidge to incriminate Brooks, Taubman and Sotheby's.

Next, Scott Muller met alone with the prosecutors, who informed him of an allegation that Brooks was making: that when Taubman had met with Tennant in 1993, Taubman had told Christie's chairman that Sotheby's and Christie's should work together to improve the bottom line, and that they should raise their seller's commissions. Muller was shocked. "I said flatly that I'd never heard such a thing and that it was not true," he recalled.[24]

The allegation was all the more startling for Muller since Brooks' lawyers had neglected to tell him of that particular wrinkle in the story, which was potentially ruinous to Taubman's defence.

When it came Weil, Gotshal's turn to plead with the prosecutors, Richard Davis tried to convince him of a supreme irony. In pursuing an antitrust policy intended to preserve competition, Greene was likely to put Sotheby's out of business, thereby creating a monopoly for Christie's, which would make a mockery of the antitrust laws. Unmoved, Greene announced that he intended to prosecute Taubman, Brooks and Sotheby's to the full extent of the law. In closing, he warned Sotheby's lawyers the Justice Department would likely seek a fine of hundreds of millions of dollars, whereupon the meeting ended abruptly.

EVEN WITHOUT the lawyers' disastrous meeting with john Greene, Fait was obvious to Sotheby's board that Brooks and Taubman should immediately step down from their respective posts as CEO and chairman.

Aside from the alarming prospect of a large criminal fine, public disgrace, irate shareholders and bewildered clients and employees who might be tempted to leave in droves, the firm was facing a mounting number of civil claims that threatened to bankrupt Sotheby's.

On Friday, the board voted to force the resignations of the accused. The company urgently needed a new chairman. Two outside directors, Henry Kravis and Ira Millstein, recommended Michael I. Sovern, the sixty-eight-year-old former president of Columbia University, who seemed just the sort of respectable figure the company needed in its moment of crisis. A legal scholar, Sovern had held several high-profile assignments. He was chairman of the New York State—New York City Commission on Integrity in Government, known as the Sovern Commission, which had been established after a municipal scandal in 1986. He also knew all about coping with unsavory allegations, having served as a trustee of President Clinton's legal-defence fund.

Ever since Brooks' revelations, Taubman had been passionately proclaiming his innocence to Sotheby's board and to anyone who would listen. But the stigma of her allegations posed too great a risk for him to remain as chairman of the board. He claimed to be dumbfounded by Brooks' claims and insisted that he had no recollection of the conversations she purported to remember.

The prospect of stepping down as Sotheby's chairman was profoundly distressing for Taubman. Sotheby's was his baby, his pride and joy. To quit was unthinkable, but he appeared to have no choice.

23

Lady Macbeth

SURPRISED ONCE AGAIN by news from Manhattan, Robin Woodhead was in his office at Sotheby's in London at lunchtime on Friday, February 18, preparing to leave for a vacation in his native South Africa, when he received a call from Dede Brooks asking him to immediately get on a plane to New York.

"Why?" he asked.

"I won't be here as of tomorrow," Brooks replied.[1]

That brief conversation, he recalled, was "the last time I ever spoke to Dede."[2] Woodhead caught the next Concorde to New York and arrived in time to join Sotheby's senior directors in the middle of an early dinner in the conference room on the eighth floor. Don Pillsbury had assembled the firm's twelve most senior executives to inform them of the shocking news that Dede Brooks and Alfred Taubman would be resigning their respective positions as the firm's CEO and chairman within the next couple of days.

"It was highly emotional," Woodhead recalled, "and there was a sense of disbelief. First, there was the enormity of what appeared to be happening, and second, what faced the company."[3]

It was an evening that would haunt those present for years to come. "It was the colour of people's faces that I remember most vividly," Diana Phillips recalled. "Hues of yellow, green, ashen, grey, white and a very occasional red. We all aged that night."[4]

The sense of bewilderment and betrayal was overwhelming.

"I remember individuals who had to walk out of the room to vomit," Bill Ruprecht recalled.[5] "You don't spend twenty years in this business believing any of this could go on," he continued. "It was hugely disorientating to people. Others got incredibly angry. People who are usually so docile and measured were screaming at the top of their lungs. Others felt there is no way that any of this could be true."[6]

The notion of Taubman and Brooks consorting with the enemy seemed unimaginable. Their imminent departures could only mean that terrible, undiscovered events had transpired. "It was the shock of knowing that Alfred and Dede wouldn't just resign unless there was some underlying reason to force them to," Susan Alexander noted. "They didn't do that out of the goodness of their heart."[7]

The sense that Sotheby's was suddenly rudderless and heading for a giant waterfall presented an unprecedented challenge. "This is a business that's necessarily always got a big measure of crisis," Ruprecht observed, "because people die and you have to rally immediately. It's the fundamental uncertainty of life that's at the core of the services we provide some families. It's the challenge of getting fifty people on a plane to-morrow morning to be some-place.

"You go ahead and *try* to show me something I can't handle. There's a sense of pride in that. But this was something that a lot of people weren't ready to cope with."[8]

The shock would have dire reverberations. "People were made *ill* by this," Diana Phillips said. "Physically, psychologically, medically ill. I have no doubt that it shortened lives."[9]

Many of Brooks' colleagues felt that she could not possibly have colluded with Christopher Davidge, if only because they could not imagine that she could have pulled off the feat of lying successfully to them for so long. "Absolutely everyone thought that Dede couldn't keep a secret," a colleague noted. "She wasn't a good actress. She couldn't keep a poker face because she had one of those faces where you *think* you can read everything."[10]

Another executive was shocked that the CEO who had always placed such emphasis on doing the right thing appeared to have been so extraordinarily deceitful. "I absolutely felt she had the highest integrity," he recalled. "I'd seen her react under pressure for fifteen years, and every single time she acted with integrity. And she wouldn't lie, which is why I was so stunned.[11]

Amid the visceral reactions, Don Pillsbury prompted a conversation about who should lead the company. After much discussion, it fell to Bill Ruprecht, who had often been first on the firing line to endure Dede Brooks' towering rages, who was chosen to replace her as CEO. After a brutal nineteen-hour day at the office, Ruprecht returned home to Greenwich for dinner with his wife, Betsy, to discuss whether he should accept the daunting job of CEO at such a hazardous moment in Sotheby's history.

"She said, 'You seem tense,' he recalled, chuckling. "I said, 'Should I do this? I think *I could* do it, but it's far from clear to me that I *want* to,' and she said, 'Do you really have any choice? *You have* to do this. These are your friends. You *have* to.'

"That's what did it, for me," Ruprecht admitted. "And I got a couple of calls from friends at Sotheby's who said, 'You don't get to talk about it, you don't get to think about it, you *must* do it.'"[12]

Having agreed to accept the job, Ruprecht sat down with Henry Kravis early in the morning on Monday, February 21, 2000—Presidents' Day—to discuss his new salary.

"You ready to do this?" Kravis asked.

"I have no idea," Ruprecht replied.

"You'll be fine," Kravis assured him.[13]

After the two men shook hands, Sotheby's board met again by telephone to accept the resignations of Brooks and Taubman in absentia, and to formally elect Bill Ruprecht as CEO and Mike Sovern as chairman. The same day, Sotheby's issued a press release announcing Brooks' and Taubman's departures from their posts.[14]

"While this clearly is not an easy decision for me," Taubman was quoted saying, "I have determined that it is time for me to step down from my role as chairman."

In resigning as president and chief executive, the press release stated, Brooks said: "I am very proud of the achievements and initiatives that Sotheby's has taken in recent years and I am confident that in the future it will build upon its great franchise and reputation for excellence. My decision is a very difficult one, but I have taken it in the best interests of the Company and of my colleagues." The reality, of course, was that neither had any choice in the matter.

The same day that Brooks stepped down as Sotheby's CEO she was also obliged to resign from Morgan Stanley Dean Witter, where she had held the distinction of being one of only two women on the powerful twelve-member board of the bank, a measure of the respect she had commanded on Wall Street.

Another key participant involved in the scandal, Sir Anthony Tennant, held a lofty position at Morgan Stanley, as a senior advisor to the firm's London branch. As a businessman living in London, where anti-trust issues were taken less seriously, he remained at the bank.

The following day, when all Sotheby's New York employees returned to work after the long holiday weekend, they found an e-mail awaiting them from Bill Ruprecht, addressed to All Worldwide Staff. "Alfred's and Dede's resignations are major changes," he wrote, "and I know that you, as I have been, will be surprised and saddened by these rapid and unexpected developments." The time ahead, he warned, "will be a very challenging period."[15]

Having digested that news, the New York staff was summoned to the tenth floor of the building for Ruprecht's first address as CEO. "*Every* member of staff was there," he recalled. "There were nine hundred to one thousand people. And I remember walking into the room and it fell absolutely dead silent. I got up and explained what had happened, and said, 'Everything's going to be all right. You're the best people in this business. You've got a lot to be proud of. This is horrible, but we're going to get through it.'"[16]

THE DAY THE NEWS that Brooks and Taubman had resigned hit the papers, Judy Taubman was skiing in Gstaad. The night before, she had attended an elegant soiree where she sat next to her friend Pete Hathaway. When Hathaway reached his hotel in Milan the following morning, he was besieged by a flood of telephone messages alerting him that Taubman and Brooks had resigned. He picked up the telephone to call his dinner partner from the night before, who had breathed not a word of the unfolding scandal.

"God, Judy! You must have been losing your mind being at this dinner and knowing what was happening," Hathaway said.

"I'm sorry I couldn't say anything to you," Judy replied. "I knew it was going to be front-page news in the morning. I'm very worried about the press with me staying here," she added, "but Alfred didn't want me coming home. It would look worse if I *did* jump on a plane."[17]

Many cynics on the slopes of Gstaad debated whether Judy had postponed her return to be at her husband's side because she did not want to miss the social event of the season, a party to celebrate the ninety-second birthday of Count Balthasar Klossowski de Rola, the painter known as Balthus. The guest list of two hundred swells included worthies such as Baron Philippe de Rothschild, Nicholas Romanov of the last Russian dynasty, and Bono of the rock group U2. *ARTIST

With such a splendid lineup, Judy could hardly resist. Alas, her presence at the party, eight days after her husband's resignation from Sotheby's, prompted more unkind society gossip that she cared more about being seen at parties than being with Alfred in his time of need.

"She's been terribly criticized for it," Hathaway noted. "I think Alfred thought of it being perceived as a terrible admission of guilt if she *did* come back. But no matter *what* Judy does, it's wrong. No matter *what* she does, it blows up in her face."[18]

"She's a very, very nice God-fearing woman," he added, "who, just because she's very beautiful and has a hundred million dollars worth of jewellery, gets a bad rap."[19]

The impact and timing of the resignations could not have been worse for Sotheby's. Like Christie's, the firm was in the midst of the crucial last two weeks of securing multimillion-dollar consignments for the all-important Impressionist, Modern and Contemporary sales in May. Sotheby's was already at a competitive disadvantage since Christie's recent announcement that it was lowering its seller's commissions. To make matters worse, Wall Street had responded with devastating speed to the news. On February

22, the day after the announcement of Brooks' and Taubman's departures, Sotheby's stock plummeted to 15 5/8.

DEDE BROOKS' private admission of guilt shocked those closest to her.

"When Dede first revealed the nature of her crime to me, I was stunned," Elinor Dwyer McKenna, her sister, recalled. "The reason being that she always had such a clear understanding of right and wrong. Other people cut corners, Dede did not. Her trademark in our home was always her honesty and forthrightness. This was such an aberration from her normal behaviour and sense of fair play."[20]

The same week Brooks resigned from Sotheby's, she and her husband Michael put their home in Greenwich, Connecticut, on the market for $4 million, along with an adjacent 2.3-acre parcel of land for $1.5 million.

Having agreed to split the proceeds from the sale, Michael Brooks bought a 3,400-square-foot, single-story house on the water in Hobe Sound, Florida, in March for $4.23 million. The three-bedroom house occupied a 2.7-acre lot overlooking the Intracoastal Waterway.

The Florida acquisition had aroused suspicion among several of Brooks' colleagues, who had overheard their CEO spending hours on the telephone trying to negotiate the acquisition of the house in Hobe Sound. "I thought, 'How can she possibly have the time and energy to buy an extra house in the middle of all this?'" a senior Sotheby's executive recalled. "Then I thought, 'She's trying to protect her assets and has something to worry about.'"[21]

Some of Dede's co-workers speculated that she was trying to take advantage of Florida's Homestead Law, which protects Florida residents from having their property seized during bankruptcy proceedings—a statute that has helped to enhance the state's reputation as a sunny place for shady people.

Brooks was upset when the press began publishing stories that she was moving to Florida to shelter her assets. The rumour was unfounded. As New York residents, Michael and Dede Brooks were ineligible for protection under the Homestead Law. With her share of the money from the sale of the Greenwich house, Brooks set aside funds to pay her legal fees, which were expected to be enormous. Brooks also wanted to have a house to escape to that was close to the year-round home of her elderly mother, who was deeply distressed by her daughter's plight.

"I know if she can take her brother's death," Mary Dwyer said, "she can take this."[22]

BROOKS TOOK NO PLEASURE in implicating Alfred Taubman in the scandal. She told friends that she felt really bad for Alfred, and sorry for the consequences he was going to have to suffer. Three days after resigning from Sotheby's, she sent her former boss and longtime mentor a handwritten note on one of her little personal stationery cards, dated February 24, 2000:

"Dear Alfred, I hardly know what to say. You have been so much on my mind that I just wanted to write and tell you that no matter what happens I will always have incredible memories of our years together. You have played an extraordinarily important role in my life. And hope-fully one day in the future we will be able to look back and share some of the amazing things we did together. Take care of yourself. With much love, Dede."[23]

The card arrived at a time when Taubman was fiercely proclaiming his innocence and telling everyone who would listen that Brooks had betrayed him to save her own skin. His assistant, Melinda Marcuse, was stunned to read Brooks' missive.

"It's Lady Macbeth," she exclaimed.[24]

MANY ART DEALERS could barely suppress their glee that the wicked auction houses had finally gotten their comeuppance. Some who had bought extensively in the salesrooms over the years relished the prospect of receiving handsome refunds when the matter got to court. "Sane men should be sickened by the mangy curs of the London art trade who now snap at Christie's and Sotheby's, sensing blood," Brian Sewell wrote in the _Evening Standard_ on February 25, 2000. "They should remember that without the

London auctioneers London dealers would count for nothing in world trade but, inspired by greed, envy and mean spirit, they have never been able to acknowledge this."[25]

Christopher Wood, who had provided evidence of an alleged conspiracy over Sotheby's and Christie's controversial introduction of the buyer's premium in 1975, took a more sanguine view. "I think the whole case has come about partly because of the difference of the laws in England and America," Wood noted. "In England collusion is not regarded as such a serious offence, but in America it's *a very* serious federal offence, and you can go to gaol.

"I think it's a lack of grasp of that fact—especially among the English people here—that led to the troubles erupting in America. There was a feeling that they could get away with it, because they'd done it once, and they felt they could get away with it again. But this time they made fatal errors. There was evidence, so they didn't get away with it. And quite right too."[26]

DAYS after the resignations of Brooks and Taubman, a federal judge held a hearing in his courtroom at 500 Pearl Street in downtown Manhattan to consider whether to consolidate the thirty-eight civil lawsuits that had been filed by disgruntled clients of Sotheby's and Christie's in the United States.

The judge was Louis A. Kaplan, a 1994 Clinton appointee known for his incisive wit. He announced his decision to appoint six law firms as interim lead counsel for the civil plaintiffs and said that he expected the case to be resolved within a year.

Lawyers for Sotheby's and Christie's immediately began trying to reach a settlement in the civil case. Based on Dede Brooks' assurances that there had been no conspiracy over the buyer's premium, Sotheby's was positioning itself to settle the civil case for what they deemed a reasonable and appropriate sum of money.

Counsel for both auction houses were apoplectic at the suggestion that their respective firms had *also* conspired to fix the buyer's premium in 1992—an allegation that had been sparked by Herbert Black's pioneering lawsuit in late January. Any proof of collusion on the buyer's side was potentially crippling to the auction houses because it could expand the liability to a far larger class of plaintiffs.

If the Justice Department or counsel for the plaintiffs could prove that the illegal activity had begun in 1992, the civil penalties could potentially bankrupt both auction houses. Unlike federal fines, damages in civil antitrust cases could be *triple* the amount of the overcharge in the alleged conspiracy. Civil cases also required a far lower threshold of proof to establish wrongdoing. With the damages estimated in the hundreds of millions, the triple-damages penalties could mean civil fines in excess of $ 1 billion.

By late February, rumours had started to fly that the government was in possession of secret documents that Davidge had turned over to Christie's. The existence of such evidence was news to Sotheby's, Brooks and Taubman, who were anxious to know the scope of the allegations likely to be levelled against them.

On April 20, Judge Kaplan agreed to grant class-action status to the suits filed on behalf of clients of Sotheby's and Christie's who had either bought or sold items offered at the two houses between January 1, 1993 (when the revised buyer's premium went into effect), and February 7, 2000 (when Christie's had altered its buyer's and seller's commissions, effectively ending the conspiracy).

Taking a novel approach, Judge Kaplan announced that the position of lead counsel for the plaintiff class would be determined by auction, with confidential, sealed bids to be submitted to his chambers. The goal, he explained, was to maximize the amount of money the plaintiffs, or "class," would receive, while assuring that the least amount possible from the settlement would be gobbled up by legal fees.

Under the terms of the blind auction, competing law firms were asked to name a dollar amount, "X," which was the minimum sum they expected they could win for the plaintiffs exclusive of attorneys' fees or expenses. The winning law firm—the one that bid the highest—would then be entitled to receive 25 percent of any monies recovered in excess of that sum, with the remaining 75 percent going to the class.

"Are the Knicks playing here this afternoon?" Judge Kaplan

quipped as he surveyed the sixty-six lawyers crammed into his courtroom on May 12, who had come to learn where they stood in the bidding process for the lucrative role of lead counsel.[27]

The hearing began with John Greene ardently entreating the court to keep twelve key documents from Davidge's trove under seal and out of the hands of lawyers for Sotheby's and Christie's until at least August, arguing that disclosure of the documents could "compromise the integrity of the grand jury."[28]

Kaplan expressed impatience with the snail's pace of the government's investigation and ordered the sensitive documents to be made available to the plaintiff's lawyers on July 18.

The auction houses were also facing related charges outside the United States. Having secured conditional amnesty from the U.S. Justice Department, Christie's lawyers had moved swiftly to try to limit the firm's legal vulnerability in other jurisdictions. The firm's outside counsel visited the European Commission on Friday, January 28, to inform its members of the turn of events. The following week, on Wednesday, February 2, Christie's met with the Office of Fair Trading in London.[29] In both meetings, Christie's lawyers pledged to cooperate fully with the competition authorities. The Australian Competition Commission was also carrying out a separate investigation into the alleged price-fixing.

Once again, being first to tap on the investigators' doors, Christie's seemed home free while Sotheby's was left to face substantial fines.

JUDGE KAPLAN HAD SET a deadline of four o'clock on May 25, 2000, for competing law firms to submit their sealed bids. The following day, after reviewing twenty-one applications, he named Boies, Schiller & Flexner LLP, of Armonk, New York, as lead counsel.

Somewhat recklessly, the Boies firm had made a bid of $405 million, thereby agreeing that any amount up to $405 million won at trial or in a settlement would go to the civil plaintiffs, and that their firm would receive 25 percent of anything in excess of that amount.

After celebrating their triumph in winning the lead counsel role,

David Boies and his business partner Richard Drubel were sobered to discover that the average bid imagined by their competitors was merely $130 million. If they failed to earn more than $405 million for the plaintiffs, their firm would receive no legal fee whatsoever.

Lawyers who had bid substantially less expressed amazement at Boies' extravagant bid. "That was magnitudes higher than I thought bids would go," admitted Lawrence A. Sucharow of Goodkind, Labaton, Rudoff & Sucharow, who expressed scepticism that such an enormous settlement could be achieved. "It's certainly not a slam dunk," Sucharow noted. "You have to have large cojones to bid $400 million in this case."[30]

David Boies was apparently equipped for the task. The fifty-nine-year-old lawyer had most recently acted as lead trial counsel for the Justice Department in its criminal antitrust suit against Microsoft, and had famously reduced Bill Gates, the world's richest man, to a blithering mess on the stand. Boies was regarded as one of the foremost trial lawyers in the nation in handling cases involving complex litigation.

His optimistic bid promised to make the auction case either one of the triumphs of his career or a huge, expensive mistake. As usual, the buccaneer of the New York bar was confident he would succeed.

AS MUCH AS HE PROTESTED his innocence, Taubman realized his lawyers were serious when they warned him that he was likely to be indicted by the Justice Department. The prospect was terrifying. He had already learned from Scott Muller that Brooks was accusing him of discussing pricing issues with Tennant in 1993, and he was worried about other allegations she might be making about his conduct. The developer had spent most of his adult life trying to burnish his reputation as a distinguished businessman and philanthropist, but this scandal threatened to destroy his public image.

Anticipating a wave of negative publicity, Taubman's lawyers engaged the services of John Scanlon, a legendary figure in the world of litigation and crisis management PR. His client list included Monica Lewinsky and Senator Bob Kerrey, and he prided himself on being on a first-name basis with every influential editor, publisher and key reporter in the country.

While waiting to go into one of his first meetings with Taubman on April 18 at the Fifth Avenue office, Scanlon turned to Chris Tennyson, Taubman's longtime press advisor, and shook his head.

"Our guy's in trouble," Scanlon said.

"Why?" Tennyson asked.

"Dede's hired this guy Kaufman," Scanlon replied. "He's a flipper." "What's a flipper?" Tennyson said, mystified.

"It's a guy who offers up the guy above you, so you can beat the charge," Scanlon replied. "Kaufman is *real* good at it. He rarely goes to court. He just makes a deal. That's why they call him a flipper."[31]

Brooks' life had become a nightmare since relinquishing her job as Sotheby's chief executive. In her heyday as the most powerful woman in the art world, she had commanded a global empire and was accustomed to having three full-time assistants scurrying to keep up with her break-neck pace. Lately, she found herself at loose ends and in a wrenching state of purgatory, confiding to friends that she was terrified of being sent to gaol.

Brooks now shunned the limelight she had craved. New Yorkers who caught fleeting glimpses of the lithe forty-nine-year-old noticed that her blond hair had turned grey and that she always seemed to be running. Since losing her job she had been spotted during the day at the Equinox Gym on Lexington Avenue, pounding away on the treadmill for hours at a time as if seeking an additional outlet for her restless competitive energy.

Sotheby's had been her life. To those who had witnessed her transformation from a glamorous executive circling the globe in fearless pursuit of multimillion-dollar art deals to a pained, lonely figure in running shoes, it was daunting to see the waste of her talents.

Between February and June, Brooks' lawyers had been trying without success to strike a favourable deal with the government for their repentant client. Through counsel, Brooks informed the prosecutor, as well as lawyers for Sotheby's and Taubman, that she was prepared to co-operate with the government even if it meant pleading guilty to conspiring to fix seller's commissions.

The Antitrust Division, however, refused to grant Brooks a cooperation agreement unless she could also provide evidence that a conspiracy had also taken place to fix the buyer's premium in 1992. In response, Brooks insisted that she knew of no illegal agreement over the buyer's premium, and the government refused to budge.

Hoping to craft a winning argument for Brooks to strike a deal, her attorneys were anxious to establish whether Davidge had already testified to the grand jury and what his version of the story might be. They now knew of the existence of Davidge's notes and were desperate to know what they contained.

Siffert finally got his hands on the elusive papers on Tuesday, July 18, when Judge Kaplan ordered John Greene to turn over copies of 153 pages from Davidge's cache of notes to counsel for Brooks, Taubman and plaintiffs in the class-action suit. Sifting through the Davidge documents, Taubman's lawyers were fascinated to discover what appeared to be three memos written by Tennant slotted into a plastic folder. Each memo was written in blue ink on white lined notepaper.

Intriguingly, the three pages of jottings that came to be known as Tennant's April 30 memo had been written on two different types of white lined paper. The lines on the first page were light blue and had a broad margin at the top and bottom. The paper used for pages two and three had grey lines and narrower margins at the top and bottom of the page. The discrepancy in the types of paper led Taubman's lawyers to conclude that the author had begun the memo after meeting with Taubman and had subsequently jotted down his ruminations after the meeting at a later date.

When Brooks learned that her lawyers had received their copy of the Davidge documents, she went immediately to Siffert's offices on Fifth Avenue, just north of the New York Public Library. She was startled by the scope of some of Davidge's papers. "I was surprised that he'd kept notes of our meetings," she told me, "and that he'd *kept* them. I wish I'd known. Then I would *never* have talked to him."[32]

A pause.

"I shouldn't have talked to him anyway," she added, "but that's another whole thing."[33]

WHILE BROOKS AND TAUBMAN mulled over the prospect of incarceration and crippling fines, others who may have had some knowledge of the conspiracy from the beginning at Christie's appeared to be thriving.

François Curiel remained chairman of Christie's Europe, a position he had held since 1999. And he continued to direct Christie's International Jewellery Department, which had led the market for the past eight years. Rumours continued to swirl over the diminutive Frenchman's amorous exploits. In an interview with *Women's Wear Daily* in the spring, he dismissed the widespread speculation that he had seduced the Parisian socialite Mouna Ayoub in order to win a consignment sale of precious jewels that she had already promised to her handsome, dashing new-best-friend Prince Dimitri of Yugoslavia at Sotheby's.

"Did I ever seduce anyone sexually to get business? The answer is a definite 'no,'" Curiel told *Women's Wear Daily*. "But if you mean did I seduce them by my enthusiasm and drive and not abandoning them until the final check is in their account, then the answer is yes.

"I have no worries about my ethics," he added. "I can look at myself shaving in the morning."[34]

Concern over his possible role in the antitrust investigation being conducted in the United States, however, meant that Curiel was obliged to step down as deputy chairman of Christie's International in July. The distinction was lost on everyone, including the majority of Christie's employees, since Curiel continued to be a very visible, dapper ambassador for the company and chairman of Christie's Europe.

As luck would have it, the same month he received his subtle demotion, Curiel was appointed a Chevalier de la Légion d'Honneur by Hughes Gall, the director of the Paris Opéra, on behalf of the president of France. The coveted award was given to Curiel in recognition of his standing as a famous auctioneer and an international authority on jewellery, who in his thirty-one years at Christie's had done so much to promote and glorify France's image abroad.

Sir Anthony Tennant was also honoured that month, when he was awarded the honorary degree of Doctor of the University of Southampton on July 19, 2000. The honour was bestowed in recognition of his "long and distinguished career in the commercial and financial sectors," and his chairmanship of the university's development trust. It was a happy occasion, and a welcome feather in Sir Anthony's cap in a year when he was forced to step down as deputy chairman of Arjo Wiggins Appleton, an Anglo-French paper company with vast interests in the United States, because he was unable to travel to America for fear of being detained by the Justice Department.

Tennant was still vexed over an incident earlier that month. Despite unpleasant newspaper headlines linking his name with a major international business scandal, he continued to work full-time as a senior advisor to the London branch of Morgan Stanley. As he was leaving his office on Upper Grosvenor Street on the afternoon of July 5, he was startled when he was confronted by Mark Castle, a private detective who had been hired to serve Sir Anthony with a subpoena issued by lawyers in New York for the civil plaintiffs.

Seeing the tall, dapper aristocrat dashing from his office and into his Saab, Castle thrust the court papers into his hand.

"Go away!" Tennant yelled, flinging the subpoena into the gutter before speeding off in his car.[35]

Learning of Sir Anthony's unwillingness to cooperate, lawyers for the class-action plaintiffs in the United States asked Judge Kaplan to enter a default judgment against Tennant for refusing to respond to their lawsuit.

CHRISTOPHER DAVIDGE was safe from criminal prosecution,

thanks to the luxury of his amnesty deal. But he was alarmed to learn from his lawyer that he had been named as a defendant in the class-action case being led by David Boies, and that he could be personally liable for millions of dollars.

Joe Linklater realized that the only way to protect his client from financial ruin was to persuade Christie's to indemnify him. But they were unlikely to oblige. There was still tremendous animosity toward Davidge at Christie's, and the Chicago lawyer was sharply rebuffed when he called Cliff Aronson of Skadden, Arps to inquire whether Christie's would consider indemnifying its former CEO.

"Absolutely not," Aronson snapped. "Don't even bother talking to me about it. My client is still *very* angry with your client. They believe it was him who got them into this mess in the first place."[36]

Linklater responded by pointedly reminding Aronson that the April 30 memo suggested that Davidge had been acting under the instructions of the firm's former chairman, Sir Anthony Tennant. Hoping to convince Christie's to reconsider its position, Linklater pointed out that Davidge had other options at his disposal.

"It's been my experience that Chris doesn't want to do anything to harm the company," Linklater said calmly, "and I think he's definitely demonstrated that in the way he handled the documents and the way he agreed to participate in the leniency programme to get you amnesty.

"But loyalty to one's employer only goes so far, even if there's a lot of money involved," he continued, tauntingly. "I understand that these plaintiffs are looking for a lot of money—somewhere upwards of half a billion dollars. Now let's see. My client's got $8 million—I think that leaves him in the hole."

Without issuing a direct threat, the Chicago lawyer hinted that if Christie's failed to cooperate, Davidge might be willing to exercise his option to come to New York to testify against his former employers to lawyers for the civil plaintiffs, in exchange for a guarantee that he would not be personally liable for civil fines.

"Now, why don't you go and have a nice conversation with

your client about possibly indemnifying my client in the civil litigation?" Linklater asked. "Don't let me twist too long on this," he
added menacingly.

To Linklater's amusement, Aronson called back within two
hours to issue a terse "Okay."[37]

Christie's took no pleasure in protecting its nemesis from financial disaster, but it had no choice. Davidge had outmanoeuvred the
auction house yet again. "The absolute beauty of that agreement
was that Christie's was once again agreeing to indemnify Chris and
to not claw back any money," Linklater noted jovially.

SOTHEBY'S ENMITY toward its own former chief executive was
just as bitter. Despite repeated entreaties, Sotheby's refused point-
blank to cover the cost of Brooks' legal bills. "I've never seen a case
where the CEO of a company was compelled to pay their legal
costs," a lawyer close to the case observed, "but Sotheby's was
chintzy with everything to do with her."[38]

Ever since the price-fixing scandal had broken in January,
Sotheby's and Christie's had cautioned their respective employees
not to discuss the subject. That silence was broken in *a New York
Times* profile of David Redden, the founder of Sothebys.com, after
he sold a rare copy of the Declaration of Independence on the
firm's Web site for $8.1 million. It was the first time that anyone
on the staff at either auction house had made a personal comment
to the press regarding the antitrust scandal that was befouling their
businesses and their daily lives.

"I was stunned by that and remain bewildered," Redden told
James Barron of the *Times*. "All I know is that two people resigned
amid allegations of what to me is inconceivable behavior."[39]

Inconceivable behaviour. Dede Brooks was hurt and angry when
she read her former colleague's words in the paper, and conveyed
her displeasure through friends. "I was speechless," Redden said,
recalling his surprise upon being upbraided, "because I thought I'd
been so restrained. It was rather an elaborate euphemism for what
I truly felt."

News of Brooks' objection convinced Redden that the former

CEO felt "no remorse, no understanding at all of what the impact was on her former colleagues."[40]

ON JULY 20, 2000, Siffert and Kaufman sat with the prosecutors—John Greene, Pat Jannaco, Phil Cody and their boss, Ralph Giordano—to deliver a full proffer of Brooks' recollections. Learning right away that Brooks was adamant that there had been no buyer's conspiracy, the prosecutors changed their tack.

They focused on a phrase that Brooks recalled Taubman telling her he had uttered to Anthony Tennant over breakfast on April 30, 1993: "It was Christie's turn to go first." To the prosecutors, that tantalizing phrase was proof that *a previous* conspiracy had existed over the buyer's premium in 1992.

Phil Cody, a seasoned prosecutor with a tall, slender physique and the lugubrious mien of a character out of Edward Gorey, probed Siffert and Kaufman on this delicate issue, trying to determine whether an inference really could be drawn from Taubman and Tennant's conversation to suggest that they had at least *known* about a previous conspiracy.

Brooks' understanding of Taubman's phrase, however, was much more innocent. She believed he had meant: "Sotheby's took the risk last time, with no assurance that Christie's would follow. So it's your turn to go first this time on a change in pricing."

Despite her lawyers' efforts to convince the prosecutors otherwise, it seemed that Brooks' only chance of avoiding gaol was to implicate Taubman in a nonexistent buyer's conspiracy. "They weren't trying to get her to lie," Siffert cautioned. "But they wanted to test whether it could be understood that there had been a pre-existing deal, even if Dede didn't know it."[41]

After listening at length to Brooks' proffer, as delivered by her counsel, the government lawyers declined to offer Sotheby's former CEO a cooperation deal that would give her immunity from prosecution. Brooks remained in excruciating limbo until late August, when John Greene called Siffert to say that he was now prepared to entertain the possibility of Brooks cooperating with the government without having to plead guilty to any involvement in a buyer's conspiracy.

Upon receiving the encouraging news, Siffert interrupted his summer vacation on Martha's Vineyard and flew back to New York on August 22 to accompany Kaufman to meet with Greene. They planned to negotiate a favourable deal for Brooks' cooperation and to make a full proffer on her behalf.

The upshot of the meeting was good news for Brooks. But not *that* good. The prosecutors wanted her to plead guilty to a felony of conspiring with Christie's to fix seller's commissions, and they expected her to cooperate by helping them to prosecute Taubman. Their only offer of leniency was to make no *specific* recommendation for her sentencing. In other words, Brooks could still go to gaol, even if she cooperated.

Kaufman was appalled at the rough terms the government was offering. "I thought that this was a very harsh deal for Dede," he recalled, "because she had no protection."[42]

ON JULY 31, 2000, Judge Kaplan compelled Christie's to hand over to lawyers for Taubman, Sotheby's and Brooks 242 boxes containing 392,500 pages of evidence, which were produced in waves, from August 17 to November 20, 2000. "It's not an uncommon tactic to overwhelm you with stuff," a Taubman lawyer noted. "Then you have to find the good stuff."[43]

Taubman's lawyers discovered that they had to fight tooth and nail to try to speed up the halting pace at which Christie's turned over its documents—a torturous process that Scott Muller described as "trench warfare with a spoon."[44]

24

A Bride with Syphilis

DAVID BOIES' RECENT VICTORY over Bill Gates and Microsoft was the stuff of legend in legal circles. Having him as an adversary in litigation was every corporation's worst nightmare. Fans who wanted to see how he would deploy his ruthless tactics in the class-action suit against Sotheby's and Christie's would not be disappointed.

In his preliminary settlement negotiations with the lawyers for the two auction houses, Boies taunted them with the threat that he was planning to take the case to court if they failed to settle with him for a suitably vast sum. Both Sotheby's and Christie's knew that the evidence against them—in the form of Davidge's documents—was so overwhelming that a jury would have no trouble finding both companies liable.

From reading Tennant's notes, Boies was confident that a conspiracy had taken place on the seller's commission, but he could find no compelling evidence of collusion over the 1993 change in the buyer's premium. When he and his colleagues examined the revenue statements for both firms they were alarmed to discover that they could substantiate total damages of only $300 million—some $200 million short of the amount they had envisaged when they bid for the position of lead counsel.

When Boies and his colleagues began serious discussions with Sotheby's and Christie's over a settlement, lawyers for the two firms stated firmly that they would consider a settlement of $100 million, but no more. Boies rejected their offers as totally unacceptable, and withdrew to consider his options. He and his partners realized that in order to improve their chances of a substantial recovery, they would have to drive a wedge between the two auction houses, forcing each to cooperate with them against the other.

Christie's seemed the liveliest prospect, since it already had Christopher Davidge, the government's cooperating witness, in its pocket. During the first week of September, Boies was on the verge of closing a deal with Christie's whereby the auction house would pay roughly two hundred million dollars in civil damages, which would be substantially reduced if the firm could supply damaging evidence against Sotheby's and Taubman.

It was a compelling offer. By mid-September, the lawyers had drawn up an agreement, which required only a signature to make it binding, but the discussions were ongoing about how much money Christie's would save by helping to nail Sotheby's.

Just when the deal with Christie's appeared to be nearing completion, Boies' law partner Richard Drubel and their junior colleagues were wading through dozens of boxes of documents furnished by Christie's. The lawyers were not expecting to find much of interest. The Davidge documents were clearly the star pieces of evidence. They figured that Christie's was so eager to prove its willingness to cooperate with Boies that they would have alerted them if there was anything of great consequence. Most of the 242 boxes contained a miscellany of papers of scant interest: office memos, press releases, executives' calendars and restaurant receipts.

Late one night, however, a paralegal piped up, "I think I've got something." Drubel rushed to take a look and found a folder that had been stuffed in a box of dull accounting records. It contained a treasure trove of handwritten notes by the punctilious Stephen Lash, laying out a devastating account of his suspicions of antitrust activity and of the complicity of his Christie's colleagues in the conspiracy.

Drubel and his colleagues were stunned that anybody would be so foolish as to commit such suspicions to paper. Apart from their incredible value as evidence, the existence of the Lash documents cast suspicions on Christie's willingness to come clean with Boies. Why had Christie's counsel failed to alert the plaintiffs' counsel about the

Lash memos? Did they seriously believe that the lawyers would not find them?

Christie's reluctance to be more forthcoming about such a major piece of evidence began to give Boies serious doubts about going ahead with the favourable deal they had been offering.

Meanwhile, Taubman's lawyers at Davis Polk & Wardwell were ploughing their way through Christie's 242 boxes and had made the same discovery. Gillian Crenshaw, a young associate, brought the Lash papers to the attention of Scott Muller, the lawyer leading Taubman's defence, who immediately shared them with the lawyers at Sotheby's.

Taubman and Sotheby's were in a dicey predicament. Lash's memos were damning evidence, because they referred repeatedly to Dede Brooks' clearly inappropriate contact with Davidge. There was no mention of Taubman's name, but it was assumed that Brooks was preparing to offer devastating verbal evidence against him if required to do so in a courtroom.

Sotheby's was especially vulnerable. As a corporation, it was liable for the illegal actions of both Taubman and Brooks. Scott Muller guessed correctly that Boies was plotting with Christie's to isolate Sotheby's and Taubman and take them to the cleaners. This potentially ruinous plan could not be allowed to succeed. Muller had worked with Boies on other cases and knew that he was brilliant. He also realized that Christie's, with its amnesty with the prosecutors and control of Davidge, was likely to use its stronger bargaining position to bury its auction rival.

Muller shared his dire prognosis with Sotheby's. "If they had settled with Christie's alone," Bill Ruprecht noted, referring to Boies' firm, "we would have been left standing with an enormous burden of liability."[1]

Boies was gleefully aware of the pressure he was exerting on Sotheby's. "If Christie's had settled and Sotheby's had not," he told me, grinning, "three things would have happened, all bad for Sotheby's."[2] First, the firm would have been liable not only for its 50 percent share of the triple civil damages, but also for the portion of damages that Christie's had not paid by settling for a lesser sum.

Second, Sotheby's would be faced with a looming multimillion-dollar liability that could cause its customers and staff to defect to Christie's, which could claim that it had settled its civil liabilities and was thus safer, more stable and a better place to do business. Third, Sotheby's would face the prospect of a civil trial in which its dirty linen would be aired for public inspection. At such a trial, with so much evidence implicating Brooks, Sotheby's would almost invariably lose, to the tune of hundreds of millions of dollars.

Muller realized that failing to settle with Boies could easily bankrupt Sotheby's. Furthermore, as the firm's major shareholder, his client Alfred Taubman could lose his entire investment if the auction house went kaput.

Trying to sound calm, Muller placed a call to Boies. "Let's resolve this," he told him. "You've got to talk to Sotheby's."[3] Boies said he might possibly be willing to entertain a resolution whereby Taubman, Christie's and Sotheby's would each pay one-third. Muller tried to nip that proposal in the bud, arguing that, in all fairness, Taubman and Sotheby's should not be held more than one-half responsible for an illegal scheme carried out by two companies.

Boies accepted Muller's invitation to get together with the Sotheby's antitrust counsel: Steve Reiss, Richard Davis and Ira Millstein of Weil, Gotshal. All the participants knew that the meeting was of pivotal importance for Sotheby's. Its lawyers had the task of persuading Boies to abandon any deal favourable to Christie's, but they had little in the way of new evidence to bargain with.

Davis and Millstein tried to cajole Boies into admitting that it would hardly benefit his plaintiffs, who were buyers and sellers of works of art, to impose a ruinous civil fine on Sotheby's that would put it out of business. They also pointed out that Christie's reluctance to alert Boies to the Lash memos proved that the firm was acting in bad faith and should not be trusted. Moreover, they argued, there were so many documents that implicated senior figures at

---

* David Boies contends that counsel for Sotheby's offered him the names of Block and Curiel as "communicators." But the Weil, Gotshal lawyers deny having done so.

Christie's that Boies would not need the co-operation of Davidge to prove his case.

In a later meeting, Boies asked Sotheby's lawyers if they could identify anyone who might have been aware of, or active in, discussing the change in the buyer's commission. The Weil, Gotshal lawyers gave him the names of François Curiel and his friendly rival at Sotheby's, John Block, who ran the Jewellery Department at Christie's and Sotheby's, respectively. The two rivals, they explained, were "communicators."*[4]

The plaintiffs' lawyers were startled. It was the first time they had heard any mention of Block's name in the context of a conspiracy. Boies was so encouraged by Sotheby's eagerness to be helpful—at a moment when the Lash documents seemed to be pointing to a far greater culpability at the rival firm—that he decided to withdraw his offer of a deal with Christie's.

Philip Korologos called Shep Goldfein, Christie's counsel at Skadden, Arps, and informed him that "things had changed." The settlement deal they had previously discussed, he explained, was no longer available. Instead, he was giving Christie's the chance to settle for a flat cash payment. Goldfein was enraged. He declined the offer, and accused Boies and Korologos of "walking out" on a deal.[5]

"How could we, when not all the terms had been agreed to?" Korologos replied.[6]

Goldfein continued to protest until Boies telephoned to spell it out for him. The deal was off. After learning the intriguing tidbit that Block and Curiel may have held illegal conversations over the buyer's premium, Phil Korologos was examining some consolidated data of the travel schedules of Christie's and Sotheby's executives. He was excited to discover that Block and Curiel had been in Florida on the same day in the spring of 1992—potential evidence that they could have been orchestrating an increase in the buyer's premium. A further search indicated that Brooks had been in Florida at the same time.

When confronted with these facts, Christie's lawyers tried to dismiss Korologos' assertion by pointing out that a Florida judge had ordered both Block and Curiel to appear before him in connection with an estate sale—a perfectly harmless explanation. Christie's lawyers realized, however, that it could be disastrous if such evidence reached a jury.

Boies played the two auction houses off against each other with notable ease during the month of September, ratcheting up the numbers by threatening each firm with the eagerness of the other to agree to a settlement that would leave the other firm out in the cold. While the negotiations continued, Boies flew to the south of France to attend a conference in Monte Carlo, where he was ensconced in a suite at the Hermitage hotel with a breathtaking view of the harbour. After evenings at the gaming tables indulging in one of his favourite pastimes, high-stakes poker, Boies repaired to his room to review the legal documents his office had faxed him, and to confer by phone with Phil Korologos and Richard Drubel. Before retiring for the evening, he fired off new suggestions and demands to the auction-house lawyers, which his office forwarded to Sotheby's and Christie's in the middle of the night in New York.

"We were largely working twenty-four hours in shifts," Ruprecht recalled, wearily.

The mood was just as tense at Christie's, where the new CEO and the company's lawyers risked incurring the wrath of François Pinault. "It was very nerve-racking, absolutely nerve-racking," Ed Dolman admitted, "and the amounts of money concerned were not insubstantial."[7]

AT ONE POINT in mid-September Boies offered Christie's the option of settling for $465 million, and they refused.

"When they said, 'Four hundred and sixty-five million is just too high,'" Boies recalled, "we went away, we waited, and we said, 'That number's off the table. The number is now five hundred and twelve million.' They said, 'You're going in the wrong direction! Four hundred and sixty-five was too high. Five hundred and twelve is even higher!'"

Christie's lawyers tried to argue that the level of damages was too punitive, but Boies refused to back down. "Our approach," he noted, "was to say, 'The new number is five hundred and twelve, and that's going to be on the table for a certain length of time. Once that number's off the table, maybe that number's going to go up ... But the number now if you want to settle is five hundred and twelve million.'"

"It was a good poker game," Soies said, grinning. "We had some good cards. You can play a poor hand well, but you can't do as well with a poor card as you can with a strong hand. And we were dealt a very strong hand. Indeed, stronger than we knew when we got into the game. We ended up with a lot of the chips."[8]

DEDE BROOKS was devastated by the harsh treatment she had received from Sotheby's since her departure, but she was going out of her way to help the company in every way she could. Over the past few months, she had referred numerous consigners to Sotheby's.

Her candid recollections of Taubman's participation in the seller's conspiracy also permitted Sotheby's to strike a hard bargain in compelling him to step up to the plate with $156 million in cash to help settle the civil suit being led by David Boies, plus an additional $30 million to settle a separate lawsuit brought by Sotheby's stockholders. In that litigation, the plaintiffs consisted of all persons who had purchased Class A common stock of Sotheby's Holdings, Inc., from the period from February 11, 1997, until February 18, 2000, inclusive, who claimed that the firm's illegal conspiracy with Christie's had depressed the value of Sotheby's stock.

Taubman agreed to dip into his pocket to hand over a total of $186 million to help Sotheby's get back on its feet. In exchange, his lawyers hammered out an agreement whereby Sotheby's agreed to indemnify him in all future related litigation.

There was little doubt that without Taubman's largesse, the company would be bankrupted. As Sotheby's majority shareholder, he was also protecting his assets. If the auction house went out of business, he would lose his entire investment, which had been worth $620·4 million during the glorious spring of 1999, when the stock was trading at $47.

In order to raise the cash for his $186 million contribution to the civil fines, Taubman quietly began selling off a few assets. In the fall of 2000, he unloaded Picasso's *L'hétaïre*, a Blue Period masterpiece depicting a flame-haired woman wearing a large yellow-and-black hat, which had hung in the living room of his Fifth Avenue apartment. In order to avoid the embarrassment of consigning such a well-known picture for auction, he sold it to his friend Bill Acquavella, the art dealer, who traded it to Gianni Agnelli for a Cubist Picasso.

ON THURSDAY, September 21, lawyers for Sotheby's and Christie's finally agreed to share a civil settlement of $512 million. The proposed settlement was designed to benefit clients who had purchased items at auction from Sotheby's or Christie's in the United States between January 1, 1993, and February 7, 2000, and those who had sold through either of the two companies between September 1, 1995, and February 7, 2000. The $256 million half-share for each company was roughly equivalent to five years of their annual pretax profits. It was excruciating to have to part with so much money. But David Boies pointed out that if the case went to trial, the damages would likely be more in the region of $1·3 billion.

The exceptionally bad news that Pinault was obliged to cough up $256 million—in addition to millions of dollars in legal fees and a crushing blow to his pride—was particularly galling to the French billionaire. No one, apparently, had thought fit to mention Christie's potential liability before he purchased the company. One wag at Sotheby's speculated that Monsieur Pinault must be livid that his investment was turning out to be so expensive.

"It's like buying a bride and finding she's riddled with syphilis," he marvelled.[9]

The prospect of a $512 million civil fine was staggering, particularly to those who recalled that the huge hue and cry over the introduction of the buyer's premium in 1975 in London had resulted in a paltry payment from Sotheby's and Christie's to cover the legal costs of enraged dealers. The feeling back then, Geraldine Norman recalled, was that "It was jolly naughty, but a fine of seventy-five thousand pounds [$152,000] should fix it."[10]

In winning a $512 million settlement, Boies' firm stood to earn a fee of $26·75 million (25 percent of $107 million—the difference between the $512 million settlement and Boies' $405 million bid). although a princely fee for a mere four months' work, $26.75 million came to only about 5 percent of the total recovery, a notably smaller proportion than rival firms had gained in similarly high-profile cases. By contrast, plaintiffs' lawyers in the antitrust suit against NASDAQ had received $143.7 million, roughly 14 percent of the $1.027 billion settlement in 1998.

Judge Louis Kaplan's novel idea of conducting an auction for competing law firms appeared to have achieved a magnificent result for the civil plaintiffs without siphoning off a disproportionate sum in legal fees to the lead counsel. Not everyone was full of praise, however. "One could argue quite strongly that it was an unjust result," a lawyer intimately involved with the case noted, "because more money was paid than was owed. Because there was *no* buyer's-premium conspiracy.

"Judge Kaplan thinks he did a wonderful job because he got more money for the plaintiffs," the lawyer added, "but one could question whether that was his job.[11]

Many people in the art and business worlds were astonished to read in the *New York Times*, the *Wall Street Journal* and newspapers around the world that Taubman had agreed to pony up $186 million—roughly one-fifth of his personal fortune—to save Sotheby's from financial ruin.

"Poor old chap," the London dealer John Baskett said. "He's probably cursing the day he ever bought it. I bet he wishes he'd stuck with root beer now."[12]

HAVING OFFICIALLY AGREED to plead guilty, Brooks sought permission from the prosecutors to allow her lawyers to inform Taubman's counsel about the allegations and recollections she was offering in her ongoing proffer sessions with the government. John Greene granted his benediction, and Siffert and Kaufman met with Scott Muller at Davis Polk to warn him of what potentially lay ahead.

"We continued to try and help Taubman understand what the evidence was going to be against him," John Siffert recalled.[13] The rationale, he explained, was that by informing him of Brooks' serious allegations against him, Taubman might agree to plead guilty, thereby giving himself and the prosecutors the benefit of avoiding a costly and taxing trial.

Brooks had a powerful motive to convince Taubman that he should plead guilty. If a case should go to trial, she would be forced to publicly admit her guilt and field withering questions under cross-examination from Taubman's lawyers that would be designed to paint her in the worst possible light. The world would learn the extent of her lies and repeated violations of U.S. laws. Without a trial, none of that embarrassing information would have to be made public.

It was worth a shot, but Alfred Taubman had no intention of pleading guilty to a crime that he was adamant he had not committed. A cloud continued to hover over his name as he waited to see whether the Justice Department would press criminal charges. Having always cared deeply about his reputation, he found the whiff of scandal attached to his name hard to take. He was so adamant that he was innocent that his lawyers suggested he might want to agree to a lie detector test. Intrigued by the idea, Taubman flew to Virginia on October 3 to meet with Paul K. Minor, the former head of the FBI's polygraph division.

"I'd never seen a polygraph machine, except on TV," Taubman recalled. "He had me in there for over an hour, all wired up. It's an awful feeling," he added.[14]

The questions were designed to try to establish his innocence beyond any doubt: (A) Did you and Tennant have an agreement regarding amounts to be charged to buyers or sellers? (B) Did you tell Dede Brooks to try to reach agreement with Davidge regarding amounts to be charged to buyers or sellers? (C) Did Dede Brooks ever tell you that she had reached an agreement with Davidge about amounts to be charged to buyers or sellers?

Taubman firmly replied "No," to each question.

"I passed this thing one hundred percent," Taubman told me proudly. "My lawyers were sitting in the next room, and he came out and said, 'This fellow doesn't know anything about this, and wasn't involved in it.'"[15]

"I didn't need that for *myself*," Taubman said. "But I felt I needed it for my family and my friends to know that I was innocent."

Minor's official report from Taubman's test showed "no deception." Nevertheless, the test was unlikely to be admissible in court.

The results were sent to Don Pillsbury, Sotheby's general counsel, who was asked to circulate them among the board of directors. Taubman also hoped that news of the encouraging results might help dissuade the Justice Department from pressing criminal charges against him.

The prosecutors were unimpressed.

MORE THAN A YEAR AND A HALF after she had been forced to relinquish her powerful position at Sotheby's, Dede Brooks appeared before U.S. District Judge Richard M. Berman in federal court on October 5 to plead guilty to one count of conspiring to violate anti-trust laws prohibiting restraint of trade.

"At the direction of a superior at Sotheby's Holdings," she said, reading from a prepared statement, "I had a number of meetings and conversations with a representative of Christie's International during which, among other things, we agreed to fix prices with respect to commissions charged to sellers."[16]

During the same court session, Don Pillsbury found himself in the uncomfortable position of standing in a courtroom to plead guilty on behalf of Sotheby's to the multimillion-dollar price-fixing scheme, and to consent to pay a $45 million fine.

"Those charged today were engaged in classic cartel behaviour," said A. Douglas Melamed, a senior Justice Department official, speaking afterward at a Washington news conference. "Price-fixing, pure and simple."[17]

When the news of Sotheby's plea reached the firm's headquarters on York Avenue, many of Brooks' former colleagues were enraged. "Our guilty plea was based solely on the actions of Mrs. Brooks!" a senior Sotheby's official fumed. "And we had no choice. Sotheby's *had* to plead guilty."[18]

Seeking to stem negative fallout from Sotheby's day in court, Bill Ruprecht issued a statement acknowledging the firm's responsibility for Brooks' illegal actions: "The behaviour that led to today's plea was wrong and is unacceptable," Ruprecht said. "On behalf of Sotheby's, I apologize to our clients for this breach of the standards of trust that they have the right to expect from us and assure them that no member of Sotheby's current management played any role whatsoever in these events or was aware at any time that they were taking place."

Following an avalanche of negative press reports that conveyed the impression that Sotheby's was an evil empire, some of the staff suddenly felt awkward about being associated with the company they had always been so proud to work for. David Redden felt self-conscious about wearing a Sotheby's T-shirt while taking a stroll in Central Park. And in upstate New York, the managing director of the Sotheby restoration workshop in Claverack, Colin Stair, began to feel awkward about driving a van whose sides were emblazoned with the word SOTHEBY'S. "People used to ask me about the paintings in the Impressionist sale," he told his father, John Stair. "Now they say, 'When's Dede going to gaol?'"[19]

Following Brooks' court appearance, many people at Sotheby's struggled to come to terms with the guilty plea of the colleague they thought they had known so well.

"I knew Dede could be reckless," a senior colleague recalled. "But I was shocked that she could do something like *this*. I didn't think anyone would be this stupid, either."[20]

Many who knew her well scoffed at the notion that Taubman had instructed Brooks to break the law.

"Dede never took orders from *anybody*," a senior executive noted.[21]

The collective rage of Brooks' former colleagues was mostly about feelings of personal betrayal. While she had been exerting tight control over Sotheby's global operations and exhorting the firm's art experts and executives to beat Christie's at every turn, Brooks had secretly been making an illegal pact with the competition that had resulted in public humiliation, legal peril and potential fiscal disaster. Worse still, she had personally lied to them repeatedly by denying that a conspiracy had taken place.

Many experts who had believed they were competing neck-and-neck with Christie's began to suspect that they had been manipulated into raising or lowering bids in order to satisfy some arrangement between Brooks and Davidge. There was also confusion and outrage among those who felt they had played an honest part in helping Brooks to reach a decision of whether to follow Christie's new charges in March 1995.

"Much about those years will always be bewildering to a lot of people who worked in this business," Bill Ruprecht noted. "What really happened? And how did it happen? We'll never know the answers, and in fact, it's not *possible* to know the answers."

Another executive wondered how Brooks' abilities as a consummate deal maker had played into her ability to mislead everyone around her. "Was Dede's extraordinary facility for navigating this artifice based on her immense skill at balancing so many variables?" he asked, rhetorically, "or was it based on the thrill of deception?"[22]

Brooks had always cultivated a reputation for unflinching honesty and integrity, and she was mortified by the groundswell of hatred directed toward her from her former colleagues at Sotheby's. Many found themselves unable to forgive her for destroying the value of their stock options by dragging the company into disrepute and for spinning a web of lies to conceal her wrongdoing.

"Dede should be boiled in oil for what she's done to the company," said Pete Hathaway, who had enjoyed a cordial relationship with Brooks for more than twenty years. "People hate her. They absolutely hate her," he continued. "She's taken a 250-year-old, very respected company and driven it into the ground. And our options are worth *nothing*. There's been terrible belt-tightening, and it's a mess. An absolute *mess*."[23]

Stock options had always made up a significant portion of compensation for senior staff, and the long-term monies they were counting on to fund their children's education or to buy their retirement homes had evaporated. "In that respect," David Redden observed, "Dede Brooks has cost people really large and important sums of money to their lives."[24]

Sotheby's intended to make Brooks pay heftily for her actions.

She had been kicked off the payroll in October 2000, just before her guilty plea, and in the process had automatically forfeited 1,930,000 stock options with exercise prices ranging from $ 10·87 to $24·25 per share. The former chief executive was also forced to relinquish 50,000 Performance Shares she had earned since 1996, which Sotheby's posted as a $1·4 million credit to its accounts.

Steve Kaufman was shocked by the zeal with which the firm sought to punish Brooks. "There are a lot of ways to spell fair," he noted, "but Sotheby's chose a version of fair which was the least kind to Dede as could conceivably be. And they did that at every step of the way."[25]

Not all Brooks' former colleagues remembered her with such venom. "I'm still fond of her," Henry Wyndham told me, sitting in his office at Sotheby's in London, surrounded by a captivating collection of Old Master drawings on the walls. "I've never met anybody like her. I think it's so tragic because she's a remarkably talented person. She set high standards, but if you worked hard there wouldn't be a problem."[26]

"I know that a lot of people have got it in for her," Wyndham noted, "but I feel I can still look her in the eye and have respect for her. Obviously, what she did was quite wrong. But she didn't include any of us in it. And *thank God* she didn't. We have that to thank her for.

"Obviously, she was too irascible with certain people," he admitted. "I think some were frightened of her. But under that facade she actually has a good heart. She's a kind person. A *very* kind person.

"What a lot of people see is not really her," Wyndham continued. "I used to play golf with her and I enjoyed her company very much. She had a good sense of humour, liked a good laugh and she was completely obsessed with Sotheby's. That's what's so sad. The hours she put in were remarkable, and her life was given over to it."[27]

"It's a real waste, this whole episode," he concluded. "It's a real waste of very intelligent people and real talent. And I think it's really sad. And the aggravation and trouble it's caused is remarkable. It's like a volcanic eruption."[28]

DAVID SOKOL was in Des Moines, Iowa, when he learned of Dede Brooks' guilty plea. The former JWP executive who had exposed crooked accounting practices at the now defunct company run by Andy Dwyer in the early nineties was amazed that corrupt business practices appeared to run in the Dwyer family.

"I can't think of another time in history," he marvelled, "where a brother who was the CEO of a company that ultimately went bankrupt from accounting fraud had a sister who was a CEO of another company who pleaded guilty to a felony. That may be a first."[29]

"There was a pretty severe arrogance between them," Sokol added. "I think sometimes arrogant people may not have caused a problem, but if they can't lower themselves to actually listen to people, the problem gets out of control on their watch."[30]

Friends of the Dwyers since childhood were also amazed at how the two competitive siblings' lives had turned out. One loyal friend, however, was kind enough to point out that Dede Brooks' crime was really not so dreadful, by comparison. "Andy did things that are a *lot* worse than what Dede did," the friend recalled. "He screwed a *lot* of people, who never got their money back. And they're still very angry at Andy. He lost his money, but he's come back, big time.

"With Dede and Andy," she noted sadly, "it was pure hubris."[31]

THE CRIMINAL CASE against Sotheby's remained open and unresolved. Even though the corporation had pleaded guilty to price-fixing in October and agreed to pay a mandatory fine of $45 million, Judge Kaplan was holding out before accepting the plea until he had determined whether the 130,000 victims of the conspiracy would be adequately compensated through the civil settlement.

Since the $45 million fine was less than the amount called for under the Federal Sentencing Guidelines, the judge also raised the threat that Sotheby's might be required to pay more.

News of that grim possibility filled Bill Ruprecht and his senior colleagues with dread.

25

'Fugitive from Justice'

EIGHT THOUSAND MILES from New York, where lawyers were battling over the multimillion-dollar repercussions of the scandal spurred by Christopher Davidge's trove of documents, he was having a splendid time in India, being fitted for a Nehru jacket and turban for his wedding to Amrita Jhaveri.

The exalted setting for their nuptials was Jagmandir, an island palace that rises majestically from the crocodile-infested waters of Lake Pichola in Udaipur. Legend has it that the palace's romantic, enchanting beauty helped inspire the Mughal emperor Shah Jahan, who took refuge there in 1623, to build the Taj Mahal.

Lit with flaming torches and visible for miles, the palace was a breathtaking sight for the two hundred wedding guests arriving by boat on the evening of December 17, 2000. Stepping onto the island, they were greeted by eight enormous elephants carved in stone standing sentinel at the gates. The seventeenth-century palace was built of yellow sandstone, inlaid with marble and crowned with an impressive dome. Within, they discovered arched pavilions adorned with frescoes and formal gardens cooled by cascades and reflecting pools, surrounded by palm trees, bougainvillea, jasmine bushes and flurries of parrots and strutting peacocks.

"It was really magical, just gorgeous," recalled an American guest who was entertained by the spectacle of hordes of visiting Englishmen decked out in turbans and Indian jackets, accompanied by gaggles of Englishwomen swathed in flowing saris, oohing and ahing as they laid eyes on the gigantic rubies, emeralds and sapphires worn by the wealthy Indians.[1]

"In India, they take jewellery *really* seriously," she marvelled. "I've never in my entire life seen jewels like the ones at this wedding. I couldn't understand how Amrita could stand up, she was so *covered* with gold and diamonds and pearls."

The host for four days of extravagant wedding celebrations was Dinesh Jhaveri, a leading diamond dealer and art collector from Bombay who was the proud father of the bride. Guests were offered luxurious shelter at the Lake Palace, the opulent, multiterraced hotel overlooking Jagmandir that was immortalized in the James Bond film *Octopussy*.

"It was an amazing display of Indian wealth," the American guest recalled. "After four days of partying, people were guessing that the wedding had cost a million bucks."

The Hindu wedding ceremony began with the entrance of the sparkling bride, dressed in traditional red and gold. Chanting in Sanskrit, the priest invoked Ganesh, the elephant-headed deity, asking him to banish all obstacles to a perfect union for the couple. The lovers then sprinkled a mixture of cumin seeds and sugar on each other's heads to symbolize their promise to support each other in good times and bad. Pledging to treat his wife as an equal and beloved partner, Davidge tied a sacred thread of gold and coral around her neck.

The groom then knelt solemnly before his bride to place silver rings on her toes. Hand in hand, with his cloak tied to her sari, they circled a holy fire seven times as they recited their marriage vows. Then, with a blessing from the priest, the bride and blissful groom were showered with rose petals.

"Later, one of the groom's best friends got up to make a toast," the American guest recalled, "and he said that no one had ever seen Christopher this happy."

Amid the merriment, murmurings were heard of Davidge's role in a loosened by champagne spilled the revelation that the bride's family was aghast that their beautiful daughter was marrying a scoundrel. "You couldn't help but pick up the gossip," the guest recalled. "We were told that the family was putting up a brave front, but they were in agony over this wedding. Chris was English, he was older, he'd been married twice before, and Amrita was gorgeous, young and beautiful and could have anybody in the world. Why him? They really couldn't understand why she'd fallen in love with Chris and was dead-set on marrying him." The frisson of scandal only added to the glamour of the wedding. Celebrations continued late into the night as fireworks soared above the palace, creating dazzling reflections in the lake. After dinner, the groom's friends watched in awe as exquisite young Indian girls rose to their feet, wearing diamond ankle bracelets that shimmered in the moonlight as they danced.

Twelve days later, £1 million ($1.5 million)—the second instalment of Davidge's severance bonanza from Christie's—was deposited into his account at Coutts.

Safe from criminal prosecution in the United States, Davidge could relax, ensconced in a luxurious apartment in the Malabar Hills section of Bombay with his beautiful young bride, having acquired a very high opinion of American justice.

SNOW WAS FALLING on the courthouse steps in New York on a bleak morning in early January 2001, when Dede Brooks appeared before a federal judge to learn when she might be sentenced to gaol. Judge Berman's dark-panelled seventh-floor courtroom was packed with journalists, many of whom were struck by the harrowing transformation in Brooks' appearance. Ashen-faced, the fifty-year-old former executive sat in silence, flanked by her lawyers. Her mane of blond hair had turned almost entirely grey.

The legal proceedings lasted only ten minutes. Citing the government's ongoing investigation, John Greene requested that Brooks' sentence be deferred, and the judge responded by issuing a new date of May 24.

As Brooks turned to leave, she pulled a black, fur-trimmed coat around her shoulders and glanced disconsolately at the wintry landscape of downtown Manhattan outside the courtroom window. Then, accompanied by her lawyers, she headed for the elevator, politely declining to answer a barrage of questions from the press.

THE USUAL SUMPTUOUS FARE of baked potatoes topped with spoonfuls of caviar was being served for dinner at the Taubmans' mansion in Palm Beach by waiters in starched white uniforms. Since twilight, a cavalcade of dark blue Mercedeses and open-topped cream-colored Rolls-Royces had been rumbling up the gravel drive, bearing 110 guests who had loyally assembled to celebrate Big Al's seventy-sixth birthday.

Such was Taubman's beaming countenance as he welcomed fellow swells with rousing handshakes and double kisses on a perfect tropical night in early February 2001, it was as if no threat of criminal indictment were on the horizon. Judy was standing at his side. Less adept at masking her emotions than her husband, she forced a smile. But her anxious brown eyes conveyed the sense that her comfortable life was crumbling around her.

Earlier that day, judge Kaplan had formally accepted Sotheby's guilty plea of conspiring with Christie's to fix commission rates charged to sellers. In imposing the hefty $45 million criminal fine for Sotheby's—on top of the crushing $512 million civil fine that the firm was obliged to split with Christie's—the federal judge called it an "especially serious" case that had been carried out at "an extremely high level."

"These were people who knew a lot better," Kaplan observed, "and they certainly didn't need the money."[2]

That afternoon, Sotheby's stock had closed at $25.85, making Taubman's controlling stake of 13.2 million shares in the company worth $341 million. Back in 1983, when he bought the auction house, Wall Street analysts had warned that it was a reckless investment. But Taubman had proved them wrong. By selling two chunks of Sotheby's stock in 1988 and 1992 and collecting annual dividends as the firm's majority stockholder, he had garnered more than a quarter of a billion dollars—$267,199,962 to be exact—a magnificent return on his original investment of a mere $38.5 million.

Sotheby's had brought him glory, but also ignominy and shame.

No kind words from devoted friends nor his own efforts to exude a blithe lack of concern for his legal woes could quite stanch his feeling of embarrassment. The one thing that mattered more to him than anything else in life was his good reputation, and that was now in tatters.

The auction scandal also threatened to undermine his legacy as a prodigious philanthropist. He had given more than $100 million over the years to the arts, medicine, education and Jewish causes. Seeing his name writ large on the front of the buildings he had endowed at the great American universities of Harvard, Brown and Michigan had brought him a deep sense of pride. Those bold capitals emblazoning his name now threatened to spell an epitaph of blight and disgrace.

In the twilight of his life, when he should be basking in the rewards of a lifetime's ambition, hard work and success, he found himself mulling the grim prospect of time in federal prison and of losing a substantial chunk of his fortune. The awkward predicament of having so many tangible assets was that he had so much to lose.

His wealth made him delicious prey now that he was the lone target of the criminal investigation led by John Greene. Taubman was quite certain he had never met Mr. Greene, who lived in a modest row house with a periwinkle-blue front door in the Bay Ridge section of Brooklyn. But his every waking moment was confounded by the relentless investigation of the resourceful prosecutor.

The government seemed intent on pressing for a conviction. Over the past ten days, Judy had been on the telephone rounding up as many friends and supporters as she could muster, urging them to come show support for her husband. He had long been accustomed to seizing all that life and business had to offer. Lately, however, he spent hours at a time slumped in his chair in despair. His lawyers at Davis Polk, who charged millions of dollars for the privilege of delivering the bad news, were gingerly preparing him for a legal bloodbath.

Hoping to banish such excruciating thoughts from his mind, he applied himself to the familiar role of genial host, exchanging jokes, offering cigars and revelling in his friends' affection. The dress code for the evening was "informal," a Palm Beach euphemism for serious jewellery and cocktail dresses for the ladies and a blue blazer, grey trousers and a tie for gentlemen. Aimee de Heeren, the Wanamaker heiress, had expected a more glamorous soiree and showed tip in a ball gown, looking resplendent in a diamond necklace that had once belonged to the Empress Eugénie. Taubman assured her that he was delighted that she had dressed so beautifully in his honour.

During dinner, Judy Taubman rose to her feet to deliver an extemporaneous toast to her husband. Wrapping her arms around his neck, she praised him to the skies. "This is the most wonderful man, who has changed my life tremendously and taught me to appreciate art and beauty," she said. "When I met him, I was a starry-eyed girl from Israel."[3]

"This was Judy's 'Stand by Your Man' speech," one dinner guest observed.[4]

After nineteen years of marriage the couple were still devoted allies, who had weathered many a storm together and who continued to share real affection for each other. Friends of Al Taubman who had previously been disinclined to give Judy the time of day were impressed with her eloquence and obvious sincerity that night. "It was incredibly heartfelt, that speech," one recalled.[5]

When Alfred Taubman rose to speak, the crowd grew silent.

"Boy ... 2000 was a lousy year!" he said, shaking his head. "As I'm sure you know, I was *not* included in Bill Clinton's final list of pardons. That's the bad news. The good news is that if I had been, I would have been in some pretty rotten company."

The reference to the fugitive billionaire Marc Rich elicited a roar of laughter from the crowd. Reassured, Taubman glanced down at the prepared script that he had spent days crafting and polishing with Chris Tennyson, his speechwriter and spokesman in Detroit. It had been almost exactly a year, Taubman told his guests, since he had first learned of the actions and allegations that had come to dominate his life and the headlines of newspapers around the world.

"This has been the most difficult time in my life," he said. Turning sentimental, he read from the opening lines of Dickens' *A Tale of Two Cities*: "It was the best of times, it was the worst of times, it was the age of wisdom, it was the age of foolishness ... it was the season of

Light, it was the season of Darkness, it was the spring of hope, it was the winter of despair."

"Friends," he said, his voice beginning to crack with emotion, "in the worst of times, you've been my season of light and my spring of hope. I want you to know that your support and best wishes mean the world to me."[6]

With thunderous applause, all 110 guests rose to their feet to give him a rousing ovation. Many had tears in their eyes, moved by the spectacle of this gruff, proud man reduced to abject humility.

"People came over and threw their arms around him and it was very emotional," recalled Pete Hathaway, who had flown from New York to attend the dinner.[7] Dolores Smithies, another close friend, was touched by the outpouring of sentiment. "There was an amazing solidarity of people around him," she recalled. "For all of us who had been at the same party five and ten years before, it was just very sad to see."[8]

WHILE TAUBMAN was languishing in the bosom of international café society in Palm Beach, Dede Brooks was leading an altogether quieter existence in Hobe Sound. *Worth* magazine had identified Hobe Sound as America's wealthiest community in 2000, but its residents claimed to abhor such vulgar publicity. Brooks sought distraction from her legal woes by finishing up the decoration of her three-bedroom house on South Beach Road, which was secluded from the street by a lush tropical landscape and a long winding gravel drive.

Brooks' luxurious exile from New York offered only fleeting distraction from her legal predicament. She was daunted by the grim reality that her only hope of avoiding gaol was to assist the government prosecutors in building their case against Alfred Taubman.

"We see Dede jogging in Hobe Sound," an heiress who lived nearby noted. "She looks miserable."[9]

AFTER MONTHS of wishful thinking that the government might drop its case against him for lack of sufficient evidence, Taubman began to realize that things were getting serious when Melinda Marcuse, his executive assistant, was summoned to appear before the grand jury in the spring of 2001. "It seemed pretty clear to me from the line of questioning that he was going to get indicted," Marcuse said.[10]

On May 2, 2001—four years after its halting investigation of Sotheby's and Christie's had begun—the Department of Justice announced its twin indictments of Alfred Taubman and Anthony Tennant.

The day before, Taubman had endured the humiliation of being taken downtown to be photographed and fingerprinted. Responding publicly to his indictment, he issued a carefully worded statement: "I am surprised and deeply disappointed by the charges made against me to-day. I am absolutely innocent, and have stated from the beginning of this investigation that whatever Dede Brooks chose to do, she did on her own and without my authorization. As confirmed by the lie detector test I have taken, the truth is on my side. While any trial is difficult, I look forward to the opportunity to clear my name in court."

Taubman had every reason to feel confident in his counsel. Muller was an exceptionally gifted lawyer who had recently been on the short-list for the job of head of the Department of Justice's Criminal Division. When the Davis Polk lawyers had met with the prosecutors early in 2001 to determine whether the government was planning to press criminal charges against Taubman, Muller had been obliged to stay away because he was still being considered for the job as head of the Criminal Division—a position that would have made him John Greene's ultimate boss, below the new attorney general, John Ashcroft.

Now that it was clear he was not moving full-time to Washington, the hotshot lawyer was working full-time on Taubman's case. And the gloves were off.

On Friday, May 4, 2001, Taubman arrived at federal court for his arraignment, dressed in a pale olive-green suit, sporting a suntan and exuding an air of bonhomie. It was his first glimpse of George B. Daniels, the forty-seven-year-old African-American federal judge who had been assigned to his case. Taubman remained silent as Bob Fiske announced his client's plea—not guilty—and asked that the defendant be permitted to retain his passport, "because it is important to him."[11] The judge agreed.

To the great surprise of reporters who knew that Taubman had retained the bulldog services of John Scanlon, his trusted PR advisor, the bearded Irish-American was nowhere to be found. It turned out that he had dropped dead that morning from a heart attack at the age of sixty-six. The tragedy of Scanlon's death, on a day when Taubman needed him most, seemed a bad omen.

Anthony Tennant had already indicated through his lawyers that he had no intention of travelling to America to stand trial for price-fixing, and he could not be extradited from Britain on the criminal charges he faced. Instead, he remained at his Elizabethan country house getting accustomed to being referred to in the press as a fugitive from justice. On the day he was indicted, Tennant sent out a letter to friends and colleagues declaring his innocence. In his letter, Tennant accused Davidge of pointing the finger of guilt at him in order to go free himself. Sir Anthony also cast doubt on the deal the government had reached with Dede Brooks. "Apparently it took some months before she claimed that she acted under Taubman's instructions," he wrote. "It is said that the Department of Justice not infrequently invites people under examination to 'refresh their memory' of events and indicate that in exchange they will recommend a relatively light sentence."[12]

Tennant speculated that the U.S. Department of Justice had brought charges against him in order to prevent him from appearing as a witness for Taubman. "It has the compelling advantage that if they did not indict me they would expect me to appear as a witness for Taubman at his trial and seriously weaken their case against him," he wrote.[13]

"Why not go to the United States to clear my name?" he asked rhetorically. "Because I would have to stay there for an unquantifiable length of time—months, possibly years, and pay huge legal bills out of my own resources. I prefer to rely on the recognition of my friends that I am innocent of these charges."[14]

When John Marion learned of Taubman's indictment, he found it hard to believe that he had broken the law. "Alfred Taubman never even once asked me to do anything illegal," Marion told me. "If he had," he added, chuckling, "I would have told him to go to hell."[15]

Like many others, Marion saw the government's case against Taubman as a witch-hunt. "They're always out for the rich guy," he noted. "That's the scalp they want on their belt. And that poor guy—his whole life's been turned upside down. He's seventy-six! At that age, he doesn't need all this. Jesus!"[16]

OVER THE SUMMER, many of the Taubmans' friends in Southampton were stunned by Judy's apparent insouciance about the court proceedings that were expected to engulf their lives that fall. "When is the trial going to begin?" a concerned Southampton hostess asked during an alfresco lunch in July.

"In October," Judy replied, "but we're trying to get it moved up to September. Because October is when we go shooting in Europe."

The clear implication that Mrs. T. regarded her husband's criminal trial as an inconvenient interruption of the social calendar filled her hostess with stifled mirth and amazement.

"Is Judy crazy?" her friend wondered. "How can she make remarks like that?"[17]

IN LONDON, Charlie Hindlip and Ed Dolman were furious that Christopher Davidge was still living on their doorstep. More than eighteen months after being forced to resign, he still occupied his comfortable two-bedroom flat in the Christie's building.

Unfazed by the wrath of his former co-workers, Davidge was taking delight in the remarkable rise of his social cachet in England, where the frisson of scandal had transformed him into a celebrity.

"It always used to puzzle me about Claus von Bülow," Davidge told his friend Amy Page, "that after that scandal he moved to London and he was everywhere in society. Now I understand it. I've been invited places by people who never invited me before.[18]

After nearly a lifetime of feeling socially downtrodden, the former street vendor was finally entering the pantheon of café society, thanks to his glamorous role as the turncoat conspirator. His ascent was altogether unpalatable for Charlie Hindlip and his colleagues, who simply wanted him out of their lives.

AS THE IMPORTANT fall auctions of 2001 approached, the art world was awash with rumours that Sotheby's was for sale. The most likely contender was still Bernard Arnault. Passionately engaged in beating his archrival François Pinault, who owned Christie's, Arnault had been spending lavishly on advertising and expensively produced catalogues. He was also throwing champagne dinner parties overflowing with Moët et Chandon, product of a company that LVMH owned.

Arnault had recruited Simon de Pury, the former chairman of Sotheby's Europe and a trilingual auctioneer, at an annual salary rumoured to be $4 million. De Pury had brought along Daniella Luxembourg, a former deputy chairman of Sotheby's Switzerland, who was getting by on $2 million a year, plus commissions for private sales, at which she and de Pury excelled. Both came with dazzling Rolodexes, and in recognition of their star power Arnault agreed to rename the firm Phillips, de Pury & Luxembourg.

Funded by Arnault's prodigious war chest, the firm's tactic of offering giant guarantees to secure first-class collections had won the upstart auction house some of the year's most enviable consignments.

To Sotheby's and Christie's, and to the rest of the art world, it was abundantly clear that there was not enough business at the top of the market for three auction houses. Ed Dolman believed that there were only fifty private collectors in the world who bought works for upward of $20 million, and fighting to consign objects to win their affections was no easy business.

Despite much carping that LVMH was trying to run Phillips like a couture fashion house—with high-price talent to pull off a dazzling show that created a lot of buzz but not necessarily any profit—there was little doubt that Phillips was giving Sotheby's and Christie's a run for their money. Hoping to cash in on Sotheby's and Christie's antitrust woes, Phillips had created an advertising campaign that was blunt but effective. At what was said to be the direct order of Bernard Arnault, the well-financed firm ran a series of full-page ads in the *New York Times* proclaiming: "Phillips, the other way to do auctions."

WITH THE THREAT of incarceration still hovering over her head as Taubman's trial approached, Dede Brooks was in a state of purgatory. "Whatever happens to her in terms of going to gaol, it can't be worse than the hell she's been through for the last year and a half," said Christopher Meigher, a close friend, who noted that Brooks had been grateful to be at liberty to attend her son's high school graduation over the summer.[19]

Brooks was carrying on with her life, finding ways to channel her competitive spirit. She won the Ladies Golf Tournament at the Rock-away Hunting Club, near her beach club in Lawrence, New York, over Labor Day weekend.

The former chief executive was nervous about the way she would be portrayed during the trial. She was hurt and angry that Taubman's team already seemed intent on assassinating her character by feeding negative stories about her to the press.

Prior to the trial, Brooks was incensed when the *Wall Street Journal* printed a riveting story revealing some of the allegations and antitrust concerns contained in Stephen Lash's notes. The article mentioned Lash's suspicions that Brooks and Davidge had reached some kind of understanding over the potential sale of artworks and artefacts left behind by Imelda and Ferdinand Marcos, the exiled premier of the Philippines.

"We never *once* agreed not to compete on a piece of business," Dede Brooks told me several months later. "I know that Stephen Lash thought we had some deal on the Philippines. That couldn't be further from the truth."[20]

Brooks ascribed Lash's speculations to his irritation at having failed to secure the consignment. "I think every time he lost a piece of business he wanted to blame it on someone," Brooks said. "And why not blame it on Davidge and Brooks making a deal? When you lose a piece of business, it's always much nicer to blame it on something other than your own personal ability to get the business."[21]

* * *

MATTHEW WEIGMAN, the head of Sotheby's Press Office for North America, was at home organizing his VCR collection one evening when he realized that one of his tapes was missing. Wondering what on earth he might have done with it, he suddenly remembered that he had lent the tape to Dede Brooks in 1997 when Sotheby's was preparing to auction off items from the estate of Marlene Dietrich in Los Angeles.

"Dede said, 'I've never *seen* a Marlene Dietrich movie,'" Weigman recalled. "I said, 'Dede, you're *kidding.*' And I happened to pick up one of my favourites, which was *Witness for the Prosecution.*"

The title seemed notably apt in light of the role Brooks was due to play in her imminent courtroom appearance as the government's star witness. In Weigman's estimation, Brooks was certainly up to the task. "She's a far better liar than any of us ever thought she was," he observed.[22]

A MONTH BEFORE his trial was due to begin, Taubman checked into the A. Alfred Taubman Health Care Centre in Michigan for a couple of days to undergo an angioplasty, an operation to clear arteries that had become clogged. It was the third invasive heart procedure he had endured in the past three years.

His doctors and lawyers were concerned about whether he would be up to getting through the trial, and how he would fare on the stand as a witness in his own defence.

"Obviously, we're willing to try this case," Muller told me shortly before the trial, "so we think we have a reasonable chance of winning it. The government indicted this case, so they must think they have a reasonable chance of winning it, too.

"One of us," he added grimly, "is going to wind up wrong."[23]

TAUBMAN'S LAWYERS were hoping to compel Lord Carrington to fly to New York to act as a witness for the defence. Carrington, they felt, could easily confirm that their client had never attempted to broach issues of profitability or economic terms with him, even during the dark days of the art-market recession in 1991 and 1992.

To their chagrin, Carrington had refused to testify willingly in the case. He had already informed the prosecutors that he had met Taubman only once, and that they had never exchanged more than a few words together. Determined to force the issue, the Davis Polk lawyers urged Judge Daniels to dispatch letters rogatory, a kind of legal summons, to try to put pressure on Carrington to come over from England to testify. Daniels declined to grant their request, however, heeding the prosecutors' argument that the proffered testimony was irrelevant to the case. It was a blow for the Davis Polk lawyers. But not necessarily a fatal one.

Simultaneously, the lawyers were mulling over the possibility of trying to compel Lord Camoys to testify on Taubman's behalf to establish that he, Camoys, had communicated with Anthony Tennant about pricing, and that he was unaware of Taubman's ever doing so.

In a sworn affidavit taken in England on December 12, 2000, Lord Camoys had stated that he had "no recollection of ever hearing of any communication between A. Alfred Taubman and any representative of Christie's on any matter relating to pricing." He also added that he and Taubman had never discussed any communication between Sotheby's and Christie's regarding pricing, nor was he aware of Taubman ever having such a conversation with anyone else.

It was information that could potentially be used to help exonerate Taubman. The only catch, however, was that Camoys was also in ill health. He had been forced to step down from the post of Lord Chamberlain of the Queen's Household in 2000 after surgery for a blood clot on the brain. Without Camoys' presence in the courtroom, it would be impossible to present his affidavit as evidence.

The same awkward rule was applicable in the case of a seemingly exculpatory letter that had been sent to John Greene shortly before the trial by Eugene Meigher, a Washington-based attorney for Anthony Tennant, in an attempt to set the record straight: "It is a fact," Meigher wrote, "that Mr. Taubman warned Mr. Tennant at one of their early meetings in 1993 that they needed to be careful to avoid discussion that would violate the United States antitrust laws."[24]

The absence of Sir Anthony Tennant and the Lords Carrington and Camoys was unfortunate for the defence. But the Davis Polk lawyers were still confident that they could exonerate their client.

26

Creative Destruction

THE MUCH-ANTICIPATED trial of *USA v. A. Alfred Taubman* began on Thursday, November 8, in federal court at 40 Foley Square in downtown Manhattan. It had been postponed for a month because of the tragic events of September 11, which had knocked out telephone lines all over downtown Manhattan and closed all federal buildings. As the defendant and his lawyers arrived at the courthouse, one could still smell the lingering stench of incinerated glass, steel and human remains.

Rifle-toting guards lined the courtroom steps, and everyone entering the building was required to pass through two security checkpoints. For his first day in court, Taubman wore a sombre grey three-piece suit with a dark blue tie and black shoes buffed to a spotless shine. He had arrived at the courthouse in a chauffeur-driven black Range Rover, having left his Fifth Avenue apartment with Muller and Fiske for the long ride downtown, navigating the roadblocks set up in the wake of the terrorist attacks.

In order to accommodate the large crowd expected, the proceedings had been moved from judge Daniels' courtroom to Room 110, an enormous panelled auditorium on the main floor that was normally reserved for the swearing-in of immigrants as American citizens.

Taubman sat solemnly at the defence table with his lawyers. Everything was riding on their expertise. It was one of the biggest, most complex and high-profile cases that Davis Polk had ever handled, and the firm was billing accordingly. In September, October and November, monthly legal bills were in excess of $1 million.

Also sitting at the table was an attractive, straw-haired lady in her mid-forties. The mystery blonde turned out to be Gail Jaquish, a jury expert, trial consultant and former assistant psychology professor at the University of Notre Dame, who was the president and founder of Jurix, Inc., of Redondo Beach, California. Dr. Jaquish was highly regarded in her field, and she prided herself on rarely losing a case.

Over the past few days, Jaquish and the lawyers had been going over the case, trying to come up with a coherent strategy for selecting jurors. After learning of Taubman's record of prodigious philanthropy to black causes in Michigan and his self-made, up-by-the-bootstraps life story, Jaquish had advised the lawyers to select as many African-American jurors as possible, preferably with little in the way of a formal education, who would look up to Taubman as a self-made man. The lawyers were relying on her to study the faces of the jurors to detect whether they believed the prosecution's case or whether they were leaning toward the defence.

Fourteen jurors, including two spares, were selected. The final list included four African-Americans—a subway-token clerk, a forklift truck operator, a childwelfare worker and an elderly healthcare aid who normally spent her days taking care of an Alzheimer's patient. There was also a young medical resident, a deputy high school principal, the owner of a gourmet store, a Web site designer, a Jet Blue aircraft mechanic and a postal worker.

"Not exactly a jury of his peers," a member of the press corps quipped.

One potential juror who escaped being assigned to the case was a dapper gentleman in a blazer, crisp white shirt and tie who turned out to be the butler of Nan Kempner, the stylish Park Avenue hostess, who was an international representative for Christie's.

The beautiful Mrs. Taubman was conspicuously absent from her husband's trial. She had been instructed to stay well away from the courthouse at the request of the lawyers. Dominick Dunne, the *Vanity Fair* columnist, ran into Judy at a party after the trial and asked why she had not been in court supporting her beleaguered husband. "No, no, I can't be seen," she told Dunne. "The media would have photographed me. It's better that I stay away."[1]

Besieged with questions from the media about Judy's bizarre absence, the mogul's spokesman Christopher Tennyson delivered the party line: "The idea was that when Mr. Taubman gets home, he doesn't want to have to think or talk about the trial," Tennyson explained. "It's more relaxing for him if Mrs. Taubman isn't in the courtroom every day."[2]

George B. Daniels, the forty-eight-year-old African-American judge presiding at Taubman's trial, had an imposing presence in the courtroom.* After calling the court to order, he called upon the prosecution to deliver its opening statement. Rising to address the jury, John Greene did a masterful job of making it seem an open-and-shut case. As he spoke, documents were projected onto a giant screen, interspersed with colour slides showing how commissions were calculated at the two auction houses.

Greene got straight to the point by establishing that Alfred Taubman and Sir Anthony Tennant had met together secretly on several occasions and implied that their rendezvous had a sinister criminal intent.

"Mr. Taubman's private diaries," Greene told the jury, "will establish that not long after Anthony Tennant came officially on board as chairman of Christie's, he got on his private jet and hustled over to London, England, and had a private meeting with Anthony Tennant."[3]

"Next it was Tennant's turn to travel," Greene continued. "Around April first of 1993 Tennant visited Mr. Taubman in New York. He met him in Mr. Taubman's private apartment here on Fifth Avenue in New York City. Again, there were no Sotheby's employees present, there were no Christie's employees present," he said in a voice loaded with innuendo. "*Just* the chairmen of the two houses."[4]

---

* Coincidentally, Judge Daniels had overlapped with Dede Brooks at Yale. Both received B.A. degrees in American studies, but Daniels graduated two years later than Brooks, in 1975. There was no glimmer of recognition in the courtroom to suggest that they remembered each other from their college days.

Next, it was Bob Fiske's turn to try to win the confidence of the jury. In his earnest, Irish-American rasp of a voice, the septuagenarian former Whitewater prosecutor painted a picture of Dede Brooks as a power-hungry monster, claiming that as CEO she had run Sotheby's "with an iron hand. It was absolutely clear to everybody that this was one hundred percent her show."[5]

"Ladies and gentlemen," Fiske announced, "Alfred Taubman is an innocent man. These charges against him are false. There *was* a crime committed here. It was committed by the two principal witnesses Mr. Greene talked about. One of them, Mr. Davidge, from Christie's, is a man who never met, never talked to Alfred Taubman once in his life—*ever* in his life—and is being paid eight million dollars to be a witness in this case. The other person, Dede Brooks, CEO of Sotheby's, is a person who has no notes, who has repeatedly lied and is testifying against Mr. Taubman in this case because that's the only way she can stay out of gaol for three years.

"So basically," Fiske said, fixing the jury with an intense stare, "Alfred Taubman is Dede Brooks' get-out-of-gaol-free card."[6]

"This is basically a one-witness case," he assured them. "The testimony of a witness like Dede Brooks, you're going to find, is not going to be enough to convict Mr. Taubman and send him to prison."[7]

Fiske also portrayed his client as a Horatio Alger hero, who had created a huge empire by dint of hard work, and was now accused of a crime committed by two despicable liars who were trying to bring a good man down to save their own skins.

After a long day in court, Taubman departed the courthouse with his retinue, including his devoted daughter, Gayle Kalisman. They hovered on the courtroom steps until Taubman's black Range Rover pulled up across the street from the security checkpoint, so he could limit his exposure to the huge phalanx of press cameras waiting to take his picture.

WHEN THE TRIAL RESUMED on Tuesday, November 9, at nine forty-five A.M., the government lawyers began delving through a pile of Taubman's diaries and typed itineraries in order to establish their contention that Taubman had met with Tennant on numerous occasions between 1993 and 1996.

Some of the scribbled and typed entries written by Taubman's various secretaries, the prosecutors noted, failed to mention Sir Anthony Tennant by name. In some places, he was referred to cryptically as "Tony," or "a gentleman." One example, the entry for Tuesday, September 7, 1993, read, "POSSIBLE meeting at the flat with a gentleman."[8] But he was referred to as "Sir Antony Tennant" in a handwritten entry in his appointment book for the same day.[9]

While hearing about Taubman's various rendezvous with Tennant, the mostly blue-collar jury received a startling picture of the tycoon's privileged existence. Taubman's itinerary for September 7, 1993, showed that Judy and Alfred Taubman had met up with Sir Angus Ogilvy, a cousin of the Queen, for a private tour of Buckingham Palace at three forty-five P.M., prior to Taubman's private meeting with Sir Anthony Tennant at the American tycoon's flat on South Audley Street at six-thirty P.M.

The notion that Sotheby's chairman had been visiting the official London residence of the Queen of England just before fitting in a bit of price-fixing with the competition had shock value that seemed potentially damaging for the defence.

Big-screen blow-ups of Taubman's appointment books revealed that his secretaries resorted to abbreviations for the Michigander's various titled friends: "L/L" denoted "Lord and Lady," while "TNT" referred to a luncheon appointment with Her Serene Highness Princess Gloria von Thurn and Taxis.

Patricia Jannaco, the prosecutor, tried to convince the jury that efforts to conceal Sir Anthony's identity pointed to a deliberate attempt to hide criminal activity. The most troubling entry for the defence was a handwritten schedule for April 1, 1993: CONFIDENTIAL 8:30 Break-fast w/ Sir Anthony Tennant. 834 Fifth. CONFIDENTIAL," which was sandwiched between an early-morning haircut and a midmorning manicure and pedicure.

Melinda Marcuse, Taubman's executive assistant and scheduler, was expected to be one of the government's most important witnesses. She was mindful of her responsibility to tell the truth, but terrified of saying or doing anything that might inadvertently harm her boss, who in his gruff, belligerent and teasing way had always treated her with respect.

Marcuse was required to wait in the government witness room, a bleak, twenty-by-twelve-foot space with a couple of windows overlooking an internal courtyard. The room's sparse furnishings included a long metal table and several uncomfortable wooden chairs. Shortly after Marcuse entered the room with her lawyer, he excused himself to escort another witness to the stand. Marcuse was left alone with a copy of the *New York Post*.

After a couple of minutes, the door cracked open, and she was joined by three middle-aged men in suits. One of them was Christopher Davidge. Horrified to find herself in the presence of the Englishman whose notes and testimony threatened to put Taubman in prison, Marcuse immediately buried her head in the crossword puzzle. Suddenly, the two other men left for the cafeteria, and to her mortification, Marcuse found herself *alone* with Davidge, whom she had known during the eighties when she had worked at Christie's.

"So now I'm sitting at the table with Mr. Davidge," Marcuse recalled, "who's known me since 1982! I used to have lunch with Chris Davidge. I knew his kids' names. I hadn't seen him since 1990, and he sat there with the *New York Times*, and I was doing the crossword."

"We sat for forty-five minutes, without a word," Marcuse continued. "Not *a word*! Not a cough, nothing. Total silence. It was just so unbelievably awkward."

Marcuse had never felt she could trust the Englishman. "Davidge was a liar from day one," she remarked. "I feared him when I worked at Christie's."

Unable to stand it any longer, Marcuse stepped out of the room to find her attorney. "You can't leave me alone like this!" she told him.[10]

Under direct questioning from Patricia Jannaco, Marcuse unwittingly supplied some of the most damaging testimony against her boss. Jannaco asked why she had specifically omitted Sir Anthony Tennant's name from her boss' calendar for a breakfast meeting between the chairmen of Christie's and Sotheby's on April 30, 1993. Looking at the documents as instructed, Marcuse acknowledged that she had written "Breakfast 'gentleman' in London apt." and that a typed-up itinerary for that day read "Breakfast meeting in AAT's London flat."

Marcuse replied that she had left out Tennant's name because she felt that the meeting could be "misconstrued."

"By whom?" Jannaco asked.

"By just about anyone, I guess, that would have wanted to misconstrue it," Marcuse stammered. "I don't know. It's my job to protect Mr. Taubman's privacy."

Prompted to explain how a reference to Sir Anthony could be misinterpreted, Marcuse fell further into the prosecutor's trap. "These were the two chairmen of two competing auction houses," she said, "and my knowledge of the business is that it's fairly gossipy and that people could be talking about things like this, and I considered that this should be kept private."[11]

By the end of the day, the government had succeeded magnificently in arousing suspicion about the purpose of Taubman's meetings with Tennant and had established that the two men had met privately in London and New York no fewer than *twelve* times.

THE DEFENDANT returned to his palatial Fifth Avenue duplex on Wednesday, November 14, after an exhausting day in court and was confronted by Judy, who had read an article in the *New York Times* that reported the news that her husband had met with Christie's chairman a dozen times.

"I didn't know it was illegal for you to meet with him," she told him.

"Judy, it's *not* illegal," Taubman replied. "There's absolutely nothing illegal about it. They made a big thing about twelve meetings to impress the jury."

Seeing that his wife was still dismayed, he continued: "If we *were* going to price-fix, we could have done that in three minutes! We wouldn't need to have twelve meetings. After the first meeting, it would be over with!"[12]

* * *

WHEN DAVIDGE took the stand as one of the government's two star witnesses, art world aficionados were astonished by his distinguished appearance and demeanour. The dignified gent in a dark blue suit and tie and perfectly trimmed white beard bore little resemblance to the feisty bantam who used to strut around Christie's in his shirtsleeves.

"Davidge did clean up good, God bless him," Alexandra Peers, a reporter for the *Wall Street Journal,* observed with a chuckle. "He's so patrician! He's really changed his look."[13]

Marion Maneker, a writer covering the trial for *New York* magazine, commented that Davidge resembled "an imperious Russian officer—picture Sean Connery's sub captain in *The Hunt for Red October,* minus the integrity."[14]

Under direct examination by John Greene, Davidge testified that Tennant had informed him that he had been introduced to Taubman shortly after it had been announced in September 1992 that he was to become the chairman of Christie's.

Davidge was taken line by line through Tennant's April 30, 1993, memo, and asked to render his opinion on the authorship and import of each sentence. At the top of the three-page memo was a section that laid out a series of agreements ostensibly made between Tennant and Taubman relating to such subjects as bad-mouthing. Nothing in that section was deemed to be illegal per se.

Under oath, Davidge asserted that he believed that Taubman had been the author of the "this quoted verbatim" section of Tennant's memo. It was a far-fetched assertion, since everything in that section seemed to point to Tennant's authorship. Davidge's willingness to go out so far on a limb made the defence lawyers wonder whether the amnesty-coddled Englishman was lying in order to make Christie's, and the government, happy.

It was clearly in Davidge's interest to pin the blame on Alfred Taubman. Christie's amnesty was contingent on the firm's representation that the collusion had been started by Sotheby's, not Christie's. To publicly suggest that Tennant had originated the conspiracy could imperil Christie's amnesty, and his own, which was bound up with that of his former employer.

Privately, Davidge confided to friends that he believed the conspiracy had not been started by Taubman.[15]

With only ten minutes left before the end of the day to begin his cross-examination, Scott Muller took a couple of swipes at Davidge, questioning why he had received an $8 million severance from Christie's, and casting doubt on the veracity of Tennant's April 30 memo.

Afterward, Joe Linklater noted that although the exchange was brief, Muller's ten minutes of aggressive, rapid-fire questioning and withering insinuation gave Davidge an opportunity to get the measure of his opponent and to prepare himself psychologically for a gruelling cross-examination the following day.

AFTER A HARROWING DAY IN COURT listening to Christopher Davidge's incriminating testimony, Taubman stood at the top of the courtroom steps waiting for his car when the diminutive white-haired Englishman and his lithe grey fox of a lawyer, Joe Linklater, emerged from the witness room and headed for the door. Noticing Taubman out of the corner of his eye, Davidge gingerly stepped past the seventy-six-year-old defendant, who stared at his accuser with palpable disgust.

Darting down the steps, Davidge glimpsed a cluster of paparazzi ready to take his picture at the security checkpoint to the south of the courthouse. Thinking quickly, he eluded the photographers by slithering through a narrow gap in the security barricade in front of the court-house and into an idling yellow cab.

For all his sharp wits, Joe Linklater was unable to match Davidge's agile footwork. As he attempted to follow his client through the barricade, the Chicago lawyer was halted in his tracks by a rifle-toting federal marshal who yelled, "No, sir!"[16]

Left with no choice, Linklater was obliged to walk around the long way—across the broad forecourt, through the white security tent, back another ninety feet—carrying his hefty suitcase and an overnight bag, before joining his client for the ride uptown to the St. Regis Hotel.

With lightning instincts and uncanny good luck, Christopher Davidge had pulled off yet another nimble escape.

MULLER'S CROSS-EXAMINATION of Davidge the next day—which the Davis Polk lawyers hoped would be an evisceration of the wily Englishman's credibility—quickly turned into a comic cat-and-mouse game, with Muller the increasingly exasperated cat as he tried to force Davidge to admit that he had lied repeatedly to Christie's outside counsel.

"You remember lying through your teeth, right?" Muller asked, sneering at the witness.

"I wouldn't say it was through my *teeth*," Davidge replied wryly, "but I did lie."[17]

Muller asked if Davidge remembered misleading John Donovan, one of the Skadden, Arps lawyers, in 1997, by pretending that there had been no illegal communications between Sotheby's and Christie's.

"You looked him straight in the eye and you said no," Muller thundered.

"I don't know if I looked him straight in the eye," Davidge quipped, "but I did say no."[18]

Davidge turned out to be an adept court jester, delivering wisecracks that made the courtroom, the judge and the jury laugh out loud. The more exasperated and accusatory Muller became, the calmer and excessively cordial Davidge made himself appear. When the Davis Polk lawyer stampeded to the witness box and flung a pile of documents at him for him to review, Davidge rearranged them in a neat pile and gave Muller the tut-tut look of a levelheaded parent bemused at the antics of a hotheaded teenager.

The Englishman's self-assured performance on the stand betrayed none of his inner turmoil, but he had been trained for courtroom combat. "I was determined not to let Muller get the better of me," he told a friend afterward. "I tend to be at my best when faced with self-opinionated people, having had to deal with so many of them during my career at Christie's."[19]

There was no question that Scott Muller was a smart lawyer.

Those acquainted with the multiple contingencies he was balancing were impressed with his ability to turn on a dime. But he was not winning fans on the jury.

"I thought he was so obnoxious," Glenn Forrester, the medical resident, said of Muller afterward.[20] Deborah Robinson, the child-welfare worker, agreed. "When he thought he was making a big point he gave us a smirk," she observed. "He was trying to get Davidge, and Davidge won every time!"[21]

Jurors were also distracted by Muller's habit of beginning a question in an accusatory tone then interrupting himself by barking out, "withdrawn." To the irritation of the jury, Muller did so eighty-two times during the trial, forty-six times while cross-examining Davidge.

The sophisticated defence planned by Taubman's lawyers hinged on testimony and evidence that the government lawyers had fought vigorously, and successfully, to exclude, including two documents in Tennant's handwriting that referred to his conversations with Lord Camoys in 1995. Taken together, they could be construed to implicate Camoys, rather than Taubman.

Judge Daniels *did* permit the introduction of Defence Exhibit #158, the memo written by Tennant to Davidge that contained the words "your friend and C." However, he refused to allow the defence lawyers to present Defence Exhibit #174, which was Tennant's summary of his conversation with Lord Camoys from their lunch at Spink on April 24, 1995, after the price changes had been announced.

The Davis Polk lawyers regarded the document as the keystone to the defence. Unlike Tennant's April 30 memo, the Spink memo referred specifically to the details of the nonnegotiable seller's commission, thus establishing an inappropriate conversation in 1995 between Tennant and Camoys, not Taubman. Without the Spink memo, the defence was unable to make use of the significant fact that Taubman and Tennant had not met between November 1994 and June 19, 1995—the period of time during which Davidge and Brooks had discussed and consummated the price-fixing agreement in detail in the parking lot at JFK.

References to Taubman in the third person in Tennant's Spink memo further indicated that the American had not been involved in carrying out the conspiracy in 1995. In sidebar conferences, the defence pulled out every stop to try to convince Judge Daniels that Defence Exhibit #174 should be admitted. But Daniels remained unconvinced. The prosecutors assailed the admissibility of the Spink memo, claiming that it was neither relevant nor a business record.

Daniels' insistence that the defence prove the admissibility of the Spink memo compelled Muller and Fiske to ask countless questions to gain admissibility throughout the entire trial that baffled the jury and the courtroom audience. "Daniels put us through those paces," a Taubman lawyer noted. "It broke that rhythm."[22] Without their document, all the other evidence and testimony the Davis Polk lawyers brought to the fore on behalf of Taubman ended up as rubble. Despite their strenuous attempts, there was no evidence that Lord Camoys was 'C' in Tennant's memo.

WHEN IT BECAME CLEAR that Davidge's star turn on the stand was coming to an end, the same question was on everyone's lips: When was Dede going to testify?

After lunch on Friday, November 16, art-world insiders became excited when they spotted Michael Brooks and Carter Brooks, Dede's husband and daughter, in the courtroom. Dressed in a blue blazer, blue-and-white striped shirt, beige slacks and brown Top-Siders, Michael Brooks was the very picture of a sporty, country club WASP. He was observed scowling at the press corps, who were sitting in the first two rows. Carter, a beautiful young woman with long blond hair pulled back into a tight ponytail, and wearing a no-nonsense ensemble of black slacks and a matching sweater, looked tense and alert. In one hand, she was clutching a copy of a book entitled *Creative Destruction*. An irreverent wag in the courtroom wondered out loud whether the book's title was actually the theme of her mother's expected testimony as a witness for the prosecution.

When Dede Brooks arrived at the courthouse to testify on Monday, November 19, she and her erstwhile co-conspirator ran into each other briefly in the government witness room.

"He was leaving and I was walking in," she recalled.[23]

"I wished her luck," Davidge remembered. "She was really gracious and congratulated me on my evidence."[24]

The dynamic executive whose presence had always enlivened every room she walked into, slunk quietly into the witness box to take the oath, looking like a penitent, broken woman. Her voice crackled with nervousness during the first volley of routine questions. Phil Cody asked Brooks to describe a conversation she remembered having with Taubman after they received a copy of Christie's press release on March 9, 1995, declaring its intention to begin charging a new set of nonnegotiable seller's commissions.

"What did you say to him, and what did he say to you?" Cody asked.

"My recollection is that I said to him, 'They did it, Christie's actually came out with an announcement on their price increase,'" Brooks recalled. "And he said to me, 'Congratulations!'"

Sitting at the defence table, Taubman shook his head in disbelief. Cody asked Brooks to recall an incident that occurred after the *Financial Times* had broken the story that Christie's had obtained amnesty. She and Taubman were scheduled to discuss a routine piece of Sotheby's business, Brooks recalled, and Don Pillsbury had insisted on joining them to ensure that nothing inappropriate was discussed. Taubman, she remembered, spoke to her just before Sotheby's general counsel entered the room. "Mr. Taubman looked at me and said, 'You know, just don't act like a girl,'" Brooks told the court.[25]

A ripple of shock went through the courtroom.

"When Mr. Taubman told you 'don't act like a girl,' what did you understand?" Cody asked.

"I think he was just telling me to be tough," Brooks replied crisply.[26]

After Pillsbury joined the meeting, Brooks testified, Taubman made another pointed remark. "Mr. Taubman had *a Financial Times,* which had a front-page picture of me on it," Brooks said. "And Mr. Taubman held the thing up and said, 'You'll look good in stripes.'"

This time there were audible gasps in the courtroom—an event that the jury could not fail to notice. For Taubman to tell Brooks not

to "act like a girl" seemed outrageously sexist. But had he *also* taunted her with the prospect of prison—when he was already part of the
conspiracy as a result of his meetings with Tennant?

Phil Cody asked the judge for a few minutes to collect his
thoughts, and it was an effective tactic. The burly American suddenly seemed like an insensitive, arrogant chauvinist.

Sitting at the defence table, Taubman stared at his accuser in
apparent astonishment. During a courtroom break, he appeared
angry and confused as he conferred with his lawyers. Brooks' recollection of his congratulating her was an utter falsehood, he told them.

"It's not true," Taubman said. "Why would I congratulate her? I
had no notion of what was going on."[27] His alleged sexist remark and
the crack about looking good in stripes was making Taubman crazy.
"That's all untrue," he told me later. "It's just not my kind of style. I
think that's all contrived. She's trying to set up this whole thing that
I was a boss beating her up because she was female. That was her
whole intent!"[28]

In court, Brooks was also asked to describe a conversation she
remembered having with Sotheby's chairman in the spring of 1993.
"Mr. Taubman told me that he had just met with Sir Anthony
Tennant," she testified, "and that they had had a very good meeting."

Taubman, she recalled, had agreed with Tennant "that we were
both killing each other on the bottom line and that ... it was time to
do something about it. He said that he and Mr. Tennant had gotten
along very well and he could see working with him."[29]

Brooks testified that Taubman had asked her to meet with
Davidge to go over the details of the various subjects he and Tennant
had discussed, including pricing. Many in the courtroom were
stunned that Dede indicated that she had felt no moral compunction
about embarking on a course of illegal activity. "You agreed to do
that willingly, did you not?" Bob Fiske asked testily, when it came
time for him to cross-examine Sotheby's former CEO.

"Yes, I did," Brooks replied. "I was nervous about it, but I agreed
to do it willingly."[30]

Those words would incite rage when repeated at Sotheby's the
following day.

"I, for one, was waiting for her to say, 'I had a crisis of conscience. I really had to work these issues through in my mind, to understand if I could really do this,'" said David Redden, the vice chairman of Sotheby's North America and chairman of Sotheby's.com. "Instead, she said, 'Davidge had been top dog for years, he was way ahead of me and I had to get up to speed before I could talk to him.' It was a moment when she *could* have redeemed herself, slightly," Redden noted. "But that passed forever. She doesn't have a shred of conscience."[31]

Redden was curious to find out where the blame really lay for the scandal that had engulfed the art world and left Sotheby's enfolded in a fog of shame. "Assuming that what was said at trial was correct and there were orders from on high," he observed, "Dede had the power, the authority and the willpower to say no. And it was her *duty* to say no."[32]

"In retrospect, Dede was truly one of those people for whom the ends justify whatever means necessary," Redden remarked, "which is one of the most dangerous things in the entire world."[33]

When asked by Bob Fiske, Brooks read out a portion of her grand jury testimony in which she had responded to questions about what had driven her to break the law.

"I think there was no question that we were extremely concerned about our financial results," she said, reading from her previous testimony, "and we saw ourselves in sort of a death struggle with Christie's in terms of the direction the business was headed in. And I think my feeling was that we weren't doing anything that was harmful to our clients."[34]

"In fact," she continued, "if we stopped some of the bad-mouthing and a lot of the other things we were doing that in fact it would be better for the business long-term and better for the clients if it was better for the business. So I guess I convinced myself that it was in the best interests of the business and our clients that we were doing it."[35]

In winding up his cross-examination of Brooks, Fiske showed the jury a video clip from PBS' *Wall Street Week with Louis Rukeyser,* where Brooks had made an appearance on December 19, 1997, to quell rumours of corruption over the art-smuggling scandal.

Up on the screen, Brooks looked confident and buoyant—a vivid contrast to the dejected witness on the stand. As the clip ended, Brooks seemed in agony and tears welled in the corners of her eyes.

"Mrs. Brooks, that is *you* giving that answer to Mr. Rukeyser, correct?" Fiske asked.

"Yes, it is," she replied, her voice breaking.

"At the time you said that you were in the middle of this price-fixing conspiracy with Mr. Davidge, were you not?"

"Yes, I was," she said, quietly.

"No further questions, Your Honour," Fiske snapped, returning to his desk, clearly savouring the death blow he felt he had just delivered to Brooks' credibility.

Brooks' two lawyers were sitting at the back of the courtroom throughout her time in the witness box. "Dede does not bear him any ill will," Steve Kaufman told me.

"She accepts that she did it herself," John Siffert continued. "She didn't have to do it. Nobody held a gun to her head. She actually *likes* the man. She doesn't want him to go to gaol. She doesn't like what he's doing to her. For the rest of his life he's going to have his press people plant stories that are untrue. And they've probably poisoned the well up at Sotheby's for her.

"She brought it on herself," he added. "She hasn't ever uttered a word to say she wants him to go to gaol, or to hope that he gets punished. She just wishes he would accept responsibility."[36]

Many of the newspaper press reports describing Brooks' testimony were balanced and respectful. The notable exceptions were the fulminations of Steve Dunleavy, a columnist at the *New York Post*, who labelled Brooks a "dragon lady"[37] and a "rat."[38] He also portrayed Taubman as the "victim of a conniving woman."[39]

"Dede Brooks," he wrote, "is an admitted third-rate crook who hid behind a skirt ... The fact that the old fella had to be put through this, rich or not, by a Wagnerian tank commander called Dede Brooks is just bloody outrageous ... He is a bit of a darling old fella—and she would eat a barracuda without taking out the bones."[40]

Brooks was hurt and confused by her merciless portrayal in Dunleavy's columns. "I could understand it if he knew me," Brooks told me afterward. "I've just never even *met* the man."[41]

Dunleavy's rants also caused considerable pain to Brooks' family and close friends. "The person who has been so ruthlessly portrayed and mercilessly attacked in the media during Mr. Taubman's trial is not my sister," Elinor Dwyer McKenna observed, "but rather a caricature of a selfish, greedy female corporate chief executive, which makes for a more dramatic story and, I guess, sells newspapers."[42]

FOR SEVERAL MONTHS, Taubman's lawyers had been debating whether to call the legendary Rosa Parks as a character witness in his trial. Parks, whose refusal to relinquish her seat to a white man on a bus in Montgomery, Alabama, in 1955 had galvanized the civil-rights movement, was more than happy to oblige.

Taubman and Max Fisher had been shocked in 1987 to learn that Parks had been mugged and badly beaten in her Detroit apartment, and they offered her a comfortable apartment in the Riverfront Tower complex that they had built in downtown Detroit. As a long-time social activist in Detroit, Parks was well acquainted with Taubman's charitable munificence in the city. He was also a generous supporter of Parks' foundation, which sent busloads of children every year to visit the place where her defiance had sparked enormous social change.

The Davis Polk lawyers were concerned that putting Parks on the witness stand might backfire if the prosecutors tried to point out just how generous Taubman had been to her. In a private conference with the opposing lawyers, however, Judge Daniels refused to allow Parks to testify. He sided with the prosecutors, who argued that her testimony as a character witness, however sincere or well intentioned, would be irrelevant to the matter of Taubman's innocence or guilt in a price-fixing case.

Judge Daniels did not rule out a court appearance by Judge Damon Keith, a sitting judge on the U.S. Court of Appeals for the Sixth Circuit, who had offered to testify on Taubman's behalf. One of the first African-Americans appointed to the federal bench, where he had served for thirty-four years, Judge Keith was a respected figure in the civil rights movement. Over the years, he had served with Taubman on numerous civic and charitable boards.

"Can you tell the jury what Mr. Taubman's reputation is in the community for honesty and truthfulness?" Bob Fiske asked.

"It is absolutely wonderful for honesty and truthfulness," Judge Keith replied, "and it's generally known that his record for honesty and truthfulness is impeccable, without a blemish on it."[43]

The defence went on to call a wide range of witnesses who testified about Taubman's passion for architecture and design and his poor head for figures. Sotheby's chief financial officer, Bill Sheridan, testified that Taubman's primary focus in board meetings was the look of Sotheby's catalogues and real-estate issues concerning the firm's New York head-quarters and the new Paris offices. And that he paid scant attention to financial matters.

"Mr. Taubman was more concerned with what time lunch was going to be served and what was for lunch," Sheridan said. "He really didn't engage very often in board discussions."[44]

THROUGHOUT THE TRIAL, the Davis Polk lawyers tried to gauge Taubman's state of mind to determine whether he was up to the stressful task of testifying on his own behalf. The indications were not encouraging. The defendant kept falling asleep during the trial—almost as much as one male juror.

The lawyers had spent countless hours coaching Taubman by peppering him with questions. During the trial rehearsals, one lawyer noted tactfully, "He didn't answer with absolute precision." His hearing was terrible; his memory was unreliable; he had trouble recalling the key details in the case; and there was a fear that if the prosecutors succeeded in making Taubman testy or angry on the stand he might alienate the jury.

In a sidebar conference with Judge Daniels, John Greene informed the Davis Polk lawyers that if Taubman was going to testify, the government would most likely keep him on the stand for two or three days. The defence lawyers were dismayed. That was a long time for an old man to have to testify in his own defence. There were also pressing concerns for his health. Taubman had been feeling sick and weak for a couple of days, and his doctors were worried about whether he might suffer a stroke or a heart attack while on the stand.

The Davis Polk lawyers had staged a couple of mock trials with a fake jury at which Taubman had *not* testified, and they had won a not-guilty verdict both times. By the third week of the actual trial itself, most of the lawyers were confident that they had established reasonable doubt.

Jim Rouhandeh, another member of Taubman's legal team, had never wavered from his belief that it was imperative for their client to testify. "This is not a reasonable-doubt case," he told his colleagues. It was vital, he argued, to give the jury an alternative scenario to that being presented by the prosecution. At present, they knew only that Taubman and Tennant had met twelve times and discussed various auction practices. After all, there was no *concrete* evidence of a conspiracy to fix prices between Taubman and Tennant, and all that was required was for Taubman to stand up and declare that he and Christie's chairman had never agreed to fix seller's commissions. "We need to give the jury something to grasp," Rouhandeh insisted. "Alfred has to testify."[45]

Finally, they decided not to put Taubman on the stand. "It was *a very* close call," Chris Tennyson noted.[46] In the final hour it was Gail Jaquish, the jury expert, who convinced the Davis Polk lawyers.

"You can only hurt yourself," she told them. "The jury *likes* him."

Jaquish was right on that score. Part of her job was to study the jury's body language, and she had deduced correctly that most of them had already formed a high opinion of him. "We called her 'Eagle Eye,'" Deborah Robinson, one of the jurors, told me afterward, referring to Jaquish.[47]

On Wednesday, November 28, Bob Fiske made a solemn announcement: "Mr. Taubman is not going to testify,"[48] Privately, Taubman feared that the decision was a mistake. "I can't believe it's adequate for me not to take the stand and look this jury in the eye and tell them I didn't do it," he told Chris Tennyson.[49]

DURING THE TRIAL, several jurors, including Mike D'Angelo, the mail carrier, repaired at lunchtime to Baxter's, a nearby bar and restaurant, where they downed pints of Guinness.

"They went to Baxter's practically every day for lunch," another juror marvelled. "I could barely keep my eyes open after having one beer at lunch."[50]

D'Angelo, a movie buff, who had urged his fellow jurors to rent *Twelve Angry Men,* the black-and-white movie classic starring Henry Fonda, was disheartened to hear that the defendant was not going to testify.

"I thought they were going to put Taubman on the stand," he told me afterward. "I had a bet with my fellow jurors, and I lost. I was so mad! They were all Guinness bets," he explained. "And we had a bet that Dede would cry. I lost that bet, too."[51]

ON THE FINAL DAY of testimony in Taubman's trial in New York, Sotheby's new salesroom on the Rue du Faubourg St. Honoré in Paris erupted with joyful, deafening applause as the gavel went down on the first lot ever sold by a foreign-owned auction house on French soil. The evening sale had begun at six o'clock with a brief address from Princess Laure de Beauvau-Craon, who had campaigned for ten years to end the 445-year-old monopoly of France's state-registered auctioneers, known as the *commissaires priseurs.* "This is a historic moment," she declared, "to know that we can finally hold a sale in our own premises and under our own control. It is a great achievement."[52]

In an elegant gesture, the first lot—a first French-language edition of a book of poetry by the Italian writer Gabriele D'Annunzio—was presented to Beauvau-Craon as a gift from Kristen van Riel, a former colleague. The auction was composed of the literary book collection of Charles Hayout, and 100 percent of the lots were sold. A copy of Marcel Proust's *Du côté de chez Swann* sold for 2,232,499 francs ($332,620), a new world record for a printed volume of French literature.

The historic sale in Paris coincided with the penultimate day of Taubman's trial. Ironically, Taubman and Tennant had spent much of the time during their twelve meetings discussing the possibility of opening up the French market—a perfectly legitimate topic of discussion between the chairmen of the two auction houses. It was a subject that the defendant could have discussed at length on the stand. Such testimony might not have convinced every juror of his innocence, but it would at least have provided *some* explanation of what the chairmen of Sotheby's and Christie's discussed during their twelve meetings.

In a further irony, Great Britain had announced the day before that it intended to institute criminal penalties for price-fixing. If such a law had only been in place a few months earlier, around the time of his indictment in the United States, Sir Anthony Tennant might be facing conviction and gaol time himself.

ONCE ALL OF THE TESTIMONY WAS OVER, lawyers for the defence and the prosecution debated over the exhibits that each side intended to present during closing arguments. Bob Fiske was incensed to discover that the government was planning to put up a slide of a quotation from *The Wealth of Nations,* written by the eighteenth-century political economist Adam Smith.

Clearly exasperated, Fiske read the offending passage out loud: "People in the same trade seldom meet together even for merriment and diversion, but the conversation ends in a conspiracy against the public or in some contrivance to raise prices."

"I mean, give me a break," Fiske exclaimed.

"You want a break now, Mr. Fiske?" the judge joked.

"This has no business here, Your Honour," Fiske replied. "It is totally inappropriate and, I think, highly prejudicial, Your Honor."[53]

Judge Daniels was unmoved by Fiske's protestations, but he made one concession: Mr. Greene would be permitted to *read* the quote out loud, but not display it on screen.

ON THE MORNING of Monday, December 3, 2001, lawyers for the defence and for the government were instructed to make their summations to the jury. It was Greene's turn to go first. The federal prosecutor poured scorn on what he derided as Taubman's "dumb and hungry" defence—a reference to Bill Sheridan's testimony that Taubman often fell asleep in meetings, that he had no head for numbers and that during board meetings he was usually more interested in what was being served for lunch. "You don't become a millionaire or billionaire without knowing how to read the bottom line," Greene told the jury.[54]

In his rebuttal, Fiske claimed that the entire case turned on "whether you believe Dede Brooks beyond a reasonable doubt when she tells you what happened at the meetings she said she had with Mr. Taubman. If you don't believe Dede Brooks' testimony beyond a reasonable doubt, you must acquit."

"Now," Fiske said, staring at the jury, "I tell you Dede Brooks is a walking reasonable doubt."[55]

AFTER THE DAY of closing arguments, a writer ran into Patty Hambrecht at an elegant dinner party held at Swifty's, the society eatery on Manhattan's Upper East Side.

"What happened in court today?" she asked.

After outlining the day's events, he congratulated her—somewhat facetiously—that her name had hardly come up at all during Taubman's trial. From the anger in her eyes, he could see that he had hit a nerve.

"I'm *furious* with Christopher Davidge," Hambrecht told him. She explained that she had been livid to hear that Christie's former CEO had cited her name as one of only two people at Christie's whom he had informed about Tennant's meetings with Taubman. Davidge had not said in court *when* he had told her, but the implication was that she had known about the conspiracy from the very beginning.

"That's a lie," Hambrecht told the writer.[57]

THE FOLLOWING MORNING, the Davis Polk lawyers urged Judge Daniels to inform the jury that meetings between competitors were not illegal per se. The critical contested issue, they pointed out, was not the existence of the meetings themselves—of which there was little doubt—but of Taubman's *intent* in meeting with Tennant.

Hoping to emphasize that point, they submitted proposed text for the judge to insert into his jury instructions: "Evidence of meetings, telephone calls, or other contacts between Mr. Taubman and Anthony Tennant and between Mr. Taubman and Diana Brooks does not by itself prove that Mr. Taubman was a participant in a conspiracy or that he had the required knowledge and intent. Competitors may have legitimate and lawful reasons to have contacts with each other or to exchange information or statements of intention. Thus you may not infer that Mr. Taubman knowingly and intentionally joined the conspiracy solely from the fact that he had meetings or other contacts with Christie's or participated in exchanges of information with Tennant."

Bowing to the government's strenuous objections, the judge declined to honour the defence's request.

27

Guilty

AS TAUBMAN AND HIS LAWYERS sat in the defence witness room awaiting the verdict, the tense silence was broken by an eruption of cheers coming from the jury room. Similar screams of delight had been heard each time one of the four black jurors agreed to find Taubman guilty. Now that there was finally a consensus, the jubilation was deafening.

The eruption of cheers made Taubman nervous. "I suspected the jury weren't on my side," he said later, "but my lawyers thought they were fine."[4] The jury's loud excitement haunted Taubman for several days afterward. "The four African-American people didn't believe I was guilty," Taubman noted wistfully, "but we could hear these cheers, where they were egging these people on, trying to get them to agree."

The jury reached its final verdict at 2:04 P.M, after ten hours of deliberations. Many of the reporters who had converged on the courthouse in anticipation of a verdict were waiting upstairs in the grim cafeteria when Kathryn Kranhold, a reporter for the *Wall Street Journal*, received an electronic alert on her BlackBerry. The jury had reached a verdict. All scurried downstairs to witness the announcement.

When the jury foreman said "Guilty," the Taubman loyalists in the first two rows to the left of the courtroom stared at one another in disbelief. The courtroom was silent except for an audible gasp from Jeff Miro, Taubman's longtime friend and confidant and the administrator of his defence, who buried his head in his hands and cried, "*No!*"

Taubman seemed unable to hear the word *guilty* and leaned over to Scott Muller with a confused look on his face. Muller whispered quietly in his ear, gripping the tycoon by the arm to prevent him from collapsing. His daughter, Gayle Kalisman, who had sat through every day of the trial, kissed his cheek and hugged him. In a brisk, businesslike manner, Judge Daniels set a sentencing date for April 2002, and the crowd slowly dispersed.

Miro looked pained as he left the courtroom. He had been instrumental in the decision to hire Davis Polk, and it suddenly looked like an expensive mistake. "Jeffrey's very upset, and surprised," Chris Tennyson noted afterward. "Very, very shaken by it."[5]

After the sixteen-day trial, the preening arrogance of Taubman's $650-an-hour attorneys had been trumped by the no-frills, matter-of-fact logic of the colourless trilogy of government lawyers.

Grim-faced, Taubman descended the courthouse steps with Fiske and Muller beside him. Ignoring the dozens of paparazzi and TV cam-eras, he sped away in his black Range Rover.

John Olsoff, one of Sotheby's in-house lawyers, had hightailed it down to the courtroom from York Avenue on the Lexington Avenue express train when he heard a verdict was imminent, and had arrived just in time. Throughout the trial, he had been tapping out regular electronic bulletins to Sotheby's on his BlackBerry. His final report came in the form of a single e-mailed message, which caused a sensation when it reached the office of Bill Ruprecht on York Avenue.

GUILTY.

"A lot of people at Sotheby's were just stunned and really, really upset," Pete Hathaway recalled. "I'm still one hundred percent behind him, and I don't understand the defense."[6]

Ruprecht was reeling from the news, and found it hard to square with his knowledge of Taubman's character and disposition. "The idea that Alfred had any appetite for managing interest-free advances or upside-or-no-upside guarantees or those kinds of financial issues is so beyond the pale," Ruprecht noted. "It's just not who the guy is.[7]

That sentiment was echoed in London by Sotheby's London chairman, Henry Wyndham. "I think we're all slightly confused," he said. "My impression was, I always thought he was totally innocent. But when it was announced that twelve meetings had taken place with Tennant, that did take us by surprise."[8]

As they emerged from the courthouse, several of the jurors in Taubman's case became instant celebrities when they paused to grant interviews to a ravenous press corps.

"If you commit a crime, I don't care how old you are, you're guilty," Mike D'Angelo, the jury foreman, told the *New York Post*. The fifty-one-year-old mail carrier with a tattoo of a snake and sword on his left biceps told reporters that the decision to convict Taubman "wasn't hard," and cheerfully noted that the art world was clearly "no different than anyplace else—they're cutting each other's throats.[9]

28

Sir Anthony Tennant

"IN SPITE OF ALL THE NONSENSE about this in court, I never called him once for an appointment," Taubman remarked about Tennant the day after the trial's conclusion. "Not once! He called every time. We could have done that thing in three minutes if we *had* done it. We didn't need twelve meetings or whatever they say I did. But they made such a big thing out of that.

"You've got to give them credit," Taubman said, referring to the prosecutors. "One of my lawyers told me, 'This guy, Greene—he's a nice guy. He's not very smart.' I said to them afterwards, 'For a guy who's supposed to be stupid—I gotta tell you something—he did a pretty good job!'"[1]

Taubman had never been troubled by the notion of getting together with Tennant. "In every industry in America, in every profession we have associations," Taubman pointed out. "Competitors get together and talk about everything in the world."

Like many other lawyers who had been paying attention to Taubman's case, David Boies was astonished by the verdict and surprised that no one appeared to have mentioned in court the simple fact that meetings between competitors were not illegal per se. "There wasn't any real evidence that they fixed prices," Boies noted, referring to Taubman and Tennant, "just that they had a lot of meetings."

It was a stunning observation coming from the lawyer who had spent the spring and summer of 2000 poring over documents and taking depositions in an attempt to establish Taubman's guilt.

Asked how he might have handled Taubman's defence differently, Boies told me that he would probably have attempted to call in
expert witnesses to establish some of the facts about how executives
and chairmen of major corporations conduct business. "You can get
a business school dean, or respected businesspeople, who say they get
together with competitors all the time," he said, "and that *of course*
they try to keep those meetings not public. That's for purely normal
competitive reasons."[2]

Boies observed that a plausible account of what the two chairmen
had actually discussed was sorely missing from the trial. "You've *got*
to have an explanation," Boies noted.

"The Davis Polk people are very smart lawyers and very decent
people," Boies noted. "But a trial is a complicated thing. In many
ways it's like a morality play. The themes and facts are important,
but the presentation is *critical*. Trying a jury case to verdict is different from a lot of other things that people do in the law."[3]

AFTER A CHANCE ENCOUNTER between the author and Sir
Anthony Tennant at an elegant lunch party in the English country-
side, Christie's former chairman finally agreed to tell his version of
the story.

The absence of Anthony Tennant—the one person who could
have furnished a plausible account of what the two chairmen had discussed during those twelve meetings—had been a devastating blow to
Taubman's defence.

Unwilling to travel to the United States for fear of being prose-
cuted, Tennant sat in England, reading daily press reports of how the
Justice Department's star witnesses were demonizing him and
Taubman in court. He was shocked to learn the verdict.

"It's beastly for Al," Tennant said. "I really do feel very sorry for
him."[4]

Taubman may have been too addled or forgetful to testify on his
own behalf. But Tennant had a clear recollection of the topics that he
and Taubman had addressed during their dozen or so meetings,
which could have provided a powerful counterpoint to the innuendo
skilfully created by the government lawyers. In addition, Tennant

had a startling perspective on the document described as his "April 30 memo." And a clear take on what he believed were Davidge's and Brooks' motives for giving false testimony in order to blame Tennant and Taubman as the prime movers of the conspiracy.

Whether true or not, Tennant's articulate reflections could at the very least have created substantial reasonable doubt in the minds of jury members, which could have resulted in an acquittal for the aging tycoon.

From the start, Tennant declared, his meetings with Taubman had been entirely lawful. "It's always been my policy in business to size up the competition," the Englishman said. "There's nothing wrong with that. First of all, I wanted to look him in the eye. See what kind of a chap he was. Secondly, I thought, and he did too, that there should be a link, chairman to chairman."

The auction world is unique, he observed, in that "it's a universal business in which there are only two major players, and where there are no trade associations. There's basically no other forum. One *had* to meet."

Consequently, Tennant noted, "all the time that I saw Al, I was talking about how to deal with inflation and taxation in this place or that place. And we used to talk a lot about complaints. Al would say to me again and again and again, 'You must stop them telling so many lies about Sotheby's.' So mostly we were dealing with complaints." The two chairmen also discussed the possibility of holding auctions in Paris, and other matters of commonplace business strategy.

Tennant's limited involvement with Christie's on a day-to-day basis meant that he relied on Davidge to furnish him with the topics he needed to discuss with Taubman.

"Most of the things I complained about were things that Davidge wanted me to put to Al," Tennant recalled. "But I had no firsthand knowledge of that kind of detail."

It was ridiculous, Tennant pointed out, to think that after only a brief acquaintance, he and Taubman would have trusted each other to break what they both knew was a federal law. "It's fairly barmy to suppose that two experienced businessmen could go straight into a deal on price-fixing when we had barely met. You can't go and meet someone and say, 'Let's fix prices.' The idea that we should suddenly go straight into a deal when we hardly knew each other is absurd."

Tennant firmly denied that he told Davidge to fix prices with Dede Brooks. "The proposition that as chairman I had given Davidge instructions is almost laughable. Davidge did whatever he wanted to and didn't inform me. I didn't see him very often," he added.

A crime had clearly been committed by Davidge and Brooks, Tennant said, but he and Taubman had nothing to do with it. "Why the hell would I want to do that sort of thing? And why would Al?" Having admitted their own culpability, Tennant observed, Brooks and Davidge "had transparently obvious reasons for putting the finger on Al and me."

On the basis of his own recollections, Tennant could only imagine that the two former CEOs had told a pack of lies at the trial. The collusion, he added, was "a bloody stupid thing to have done, because it was quite unnecessary. It's sort of naive and rather indicates that neither of them was very businesslike."

Tennant was astonished by all the fuss in court over his so-called April 30 memo.

It was never a memo, he said. "I don't think I've ever sent a memorandum without signing it or addressing it to someone. I don't think anyone does. And there's no record of any offer, or any acceptance of an offer or agreement, in that thing. They made it seem to be a very sinister document. And that suited everybody, except poor Al, who didn't know what the hell it was about, I imagine."

Instead, the "memo" was merely three pieces of paper on which Tennant had jotted down a series of notes over several days, weeks or months—an assertion that appeared to square with the discovery by Taubman's lawyers that the two different kinds of paper had been used: one sheet had faint blue lines, and the other two, faint grey lines. The various unrelated paragraphs, Tennant said, "were all written at different times.

"It was my habit to make notes on an ongoing basis when I

thought of something or saw somebody, so that when I returned to it three or five days later I could refresh my memory. And I would jot down what people told me. A lot of it is what I gleaned from other people at Christie's."

When he met with Taubman for breakfast on April 30, 1993, Tennant recalled, "I had spent a total of about ten days' work on Christie's. That was partly because I was only a non-executive director. I hardly set foot there. And I had at least three things which were more important to me than Christie's, all of which were buzzing at the time."

He was baffled by the weight attached to his jottings. "I naturally didn't recollect this 'memorandum,' these bits of paper," he said, "until I saw what they were making of them in the trial. I personally think that it was shorthand notes that I made for myself, and that it was largely composed of what Christie's people told me."

Under the heading "Paper given April 30," Tennant had written an opening section of eighteen lines that appeared to detail various benign agreements between the two auction houses, most of which were never put into practice. That section, identified in Tennant's notes as "This quoted verbatim," was, he said, "probably from a briefing note from Davidge. Because he knew those points, and I didn't. I didn't have the foggiest idea about any of them.

"This group of papers couldn't possibly constitute instructions, because it doesn't say go out and do anything. It's not addressed to anybody. Much of it is innocuous, and much of it's incorrect."

In court, Davidge had stated that Tennant had brought the April 30 memo into Davidge's office for him to read. The implication was that he had left it with the CEO, who had carefully held on to it. That impression, Tennant believed, was false.

Tennant had no idea how Davidge had got hold of the memo pages. He had no recollection of ever showing, or giving, them to him. According to Tennant, Davidge was the only person who knew the secret combination number that opened the door to the chairman's private office.

The whole sordid matter had seriously dented Tennant's reputation as a brilliant businessman. But the outcome proved disastrous for Taubman, whom he referred to as "a nice chap."

From his removed perspective in England, Tennant surmised that there had been an attempt to prejudice the jury against Taubman, and that his fate had rested on their unfavourable impression of his character.

"The trial was all about him being a filthy-rich Jew," Tennant said in a mellifluous, aristocratic tone. "That was really all they wanted to focus on. The whole message of the trial was to do that."

The Englishman was wrong on that score. In the minds of the jurors, ethnicity had nothing to do with it. Their perception of Taubman's guilt had hinged on three elements: the fact of twelve meetings; the April 30 document, which suggested a dialogue between the two chairmen; and the testimony supplied by Brooks and Davidge.

According to Tennant, that was all bunk. But the indictment that prevented him from travelling to the United States had made it unwise for him to make any of the assertions that might have vouchsafed Taubman's liberty.

IN DEFEAT, the Davis Polk lawyers had to endure the humiliating epithet that had caused peals of laughter when repeated in the courtroom during the last days of the trial—that Taubman had "the worst defence money can buy."

As accounts of their lacklustre performance began appearing in newspapers and magazines everywhere, the lawyers quietly complained that the judge had stumped their every attempt to offer an alternative narrative to the one portrayed by the prosecutors. "We weren't allowed to put in our defence," Jim Rouhandeh explained. "It was not a fair fight." Frustrated by several of Daniels' exclusionary decisions, they vowed to mount an appeal.

"I can't tell you how infuriating it is to have to sit and read article after article about how our defence was too stupid," another lawyer told me. "It just *wasn't* our defence. It's just that when you got finished, that's all that was left."[5]

The lawyers were particularly upset that Judge Daniels had forbidden them from introducing the Spink memo—which they believed could have been used to prove that a collusive dialogue had existed between the two English auction officials in 1995 that did *not* involve Taubman.

Jim Rouhandeh corrected the misperception that appeared to have been held by some of the jurors, judging by interviews they had given on the courtroom steps after pronouncing their verdict. "We weren't simply resting just on saying that Davidge and Dede are liars," Rouhandeh explained. "We had two components, one of which was that Taubman and Tennant met legitimately. And when it came to fix prices it was Camoys and Tennant in 1995. Not Alfred and Tennant in 1993. We got clobbered."[6]

Taubman was altogether more generous on the subject of his lawyers' efforts, even though, he noted laughing, "I had lawyers coming out of my ears!

"I feel in all honesty that they did the best job they knew how to do," he told me. "I believe they were probably too straightforward with this. But that's my only criticism. I couldn't expect anything more of them."[7]

AFTER HIS BRAVURA courtroom performance, Davidge had flown to London to spend a few days before travelling to Bombay on December 5, the day the verdict was announced.

Keen to put the past behind him, the Englishman was happily setding into the exotic Indian city he now called home. He and Amrita had recently moved into a two-bedroom apartment in a 1950s building, which he had purchased for $2.1 million. The couple's new home was near the formal Hanging Gardens at the top of Malabar Hill, which abutted the famous Towers of Silence, where Parsees, who hold fire, earth and water to be sacred, lay out their dead to be picked clean by vultures.

Davidge felt far removed from the cares of his frantic working days at Christie's, but he continued to be fascinated by the legal bloodbath he had just witnessed in New York.

"I was surprised by Taubman's poor defence," he told a friend. "And I feel sorry not only for Taubman and his family but also for Dede."[8]

Davidge believed that Taubman had come up with a phrase that had appeared in Tennant's handwritten notes from April 30, 1993, a proposal that "we should get back to the published terms and conditions of sale."

"In other words," he noted, "'charge what we say we charge.'" Leaving their discussions at that simple conclusion would have saved Taubman—and everyone else—an awful lot of trouble. "I have always thought this was the mind of someone with a retail background who understands how you get the consumer's confidence," Davidge told a friend. "Do you need to send a man of Taubman's age to prison for promoting the very ideals that the antitrust laws seek to promote—especially after paying such a vast fine and damage to his life's reputation? No way![9]

"I tried to reason with John Greene," Davidge claimed, "but he was not prepared to look beyond the 'crime' and judge the effect. Surely the law is fairer than that!"[10]

Since the discovery of the conspiracy, Davidge observed, vendor's commissions were pretty much back to the old arrangement. Fat cats got richer and Joe Public was again disadvantaged. Christie's and Sotheby's had profited in the short term from the collusion he and Brooks had carried out. But this fiscal advantage had soon been eroded by competing on improved services, all to the advantage of each firm's clients.

"The Justice Department was determined to get a scalp," Davidge observed. "What better than a high-profile industry with virtually no political clout or public sympathy? Would they be so keen on pursuing Pepsi and Coke if they knew they colluded on price-fixing?

"Going to gaol is the final undeserved insult," Davidge said of Taubman. "I do feel very sorry for him."[11]

DEDE BROOKS RECEIVED a terrible shock went she went to the doctor's on December 6, the day after Taubman was convicted. Her ob/gyn appointment had originally been scheduled for November 6, but she had postponed it because she was working with her lawyers in anticipation of the trial. After the examination, her doctor broke the alarming news. He had discovered two ovarian tumours and needed to operate in order to determine whether they were benign or malignant.

Terrified of what the doctor might find, Brooks underwent a radical hysterectomy at New York Hospital a few days later.Fortunately, the tumours turned out to be benign.] The surgeon's task was made especially daunting due to the ten-inch-long, two-inch-deep scar on her abdomen, which she had lived with since her surgery for Crohn's disease in 1975.

News of Brooks' cancer scare elicited conflicting emotions at Sotheby's when it appeared as a gossip item in the boldface-names section of the *New York Times*.

"You certainly well up with sympathy for the old girl, don't you?" a Sotheby's executive said, noting that Brooks still faced the possibility of spending three years in gaol and an enormous fine at her upcoming sentencing in the spring. "Can you imagine if they'd found the tumours on November 6?" he added. "They would have put off the whole trial!"[12]

While Dede Brooks was grappling with issues of life and death, Taubman was bringing a chapter of his professional life to a grim conclusion. Six days after the verdict, he stepped down as chairman of Taubman Centres, Inc., the billion-dollar shopping-mall empire he had started in 1950 with a $5,000 loan. His son Bobby, who had had day-to-day control of the company for a decade as the firm's president and chief executive officer, was announced as the new chairman of Taubman Centres.

Taubman's trial continued to have rippling effects. François Curiel was dismayed to learn that Davidge had identified him in court as someone who had known about the conspiracy prior to the revelations of January 2000. When pressed, Curiel admitted that Davidge had given him some notion of what transpired. "He told me *some* things," Curiel told me, "but not enough to know the extent of what he was doing. He very cleverly parcelled out information—enough to make me feel very, very important. I believe he did the same to Patty, and Christopher Burge and others."

"Chris is a chief manipulator with a capital C," Curiel added. "He did it very, very cleverly."[13]

As Judy Taubman had feared, her husband's legal woes were beginning to cramp her style. When she flew to Gstaad in early 2002 to do some skiing and après-skiing, she suffered the indignity of being turned down for membership at the Eagle Club, the most prestigious social club in town. It was a startling reminder that life could never be the same again.

Many of Judy's friends in New York wondered how she would fare in society after Alfred's conviction. Sotheby's had been her great calling card. But her husband was no longer chairman, and now it seemed likely that he was going to gaol. Some predicted a chilly reception.

"Sotheby's was her Blenheim," *Vanity Fair*'s Dominick Dunne observed.[14]

Alfred remained a member of several prestigious clubs, including the National in Southampton and Deepdale in Manhasset. But he had been asked to resign his membership in the Atlantic Golf Club in Bridgehampton, Long Island. It was a bitter blow to the mogul, who had put up seed money for the club in 1992.

THE NEGATIVE WORLDWIDE PUBLICITY for Sotheby's during Taubman's trial was troubling to many of its employees, who feared how the scandal might impact their ability to win business. Christie's, by virtue of its amnesty, appeared to be getting away relatively unscathed.

The verdict shook everyone's confidence at Sotheby's, but many people were blaming its former chief executive, not the recently convicted chairman. "A lot of stuff happened that was really awful and really tragic that hurt a lot of people, clients and staff," Ruprecht said. "But you know what? I didn't do it. It's time for me to focus on what we can do to make things good, rather than how or why this happened."[15]

Brooks' name seemed indelibly linked with Sotheby's, never more so than when she made worldwide television appearances with the Jacque-line Kennedy Onassis sale. Since the scandal, however, the firm made strenuous efforts to erase any memory of the fallen executive. And she had been forced to give up all her

Sotheby's shares, which only two years earlier had been worth between $35 million and $40 million.

On March 12, 2002, Sotheby's released its annual report for 2001, announcing that the firm had slashed its costs and drastically reduced its losses. The company also announced it was raising its buyer's premium.*

Three weeks later, on April 9, Christie's exactly matched Sotheby's new rates, which were to become effective on April 15. (Since February 7, 2000, Christie's premium had been 17:5 percent on the first $80,000 and 10 percent on any amount above.[16] Christie's new rates were applied to its two principal salesrooms, on King Street and in Rockefeller Centre, as well as in Los Angeles, Hong Kong, Geneva, Zurich, Amsterdam and Tel Aviv.)

This time around, Christie's was following Sotheby's in altering its commissions—a reversal from the troublesome change in 1995. Once again, the auction houses were responding to economic necessity. The great irony was that Sotheby's and Christie's were keeping their prices in line because of normal market forces, proving once again that the collusion in 1995 had been entirely unnecessary.

DESPITE THE NEGATIVE PRESS, Sotheby's had landed a dazzling series of collections for the spring sales of 2002. The feeling of elation was dashed, however, when the Second Circuit announced that the appeal for foreign claims had been accepted. This necessitated yet another civil fine for the auction houses. Arriving at a moment when Sotheby's seemed to be set on the right path, the news was hugely depressing for the staff.

"With Phillips choking on its own bile and Sotheby's getting all the great consignments for the spring, its seems like we're moving in the wrong direction with this legal decision," a Sotheby's executive lamented.[17]

---

* Since April 1, 2000, Sotheby's had been charging a three-tiered buyer's premium of 20 percent for the first $15,000; 15 percent for amounts between $15,001 and $100,000; and 10 percent for everything above $100,000. With the new rates, Sotheby's would charge 19.5 percent of the first $100,000 of the hammer price, and 10 percent of the price in excess of $100,000 at its major salesrooms in New York, Geneva and London.

* * *

IN AN INTERVIEW that appeared in the *Sunday Telegraph* on I March 3, 2002, Lord Hindlip revealed that he had been aware of his colleagues' price-fixing activities.

"I've never tried to deny that I knew something of what was going on," Christie's chairman declared. "I've also never tried to deny that I told them I didn't think it was a very clever idea. Because it would have happened [anyway]. If we'd said what we were going to do, Sotheby's would have followed. And that would not have been criminal. It would not have broken any law at all."[18]

"It was such a blinding failure," Hindlip continued. "It was perfectly obvious it wasn't going to work. Well, perfectly obvious to *me* it wasn't going to work."[19]

IT WAS A LONG SHOT, but Taubman and his lawyers figured it was worth petitioning Judge Daniels to overturn the conviction against Sotheby's former chairman and to grant a new trial. They argued that the judge had erred in failing to allow documents and testimony regarding Lord Camoys; and in declining their request to explain to the jury that meetings between competitors were not illegal per se. In denying Taubman's request, Judge Daniels derided the lawyers' argument that the jurors had been wrongly instructed as a "simplistic mischaracterization of the jury's verdict. It ignores the jury's thorough analysis of the totality of the evidence during their deliberations."[20]

Much worse for Taubman—and a harrowing hint of what was to come in his upcoming sentencing—Daniels remarked that the evidence had revealed that Taubman was "not merely a member of the conspiracy, but rather, the initiating and driving force behind it."[21] It was a particularly harsh pronouncement, and one that not even Christopher Davidge or Dede Brooks agreed with, in private.

In anticipation of Taubman's sentencing by Daniels on April 22, the Davis Polk lawyers submitted to the court a tome that was roughly the size of the Manhattan telephone directory. It contained ninety-one letters from his family and powerful friends, all attesting to his fine character and appealing for leniency for the seventy-eight-year-old. The hefty collection included tributes from such public figures as former President Gerald Ford, Henry Kissinger, Barbara Walters and Queen Noor of Jordan.

One of the most dramatic and touching letters was from his wife. "Our lives are shattered forever," Judy Taubman wrote to Judge Daniels. "My husband is a broken man. Mentally and health-wise. He hardly sleeps at night, and spends a great deal of the day lethargically staring at the ceiling.[22]

"We both try to hide our pain in public," she added. "The past two years have been hell on earth for him and his family. He is a sick 78-year-old man. Please, please show mercy on him."[23]

Taubman's daughter, Gayle Kalisman, tried to impress upon the judge that "there is no greater irony that a man who has given so much to so many has now lost the one thing, other than his family, that he valued above all else. My father's reputation and good name are seriously tarnished forever."[24]

The Federal Probation Department recommended no prison time for Taubman after reviewing his medical records and extensive philanthropy. But the prosecutors disputed the suggestion and argued that Taubman should get the maximum three-year prison term and a criminal fine of $1.6 million to $8 million. To bolster their argument, the government lawyers submitted their calculations that sellers at Sotheby's had been overcharged by $43.8 million during the alleged six years of collusion.

Fiske tried valiantly to make a case that his client should be sentenced to probation, as the Probation Department had recommended, and not time in prison. Trying to play up the issue of Taubman's great antiquity as an argument that he should not be sent to prison, his attorneys announced that he was seventy-eight. The news came as a considerable surprise to friends who had attended his seventy-seventh birthday party in Palm Beach only three months earlier.

Leveraging against the tycoon's newly advanced age, Fiske cited an array of maladies that his client suffered, including diabetes, renal failure, heart disease, hypertension and sleep apnea.

For the momentous occasion of his sentencing on April 22, 2002, Taubman showed up with every member of his family. They sat in the front row and stared straight ahead, or talked quietly among themselves, careful not to engage the glances of reporters and other court-room gawkers.

Addressing the court, Bob Fiske made a passionate argument that Taubman should be given probation. "Mr. Taubman stands before this court at seventy-eight years of age with a number of interrelated and very serious medical conditions," Fiske told the judge. "After tirelessly dedicating himself to philanthropic causes, he now stands in the twilight of his years stripped of his reputation and good name."[25]

When it was his turn to speak, John Greene ridiculed the suggestion that Taubman was too sick to spend time in gaol. "Look at his lifestyle!" Greene exclaimed. "He hunts, he fishes, he plays golf. So he is not as infirm as we are led to believe."[26] The prosecutor argued that merely placing Taubman on probation would send a clear message to other white-collar criminals that they were home free. "The public would be ill served," he noted, "by the perception that a man can steal millions of dollars and still escape prison after a jury has convicted him."[27]

Before pronouncing sentence, the judge asked Taubman if he wished to say anything.

"No sir, Your Honour. Thank you," he replied.

Daniels acknowledged Taubman's history of civic and charitable contributions was impressive. "But the law does not countenance a Robin Hood," he said. "One cannot give to the poor and steal from the rich. Price-fixing is a crime whether it's committed in the local grocery store or the halls of the great auction houses."[28]

"This was a deceitful, secretive criminal scheme whose object and purpose was illegal profit. This was not a crime motivated by desperation or need, but by arrogance and greed," the judge declared.[29] "When those of accomplishment commit criminal misdeeds, it always seems wasteful and tragic, but regardless of what heights we may attain in life, not one is above the law."[30]

Daniels criticized Taubman for failing to admit his culpability. "There is a lack of contrition demonstrated," he noted gravely. "He has continued a conspiracy of denial, portraying himself as the victim of a scheme of perjury and lies to frame him ... He has neither acknowledged responsibility nor shown any remorse."

Taubman was told to report to gaol on August 1 to begin serving a one-year term. He was also ordered to pay a fine of $7·5 million, equal to 5 percent of the estimated $150 million volume of commerce affected by the conspiracy.

"Excuse me, Your Honour," Bob Fiske said, jumping to his feet. "Could you make that a year and a day?"

"Certainly," Daniels replied.

Many people in the courtroom stared in confusion. The reason, it turned out, was that under federal guidelines, a sentence in excess of one year would make Taubman eligible for time off for good behaviour.

As Taubman stood and turned to leave the courtroom, he whispered, "Sorry," to his stunned, weeping family.

THE FOLLOWING DAY, Taubman sat in his office, still protesting his innocence. "It's fascinating to me. He chewed me out in court for the fact I wouldn't stand up and say I was guilty. But if I'd said that, I'd be lying and then he'd have to send me to gaol for perjury! You don't win on that one, I'll tell you. That was such an outrageous thing.[31]

"I don't know what I did," he added. "I sure as hell didn't send her to do it, that's for sure."[32]

Many people at Sotheby's were stunned to learn of his sentence.

"I think a lot of people feel sorry for Alfred," Henry Wyndham said. "To send a seventy-eight-year-old man to gaol seems to be a complete waste of time. It's very, very tragic and I think we're all sympathetic to him."[33]

Some other people, however, could barely contain their satisfaction.

Pauline Pitt, the ex-wife of Taubman's close friend Dixon Boardman, was also the widow of his former best friend Bill Pitt. Wintering in Palm Beach, Pitt was incensed to read Steve Dunleavy's encomiums of Taubman in the *New York Post*. Determined to set the record straight, as she saw it, she wrote the

columnist a poison-pen letter, which wound up in the gossip column of Neal Travis, a fellow Australian-born scribe, in the *Post*.

Pitt's letter, written in a backward-slanted debutante scrawl,
pulled no punches. "Alfred Taubman (AAT) has an ego the 'size of
the Grand Canyon,'" she wrote. "His motto has always been 'If it is
a good idea, it is his idea—if it is a bad idea, it is someone else's
idea.'"

"I have had two husbands, both have been very close to AAT at
various times—neither of them have had good things to say of his
ethics ... People in high places are saying 'Poor Alfred,' whilst whis-
pering, 'I know he is guilty,'" Pauline Pitt continued. "It is chic to
be sorry for him. Were you ever to dig deeper into AAT's track
record—the guy is a pig and *never* does the right thing unless it looks
better in 'high society.'"[34]

NOW THAT TAUBMAN was on his way to gaol, it was Dede
Brooks' turn to be sentenced. The probation office had recommended that Brooks, like Taubman, should serve no gaol time. But
there was no guarantee that she was off the hook. On March 29,
2002, a month before she was due to be sentenced, Sotheby's had
entered a final Settlement Agreement with Brooks requiring her to
repay a total of $3.25 million to the firm.

In the sentencing report that John Siffert and Steven Kaufman
submitted to Judge Daniels on their client's behalf, the lawyers
pointed out that the sum of $3.25 million represented restitution of
every dollar of the after-tax compensation she had received since
1993, when her part in the price-fixing conspiracy had begun.[*]
"Together with the return of her stock options earned since 1992,"
the lawyers wrote, "Mrs. Brooks has disgorged every penny she
earned from Sotheby's from before the conspiracy started."[35]

Unlike Christopher Davidge, who had earned a lot of money,
Brooks had been compelled to pay all of her own lawyers' fees and
had had to forfeit an estimated $13.25 million in salary, stock

---

[*] Brooks' pretax Sotheby's earnings between 1993 and 2000 were $6,151,800, and after tax,
$3.25 million.

options and bonuses. Davidge, meanwhile had actually *gained* nearly $13 million, including the $8 million from his severance agreement with Christie's, $2 million from his three-year consultancy with Artémis, plus a pension in the form of a capital sum of $1.6 million plus $339,000 a year.

Back in August 2000, the prosecutors had offered Brooks the tough deal that in exchange for her cooperation the government would merely make no specific recommendation regarding her sentencing. However, in a letter to Judge Daniels dated April 23, 20002, the prosecutors wrote that Brooks' "cooperation was excellent, wholehearted and unequivocal," noting that by providing crucial information and "critical testimony" she had provided substantial information and assistance under the sentencing guidelines.

The collection of letters written in support of Brooks was not as large as the one submitted on behalf of Taubman. But it was nevertheless impressive. A testimonial from her husband was extremely moving. In his letter to the judge, Michael Brooks wrote of his wife's "superior intelligence, strong moral fibre." Without mentioning Taubman by name, he noted that Dede had been the only person in this difficult situation who "had the integrity and self-respect to do what was right.[36] "It is painful to watch others denigrate the reputation of someone you love," Michael added.

The letters submitted on Brooks' behalf revealed that she had some powerful allies who thought the world of her. Michael Bloomberg, New York's billionaire-businessman-turned-mayor and a longtime friend of Dede's, wrote as a private citizen. "I believe she has learned and will continue to learn life lessons from her serious mistakes. I sincerely believe Dede has much to give to society."

Judge Daniels also received an unsolicited letter from Matthew Weigman, the head of Sotheby's New York Press Office, imploring the federal judge to send Brooks to gaol. "I draw your attention," Weigman wrote, "to the damage done by the actions of Ms. Brooks to a class of victims who will benefit from no legal settlements and whose interests have been largely ignored by the media who have so avidly covered every other aspect of the scandal and trial. The class of victims I refer to is the employees of Sotheby's."[37]

"I am one of about 2,000 people who have borne professional, emotional and economic consequences of the illegal activity carried out by the very person whose primary responsibility it was to forward the best interests of the company," he continued. As a result of the devastating scandal, Weigman explained, 375 Sotheby's employees had lost their jobs in the past year. And the stock options that had formed part of the staff's compensation for the past fourteen years had been rendered "virtually worthless."

BROOKS' SENTENCING was scheduled for April 29, 2002, one week after that of her former boss, and almost exactly eight years after Taubman and Tennant's pivotal breakfast meeting in London on April 30, 1993.

Wearing an olive green suit, the fifty-one-year-old former executive walked into the courtroom surrounded by her family and friends. When the court was called to order, Patricia Jannaco spoke briefly on behalf of the government, pointing out that Brooks had rendered substantial assistance in the investigation and successful prosecution of Alfred Taubman. As required to do so by law, the prosecutors had submitted an official estimate that the amount that Sotheby's sellers had been overcharged as a result of the conspiracy between 1995 and 1999 was $43.8 million. By that reckoning, Brooks could be liable to a federal fine of twice the illegal gain, or $87.6 million.

In requesting leniency, John Siffert told the court that Brooks "will always bear the stigma of being a convicted felon, which will have collateral consequences for the rest of her life."[38]

Siffert noted that his client had already been humiliated by a publicity campaign waged against her by Taubman's advisors. "For two years she was subjected to a sophisticated and calculated campaign of character assassination," he said. "She bore the attacks in dignity and let her testimony speak the truth.

"She now owns only what she earned before the conspiracy and what her husband gifted to her in their thirty years of marriage," he added. "To make her serve time in gaol now, I submit, would be cruel and unnecessary, considering what she has suffered."[39]

When it came time for Judge Daniels to speak, everyone in the courtroom was riveted.

"Diana Brooks," the judge said, as the former executive bowed her head, "by your own actions, you have traded your title of CEO to be branded a thief and common criminal. Blinded by ambition, you substituted shame for fame ... You allowed yourself to go from respected, successful executive to being ridiculed as a caricature for a melodrama. The notoriety you have gained will outlive you.

"Your words are the all-too-familiar refrain of the white-collar criminal; the rationalization that somehow their theft is less serious because theirs is not a crime of violence and is committed while wearing a business suit.

"Let us not forget that you did not voluntarily disclose, motivated by remorse, an offence that otherwise would have remained undisclosed. Although your decision to cooperate was the right one, it was not a noble gesture, motivated by a guilty conscience. Once the finger of guilt was pointed in your direction, your decision to cooperate was self-serving, not self-sacrificing.

"You have not earned absolution," he continued. "The debt you owe to society may never fully be repaid."[40]

Daniels then asked if Brooks would like to say anything before he passed sentence.

"I would like to apologize to all the people who I've hurt," Brooks said, in a pained voice. "I accept responsibility for what I have done. I will forever bear the burden for what I've done and I will accept whatever sentence Your Honour feels is appropriate."[41]

As Brooks remained standing, the judge imposed a term of three years' probation, including six months of home detention, plus one thousand hours of community service and a criminal fine of $350,000.

It was wonderful news for Brooks that she would not have to go gaol. But she was distraught by the fire-and-brimstone language that Daniels had used. "The judge said there's no redemption in my lifetime," Brooks said to Siffert as they walked from the courtroom to the probation office next door. "That's not right, John, is it?"

"He's only a judge," Siffert replied, startled that Brooks seemed to be taking the judge's admonition so much to heart.[42] In the probation office, Brooks learned that she was to wear an electronic monitoring device during the period of her home confinement.

When she left the probation office, Brooks and her family took the subway, heading for their $5 million co-op apartment on East Seventy-ninth Street.

"I made some bad mistakes," Brooks said later that day, "so I've suffered the consequences. The good news is that I'm healthy and I've got my whole life ahead of me. Now I've just got to do something with it.

"For my children and my husband, I'm just so glad this part is over. They didn't do anything wrong, and it's been very, very difficult for them. Now they've got me home, and I can cook."[43]

THE MOOD WAS LESS BUOYANT on York Avenue. "Dede betrayed Sotheby's clients, the employees and the stockholders," a former staffer noted. "She should be in gaol for twenty years."[44]

Another was similarly incensed. "This is a catastrophe she caused with her eyes wide open. What she can't possibly know is the daily consequences that we've had to live with for three years. And that is very hard ... There is so much pain, for so many people."[45]

29

Hurt

DEDE BROOKS' SIX-MONTH home detention began officially on May 8, 2002, the day she was outfitted for the electronic bracelet, which she wore around her left ankle. The large black transmitter, which resembled an oversized wristwatch, communicated with a base that was plugged into a telephone line in her apartment. The device tracked Brooks' whereabouts to make sure she did not leave home without permission.

Sotheby's former CEO was perfectly happy spending time in her spacious apartment. She was allowed to receive visitors, except for ex-convicts, and she was permitted to leave her apartment for two hours on Friday afternoons, between two and four, to run errands to the grocery store. The terms of her probation also meant that she could attend church services. Three afternoons a week, she took the subway to East Harlem, where she continued to work as a volunteer school tutor. For doctors' appointments, she was required to get permission forty-eight hours in advance.

Three weeks later, sitting at home under house arrest, Brooks appeared to still be exasperated and deeply hurt by the attitude of her former close colleagues.

"From day one I have tried to be helpful to Sotheby's," she said solemnly. "And for whatever reason, the hostility from the top management that existed the day I left the company is as dramatic as ever, if not more so. And for the life of me I don't know why.

"For me, that's the hardest part. I realize that I really screwed up, and I will pay for it for the rest of my life. But I didn't do it to hurt the company. I didn't do it to help myself. I did it because I used poor judgment, and I thought that I was doing something that was helpful to the company. And that was wrong.

"But the personal nature of the anger that people at the top management feel is the hardest thing for me to deal with. And the only thing I can imagine is that it's Taubman who still owns the place, and they're all being paid by him."[1]

Brooks' light sentence was irritating to many people at Sotheby's. But what really enraged them was that Christie's and its top executives appeared to be getting off scot-free.

"What I find unacceptable," a senior Sotheby's expert told me, "is that Stephen Lash, Charlie Hindlip and Christopher Burge are still at Christie's. I find that despicable."[2]

David Redden agreed. "If Christie's were a public company, some people wouldn't be there anymore," he observed. "Knowing about the conspiracy means they participated in the conspiracy. Those same people were business-getters. They negotiated contracts with clients on the basis of commissions that they knew were fixed. Which means they were active participants in the conspiracy. They were not bystanders. It's important to recognize their culpability, too."[3]

Dede Brooks had the good grace not to lash out at those who had escaped censure. "It seemed pretty surprising to me that they're still in their jobs," she said. "One thing I've learned," she added, "is that being angry or bitter or hurt doesn't help. All it does is destroy you. It just doesn't help anybody."[4]

Brooks said she did not feel betrayed by Christopher Davidge.

"I feel like I betrayed myself. When you go through something like this, you have a choice. You can either blame all your mistakes on someone else, or accept that regardless of what other people did to you, it doesn't take away from the fact that I shouldn't have done what I did. So I found that it's an easier way to live not to blame anyone but myself.

"He made terrible mistakes," she added. "Just like I did."[5]

Trying to rise above the negative press that continued to rain down on her was a greater challenge for the sensitive, thin-skinned

Brooks, who had recently been referred to by the *Times* of London as "the reincarnation of Cruella De Vil."[6]

BROOKS' HOME-CONFINEMENT SENTENCE, with its requirement of an ankle bracelet, inspired mirth in some circles. Three weeks after Brooks' sentencing, Patty Hambrecht made a spectacular entrance at the fiftieth wedding anniversary of Nan and Tommy Kempner—one of the most glamorous society events of the spring—wearing a matching diamond-and-ruby necklace, earrings and bracelet from Harry Winston, the world-famous jewellery company of which she had become president since leaving Christie's.

"You look fabulous!" a Park Avenue socialite said, dazzled by her finery.

"Thank you," Hambrecht replied. "It's all from Harry Winston." "Do you have the ankle bracelet, too?" the socialite asked jokingly. "No," Hambrecht said, quick as a flash. "The one wearing the ankle bracelet is Dede Brooks."[7]

DESPITE THE SCANDAL that had raged in the press since January 2000, Sotheby's and Christie's business did not appear to be adversely affected. "I think people realize that if they want to sell their art, they've not got too many avenues to pursue," Henry Wyndham, Sotheby's London chairman, observed. "Sotheby's and Christie's are two great institutions and have tremendous experts. And I think most people believe that they're ethical businesses," he added, hopefully.[8]

Even so, he admitted, "the industry has been tainted. The scandal hasn't done anyone any particular good. But we seem to have survived it.

We're still in business. We're still here and we're still selling pictures for lots of money."[9]

ON TAUBMAN'S LAST DAY in New York—three days before he was expected to report to gaol—he was sitting at his huge desk in his magnificent corner office on Fifth Avenue.

"It's like dying," he joked. "All my friends have been great. They know I would never do such a stupid thing. And they've been very supportive. You assume that all your friends will remain your friends, and that's what's happened. It's pretty extraordinary, the amount of people who step up."[10]

Taubman continued to be confounded by the testimony the government's star witnesses had given against him in court. "He is an evil guy," Taubman said of Davidge. "Dede is evil, too, although I never believed she was. They're an evil pair!"[11]

Having developed much affection and admiration for Dede Brooks during the seventeen years he had worked with her—acting as her mentor, fostering her career and ultimately promoting her to worldwide CEO—Taubman seemed truly devastated by what he perceived as her betrayal.

"I feel sad about it, I really do," Taubman he told me. "This woman ruined her life. She hurt everybody who was supposed to be her friend and her associates and colleagues at Sotheby's. She hurt people in the business. She destroyed her relationships with her family and everybody else.

"Why she did this, I don't know. I assume it was greed and power. She thought she was so big and strong and such a big deal, and that she was beyond anyone touching her in any way.

"I'm taking her place in gaol," he said.[12]

"On the other hand," he added, "I'm not a bitter person. I understand that she traded. She didn't want to go to gaol, and she was frightened about it. Which I can understand. I think she just decided that whatever it takes, she was going to do. And this was a way she could find her way out. That was it.

"But I don't sit here with the idea that I hate *anybody*."

Taubman explained that the startling events of the past six months had taken him completely by surprise. "I didn't give this trial that much credence," he admitted. "I never really believed that they could possibly convict me of anything. Because I knew I didn't do anything wrong. I went down there to make sure that everyone around me also knew it."

Taubman sounded resigned to his fate.

"I've been in business fifty-two years. I've spent my life trying to be honest, courageous and a good citizen, a good businessperson, a good person, a good friend and a family person. I've tried to be those things all my life. And I find myself at this stage of my life ..." He trailed off, apparently unwilling to utter the word "prison."

"My name was very important to me all my life," he continued. "There's no question that it's been hurt badly. But my family have been incredible. They've never questioned my integrity. They knew I wasn't involved. And my friends know I'm not involved. And I can't ask for anything more."[13]

30

Gaol

IT WAS A GLORIOUS SUMMER DAY in Bloomfield Hills when Taubman left his lakeside house at eleven-thirty A.M., kissing his wife Judy in a tearful farewell. The household staff stood at the portico, waving good-bye. He climbed into his chauffeur-driven Lincoln Navigator for the twenty-minute ride to the private Taubman Air Terminal at Oakland County Airport in Pontiac, where he met up with Bobby, his oldest son, and Jeff Miro, his lawyer and confidant, for the forty-minute flight to Rochester, Minnesota.

It was the worst day of his life. But at least, Taubman told himself, he was going to gaol in style, in his magnificent jet, a silver-painted Gulf-stream IV, which the crew at Taubman Air called the *Silver Bullet*. Taubman and his two companions sat in the front cabin, a travelling office with four armchairs and a desk, all tastefully decorated in dove grey. Once they were airborne, a butler set the table with fine china and linens, and Taubman tucked into a Last Supper with two of his favourite foods: hot dogs and caviar.

A limousine was waiting on the tarmac to take them for the four-minute drive to his new temporary abode: Rochester Federal Medical Centre, known as the FMC. As they approached, Taubman was dismayed to see two rows of ten-foot fences topped with concertina razor wire that seemed to stretch for miles. His criminal lawyers had told him it was going to be more like a hospital. But this certainly had all the grim outward trappings of a gaol.

Upon arriving, Taubman followed the narrow sidewalk to the front door of the prison, past the double fence, the rings of razor wire and NO TRESPASSING signs. Burly guards were standing behind thick security glass with crackling radios and keys jangling from their waists. They pointed him toward a lobby with stale air and rough wooden benches.

Like every new arrival, the seventy-eight-year-old multimillionaire was strip-searched and given a uniform of a khaki shirt and pants. He was allowed to keep only his eyeglasses and his hearing aid.

Quite literally stripped of his dignity, Taubman became one of 780 prisoners serving time that week at the FMC. He was assigned to the medical-surgical unit of the prison. After a one-hour physical he was judged not to have any urgent medical problems, but he was allowed to stay in the medical unit because of his advanced age.

"Where were you before?" an inmate asked him on his first day.

Taubman did not know how to respond. What should he say? Bloomfield Hills, Fifth Avenue, Southampton, Palm Beach, London or Gstaad?

"Detroit," he finally blurted out.

Sensing Taubman's confusion, the inmate explained that the majority of inmates in the medical wing had served time at other prisons before being transferred to the FMC on account of illness. "Where were you before?" he explained, was the first question every inmate asked a new arrival, meaning "Where were you incarcerated before?"

Taubman told him that he was new to the prison system.

Then came the inevitable second question.

"So what are you in for?" the inmate asked.

"Price-fixing," Taubman replied.

"What the hell's that?"

When Sotheby's former chairman explained that he had been convicted of fixing seller's commissions with the chairman of Christie's, the inmate seemed incredulous.

"That's *a crime*?" he asked.

"Yeah. But I didn't do it," Taubman said.

"That's what everyone says," the inmate told him, laughing. "Ask anyone here, they'll tell you they didn't do the crime. They're totally innocent. They were framed."[1]

Taubman soon began making friends, including Jim, a cheerful, hulking inmate with a giant scar running up the left side of face and down his neck—a grim souvenir of an operation to remove a tumour. Jim explained that he was serving a fourteen-year sentence in connection with his former career as a drug pilot.

On his first day, Taubman began adjusting to the grim realities of his new existence as inmate number 50444-054. He was obliged to shave and shower in a communal bathroom and eat in a chow hall with convicted armed robbers, arsonists and drug dealers. Jim quickly became Taubman's protector. Shortly after the tycoon arrived, a tall, burly black inmate cut in right in front of him on the line for the cafeteria.

"Hey, buddy," Taubman growled, "the line starts back there."

Jim poked him in the ribs. Prison was no place to assert his sense of fair play.

"Alfred, keep it quiet," Jim whispered in his ear. "You want trouble?" "What's the matter?" Taubman quipped. "You've got my back covered."

"Thanks, Alfred!" Jim replied, laughing.[1]

Taubman learned that there were strict rules for everything. He was expected to be in his cell at the appointed time four times a day for head count. He was assigned a bunk in a spartan room that looked more like a hospital room than a cell. There was a door with no lock and a window without bars. The room contained only a few beds, a desk, a shelf for books and a simple clothes closet. As an architect, Taubman was critical of the poor design that made it impossible to read in bed because the dim overhead lighting was across the room.

Rochester's FMC was a former state mental hospital. There were six low-lying beige buildings within a fifty-three-acre compound, where the lawns and hedges were meticulously maintained. On the day Taubman arrived, he found flower beds brimming with hollyhocks, cosmos, bee balm and impatiens, all tended by the prison's mentally ill inmates, who carried out the weeding and mowing and picked up cigarette butts.

Taubman's vast fortune, which *Forbes* had recently estimated at around $700 million, was of little use to him in gaol. Inmates were allowed to spend no more that $200 a month in the commissary, and everyday purchases were made through vending machines that accepted only quarters.

The septuagenerian slept badly during his first two months in prison because of bureaucratic stubbornness over the machine he needed to breathe at night. A longtime sufferer of severe sleep apnea, he had arrived at the prison with his portable device, but the guards refused to let him bring it in. Taubman tried to explain that the machine was necessary for him to be able to breathe properly, but the guards were adamant.

"We'll get you one," a corrections officer told him. "Don't worry about it."

"This is so stupid!" Taubman replied. "Why should it cost the prison system more money? I have the damn equipment!"

No, he was told.

The only way Judy Taubman could get the machine to her husband, they told her, was to send it by mail. Judy was incredulous, but she contained her temper. When she left the prison she went directly to the Mail Boxes Etc. store in Rochester and sent the machine by UPS. It was delivered to the prison the following day, but it took two weeks to reach Taubman.

"He finally got it," a family friend noted. "But it's unbelievable—the sheer stupidity and meanness of it."[3]

As the philanthropist who had given $3.05 million to found the A. Alfred Taubman Health Care Centre at the University of Michigan, he was keenly aware of the high costs of medical care. He had arrived with thirty critical drugs that his doctors had prescribed for him, but they too were denied entry.

"Why can't I bring my own medications?" he asked a prison doctor. "Why should I cost the corrections system money? I have the means to buy my own meds!"

No, he was told, again.

The arrivals of friends and family were the bright spots in Taubman's otherwise dreary existence. Visitors' names had to be cleared a month in advance. First-timers had their picture taken, which was stored in the prison computer. They were asked to fill in a form which was turned over to the corrections officer on duty to ensure the visitors had been cleared. Next, they had to surrender all personal belongings except a locker key and the $20 in quarters that they were allowed to bring in for the vending machines. Then they had to pass through a metal detector and sign a visitors' book before being given a glow-in-the-dark hand stamp. After those formalities, they had to wait to be escorted outside through a windy courtyard to enter the visitors' centre.

One visitor's grim impression of the prison was of a seething netherworld of "tattoos, long hair, ponytails and grey teeth."[4]

Judy Taubman tried to put a positive spin on the matter when describing her husband's place of incarceration. "It's like a sanatorium in Europe," she told a friend.[5]

The Rochester FMC wasn't exactly Baden-Baden. But it proved to be an ideal setting for Taubman to lose some of the weight he had vowed to shed during his time in Rochester.

"Quite honestly, you look better now than in the ten years I've known you," Melinda Marcuse, his executive assistant, told her boss when she visited him in December.[6] Taubman recounted the secret of his weight loss: a powerful aversion to prison food and exercising three times a week pedalling furiously on an exercise bike. Within six months, the portly mogul had lost thirty-two pounds.

Taubman looked well in prison, but his hair had reverted to its natural white. "It's normally dyed a distinguished grey," a visitor recalled. "The white is a little stark."[7]

As a person accustomed to travelling on his private plane every three or four days—to Michigan, New York, Florida, Europe or wherever the fancy took him—it was extremely challenging to find himself cooped up in one place for months on end. He was used to calling the shots, and he found it hard to adapt to the prison's mind-numbing regulations.

"This is such a tremendous waste," Taubman told a friend visiting from New York. "There are some really bright guys in here. Is it really serving society to lock us up like this when we could be outside doing better for the community?"

Taubman did not appear to be feeling sorry for himself, the friend noticed. Rather, he seemed perplexed. "I have times when I wonder, how did this happen?" the tycoon told him. "Then I replay it in my head and it drives me crazy. So I just read something and count the days till I go home."

He played bridge with a few inmates twice a week to help keep his mind alert, and he boasted to visitors that he was trouncing them on a regular basis. On days when he was without a visitor, Taubman spent much of his time reading. He had subscriptions to the *New York Times,* the *Wall Street Journal* and the *New York Post,* which arrived two days late.

Judy Taubman visited her husband twice a month and soon got the hang of operating the vending machines, which were always running out of items. She also became adept at microwaving her husband's ham-burger in the prison's populous visitors' room. "It's the first time she's cooked in their twenty-year marriage," a family friend quipped.[8]

Concerned pals wrote frequently to Taubman and went out of their way to fly to Minnesota in their private jets for a visit. Parker Gilbert, the former chairman of Morgan Stanley Dean Witter and a director of the Taubman Company, was happy to receive a call from Taubman, whom he was planning to see the following week.

"Is there anything I can bring you?" Gilbert asked.

"Yes," Taubman replied. "Twenty dollars in quarters."

WHILE TAUBMAN SUFFERED in federal prison, Dede Brooks was performing one thousand hours of community service in New York, making occasional trips to Florida with the permission of her probation officer. Thousands of miles away, Sir Anthony Tennant and Christopher Davidge continued their lives unscathed.

Acknowledgements

I would like to express my profound thanks to those who helped me during the research and writing of this book. In my quest to discover the truth of what really happened in the Sotheby's-Christie's price-fixing scandal—and to comprehend the characters of the well-dressed criminals in this drama—I conducted more than twenty-four hundred interviews with more than three hundred sources over a period of two and a half years. As these statistics indicate, several people granted me dozens of interviews. Some spoke for hours, some for only a few minutes. Some provided snippets of information in passing, or merely confirmed reports from other sources. Many, alas, provided intelligence that wound up on the cutting-room floor.

I am grateful to Alfred Taubman, Dede Brooks and Sir Anthony Tennant for allowing me to interview them directly. I have endeavoured to render a fair and balanced account, and to ensure that their very different versions of events are faithfully represented here. I am particularly thankful to Mr. Taubman and Ms. Brooks for giving me unfettered access to their legal counsel. Scott W. Muller and James P. Rouhandeh at Davis Polk were unfailingly generous in assisting as I navigated the legal complexities of the federal and civil cases against their client. John S. Siffert and Stephen E. Kaufman, Ms. Brooks' attorneys, were also very helpful, and I offer them my sincere thanks.

At Sotheby's, Diana Phillips and Matthew Weigman, the worldwide and American heads of the press office, respectively, were unfailingly gracious and professional. Their patience has surely earned them a delectable placement in heaven. Andrée Corroon, the head of Christie's press office, has been in her job for a much shorter time, and she was constrained by a companywide edict that forbade discussion of antitrust matters. Despite such constrictions, she was always kind and helpful.

Christopher Tennyson, Mr. Taubman's longtime spokesman, granted me more than fifty interviews. I must have driven the poor guy nearly crazy. William J. Linklater, counsel for Christopher Davidge, was a wry interviewee. I appreciate his candour. David Boies was generous with advice and assistance in understanding the subtleties of the civil plaintiffs' legal action. And federal prosecutor John J. Greene and his boss, Ralph T. Giordano, were generous in granting me an interview to clarify aspects of their case.

My research took me to London, Paris, Detroit, Long Island and Palm Beach. For their hospitality along the way, I am very grateful to Peter Bacanovic, Barbara Bancroft, Joan Davidson, Joan and John Hotchkis, Pauline Karpidas, Jill Krementz and Kurt Vonnegut, Rachel and Jean-Pierre Lehmann, Ivana Lowell, Christopher Shaw, Graham Snow, and Barbara and Donald Tober.

Five weeks after twelve jurors rendered their guilty verdict in the case of *USA v. A. Alfred Taubman,* I attended a jury reunion held at Willy Nicks, a restaurant in Katonah, New York, run by Jeffery Goodwin, one of the jurors. For their forthrightness, I am particularly grateful to the foreman, Mike D'Angelo, and to Dr. Glenn Forrester, Dorothy Fronk, Deborah Robinson and Mr. Goodwin.

David Highfill, my editor at G. P. Putnam's Sons, was supportive and a delight to work with, as was his enchanting assistant, Sarah Landis. And I'm grateful for the efforts of Marilyn Ducksworth and Steve Oppenheim in Putnam's publicity department. Todd Shuster, my literary agent at Zachary Shuster Harmsworth, spent many hours patiently helping me to germinate the ideas that became this book, and provided encouragement when I thought my labours would never cease.

My special thanks go to historian and author Amanda Foreman, who encouraged me to write this book in the first place. She read the manuscript and made invaluable suggestions, and I will always be grateful for her guidance.

I am indebted to Graham Snow, a friend of more than twenty-five years, who invited me to stay at Hinton Ampner, the home of the financier Christopher Shaw in Hampshire, over Christmas 2003 and New Year's. In that elegant setting I met Sir Anthony Tennant, who had previously eluded my requests for an interview. At the very last moment he agreed to speak, and his perspective radically altered my perception of the case.

I would also like to thank Georgina Adam, Brooks Adams, Frances Beatty Adler, Julian Agnew, Michael L. Ainslie, Susan Alexander, the Hon. Henry Allsopp, the Hon. Kirsty Allsopp, Tim Ambler, Alex Apsis, Clifford H. Aronson, Steven M. L. Aronson, Abigail Asher, Barbara Ashley, Caroline Atkinson, Bart Auerbach, Peter Bacanovic, Sir Jack Baer, Barbara Bancroft, Fred Bancroft, Godfrey Barker, Jonathan Barton, John Baskett, Douglas Baxter, Amir Ben-Zion, Brigid Berlin, William L. Bernhard and Catherine G. Cahill, Marion Bevan, James Biddle, Herbert Black, John D. Block, Marc Blondeau, Ralph Blumenthal, Dixon Boardman, Maria Bockmann, R. Louis Bofferding, Sue Bond, David Brewerton, Debra C. Brookes, Mario Buatta, Jacob Buchdahl, Jay Cantor, Barbara Cates, Edward Lee Cave, Joshua Chaffin, Christine Chauvin, Heather Cohane, Lou Colasuonno, Virginia Coleman, Joanna Coles, Joe Colman, Joanne Creveling, Muffie Cunningham, François Curiel, D. C. Cymbalista, Olga Davidge, Olive Davidge, Joan Davidson, Daniel P. Davison, James de Givenchy, Bernard de Grunne, Margo de Peyster, Andrew Decker, Barbara Deisroth, Beth Rudin DeWoody, Jennifer Dixon, Joe Dolce, Ben Doller, Edward Dolman, Colin Donnelly and Andy Yeatman at the British Meteorological Office, Kathy Doyle, Maldwin Drummond, Anthony du Boulay, Tiffany and Louis Dubin, Dominick Dunne, Korieh Duodo, Pierre Durand, Gary Dycus, Polly Earl, Lynn Einsel, Ed Epstein, James Espey, Anthony Fair, James Fallon, Richard Feigen, Rupert Fennell, Charlie Finch, Jimmy Finkelstein, Eileen Finletter, Robert B. Fiske, Jr., Bert Foer, Fiona Ford, the late John Galliher, David Gaskin, Hillary Geary, Kristin Gelder, Monica Gerard-Sharp, Pedro Girao, Manuel Gonzalez, Marco Grassi, Jim Gray, Alexis Gregory, Peter Gregory, Geordie Greig, James M. Griffin, Mac Griswold, Pamela Gross, Joel Gunderson, Fernando Gutierrez, Patty Hambrecht, Amey Harrison, Kevin B. Hart, Nick Harvey, Mallory Hathaway, Phillips Hathaway, Ashton Hawkins, Amanda Haynes-Dale, John Herbert, Frank Herrmann, C. Hugh Hildesley, Glenn Hinderstein, Lord and Lady Hindlip, Jeffrey Hogrefe, Philip Hook, Maury Hopson, Anne E. Horton, Betsy Huber, Tom Jago, Paul Jeromack, Na-dine Johnson, Richard Johnson, Arnold M. Kagan, Melik Kaylan, Nan Kempner, Ian Kennedy, Jack Kilgore, Joel Klein, Cliff Klenk, Jill Kopelman, Kathryn Kranhold, Jill Krementz, Jud Laird, Kenneth J. Lane, Sir Hugh Leggett, Rachel and Jean-Pierre Lehmann, Susan Lesovicz, Dominique Levy, Mary Libby, Monique Lodi, John L. Loeb, Prince Antoine Lopkowicz, Roberta Louckx, Ivana Lowell, Leila Hadley Luce, Daniela Luxembourg, Barrie Macintyre, Huon Mallalieu, Marion Maneker, Roberta Maneker, Bill Mapel, Melinda Marcuse, Patricia Marshall, Sophie Martin, John D. Mashek, Jr., David Mason, Stephen C. Massey, Steven Mazoh, Boaz Mazor, Mary McFadden, Barbara McIntyre, Duncan McLaren, Pravina Mecklai, S. Christopher Meigher III, Todd Merrill, David Metcalfe, Tobias Meyer, Thierry Millerand, Jeffrey H. Miro, Deborah Mitchell, Lucy Mitchell-Innes, Charles S. Moffett, Susan Moore, Len Morgan, Senga Mortimer, Laura Murray, David Nash, James Niven, Robert Noortman, David Norman, Geraldine Norman, Guy Norton, David Ober, Manoli Olympitis, Flavia Ormond, Amy Page, Judith Peabody, Tito Pedrini, Alexandra Peers, Ray Perman, Robert Peston, Donaldson C. Pillsbury, Betsy Pinover, Ariadne and Mario Platero, Michael Plummer, Ron Portante, Neal A. Potischman, David Price, Christopher Proudlove, Kathy and Billy Rayner, David Redden, Gila Reinstein, Steven A. Reiss, Matthew Rice, J. Douglas Richards, John Richardson, the late Khalil Rizk, Michael Roberts, Princess Mimi Romanoff, Nick Rossiter, James Roundell, William E Ruprecht, Jean-Renée Saillard, Warren St. John, Ewoud Sakkers, the late John Scanlon, Fred H. Scholtz, Susan Seidel, Christopher Shaw, Peggy Siegel, Stanley Siegel, Linda Silverman, Dolores C. Smithies, David L. Sokol, Carlene Soumas, Pat Spain, Jill Spalding, Peter Spira, John Stair, Garrick Stephenson, Fran Sternbach, Gina Talamona, Lady Rosemary Tennant, Christopher Tennyson, Andrew Terner, Vance Thompson, Barbara B. Toole, Ivana Trump, Judd Tully, Sidney Unobsky, Hugo Vickers, Steven Vincent, Carol Vogel, Paul E Walter, Beth Gates Warren, Peter Watson, Harriet Weintraub, Howard Weiss, Jackie Weld, Alex Wengraf, Jeremy Wiesen, Angus Wilkie, Dave H. and Reba White Williams, Natalie Williams, Elizabeth B. Wilson, Michael Wolff, Bruce Wolmer, Christopher Wood, Robin Woodhead, Henry Wyndham and David Yudain.

Notes

The information on which Lords and Liars is based includes more than 2,400 interviews conducted by the author (CJM) with more than 300 sources; 2,145 pages of transcripts and 300 documents from the Taubman trial; 1,848 pertinent press clippings; and Sotheby's and Christie's annual reports. Some sources prefer to remain anonymous, and they have been listed as such below.

For the purposes of creating a lively narrative, the author has extrapolated (recreated) dialog from conversations referred to during testimony, interviews he conducted, press reports and legal documents. Great care has been taken to ensure that the reported dialog adheres closely to the original source, which is indicated in the notes.

For the leading players and publications, the following abbreviations have been used:

DDB	Diana "Dede" Brooks	AP	Associated Press
CMD	Christopher Davidge	FT	*Financial Times*
AAT	Alfred Taubman	IHT	*International Herald Tribune*
AJT	Anthony Tennant	NYT	*New York Times*
		T&C	*Town and Country*
		WP	*ashington Post*
		WSJ	*Wall Street Journal*
		WWD	*Women's Wear Daily*

Documents from the Taubman trial are referred to as either GX (Government Exhibit) or DX (Defendant's Exhibit).

PROLOGUE

1. AJT, handwritten notes identified as "Paper given April 30." GX#48. Hereafter referred to as "AJT April 30 memo."
2. PR Newswire, 1/12/2000.

CHAPTER ONE

1. Dialogue extrapolated from AAT interview with *Irish Times*, 1/20/93.
2. John Stair to CJM, 4/17/01.
3. Thierry Millerand to CJM, 8/22/01.
4. John Marion to CJM, 4/23/01.
5. *Fortune*, 5/31/82.
6. Anonymous to CJM, 8/22/01.
7. David Metcalfe to CJM, 5/23/02.
8. AAT comment to David Metcalfe recalled by Metcalfe to CJM, 5/23/02.
9. David Metcalfe to CJIVM, 5/23/02.
10. Anonymous source close to AAT, to CJM, 3/21/03.
11. *Corporate Detroit Magazine*, 4/93.

12. Anonymous source close to AAT, to CJM, 3/21/03.
13. Henry Ford, Sr., *The International Jew: The World's Foremost Problem.*
14. Anonymous source close to AAT to CJM, 7/6/01.
15. WP112/4/01.
16. Joan Didion, quoted by WP88/1/80.

CHAPTER TWO

1. Dialogue extrapolated from David Metcalfe interview with CJM, 5/23/02.
2. John Marion to CJM, 4/23/01.
3. Conversation between Jeffrey Miro and John Marion recalled by Marion to CJM, 4/23/01.
4. John Marion to CJM, 4/23/01.
5. Ibid.
6. Conversation between AAT and John Mar-ion recalled by Marion to CJM, 4/23/01.
7. John Marion to CJM, 4/23/01.
8. Ibid.

9. *NYT,* 5/19/83.
10. John Marion to CJM, 4/23/01.
11. *NYT,* 6/10/83.
12. *Fortune,* 12/18/2000.
13. AP, 12/19/83.
14. Ibid.
15. *NYT,* 12/16/83.
16. AP, 12/19/83.
17. Anonymous to CJM, 5/3/03.
18. Ibid.
19. Anonymous to CJM, 5/5/03.
20. Professor Sir John Hale anecdote, and re-ported speech, per Anonymous to CJM, 5/22/03.

CHAPTER THREE
1. AAT to CJM, 4/23/02.
2. Christopher Tennyson to CJM, 9/18/01.
3. DDB to CJM, 4/29/02.
4. Sentencing Memorandum on behalf of DDB, 4/25/02, p. 2.
5. Elinor Dwyer McKenna, letter to Judge George B. Daniels, 3/26/02.
6. DDB to CJM, 11/7/02.
7. *USA Today,* 1/27/92.
8. Elinor Dwyer McKenna, letter to Judge George B. Daniels, 3/26/02.
9. *People,* 10/23/2000.
10. Fred Scholtz to CJM, 9/1/01.
11. Ibid.
12. Ibid.
13. Ibid.
14. DDB, speech given as a Gordon Grand Fellow at Pierson College, Yale, 4/18/91.
15. Ibid.
16. Anonymous to CJM, 4/12/02.
17. Susan Alexander to CJM, 4/12/02.
18. Ibid.
19. Fred Scholtz to CJM, 9/1/01.
20. John Marion to CJM, 4/23/01.

CHAPTER FOUR
1. *NYT,* 2/3/85.
2. Ibid.
3. Michael Ainslie to CJM, 1/25/01.
4. Ibid.
5. Michael Ainslie, testimony at AAT trial, p. 1320.
6. Ibid.
7. Michael Ainslie to CJM, 1/11/01.
8. Michael Ainslie, testimony at AAT trial, pp. 1307-1308.
9. Ibid., p. 1308.
10. *WWD,* 3/30/84.
11. *NYT,* 4/25/85.
12. *NYT* 2/3/85.

CHAPTER FIVE
1. *NYT,* 9/25/84.
2. Boaz Mazor to CJM, 8/30/01.

3. Anonymous to CJM, 12/23/02.
4. Judy Taubman, letter to Judge George B. Daniels, 3/14/02.
5. Anonymous to CJM, 12/31/02.
6. Anonymous to CJM, 7/6/01.
7. Anonymous to CJM, 6/26/03.
8. Anonymous to CJM, 5/16/03.
9. Alexis Gregory to CJM, 5/10/03.
10. *NYT* 2/3/85.
11. Ibid.
12. Ibid.

CHAPTER SIX
1. WP, 7/11/85.
2. Ibid.
3. Ibid.
4. Ibid.
5. John Herbert, *Inside Christie's* (St. Martin's, 1990), p. 292.
6. Anonymous American former colleague of Jo Floyd, interview with CJM, 1/21/03.
7. *Guardian,* 9/24/92.
8. *NYT,* 7/20/85.
9. *NYT,* 7/12/85.
10. *NYT,* 4/10/86.
11. *Sunday Business Post,* 4/28/02.
12. *Sunday Telegraph,* 3/7/93.
13. *FT,* 4/27/96.
14. *Art & Auction,* 3/92.
15. Ibid.
16. Henry Wyndham to CJM, 6/13/02.
17. Ibid.
18. *Straits Times,* 5/29/93.
19. *Sunday Telegraph,* 3/7/93.
20. Olga Davidge to CJM, 7/23/02.
21. *Art & Auction,* 3/92.
22. Ibid.
23. Ibid.
24. Ray Perman to CJM, 3/19/01.
25. Olive Davidge to CJM, 8/2/02.
26. Christopher Wood to CJM, 6/6/01.
27. Ray Perman to CJM, 3/19/01.
28. Anthony du Boulay to CJM, 6/27/02.
29. *FT,* 4/27/96.
30. Anonymous to CJM, 3/28/01.
31. Ray Perman to CJM, 4/4/02.
32. Anthony du Boulay to CJM, 6/27/02
33. Ibid.

CHAPTER SEVEN
1. Melinda Marcuse to CJM, 4/24/02.
2. Ray Perman to CJM, 3/19/01.
3. Ibid.
4. John Herbert, *Inside Christie's* (St. Martin's, 1990), p. 215.
5. Lord Hindlip to CJM, 6/18/02.
6. Anthony du Boulay to CJM, 6/27/02 and 8/20/02.
7. Anthony du Boulay to CJM, 6/27/02.

8. Ibid.
9. John Herbert, *Inside Christie's,* p. 218.
10. Sir Hugh Leggatt to CJM, 3/26/01.
11. Christopher Wood to CJM, 8/21/02.
12. Anonymous to CJM, 3/30/01.
13. CMD, e-mail to Anonymous, 1/5/03.
14. Ibid.
15. John Baskett to CJM, 9/7/01.
16. Ibid.
17. Ibid.
18. Ibid.
19. Richard Crewdson to CJM, 8/20/02.
20. *EuroBusiness,* 9/94.
21. *T&C,* 9/94.
22. *NYT,* 10/4/98.
23. Article by CJM, *New York* magazine, 1/24/2000.
24. Ibid.
25. Ibid.

CHAPTER EIGHT
1. Deposition of Lord Carrington, held at Christie's on 12/13/2000.
2. Dialogue between AAT and Lord Gowrie, extrapolated from Lord Gowrie interview with CJM, 8/12/02.
3. Lord Gowrie to CJM, 8/12/02.
4. Pamela Gross to CJM, 8/21/01.
5. PR Newswire, 3/30/87.
6. *Sunday Telegraph,* 3/3/02.
7. *NYT,* 4/1/87.
8. CMD, e-mail to Anonymous, 1/5/03.
9. Ibid.
10. *Daily Telegraph,* 6/26/89.
11. Anonymous to CJM, 5/8/02.
12. François Curiel to CJM, 10/17/02.
13. *NYT,* 2/17/88.
14. *NYT,* 4/2/89.
15. *NYT,* 3/12/90.
16. Ibid.
17. Ibid.
18. Ibid.
19. *Business Week,* 11/26/90.
20. Anonymous to CJM, 7/6/01.
21. AAT's jokes over Lord Gowrie's press humilia-tions recalled by source close to AAT, to CJM, 8/22/02.
22. *Daily Telegraph,* 3/25/91.
23. CMD, e-mail to Anonymous, 1/5/03.

CHAPTER NINE
1. CMD, e-mail to Anonymous, 1/5/03.
2. Ibid.
3. Ibid.
4. Ibid.
5. Ibid.
6. Ibid.
7. Ibid.
8. Ibid.

9. AJT, letter to Lord Carrington, 5/18/92.
10. GX#20.
11. John Block, testimony at AAT trial, pp. 1448-1450.
12. Ibid., pp. 1463-1464.
13. *Daily Telegraph,* 9/18/92.
14. *Independent* 11/3/92.
15. Ibid.
16. Ibid.
17. *NYT,* 12/18/92.
18. Ibid.
19. John Block, testimony at AAT trial, 1480.
20. Ibid.
21. CMD, e-mail to Anonymous, 1/5/03.
22. CMD, e-mail to Anonymous, 1/10/03.
23. *NYT,* 12/23/92.
24. Ibid.

CHAPTER TEN
1 Conversation between AAT and Tennant recalled by AAT to CJM, 7/29/02.
2. AAT to CJM, 7/29/02.
3. Ibid.
4. AJT to CJM, 1/3/04.
5. Dialogue extrapolated from CMD testimony at AAT trial, p. 306.
6. Dialogue extrapolated from anonymous source close to AAT, 10/25/02.
7. Dialogue extrapolated from Lord Gowrie comment to *Sunday Times,* 11/8/92.
8. Michael Ainslie, testimony at AAT trial, p. 1330.
9. Dialogue extrapolated from Michael Ainslie testimony at AAT trial, p. 1330.
10. Dialogue extrapolated ibid., p. 1331.
11. Michael Ainslie, testimony at AAT trial, pp. 1331-1332.
12. Dialogue extrapolated from DDB comment to *Evening Standard,* 4/1/93.
13. CMD, e-mail to Anonymous, 1/5/03.
14. Ibid.
15. Lord Hindlip to CJM, 6/17/02.
16. *Art & Auction,* 3/92.
17. *Sunday Telegraph,* 3/7/93.
18. Olga Davidge to CJM, 7/23/02.
19. Olga Davidge to CJM, 8/27/02.
20. CMD, e-mail to Anonymous, 1/3/03.
21. Olga Davidge to CJM, 7/23/02.
22. *New Straits Times,* 5/29/93.
23. Olga Davidge to CJM, 7/23/02.
24. Anonymous to CJM, 1/23/01.
25. Anonymous to CJM, 6/17/02.
26. Anonymous to CJM, 6/17/02.
27. CMD, e-mail to Anonymous, 1/3/03.
28. Olga Davidge to CJM, 7/23/02.
29. Ibid.
30. Olga Davidge to CJM, 8/27/02.
31. CMD, e-mail to Anonymous, 1/3/03.

32. Olga Davidge to CJM, 7/23/02.
33. Dialogue extrapolated from AAT interview with CJM, 7/29/02.
34. AAT to CJM, 7/29/02.
35. CMD, e-mail to Anonymous, 1/5/03.
36. Ibid.
37. Dialogue extrapolated from CMD testimony at AAT trial, p. 307.
38. Dialogue extrapolated ibid., pp. 307-308.
39. CMD, e-mail to Anonymous, 1/5/03.
40. CMD, e-mail to Anonymous, 1/10/03.
41. CMD, e-mail to Anonymous, 1/5/03.

CHAPTER ELEVEN
1. CMD, e-mail to Anonymous, 1/5/03.
2. Ibid.
3. CMD, fax to AJT, 4/8/93. GX#28.
4. Dialogue extrapolated from CMD testimony at AAT trial, pp. 310-311.
5. E-mail from Patty Hambrecht to Irmgard Pickering, 4/15/93. GX#27.
6. Dialogue extrapolated from CMD testimony at AAT trial, p. 321.
7. Dialogue extrapolated ibid., p. 321-322.
8. Letter from Timothy Sammons of Sotheby's to Iain Wotherspoon, Esq, executor for the Countess of Lovelace. GX#31.
9. Dialogue extrapolated from CMD testimony at AAT trial, p. 322.
10. Dialogue extrapolated ibid., pp. 321-323.
11. Dialogue extrapolated from CMD comment to NYT, 12/25/92.
12. Dialogue extrapolated from CMD testimony at AAT trial, p. 316.
13. Quotation from Sotheby's proposal for Hunt collection. GX#26.
14. Dialogue extrapolated from CMD testimony at AAT trial, p. 318.
15. Dialogue extrapolated ibid., p. 321.
16. Dialogue extrapolated ibid., p. 328.
17. Dialogue extrapolated from AJT Apr. 30 memo.
18. Dialogue extrapolated from AJT undated, handwritten note. GX#30.
19. Dialogue extrapolated from AJT Apr. 30 memo.
20. Dialogue extrapolated ibid.
21. Dialogue extrapolated from DDB testimony at AAT trial, p. 833.
22. GX#47.
23. AJT April 30 memo.
24. AJT's words as recalled by CMD in testimony at AAT trial, p. 332.
25. CMD, e-mail to Anonymous, 1/10/03.
26. CMD, e-mail to Anonymous, 1/5/03.
27. CMD, testimony at AAT trial, p. 811.
28. Ibid., pp. 349-350.
29. Ibid., p. 811.
30. CMD, e-mail to Anonymous, 1/5/03.
31. Ibid.
32. Lord Hindlip to CJM, 11/25/03.

33. CMD, e-mail to Anonymous, 1/5/03.
34. Ibid.
35. Ibid.
36. Ibid.
37. Anonymous British publisher to CJM, 7/15/03.
38. Dialogue extrapolated from DDB testimony at AAT trial, pp. 831-832.
39. Dialogue extrapolated ibid., p. 833.
40. DDB to CJM, 4/29/02.
41. DDB, testimony at AAT trial, p. 834.
42. Ibid., p. 998.
43. *Computer Reseller News,* 4/5/93.
44. Anonymous Sotheby's source to CJM, 5/30/03.
45. *Independent,* 10/24/93.
46. Lady Hindlip to CJM, 6/18/02.
47. Lord Hindlip to CJM, 6/18/02.
48. Ibid.
49. *Sunday Telegraph,* 3/7/93.
50. Lady Hindlip to CJM, 6/17/02.
51. Lord Hindlip to CJM, 6/17/02.
52. Dialogue extrapolated from CMD testimony at AAT trial, p. 352.
53. CMD, testimony at AAT trial, p. 354.
54. CMD, e-mail to Anonymous, 1/5/03.
55. Ibid.
56. CMD, testimony at AAT trial, p. 354.
57. Dialogue extrapolated from DDB testimony at AAT trial, pp. 842-843.
58. Dialogue extrapolated ibid., p. 843.
59. Dialogue extrapolated ibid.
60. Dialogue extrapolated ibid., pp. 843-844.
61. Dialogue extrapolated ibid., p. 844.
62. Dialogue extrapolated ibid., p. 843.
63. Dialogue extrapolated from CMD testimony at AAT trial, p. 355.
64. Dialogue extrapolated from DDB testimony at AAT trial, pp. 844-845.
65. William F. Ruprecht to CJM, 4/10/02.

CHAPTER TWELVE
1. DDB to CJM, 5/31/02.
2. Ibid.
3. Anonymous to CJM, 5/31/02.
4. Dialogue extrapolated from CMD testimony at AAT trial, p. 358.
5. Dialogue extrapolated ibid.
6. Dialogue extrapolated ibid., p. 366.
7. Dialogue extrapolated from DDB testimony at AAT trial, p. 849.
8. Dialogue extrapolated ibid., p. 850.
9. Dialogue extrapolated ibid., pp. 952-953.
10. Dialogue extrapolated from CMD memo summarizing a meeting with DDB.
11. Dialogue extrapolated from CMD testimony at AAT trial, p. 364.
12. Quotation attributed to DDB combining recollections of DDB and CMD. DDB says it was made at the Stafford Hotel some-time in November. CMD says that it came at their

subsequent meeting at DDB's Lon-don flat in December. DDB, testimony at AAT trial, pp. 841-842; CMD, testimony at AAT trial, pp. 363-364.

13. DDB to CJM, 5/15/02.
14. DDB to CJM, 7/12/02.
15. Dialogue extrapolated from DDB testimony at AAT trial, p. 849.
16. Dialogue extrapolated from CMD testimony at AAT trial, pp. 356-366.
17. Melinda Marcuse to CJM, 10/25/02.
18. Ibid.
19. AAT to CJM, 7/29/02.
20. Ibid.
21. Ibid.
22. Christine Chauvin to CJM, 9/9/01.
23. Ibid.
24. Anonymous art-world observer to CJM, 5/10/01
25. Anonymous Christie's director to CJM, 6/28/01.
26. CMD, e-mail to Anonymous, 1/5/03.
27. Ibid.
28. AP, 5/12/94.
29. Ibid.
30. Dialogue extrapolated from Susan Alexander testimony at AAT trial, p. 1143.
31. Susan Alexander to CJM, 4/12/02.
32. Dialogue extrapolated from DDB reading of Sotheby's 6/22/94 hoard meeting minutes during testimony at AAT trial, p. 851.
33. DDB, testimony at AAT trial, p. 856.
34. Ibid., p. 857.
35. Ibid.

CHAPTER THIRTEEN
1. DDB, testimony at AAT trial, pp. 1045-1047.
2. Dialogue extrapolated from DDB interview with CJM, 5/31/02.
3. DDB to CJM, 5/31/02.
4. Henry Wyndham to CJM, 6/13/02.
5. Lord Hindlip to CJM, 6/17/02.
6. Lord Hindlip to CJM, 6/18/02.
7. Ibid.
8. CMD, e-mail to Anonymous, 1/10/03.
9. Stephen Lash memo, 1/21/95.
10. Phillips Hathaway to CJM, 9/10/01.
11. Anonymous Christie's paintings expert to CJM, 6/18/02.
12. Lord Hindlip to CJM, 6/17/02.
13. DDB to CJM, 7/12/02.
14. Daniel P. Davison to CJM, 11/3/02.
15. DDB to CJM, 5/15/02.
16. CMD, e-mail to Anonymous, 1/5/03.
17. CMD, testimony at AAT trial, 374-375.
18. DDB to CJM, 4/29/02.
19. Dialogue extrapolated from DDB testimony at AAT trial, p. 862, and from DDB interview with CJM, 4/30/02.
20. DDB to CJM, 4/30/02.
21. DDB, testimony at AAT trial, pp. 859-862.

22. Dialogue extrapolated from DDB testimony at AAT trial, pp. 859-862.
23. Dialogue extrapolated from CMD testimony at AAT trial, pp. 374-375.
24. DDB, testimony at AAT trial, pp. 862-863.
25. DDB, testimony at AAT trial, pp. 1051-1053.
26. *Fortune,* 12/18/2000.
27. Michael Ainslie to CJM, 12/14/01.
28. CMD, testimony at AAT trial, p. 375.
29. Christie's press release, "Christie's International PLC Announces Change in Auction Charges to Sellers," 3/9/95.
30. DDB, testimony at AAT trial, p. 866.
31. Susan Alexander, testimony at AAT trial, p. 1169.
32. Henry Wyndham to CJM, 6/13/02.
33. William F. Ruprecht, *A Crime Amongst Gentlemen,* BBC, 5/9/02, transcript pp. 17-18.
34. Susan Alexander to CJM, 4/9/01.
35. DDB, testimony at AAT trial, p. 867.

CHAPTER FOURTEEN
1. Dialogue extrapolated from Godfrey Barker conversation with CJM at AAT trial, 11/9/01.
2. Godfrey Barker to CJM, 11/6/01.
3. *Daily Telegraph,* 3/10/95.
4. Anonymous former Christie's paintings expert to CJM, 1/8/01.
5. DDB, testimony at AAT trial, p. 907.
6. *NYT,* 3/17/95.
7. Dialogue extrapolated from Phillips Hathaway interview with CJM, 2/12/01.
8. Robert Fiske, quoting DDB, unsealed transcript from AAT trial, pp. 1099-1100.
9. Anonymous to CJM, 1/8/01.
10. Anonymous Sotheby's executive to CJM, 5/29/03.
11. Dialogue extrapolated from minutes of 3/29/95 meeting of Board of Directors of Sotheby's Holdings, Inc. DX#170.
12. Sotheby's press release, "Sotheby's Announces Changes in Seller's Commission," 4/13/95. GX#2.
13. AJT, undated, handwritten memo. DX#174.
14. *Daily Mirror,* 5/12/95.
15. DDB to CJM, 5/15/02.
16. Dialogue extrapolated from DDB testimony at AAT trial, pp. 878-879.
17. DDB to CJM, 5/15/02.
18. Lord Hindlip to CJM, 6/18/02.
19. Ibid.
20. Lord Hindlip to CJM, 6/17/02.
21. William F. Ruprecht to CJM, 4/9/02.
22. Phillips Hathaway to CJM, 3/25/02.
23. Susan Alexander to CJM, 4/12/02.
24. Ibid.
25. William F. Ruprecht to CJM, 4/9/02.
26. Ibid.
27. Susan Alexander to CJM, 4/12/02.

28. *Fortune,* 12/18/2000.
29. Lucy Mitchell-Innes to CJM, 2/7/01.
30. Susan Alexander to *CJM,* 4/12/02.
31. Ibid.
32. William F Ruprecht to CJM, 4/9/02.

CHAPTER FIFTEEN
1. *T&C,* 1/97.
2. Todd Merrill to CJM, 1/22/01.
3. Anonymous Christie's director to CJM, 6/28/01.
4. *T&C,* 1/97.
5. Fernando Gutierrez to CJM, 1/14/01.
6. Dialogue extrapolated from DDB testimony at AAT trial, p. 885.
7. Dialogue extrapolated ibid.
8. CMD, testimony at AAT trial, p. 809.
9. Anonymous to CJM, 9/11/02.
10. Ibid.
11. Herbert Black, A *Crime Amongst Gentlemen,* BBC, 5/9/02, transcript p. 19. The following account of Black's conversation with DDB, and the reported dialogue, are based on the same source.
12. CMD, e-mail to Anonymous, 1/5/03.
13. Stephen Lash, memo about conversation with Daniel P. Davison, dated 1/14/96.
14. Stephen Lash, memo to himself, dated 1/14/96.
15. CMD, e-mail to Anonymous, 1/5/03.
16. Ibid.
17. *NYT.* 12/22/95.
18. Chairman's Statement, Christie's Annual Report 1995, p. 4.
19. *NYT* 12/22/95.
20. Lord Hindlip to CJM, 6/18/02.

CHAPTER SIXTEEN
1. Stephen Lash, memo about conversation with Daniel P. Davison, dated 1/14/96.
2. Ibid.
3. Stephen Lash memo, CHR 060635.
4. Ibid.
5. Stephen Lash memo, CHR 060636.
6. Daniel P. Davison to CJM, 11/7/02.
7. Stephen Lash, draft of letter to CMD, 3/1/96.
8. Stephen Lash memo, CHR 060638.
9. Daniel P. Davison, letter to AJT, dated 3/5/96.
10. AJT, memo to Colin Forbes, 3/1/96. CHAPTER EIGHTEEN GX#43.
11. GX#43, penultimate paragraph.
12. DDB, letter to Deloitte & Touche LLP, 2/28/96.
13. AAT to CJM, 7/29/02.
14. Susan Alexander to CJM, 4/12/02.
15. Anonymous Sotheby's executive to CJM, 12/21/01.
16. Ibid.
17. *T&C,* 1/97.
18. Anonymous Sotheby's executive to CJM, 4/9/02.
19. Ibid.

20. Ibid.
21. CMD, e-mail to Anonymous, 1/6/03.
22. Ibid.
23. *Extel Examiner,* 3/12/96.
24. Daniel P. Davison, letter to AJT, dated 5/13/96.

CHAPTER SEVENTEEN
1. Office of Fair Trading, letter to DDB. DX#361.
2. Scott Muller, cross-examination of CMD at AAT trial.
3. DX#361.
4. *WSJ,* 8/17/01.
5. *NYT,* 1/24/97.
6. DDB to CJM, 7/14/02.
7. Stephen Lash memo, CHR 060652.
8. CMD, testimony at AAT trial, p. 391.
9. *WSJ,* 8/17/01.
10. Anonymous Christie's director to CJM, 6/28/01.
11. CMD, e-mail to Anonymous, 1/5/03.
12. Ibid.
13. *Evening Standard,* 2/7/97.
14. Ibid.
15. *WSJ,* 2/7/2000.
16. Jim Griffin, *A Crime Amongst Gentlemen,* BBC, 5/9/02, transcript p. 21.
17. Diana Phillips to CJM, 5/29/03.
18. U.S. District Court Subpoena, 4/25/97. DX#392.
19. Ibid.
20. Rena Neville, testimony at AAT trial, pp. 1495-1496.
21. DDB to CJM, 5/15/02.
22. DDB to CJM, 7/12/02.

CHAPTER EIGHTEEN
1. Patty Hambrecht to CJM, 5/29/03.
2. Ibid.
3. Ibid.
4. Background Note for the European Commission, 2/18/2000, p. 7.
5. CMD, e-mail to Anonymous, 1/5/03.
6. Lord Hindlip to CJM, 6/18/02.
7. Olga Davidge to CJM, 7/23/02.
8. Lady Hindlip to CJM, 6/17/02.
9. François Curiel to CJM, 10/17/02.
10. *NYT,* 6/8/97.
11. *Mirror,* 6/25/97.
12. Olga Davidge to CJM, 10/31/02.
13. Steve Reiss, testimony at AAT trial, p. 1774.
14. Ibid., p. 1776.
15. Lord Hindlip to CJM, 6/18/02.
16. Anonymous Christie's insider to CJM, 5/8/02.
17. Lord Hindlip to CJM, 6/18/02.
18. Lord Hindlip, letter to CMD, 12/97.
19. CMD, e-mail to Anonymous, 1/5/03.
20. DDB, memorandum to Sotheby's staff worldwide, 12/16/97.
21. Ibid.
22. DDB, *Wall Street Week,* 12/19/97, transcript p. 6.

23. Donaldson Pillsbury, testimony at AAT trial, p. 1252.

CHAPTER NINETEEN

1. Anonymous Sotheby's executive to CJM, 4/9/02.
2. DDB, testimony at AAT trial, p. 1803.
3. William Sheridan, testimony at AAT trial, p. 1804.
4. Olga Davidge to CJM, 10/31/02.
5. Ibid.
6. CMD, e-mail to Anonymous, 1/5/03.
7. Anonymous to CJM, 6/28/01.
8. CMD, e-mail to Anonymous, 1/5/03.
9. Olga Davidge to CJM, 7/23/02.
10. Charlie Finch, "The Royal Flush," artnet. corn, 8/24/98.
11. Olga Davidge to CJM, 7/23/02.
12. Anonymous American art journalist to CJM, 9/24/01.
13. Lord Hindlip to CJM, 6/17/02.
14. CMD, e-mail to Anonymous, 1/3/03.
15. Pravina Mecklai to CJM, 4/4/02.
16. Phillips Hathaway to CJM, 3/25/02.
17. "Diana D. Brooks Communications with Christie's." DX#359.
18. Phillips Hathaway to CJM, 3/25/02.
19. Phillips Hathaway to CJM, 2/12/01.
20. Ibid.

CHAPTER TWENTY

1. Anonymous friend of CMD to CJM, 5/8/02.
2. Ibid.
3. CMD, e-mail to Anonymous, 1/6/03.
4. Lord Hindlip to CJM, 6/18/02.
5. CMD, testimony at AAT trial, p. 398.
6. Anonymous Christie's source to CJM, 1/8/02.
7. Anonymous Christie's director to CJM, 6/28/01.
8. Lord Hindlip to CJM, 6/17/02.
9. Lord Hindlip to CJM, 6/18/02.
10. Lord Hindlip to CJM, 6/17/02.
11. Ibid.
12. Lord Hindlip to CJM, 6/18/02.
13. Lord Hindlip to CJM, 6/17/02.
14. Lord Hindlip to CJM, 6/18/02.
15. Lord Hindlip to CJM, 6/17/02.
16. CMD, e-mail to Anonymous, 1/5/03.
17. Lord Hindlip to CJM, 6/17/02.
18. *NYT,* 7/16/99.
19. Lord Hindlip to CJM, 6/17/02.
20. *NYT,* 7/9/99.
21. François Pinault comment to Lord Hindlip recalled by Lord Hindlip to CJM, 6/17/02.
22. *NYT,* 1/16/2000.
23. Edward Dolman to CJM, 11/4/01.
24. Anonymous to CJM, 1/5/03.
25. Edward Dolman to CJM, 11/4/01.
26. Clifford Aronson, written response to questions from CJM, 1/02.
27. Lord Hindlip to CJM, 6/18/02.
28. Ibid.
29. Edward Dolman to CJM, 11/4/01.
30. CMD, e-mail to Anonymous, 1/5/03.
31. Clifford Aronson, written response to questions from CJM, 1/02.
32. CMD, testimony at AAT trial, p. 490.
33. Conversation between CMD and William J. Linklater recalled by Linklater to CJM, 12/6/01.
34. Termination agreement between Christopher M. Davidge and Christie's. DX#267.
35. William J. Linklater to CJM, 3/11/02.
36. William J. Linklater to CJM, 7/12/02.
37. William J. Linklater to CJM, 3/11/02.
38. Ibid.
39. CMD, e-mail to Anonymous, 1/5/03.
40. CMD, e-mail to Christie's staff, 12/24/99.
41. Conversation between Clifford Aronson and William J. Linklater recalled by Linklater to CJM, 12/6/01.

CHAPTER TWENTY-ONE

1. William J. Linklater to CJM, 12/6/01.
2. Anonymous to CJM, 9/20/02.
3. DDB to CJM, 5/31/02.
4. DDB to CJM, 4/29/02.
5. Ibid.
6. Dialogue extrapolated from John Siffert interview with CJM, 5/21/02.
7. Ibid.
8. DDB to CJM, 5/31/02.
9. Ibid.
10. John Siffert to CJM, 5/31/02.
11. William F. Ruprecht to CJM, 2/22/02.
12. Diana Phillips to CJM, 4/9/02.
13. John Siffert to CJM, 5/21/02.
14. William F. Ruprecht to CJM, 2/22/02.
15. Susan Alexander to CJM, 4/9/02.
16. Robin Woodhead to CJM, 6/9/01.
17. Jeffrey Miro to CJM, 7/6/01.
18. Jeffrey Miro to CJM, 7/18/02.

CHAPTER TWENTY-TWO

1. Anonymous to CJM, 9/2/02.
2. Christie's antitrust statement, 1/28/2000.
3. Herbert Black, *A Crime Amongst Gentle-men,* BBC, 5/9/02, transcript pp. 33-34.
4. Ibid.
5. *Art & Auction,* 3/2000.
6. Article by CJM, *New York* magazine, 3/20/2000.
7. Edward Dolman to CJM, 11/4/01.
8. Henry Wyndham to CJM, 6/13/02.
9. *Gazette* (Montreal), 2/4/2000.
10. *Observer;* 2/27/2000.
11. Ibid.
12. Ibid.
13. Lord Hindlip to CJM, 6/18/02.
14. Judy Taubman, letter to Judge George B.

Daniels, 3/14/02.
15. Melinda Marcuse to CJM, 5/16/03.
16. David Redden to CJM, 11/15/02.
17. DDB to CJM, 5/15/02.
18. William E Ruprecht to CJM, 2/22/02.
19. John Siffert to CJM, 5/21/02.
20. Ibid.
21. DUB to CJM, 5/31/02.
22. Ibid.
23. John Greene to CJM, 7/23/02.
24. Scott Muller to CJM, 6/2/02.

CHAPTER TWENTY-THREE
1. Robin Woodhead to CJM, 6/9/01.
2. Robin Woodheacl to CJM, 5/8/02.
3. Ibid.
4. Diana Phillips, e-mail to CJM, 8/12/03.
5. William F. Ruprecht to CJM, 4/9/02.
6. Ibid.
7. Susan Alexander to CJM, 4/9/02.
8. William F. Ruprecht to CJM, 4/9/02.
9. Diana Phillips to CJM, 4/9/02.
10. Anonymous to CJM, 4/17/02.
11. Anonymous Sotheby's senior executive to CJM, 11/20/01.
12. William F. Ruprecht to CJM, 2/22/02.
13. Ibid.
14. Sotheby's press release, 2/21/2000.
15. William F. Ruprecht, e-mail to Sotheby's staff worldwide, 2/21/2000.
16. William F. Ruprecht to CJM, 2/22/02.
17. Phillips Hathaway to CJM, 2/12/01.
18. Ibid.
19. Ibid.
20. Elinor Dwyer McKenna, letter to Judge George B. Daniels, 3/26/02.
21. Anonymous to CJM, 4/9/02.
22. *People,* 10/23/2000.
23. DDB, letter to AAT, dated 2/24/2000.
24. Melinda Marcuse to CJM, 8/5/02.
25. Brian Sewell, *Evening Standard,* 2/25/2000.
26. Christopher Wood to CJM, 6/27/01.
27. *NYT,* 5/13/2000.
28. Ibid.
29. The grim possibility that a separate investigation might be carried out by the British government miraculously disappeared when a new Competition Act came into effect in the U.K. on March 1, 2000. It carried much stiffer penalties for price-fixing, in line with European laws. Happily for Sotheby's and Christie's, the Office of Fair Trading admitted in late February that it had "closed the case" because the new law did not allow retrospective investigations.
30. *New York Law Journal,* 11/22/2000.
31. Christopher Tennyson to CJM, 7/30/02.
32. DDB to CJM, 5/15/02.
33. Ibid.
34. *WWD,* 3/2/2000.

35. *Daily Telegraph,* 8/10/2000.
36. William J. Linklater to CJM, 12/12/01.
37. Dialogue between Clifford Aronson and William J. Linklater extrapolated from Linklater interviews with CJM, 12/12/01 and 2/15/02.
38. Steve Kaufman to CJM, 5/21/02.
39. *NYT,* 7/4/02.
40. David Redden to CJM, 11/15/02.
41. John Siffert to CJM, 5/21/02.
42. Ibid.
43. Anonymous to CJM, 7/2/02.
44. Scott Muller to CJM, 7/2/02.

CHAPTER TWENTY-FOUR
1. William F. Ruprecht, *A Crime Amongst Gentlemen,* BBC, 5/9/02, transcript p. 36.
2. David Boies to CJM, 4/25/02.
3. *New Yorker;* 10/15/01.
4. Ibid. This account, and the use of the word "communicators," were confirmed by David Boies in an interview with CJM on 4/25/02. As previously noted, the Weil, Gotshal lawyers deny this.
5. *New Yorker;* 10/15/01.
6. Ibid.
7. Edward Dolman,A *Crime Amongst Gentle-men,* transcript p. 35.
8. David Boies, *A Crime Amongst Gentlemen,* transcript p. 38.
9. Anonymous to CJM, 11/20/01.
10. Geraldine Norman to CJM, 3/15/01.
11. Anonymous to CJM, 5/21/02.
12. John Baskett to CJM, 3/19/01.
13. John Siffert to CJM, 5/21/02.
14. AAT to CJM, 7/29/02.
15. Ibid.
16. Reuters, 10/5/2000.
17. Ibid.
18. Anonymous to CJM, 9/27/02.
19. John Stair to CJM, 4/17/01.
20. Anonymous Sotheby's executive to CJM, 5/29/03.
21. Anonymous to CJM, 11/15/02.
22. William E. Ruprecht to CJM, 4/9/02.
23. Phillips Hathaway to CJM, 2/12/01.
24. David Redden to CJM, 11/15/02.
25. John Siffert and Steve Kaufman to CJM, 5/21/02.
26. Henry Wyndham to CJM, 6/13/02.
27. Ibid.
28. Ibid.
29. David L. Sokol to CJM, 5/13/02.
30. Ibid.
31. Childhood friend of DDB and Andy Dwyer to CJM, 5/5/03.

CHAPTER TWENTY-FIVE
1. Anonymous wedding guest to CJM, 1/8/01. All quotations in this description of the Davidge

nuptials are from the same source.
2. The Honorable Lewis A. Kaplan, District Judge, court transcript, *United States of America v. Sotheby's Holdings, Inc.,* 2/2/01, p. 6.
3. Judy Taubman's toast at AAT's seventy-sixth birthday party, per anonyrnous guest to CJM, 2/12/01.
4. Anonymous to CJM, 3/12/02.
5. Anonymous to CJM, 2/15/01.
6. AAT, speaking from prepared notes at his seventy-sixth birthday party. Copy obtained by CJM.
7. Phillips Hathaway to CJM, 2/12/01.
8. Delores Smithies to CJM, 6/27/02.
9. Anonymous Hobe Sound heiress to CJM, 1/31/02.
10. Melinda Marcuse to CJM, 1/24/03.
11. Robert Fiske, speaking to Judge George B. Daniels in court, witnessed by CJM, 5/4/01.
12. "A Statement from Sir Anthony Tennant," 5/01.
13. Ibid.
14. Ibid.
15. John Marion to CJM, 4/23/01.
16. Ibid.
17. Dialogue extrapolated from conversation recalled by a Southampton hostess to CJM, 7/20/01.
18. Amy Page to CJM, 11/18/02.
19. Christopher Meigher to CJM, 10/11/01.
20. DDB to CJM, 7/12/02.
21. Ibid.
22. Matthew Weigman to CJM, 8/22/01.
23. Scott Muller to CJM, 9/5/01.
24. Letter from Eugene J. Meigher, attorney for AJT, to John Greene, 10/18/01.

CHAPTER TWENTY-SIX
1. Dominick Dunne to CJM, 4/5/02.
2. Christopher Tennyson to CJM, 8/29/03.
3. John Greene, opening argument at AAT trial, p. 16.
4. Ibid., p. 17.
5. DDB, testimony at AAT trial, p. 43.
6. Robert Fiske, opening argument at AAT trial, p. 35.
7. Ibid., pp. 28-29.
8. AAT itinerary for 9/7/93, GX#63, read by Melinda Marcuse, testimony at AAT trial, p. 196.
9. AAT appointment book entry for 9/7/93, GX#86B, cited during Melinda Marcuse testimony at AAT trial, p. 196.
10. Melinda Marcuse to CJM, 4/24/02.
11. Melinda Marcuse, testimony at AAT trial, pp. 193-194.
12. AAT to CJM, 7/29/02.
13. Alexandra Peers to CJM, 11/18/01.
14. *New York* magazine, 12/3/01.
15. CMD, e-mail to Anonymous, 12/15/02.

16. Overheard by CJM.
17. CMD, testimony at AAT trial, p. 477.
18. Ibid.
19. CMD, e-mail to Anonymous, 1/5/03.
20. Glenn Forrester, ruminating at 1/12/02 jury reunion, attended by CJM.
21. Deborah Robinson, ruminating at 1/12/02 jury reunion, attended by CJM.
22. Anonymous to CJM, 7/24/02.
23. DDB to CJM, 4/29/02.
24. CMD, e-mail to Anonymous, 1/5/03.
25. DDB, testimony at AAT trial, p. 900.
26. Ibid.
27. AAT to CJM, 7/29/02.
28. Ibid.
29. DDB, testimony at AAT trial, pp. 831-832.
30. Ibid., p. 998.
31. David Redden, interview with CJM, 11/15/02.
32. Ibid.
33. Ibid.
34. DDB, testimony at AAT trial, p. 999.
35. Ibid., pp. 1069-1070.
36. John Siffert and Steve Kaufman to CJM, 5/21/02.
37. *Nett, York Post,* 11/25/01.
38. *New York Post,* 11/27/01.
39. Sentencing Memorandum on behalf of DDB, 4/25/02, p. 14.
40. *New York Post,* 4/19/02.
41. DDB to CJM, 4/29/02.
42. Elinor Dwyer McKenna, letter to Judge George B. Daniels, 3/26/02.
43. Judge Damon Keith, testimony at AAT trial, p. 1246.
44. William Sheridan, testimony at AAT trial, pp. 1798-1799.
45. Anonymous to CJM, 11/11/02.
46. Christopher Tennyson to CJM, 8/12/02.
47. Deborah Robinson, ruminating at 1/12/02 jury reunion, attended by CJM.
48. Robert Fiske to the Court at AAT trial, p. 1594. Sealed transcript.
49. Christopher Tennyson to CJM, 8/12/02.
50. Jeffery Goodwin to CJM, 1/16/02.
51. Mike D'Angelo at 1/12/02 jury reunion, attended by CJM.
52. Agence France-Presse, 11/19/01.
53. Exchange between Robert Fiske and Judge George B. Daniels, AAT trial, p. 1931.
54. John J. Greene, closing argument at AAT trial, p. 2153.
55. Robert Fiske, closing argument at AAT trial, p. 2110.
56. Patty Hambrecht to CJM, 12/3/01.
57. Ibid.

CHAPTER TWENTY-SEVEN
1. AAT to CJM, 7/29/02.
2. Christopher Tennyson, 1/15/02.

3. Phillips Hathaway to CJM, 3/25/02.
4. William E Ruprecht to CJM, 2/22/02.
5. Henry Wyndham to CJM, 6/13/02.
6. *New York Post,* 12/6/01.
7. *NYT,* 12/6/01.
8. National Public Radio, 12/6/01.
9. *New York Post,* 12/6/01.
10. Jeffery Goodwin to CJM, 12/13/01.
11. Glenn Forrester to CJM, 1/12/02.

CHAPTER TWENTY-EIGHT
1. AAT to CJM, 7/29/02.
2. David Boies to CJM, 4/25/02.
3. Ibid.
4. Quotations here are based on AJT's interviews with CJM, 12/28/03 to 12/21/04.
5. Anonymous to CJM, 7/2/02.
6. James Rouhandeh to CJM, 7/2/02.
7. AAT to CJM, 7/29/02.
8. CMD, e-mail to Anonymous, 1/5/03.
9. Ibid.
10. Ibid.
11. Ibid.
12. Anonymous to CJM, 12/13/01.
13. François Curiel to CJM, 10/17/02.
14. Dominick Dunne to CJM, 7/11/02.
15. William E. Ruprecht to CJM, 2/22/02.
16. *NYT,* 3/20/02.
17. Anonymous to CJM, 3/18/02.
18. *Sunday Telegraph,* 3/3/02.
19. Ibid.
20.. George B. Daniels, District Judge, Memorandum Decision and Order, 4/11/02, p. 28.
21. Ibid.
22. Judy Taubman, letter to Judge George B. Daniels, 3/14/02.
23. Ibid.
24. Gayle Kalisman, letter to Judge George B. Daniels, 2002.
25. Robert Fiske at AAT sentencing, 4/22/02.
26. John Greene at AAT sentencing, 4/22/02, p. 32.
27. Ibid., p. 33.
28. Judge George B. Daniels at AAT sentencing, 4/22/02, p. 42.
29. Ibid., p. 43.
30. Ibid., p. 44.
31. AAT to CJM, 7/29/02.
32. AAT to CJM, 4/23/02.
33. Henry Wyndham to CJM, 6/13/02.
34. Pauline Pitt, letter to Steve Dunleavy at *New York Post,* 4/23/02. Copy obtained by CJM.
35. Sentencing Memorandum on behalf of DDB, 4/25/02, p. 16.
36. Ibid., p. 4.
37. Matthew Weigman, letter to Judge George B. Daniels, 3/28/02. Copy obtained by CJM from the Court.
38. Transcript of DDB sentencing, 4/29/02, p. 7.
39. John Siffert at DDB sentencing, 4/29/02.
40. Judge George B. Daniels at DDB sentencing, 4/29/02, p. 11.
41. DDB at sentencing, 4/29/02, p. 11.
42. John Siffert to CJM, 5/21/02.
43. DDB to CJM, 4/29/02.
44. Anonymous to CJM, 9/9/02.
45. Anonymous to CJM, 11/15/02.

CHAPTER TWENTY-NINE
1. DDB to CJM, 5/31/02.
2. Anonymous Sotheby's expert to CJM, 5/12/02.
3. David Redden to CJM, 11/15/02.
4. DDB to CJM, 4/29/02.
5. DDB to CJM, 5/15/02.
6. *Times* (London), 4/30/02.
7. Anonymous to CJM, 5/17/02.
8. Henry Wyndham to CJM, 6/13/02.
9. Ibid.
10. AAT to CJM, 7/29/02.
11. Ibid.
12. Ibid.
13. Ibid.

CHAPTER THIRTY
1. AAT conversation with fellow inmate, according to source close to AAT, interview with CJM, 9/30/02.
2. Anonymous to CJM, 4/16/03.
3. Anonymous to CJM, 12/23/02.
4. Anonymous to CJM, 7/31/02.
5. Anonymous to CJM, 12/23/02.
6. Melinda Marcuse to CJM, 12/17/02.
7. Anonymous to CJM, 6/6/03.
8. Anonymous to CJM, 9/17/02.

Index